D0629788

*Forgeries, Fakes, and Reproductions*

*By the same author*

Eighteenth Century German Porcelain
Eighteenth Century English Porcelain
Seventeenth and Eighteenth Century French Porcelain
Art and Antique Restorer's Handbook
The Antique Collector's Handbook

The end of the road: Han van Meegeren listens to the evidence at his trial in Amsterdam. In the background is "The Blessing of Jacob", sold in 1942 as the work of Vermeer.
[*Ullstein*

GEORGE SAVAGE

# *Forgeries, Fakes, and Reproductions*

## A HANDBOOK FOR THE ART DEALER AND COLLECTOR

FREDERICK A. PRAEGER, *Publishers*
NEW YORK · WASHINGTON

BOOKS THAT MATTER

Published in the United States of America in 1964
by Frederick A. Praeger, Inc., Publishers
111 Fourth Avenue, New York 3, N.Y.

Library of Congress Catalog Card Number: 64-25426

Printed in Great Britain

The eye sleeps, until the spirit awakes it with a question.

MAX FRIEDLÄNDER

*Contents*

*Illustrations*

## *Preface*

This book is not intended to be sensational. It is a serious study of a subject of unusual interest and nothing more.

Naturally a book dealing with forgeries must discuss its subject to the exclusion of a vast number of genuine objects. No matter how carefully an author chooses his words he is certain to give the impression that dangerous forgeries are more numerous than they are. In fact they are much rarer than many people suppose, although superficially deceptive reproductions, some made for more or less honest purposes, are common.

This situation has been made more difficult by distorted reports in some sections of the popular press. An excellent example of this tendency is the treatment given to Han van Meegeren. This man was not an especially clever forger, certainly not on the same plane as Bastianini or even Rouchomowsky later discussed. If anything is to be learned from this episode at all it is that a combination of circumstances may sometimes favour the acceptance of forgeries which sail into our ken with every conceivable danger-signal flying. That these were ignored is inexplicable on rational grounds; that the tests which could have been applied were disregarded is something which defies comment. The subsequent sensational discussion of the case can only be deplored.

Few forgeries are dangerous to the sceptic who has taken the trouble to acquire some knowledge of the objects in which he is interested, and who possesses a modicum of worldly wisdom. Their existence at first seems a formidable obstacle to the novice, who is sometimes at a loss to see why one thing is accepted and another rejected, but he learns to tolerate spurious works, and to accept them as adding spice to his chosen pursuit. The conversation of two veteran collectors soon turns to the subject of forgeries past and present, and they undoubtedly cause works of art to be studied more closely in some aspects than might otherwise be the case. The acquisition of knowledge and the ability to discriminate would be less worth while if there were no opportunities for exercising them.

This book discusses the making of forgeries, fakes, replicas, reproductions, and deceptive copies in a way which is intended to help the collector to avoid them. That is its purpose, and I have been content to leave the exploitation of the sensational aspects to others. Not all the objects mentioned are forgeries; some are reproductions made for honest commercial purposes to meet a demand for decoration. They are, however, no less important, because in certain circumstances they can be used by others for dishonest reasons.

The amount of space which has been devoted to paintings of all kinds is relatively small, although I hope that my general remarks will be useful to the collector in this field and provide him with some food for thought. To treat this subject in the same way as the others discussed would have been impossible in the compass of a single volume, nor is any one person competent to do it in such detail. Much more has been written about forged paintings, however, and the reader can profitably pursue this aspect elsewhere.

What follows is a distillation of the experience of many years spent in the study of those forgeries and reproductions which have come my way, some of which I have had the salutary experience of buying. To make it as complete as possible, and to fill the gaps in my own knowledge, I have also drawn on the work of those authorities who seemed to approach the subject with the same desire to be informative about methods. Throughout, I have tried to verify statements about the provenance of spurious works, but this has been unusually difficult. We are, after all, discussing what are in many cases essentially criminal activities, and criminals do not advertise.

It is, perhaps, a common defect of our time that in some quarters these activities are regarded as rather less morally reprehensible than other forms of crime. The statement of Van Meegeren that he indulged in forgery because his own work was insufficiently appreciated is, for example, accepted almost as a legitimate excuse. Acquaintance with his work, however, suggests that there was very good reason for the neglect; it is both trivial and sentimental. It is at least possible that some burglars follow their chosen vocation because they feel themselves similarly unappreciated. There is no reason why art-forgery should not be punished as severely as cheque-forgery, larceny, counterfeiting, or fraud, since there is no moral difference between any of them.

The collector may take heart from the fact that at no time during the history of the art-market has forgery been so difficult as it is now, or more likely to be detected, and the forger's task is becoming continually more difficult.

G. S.

*Guestling,*
*Sussex.*
*January,* 1963.

## *Acknowledgements*

My thanks are due to the Ullstein Picture Library, the Victoria and Albert Museum, and Engelhard Hanovia Lamps for permission to use many of the photographs.

I am also grateful to my friends for advice and assistance; especially to Gerald Reitlinger, John Cushion, and Diana Imber; and to Wilfrid Walter, who photographed objects not otherwise acknowledged and gave me much useful information about the art of photography.

## *Introduction*

> Hast thou betrayed my credulous
>   innocence
> With vizor'd falsehood and base
>   forgery?
>
> MILTON, *Comus*

This volume is mainly concerned with the detection of forgeries, and it is desirable to begin with some definitions of the terms which will frequently be used.

Forgeries are copies of works of art or craft made for fraudulent purposes; fakes are genuine works which have been altered in character, or added to, for the purpose of enhancing the value; reproductions are copies made for honest purposes which may subsequently be used by others for dishonest reasons; replicas are contemporary reproductions.

The term "forgery" needs to be used with great care, because the intention is all-important. The Vermeers of Han van Meegeren are, of course, examples of forgery with no mitigating circumstances. His intention was not only to reproduce the appearance of a Vermeer, but to sell it as the work of Vermeer at a high price. There have, however, been many cases of artists making reproductions of old work with honest intentions which have later been used by others for fraudulent purposes. During the Renaissance it was by no means unknown for an artist of note to make a replica of the work of another to fulfil a patron's order.[1] Whatever it might have been called at the time, it would hardly be regarded as a forgery today. But if a copyist of an Old Master takes great pains not only to imitate his style, but his

[1] There were, of course, no Copyright Acts.

materials, his methods of working, and the effect of time on his work, then the inference to be drawn is obvious.

In many other instances, however, the problem is primarily one of attribution. Until the eighteenth century painters of pictures were regarded as socially equivalent to other craftsmen—to the goldsmith, the cabinet-maker, and the sculptor. They were often highly skilled in several related crafts, and were commissioned by patrons who exercised some measure of control over the finished work. They might be called upon to paint walls, to decorate furniture panels, to supply designs for *fêtes* and pageants or for work to be carried out in other media. The artist was usually a member of a guild, a trade union which often controlled the materials used and the terms of sale, examining the quality of the work produced and condemning inferior objects. He was an employer of labour, and his work was done in a studio with the aid of employees and apprentices.

Therefore, the problem is often whether or not the work is wholly by the hand of a Master or executed in part by one of his workmen. Naturally his influence predominates in the style of the work, but, particularly in portraiture, only the face may have been executed by him, the drapery being by another hand. Backgrounds, too, were often filled in by an assistant. Replicas of paintings and portraits were ordered from the artist and carried out by a workman under his supervision. The buyer at the time was under no illusion as to the nature of his purchase, and he did not demand that the artist should carry out every operation with his own hand, from the priming of a canvas to the final date and signature. The signature was not the hall-mark of genius, it was the trade-mark of the studio.

The modern fashion is for what has been well called the "personality cult". The demand among collectors is for the unaided work of the artist, which is assumed to possess qualities missing from composite works. This is becoming extremely noticeable in other fields than painting, high prices being realized for silver and porcelain, for example, to which the name of an artist can be attached, and this is often irrespective of the quality of an object. The vogue is probably a reaction from the deadening uniformity which the modern state seeks to impose, and emphasizes the value of the individual against the mass. To this extent it is a healthy sign, but the nature of most early work is at variance with the trend.

1. Forgery of an Etruscan sarcophagus in *terracotta*, probably by the Pinellis. c. 1863. The Pinellis worked for the Marchese di Cavelli who owned a *terracotta* factory.

[*Ullstein*

2. The Bushell Bowl, thirty-three inches in diameter, was bought in 1870 when little was known of early Chinese bronzes, and came from the collection of the Princes of Yi, descendants of the Emperor K'ang Hsi. It arrived in a case lined with embroidered yellow silk. For many years this bowl was regarded as one of the important treasures of the South Kensington Museum, until, with the advance of knowledge, its spurious nature and modern manufacture were recognized.

[*Victoria and Albert Museum*

3. Two figures of "Minerva" in bronze. Left, is a copy by Solomon Weininger of Vienna made about 1870. The original is by Tiziano Aspetti (1565-1607). [*Ullstein*

The detection of forgeries in any media is, above all, a matter of drawing the correct inferences from observation. A book such as this can suggest lines of inquiry by recording what has been done in the past, but each suspected object has to be examined afresh with all the possibilities in mind.

Three points are of outstanding importance:

(*a*) the materials used
(*b*) the style or manner of using them
(*c*) the effects of time and its vicissitudes.

Objects of art are made with a great variety of materials in many different ways and with a diversity of tools. It is, therefore, essential to determine as closely as possible not only what an object has been made from, but how it was made, and to relate these to an object known to be genuinely of the period.

A forgery, if it is to pass expert examination, needs to deceive on all these three points. This in most cases is completely impossible if the work imitated is older than a century or so. During the nineteenth century rapid strides were made in the production of synthetic substances of all kinds, and in the production and refinement of pure materials. Until this time materials which were technically pure were impossible to obtain.[1] Craftsmen sought out natural deposits of suitable substances, and these were greatly valued when they yielded reasonably consistent results. Even today such industries as glass-making tend to do the same, beds of sand varying considerably in their value. Natural materials contained impurities of one kind or another which affected the final result. Some old glass, for instance, has a steely blue colour, whilst other specimens have an orange fluorescence under ultra-violet light. These properties can be reproduced in modern glass, but not in the same way, and for this reason there is a perceptible difference from old glass. A forger, therefore, is usually accused by his materials, especially if a chemical analysis can be compared with that of genuine work.

The point can be well illustrated by repeating an instance of the effect of impurities on materials given by H. Stafford Hatfield.[2] A

[1] "Chemically pure" materials, that is with virtually no impurities, are only used for special purposes.
[2] *The Inventor and His World*. Harmondsworth, 1948.

man devised a new kind of floor-covering which yielded excellent results. After demonstration with a small quantity he was given a large contract, and to fulfil this he ordered commercial quantities of the substances necessary to make it, only to find that his formula would not work. His previous success was traced to an impurity occurring in one of the original substances used, but it was no longer possible to buy from the former source, he had none left which could be subjected to chemical analysis, and the origin could not be traced. In the circumstances the problem was insoluble, but it serves to stress the important effect of trace-elements occurring as impurities.

The problem is, essentially, the one which faces the forger. Unless he draws on the original sources for his materials, and this is still possible in a few cases, he cannot reproduce the object. He can only imitate its appearance in other substances. However, assuming it possible to reproduce an object successfully in the original materials, the forger still has something which is entirely new. Time affects most things, sometimes very considerably. Bronze is an excellent example. No doubt, given an analysis of an ancient bronze, the metal could be reproduced more or less accurately. The object could even be reproduced from moulds taken from a genuine piece, but the corrosion (referred to as patina) which is an essential quality of much old bronze is often the product of many centuries. It varies considerably because it arises from exposure to different circumstances which are later discussed, and these cannot be reproduced satisfactorily.

There remains to be considered the question of the style or manner in which the materials have been used. Here we move on to more difficult ground. To take as an example the difference between a picture by a Master and a replica by someone working in his studio, it is obvious that the materials will be the same in each case, and the effects of time will be at least comparable. If, therefore, we are to express an opinion on the authorship of a painting in these circumstances the style in which it is executed will be of paramount importance. At first sight it might be thought that the more skilled the execution the more likely that the work came originally from the principal artist. This is not necessarily the case. A portrait undertaken as a commission was not always regarded by him as sufficiently important to warrant great pains being taken with it, whereas the workman had to satisfy his master. Therefore, in some cases the lesser man worked more carefully, and with greater precision. Whatever may be the market value of a great name, every artist must at some point have worked when he was suffering from toothache or constipation and his work must have suffered in consequence.

The manner in which the paint was applied, however, and the handling of small details, is never the same from one individual to another, and these are, in fact, almost as idiosyncratic as a fingerprint. Experts often have large collections of photographs and microphotographs of small details which help to establish the hand of the artist. This method can equally well be applied to the detection of modern forgeries of old paintings and to those of contemporary work. Scientific methods of approach are almost the only way of elucidating problems relating to materials and the effects of time; it is more difficult, though not impossible, to apply them to questions of style.

An easy exercise for the novice in stylistic differences is provided by European engravings copied in Canton on Chinese export porcelain of the eighteenth century.[1] The eye is accustomed to the European idiom and can see with ease the distinctively Chinese flavour in the drawing of the features and the delineation of architectural details. Unlike Europeans, the Chinese were not interested in linear perspective and *chiaroscuro*, and this led to ludicrous misinterpretations of detail. To put the process into reverse, and to examine European copies of Chinese porcelain, is a slightly more advanced exercise, since it presupposes a closer acquaintance with the Chinese idiom. Yet the same thing can be distinguished. Chinese features have a European cast, and such things as dragons and the less well-known symbols are often comically misunderstood.

The approach to European forgeries of Chinese work is probably best made by way of certain varieties of early European porcelain which were frankly based on Chinese models.[2] This can be well seen in the work of the Worcester porcelain factory between 1751 and 1760, when Chinese patterns were much used. An equally marked divergence in style will be found in modern reproductions from the old moulds of the Victorian figures from Staffordshire known as "flat-backs". The difference in the painting of the features, especially the mouth,

[1] There is a large collection in the Victoria and Albert Museum.

[2] The *Treatise on Japanning* (see footnote, page 50) has many amusing examples of seventeenth-century English work in the Chinese manner.

between the nineteenth-century examples and those made today is especially obvious.

This preliminary study may be carried further by comparing objects known to be genuine with forgeries. The facial expression of the archaic Greek *kore*, which has been referred to as the "smile", has proved the undoing of a number of skilful forgers, and few have attempted to reproduce it. Even when a fairly deceptive resemblance has been achieved on a frontal view, the profile invariably differs from that of ancient work. An attempt made by Alceo Dossena, later discussed, ought not to have deceived anyone acquainted with ancient sculpture. Then, too, the forger of early sculpture of this kind overlooks the ideal of feminine beauty of the period. As the social customs of the Greeks suggest, this tended to disregard curves in favour of straight lines. But feminine curves are fashionable at present, and have been for a long time. It is hardly surprising, therefore, that the forger finds it difficult to keep them from his work. Curves were out of fashion during this century for a few years in the 1920s. The straight lines in the design of feminine costume of the period is so obvious a key to the dating of a drawing that we can hardly miss it. The possibility of a forger in two or three hundred years time adding "1960" to such a drawing is amusing to contemplate. It would not be difficult for the expert of the day well-versed in twentieth-century costume to detect the discrepancy.

Much the same may be seen in later copies of Egyptian sculpture and bronzes, where a certain realism totally out of keeping with the rigidly hieratic style of official Egyptian art of the period has crept into the design.

It is essential in considering a work of decorative art to understand the purpose for which it was originally intended. Some were made to be applied as decoration to other objects, such as bronzes for application to furniture or as chariot-fittings, and they will, for this reason, be provided with the means of attachment in the form of lugs, holes, and so forth. Copies in the same, or in some other medium, however, may not have this provision because the forger lost sight of the original purpose, his work being intended rather for the cabinet of the collector. The spurious nature then becomes obvious. An example may be found in jade copies of ancient Chinese bronze ornaments which seem impressive enough until one realizes that they could fulfil no apparent purpose except the original one, and that the necessary holes have not been provided for attachment. Much the same might be said for certain copies of Renaissance bronze decorative fittings.

The nature of materials plays a far greater part in forming the style in which works of art are executed than is generally supposed, and it is sometimes possible to see that an object has been translated from one medium into another. For instance, a sculptor trained to the use of such soft stones as sandstone, limestone, and marble will develop a very different style from one whose work has been predominantly in granite and the harder stones. The techniques are completely different. A sculptor who switches from one type of stone to another, or from stone to bronze, will necessarily change his style to suit the medium. This can be well seen from a comparison of the bronzes and stone-carvings of Sir Jacob Epstein, and this aspect of his work is worth study.

The forger's task has been made much easier by the scholar's reluctance to descend from his ivory tower into the market-place, and by the existence of what has been aptly termed the "two cultures". The market-place, if they but knew it, is fascinating in itself, and, until recently, it has been the place of resort for artist and patron alike. Even in the nineteenth century many artists (the successful ones, at least) were good business-men, as Picasso and Dali are today, and it is only within the last few decades that it has been thought bad taste in more refined quarters to discuss art and what it takes to buy it in the same context. The result has been that those whose talents have best equipped them to thwart the schemes of the forger have been largely uninterested in the problem.

More serious, perhaps, has been the growing division between students of the arts and those of the sciences—a gap bridged only in part by such quasi-sciences as psycho-analysis, which is disposed to value art for its diagnostic and therapeutic possibilities. I am inclined to think that this is hardly the fault of the scientist, whose contributions to the problem have been too often belittled and neglected. I have known many workers in the scientific field who have been interested in the arts, and they have freely put their experience at my disposal. That I have not been able to profit to a greater extent by their help has been due to my own limitations rather than to any lack of willingness to explain the methods which science can bring to bear on this and allied problems.

In these days of specialization it is impossible for those who have made the arts their field to gain sufficient knowledge of all the scientific techniques which could help them in enough detail to use them effectively. Indeed, the degree of specialization is often such that a critic or historian of painting will know little or nothing about the related decorative arts, such as furniture, silver, and ceramics, which in former times were often given equal status. The tendency, in fact, is to know more and more about less and less. Perhaps in time it will be realized that the true aim of education should not be to cram the mind of its unfortunate victim with facts, but to teach him where to find the facts when he wants them, and to value them at their correct significance. The student who can move at ease through a good reference library ultimately has an advantage over one with a head stuffed with details about one small corner of the subject.

The word "science" is used throughout to mean an organized body of exact knowledge. "Scientific methods" are those whereby this knowledge can be assembled and applied, and range from X-ray apparatus to systematic schemes of classification such as those possible with fingerprints.

Anyone wishing to specialize in the detection of forgeries needs many of the attributes of a good detective, because the work, in its essentials, is similar. The perusal of one of the standard works on criminology, such as Gross's *Criminal Investigation*, provides a valuable background to the further study of our present subject. In addition to being a keen observer of small details, able to draw correct inferences from the results of the physical examination of an object, the expert needs a reservoir of historical and technical knowledge, and access to a large and varied library. Detailed knowledge is not so essential as a broad acquaintance with art-history and the ability to find required references. He does not need to specialize in any branch of science, although knowledge of scientific method is essential. He needs to know which specialist can give him the information he requires; he must be able to put the problem clearly, know the limitations of the method it is proposed to use, and be able to evaluate the results. The specialist is merely concerned with providing information on the problems referred to him. A chemist, for example, can provide an analysis of a porcelain figure, but unless he is a porcelain collector he will not be able to say what his analysis reveals. He can answer questions put to him; only the expert knows which are the right questions.

It is not generally possible to make detailed examinations by scientific methods of objects offered for sale unless it is made a condition of purchase. Most objects which fall to be examined in this way have been bought and later suspected for one reason or another. They are, therefore, already in dispute. There are certain methods which can be employed without affecting the object itself. These vary in the information they are able to provide, but ultra-violet light (see Appendix 3) is probably the most useful general-purpose tool. After purchase an owner is rarely willing to allow a detailed examination unless he is also in a position to make a successful claim on the seller in the event of it being unfavourable. If an object is proved to be a forgery he can only resell it as genuine by becoming party to a fraud. Whilst proof is lacking he is under no such disability.

Art-criticism, in these days especially, tends to be a hotch-potch of art history and biography, with dashes of psychiatry and ill-digested metaphysics thrown in for good measure. In some cases even the most concentrated effort to understand what is said results in confusion,[1] whilst in the journals of the *avant-garde* criticism becomes a vehicle for economic theory, in particular that of the Left.

Criticism, properly so called, is a process of comparing one work with another with the object of appraising its value, using the term in its widest sense. A unique entity could not be criticized or appraised, because there would be nothing with which to compare it. Legitimately reduced to its simplest possible terms, one painting is preferred to another by an individual critic because its subject and technique give him the greater satisfaction for entirely personal reasons. Criticism which is universally valid cannot exist, at least until man is able to assume the prerogatives of the Deity.

It is impossible to think in these terms as a foundation for the study of forgeries and imitations. Here we are concerned with objective truth which, for present purposes, may be defined as a fact consistent

[1] For instance, the following extract from the catalogue to an exhibition, quoted by the *Daily Telegraph*: "In the heat of his discovery of a new resin it was natural that all figuration should melt", the discovery being "not of conventional assemblage mannerisms . . . but of the powerful transfigurations of these materials in a new visual unity, where identities are lost only to be regained in the very act of their metamorphosis". In the vernacular this is aptly described as "blinding with science".

with all other known facts, and art-criticism as a process of comparison assumes much greater importance.

The specious argument is often advanced that if a forgery deceives the critics and the experts it is as valid as the original work, which is strictly equivalent to saying that if a forged cheque deceives a bank clerk it ought to be honoured. This retort, however, is almost as specious as the argument which provokes it. Much more important as a refutation is that the life of any forgery is rarely more than a generation. Left alone it will expose itself merely by existing. Even those who accepted it at first, if they live long enough, will realize its fraudulent nature. Moreover, a case in which a forgery has been universally accepted is virtually unknown. At best it can be said to have deceived some of the experts for some of the time. Not everyone accepted the Vermeers of Van Meegeren[1]; the tiara of Rouchomowsky (page 76) was hotly contested. A forgery, even the best, can hardly be said to exist on the same plane as a genuine work of art.

If we are to accept fraudulent copies as worth as much as original works, financially or aesthetically, our whole system of values painfully built up over millennia must be discarded, and replaced by that of the two young men in New York who opened a shop which they called "Fabulous Fakes", proclaiming that "the best things in life are fake", with beautiful twelfth-century manuscripts at £3, excellent copies of Michelangelo drawings for £10, and copies of Rembrandt for £30.[2]

Let us digress, and remove this discussion from the realm of art to that of literature. The problems facing a man who proposes to write a spurious play by Shakespeare are parallel in many ways to the difficulties of the picture forger. First, it is necessary to select a subject. Shakespeare habitually took his from old chronicles and romances, and we know enough about the themes which attracted him to look suspiciously on any sudden discovery out of character. The forger, therefore, would be certain to select a historical subject as presenting fewer difficulties.

Although *pastiches* exist, they only serve to prove that it is impossible for any modern writer to think his way into the mind of one of the

[1] Duveen's agent is reputed to have cabled that the "Christ at Emmaus" was an obvious fraud.

[2] Reported in the *Daily Telegraph*.

sixteenth century, and certainly not into that of Shakespeare. Even though he had, for many years, saturated himself in the imagery of the plays, he would still have to comb them for likely snippets and join them together like a patchwork quilt. Any student of Shakespeare would be able to trace the origin of most of them. The play would seem stilted in form and language, and bear traces of another hand at almost every point.

Then the problem of presenting it to the world would arise. Either the forger would need to transcribe it on sixteenth-century paper in a hand which bore a colourable resemblance to that which could reasonably be associated with Shakespeare, or he could have it printed in imitation of an early edition of the plays. For the latter he would need a type-face of a kind which no longer exists, hand-set in the fashion of the period which would take into account the typographical customs of the time.[1] For this he would require a supply of blank paper of the late sixteenth or early seventeenth century, and it would be necessary to fake signs of age to the binding convincing to an expert. Assuming, however, that all these difficulties could be overcome, the work would then have to be "discovered". Whatever method the forger might select, suspicious bibliophiles would want to know how it came to remain out of the light of day for 350 years or so. Of course, the problem is virtually insoluble, which is why there are no modern forgeries of Shakespeare's plays despite the price that would be paid for a genuine discovery of this nature.

The problems raised by this hypothetical forgery are closely related to those facing the modern forger of antique painting or sculpture. He has to do something equivalent to all I have outlined, and his work, when it is completed, is just as worthless.

The history of the more spectacular works of art ought to be especially valuable in helping to determine whether or not they are genuine, but this is often absent, and, when present, is frequently unreliable. Impoverished families have sometimes had copies made

[1] Since these lines were written there have been two developments worthy of note: first folio typography has been studied in fascinating detail by Charlton Hinman (*The Printing and Proof Reading of the First Folio of Shakespeare*, Oxford, 1963) and the computer has been adapted to detecting and recording stylistic idiosyncrasies by which, it is claimed, the authorship of disputed books and manuscripts can in some cases be verified.

before selling originals, and have even made it part of a bargain with a purchaser that a copy be provided.

Works of art of considerable importance are frequently found in unlikely places, their history having been completely lost. The reason for this is usually to be sought in the orgy of looting which occurred during the French Revolution and the Napoleonic Wars. The custom of taking works of art of importance as a perquisite of conquest is not particularly new; it dates back to the rise of the first fortified settlements, when these things were collected together as objects of household furnishing and ornament. During the preceding five hundred years or so victorious princes who exacted contributions of this kind had removed them to their own palaces. They were legitimate spoil of war, and it was not difficult to trace possession from one to another.

The French Revolution, however, was essentially a mob-uprising in which those who seized power had small respect for the possessions they acquired by so doing. Much was destroyed, especially those things which bore evidences of former ownership, such as coats-of-arms. Much, too, was sold clandestinely by the owners, often at absurdly low prices. The dispersal of the important French Royal Collections took place at this time.

In June 1794 a French Committee for the education of the people first proposed sending knowledgeable persons charged with the special duty of looting the cream of the art-works from occupied countries, and an Army Order was issued shortly afterwards putting the plundering of invaded territory on an organized basis. Soon the loot began to pour into Paris in long trains of wagons. From this treatment paintings probably suffered least. Other works of art were rudely torn from their settings, and silver was sometimes hammered flat for transport.

When an army issues orders of this kind officially, it is to be expected that officers at least will follow the example. In the French Army at this time many of the officers were appointed for political reasons and their only qualification, as often as not, was political reliability. They did not miss the opportunity offered to "acquire" objects for themselves. One of the offenders was Marshal Ney, who appropriated pictures belonging to the King of Naples. The process of acquisition was accelerated by the activities of the Baron Vivant

Denon. He was a protégé of Jacques-Louis David, who had been prominent in the clamour for the death of Louis Seize. Perhaps as a reward David was given a position which made him virtual dictator in the field of the arts, and Denon was Inspector-General of French Museums whose activities abroad earned him the soubriquet of "The Packer". He organized plunder on a vast scale, especially in Germany and Austria.[1]

In Italy particularly English art-buyers moved ahead of Napoleon's armies, and bought paintings for what were often ludicrous prices from owners fearful of losing their property. Even during periods of hostilities Englishmen were able to move about the Continent. The difficulties were greater, but it was still possible to trade, and their acquisitions were shipped back by devious routes. Sometimes they even bought from the looters. Total war, with all its implications, had not yet made its appearance, although it was to do so before the end of the next decade. Circumstances were not propitious to close examination, even had the buyers possessed the scholarship and time to consider their purchases carefully, and Italian forgers undoubtedly took advantage of the opportunity offered to unload their wares on unwary buyers, just as Van Meegeren one hundred and fifty years later used the German Occupation to sell pictures which, in other circumstances, must have been recognized immediately.

During the first half of the eighteenth century Italy had been the most flourishing section of the art-market, and forgery was rife. The younger members of aristocratic families making the Grand Tour bought works of art and became collectors in consequence. Immense quantities were sold to Germany and the northern countries, as well as to France and England, and much which left Italy in this way was of recent manufacture. Count Algarotti, who was in Italy in 1743 as a purchasing agent for the Saxon Court, wrote to Augustus III that

[1] The following is offered without comment:

"People of Italy, the French Army has come to break your chains. Advance and meet it with confidence. Your possessions, your religion, your customs, will not be touched."

—Proclamation of Bonaparte

"Italy owes much of its wealth and fame to the fine arts . . . some of its beautiful statues, medallions, libraries, bronzes, and silver Madonnas will compensate us for the expense of a visit to Rome."

—Lazare Carnot to Bonaparte

there were "many copies, many fakes, many poor and patched-up originals". There is no reason to suppose that the situation had altered by the end of the century, and the forgers of Rome, Naples, and elsewhere were no doubt still as industrious. After Waterloo Blücher's Prussians not unnaturally looted enemy works of art, although on a relatively trivial scale, and these were sent to Germany and not returned.

There is no reason for complacency about the record of English troops, who were accomplished looters. Many works of art found their way to England as the result of the looting of the Summer Palace at Peking in the middle of the nineteenth century. Lacquer, jade, and rock-crystal went into the soldiers' knapsacks. Axes were used to prise precious stones from their settings in the furniture, although their value in comparison with that of the object in a complete state must have been small. Auctions were held in the field, at which the plunder was sold. The largest and flashiest objects went to the generals, since they were in a position to order their inclusion in the baggage-train. Privates often had to be content with, perhaps, a small piece of porcelain which, today, could be sold for prices exceeding those for the officers' loot. It is probable that as a result of nineteenth-century European exploits in China the number of important works removed to the West was greater than that of those remaining. There is always the possibility, therefore, that an important object may come to light suddenly in an unexpected place. I had the experience a few years ago of seeing two fine Chinese bronzes of the Chou dynasty in a small country cottage. The owners did not know what they were, or their value, but there was a history of receiving them by way of a grandfather who had been in China in the middle of the nineteenth century. It is possible that they were part of the loot of the Summer Palace.[1]

[1] An indication of the attitude to the acquisition of works of art in this manner is to be found in the *Connoisseur* as late as December 1901: "At the time of the sacking of the Summer Palace in 1860 there were many opportunities for those on the spot to acquire rare and beautiful specimens of Chinese art." Illustrated are several specimens thought to have been "acquired" from this source. Captain Gordon (later General "Chinese" Gordon, killed at the siege of Khartoum), who was present, wrote: ". . . in fact the palaces were so large and we were so pressed for time that we could not plunder them completely. . . ."

It is, of course, this kind of situation which often baits the forger's trap. The history of the migrations of works of art can be read with profit by the student. They are discussed in detail by Wilhelm Treue in his book, *Kunstraub* (Dusseldorf, 1957).[1]

The full story of the dispersal of works of art during the Nazi régime will probably never be told. Some of the salient facts deserve brief mention here, if only because lost works undoubtedly remain to be discovered, and the circumstances of the time may be used by forgers to explain the lack of a reliable history.

Even before the war there are instances of the expropriation of Jewish collections in Germany, and the hostility of Hitler[2] and others to modern art resulted in the confiscation of paintings regarded as decadent. Some of these were auctioned in Lucerne in 1939. About one thousand oil-paintings and nearly four thousand watercolours, all regarded as "degenerate art", were burned in March 1939 in Berlin. Some may have escaped, stolen by those charged with the operation of burning them.

Reliable sources suggest that about 22,000 works of all kinds were removed from France and sent to Germany by the Rosenberg organization. Principally they came from Jewish collections, the Rothschild family being an especial sufferer. Both Göring and Frank took some of these things for their own collections. At Nuremberg thirty-nine volumes of reproductions were produced, which contained a total of 2,500 looted works of art. The full total could probably be multiplied by twenty at least.

We do not know how much was destroyed by the advancing Russians. Museums at Königsberg, Stettin, Danzig, and Breslau were destroyed, with such of the contents as remained. The numerous castles, palaces, and churches of Prussia were plundered and burnt.

The destruction of Dresden by the American Air Force, said to have been undertaken at the request of the Russians, which was

[1] An English translation, entitled *Art Plunder*, was published in London in 1960.

[2] If we are to believe the evidence of Reinhold Hanisch, the Führer made a precarious living in Linz and Vienna by forging oil-paintings and heating them in an oven to simulate the appearance of an old varnish. According to Hanisch, Hitler claimed to have been successful in selling them as antique to dealers. "I suggested to Hitler", said Hanisch, "that it would be better to stay in an honest trade and paint postcards."

without any perceptible military necessity, resulted in the destruction of works of art as well as of superb buildings. Many important paintings were shipped to Russia, among them Raphael's "Madonna", goldsmiths' work, and precious stones and jewellery from the Grüne Gewölbe. Since Stalin was succeeded by Krushchev some of these things have been returned, although how many is unknown. Some, particularly objects of silver and gold, probably disappeared long before they reached the Russian border.

Vast numbers of important objects from Germany and the occupied countries were stored in the salt-mines at Salzburg, and it was only good fortune, and the last-minute intervention of Kaltenbrunner, which saved them from deliberate destruction by fanatics. This much can be put to the credit side of a misspent life.

Works stored in the Flakturm Friedrichshain in Berlin were less fortunate. Some of the large number stored here were removed during March 1945 to a place of greater safety. A small number were subsequently damaged and destroyed by an incendiary bomb, but almost all that remained were destroyed by fire during the occupation of the city by Russian troops, although a few things were salvaged by looting civilians and one painting was later found in the possession of a dealer in the American sector. How many of the four hundred paintings which still survived before the last fire escaped to be subsequently looted is unknown, but it is probable that the number was not great. Elsewhere the same story was repeated with minor variations. Much went to Russia, nearly everything without proper packing and protection, and most of it is hardly likely to have survived. Such things as coins of valuable metal were put into sacks to be melted. As this manuscript was being prepared for the printer two paintings by Antonio Pollaiuolo emerged from obscurity in the United States. They were originally removed from the Uffizi Gallery in Florence during the last war and transferred to a place of safety. They were, apparently, then taken by the retreating German Army, and reports suggest that they first found their way into the possession of Hermann Göring, after which they disappeared completely. They came to light in California in 1963 in the possession of German immigrants and were returned to Italy.

Works offered without a history, but with the tacit suggestion that they have been smuggled from Greece or Italy, are spurious as often as not. Nevertheless, the number of genuine objects procured in this way is large. A report in *The Times* of January 1963 discussed the thriving trade in smuggled antiquities from Greece where, as in Egypt, clandestine digging for works of art is almost a family tradition. It was suggested that between eighty and ninety per cent of the (adult) population of Attica is engaged in this trade, a barely credible figure which must be accepted with some reserve. Much more believable, however, was the statement that they do irreparable damage in their searches. Undoubtedly they are encouraged by the lightness of the penalties imposed for contravention of the existing laws relating to the export of works of art. "What man," commented a police official, "having honey on his hands will not lick it off?", a remark capable of much wider application. Foreign yachts were named as one of the principal routes by which antiquities found their way out of the country, and Switzerland was said to be one of the most active clearing-houses. The extent of the traffic may be judged from an estimate that £17 million worth of ancient bronzes had been illegally exported in the decade from 1930 to 1940, and foreign museums were named among the chief purchasers. Figures of this kind must be accepted with reserve because they can only be estimates based on incomplete information, but even half the amount would be impressive. Byzantine art and medieval manuscripts are now being smuggled out as the demand extends to the later periods.

Works of this kind, although they may be perfectly genuine, will lack a history. There is no way in which a purchaser can tell how they have been acquired, and he can only judge the authenticity from an examination of the objects themselves. If, however, they prove to be spurious, they have certainly not been smuggled, and the purchaser is entitled to whatever protection from the law he can get.

There are no estimates for the number of works smuggled from Italy, but it is probably fewer because the frontiers are less difficult to control. It has been said in the past that Italian Customs officials have connived at the export of spurious works from Italy, and that dealers have confidently produced proof that the works they intended to export were forgeries in order to get the necessary clearance documents.[1] It is obvious, therefore, that official documents of this kind cannot be regarded as proof of authenticity. In fact, since the export

[1] Ricardo Nobili: *The Gentle Art of Faking*. London, 1923.

of genuine works is, for the most part, prohibited, they may even be proof in some cases that objects are spurious.

The claim that forgeries are extremely numerous is sometimes made by writers on art who are anxious to emulate Dickens' Fat Boy. The flesh of those who have considered the subject with the greatest attention, however, refuses to creep. If we look at the sum total of forgeries, fakes, and replicas it is without doubt enormous, although it is small in comparison with that of genuine works. But this aspect is not very important. Works of art will always be copied by those who have not the originality to produce something of their own, or who are attempting to meet a fashionable demand. The essential question is, *How many of these works are capable of deceiving unbiased specialists who are prepared to take advantage of the resources of modern science in appropriate cases?* The answer must certainly be, *Very few*. A number of cases are cited elsewhere in this book. In every one the works in question were not universally accepted, and even the most deceptive found those who were prepared to contest them. But the number of instances in which some experts have been deceived, have proceeded to spend their own or somebody else's money, and have then defended their purchase tooth and nail, are very large. There are always danger-signals accompanying even the cleverest forgery for those who are looking for them. The fact, for instance, that several experts accept an object but disagree about its period often means that it is a compound of elements taken from several sources which do not agree in date. If a work is important a history which is insufficient and unable to stand close investigation is suspicious to say the least, although it is not proof of fraud in every case. The junk-shop Rembrandt may exist, but no experienced buyer would accept it without the most stringent tests. The final attribution to Rembrandt rather than to a seventeenth-century painter in his style may be a matter of opinion, but it is possible to be certain that it is a seventeenth-century canvas, painted with pigments of the period, and in a style which does not conflict with what we know of the artist.

Price, too, is important. Forgeries are usually offered at a price sufficiently below market value to tempt an incautious buyer, but not so low that they are immediately marked as spurious. The buyer should ask himself why, if a higher price could be obtained in a reputable sale-room, it has been offered to him. Clandestine offers are

4. (*Left*) "Medieval" medallion in cock-metal by Billie and Charlie, made about 1860. The inscription is gibberish, the date in Arabic figures ought to be in Roman numerals, the helmets are a gross anachronism, the armour an absurdity. It shows in an exaggerated form almost every mistake a forger can make.
[*Author's Collection*

5. (*Right*) Head in the antique style by Dossena. The features are a travesty of genuine work, and it is obviously of twentieth-century manufacture.
[*Ullstein*

6. Alceo Dossena (1878-1937), the Italian forger of classical, medieval, and Renaissance sculpture. See Chapter IV. [*Ullstein*

rarely made if the object is genuine. At best it will be stolen property, or the sale may, for some reason, be illegal. A collector acquiring an object in circumstances which place him outside the protection of the law is certainly buying trouble of one kind or another.

Many of the circumstances in which forgeries are offered do not need expert knowledge to evaluate them; they need only a little worldly wisdom and a knowledge of human nature. The suspicious buyer may sometimes pass a bargain; he will certainly save himself loss in other cases, and the two will cancel each other out.

A word needs to be said on the peculiar position of some contemporary art, particularly that of the *avant-garde* variety. In this field it is difficult to see what the future is likely to bring. The element of craftsmanship, essential to the detection of forgeries, seldom exists. For instance, the effects of paint dripped on to a canvas, or squirted at it, are so easy to reproduce that there can be no defence against forgery on a massive scale provided the rewards are sufficiently worth while. Much the same applies to certain kinds of sculpture, and to decoration which passes under that name. Obviously "sculpture" produced by welding together selected pieces of scrap-metal will not present the forger with any considerable problems. He only needs access to a scrap-yard and an hour or two's instruction in elementary welding. Forgeries of paintings and sculpture based on abstract forms and patterns also present difficulties to the expert which it seems almost impossible to resolve, unless the history of any particular object can be traced from the moment it leaves the studio.[1]

If a work has received so slight an impress from the hand of its maker that it can be imitated without fear of detection by someone with even a trivial degree of technical competence, it is probably, of itself, trivial and unimportant.

Much contemporary work is no more than a pathological aberration in the long course of art history, fit only as material for the psychiatrist. It does not even provide grounds for healthy controversy between critics and historians, and those who write about it are reduced to

[1] A healthier sign, noticed as this book was being completed, is provided by the statement of producers of mural decorations in the *avant-garde* style, who said: "We don't call them modern art; they're room decoration." It is to be hoped that this refreshing candour will eventually lead to less pretentious nonsense in other quarters.

stringing together meaningless words and phrases. If the practitioners of this kind of nonsense were deceiving only the public and the more obtuse of the critics it would be serious enough, but many of them are deceiving themselves. They are charlatans and do not know it.

Art-dealers anxious for the reputation of their profession, collectors, museum officials, and auctioneers are all vitally concerned in the suppression of forgeries and all forms of fraud in connection with the sale of works of art. It is, however, a complex subject about which little has been published in an accessible form calculated to make the life of the criminal more difficult. Despite the tendency among popular writers to gloss over the nature of these spurious works, and the reasons for which they are fabricated, they cannot be regarded as other than fraudulent. The successful prosecution of the forger, however, is by no means easy. It would be difficult to convince a jury, and a reasonably cautious member of the judiciary, that a clever copy was spurious merely on grounds of style, because attributions of this kind must always be a matter of opinion. Unless objective facts about the nature of a disputed specimen are presented in evidence there is little upon which a judgement could be based. Judges habitually distrust expert opinion which is not manifestly founded on fact, and experience gives them good reason for doing so. It would not be difficult to cite numerous cases in other fields where experts, even those officially appointed, have been wrong. Facts must point overwhelmingly to a definite conclusion if a decision is to be reached.

The steps necessary to complete a successful prosecution for forgery are, first, to prove beyond reasonable doubt that the object is spurious, and then to connect it with the perpetrator. The first step will usually be easier than the second, unless reputable witnesses are prepared to come forward, or, as in the case of Van Meegeren and others, there exist strong and compelling reasons which induce the forger to admit the fraud. So far as the sale of a spurious object is concerned, although the vendor might be compelled to return the money, it would be necessary to prove that he knew he was offering a forgery and had described it inaccurately before he could be successfully prosecuted for fraud. In the case of a dealer specializing in a certain kind of object who sold a blatant forgery (an unlikely occurrence) this might not be difficult, but if it were unusually deceptive it seems likely that a defence that he, also, was deceived would succeed.

The dealer turned rogue is more likely to use a cat's-paw than to sell spurious objects himself. The notable case of Dickins *v.* Ellis early this century is an apt illustration. A well-known dealer of the time employed Ellis, a young man of good presence but little knowledge, to foist on to the founder of Dickins and Jones large quantities of spurious Sèvres and Meissen porcelain at grossly inflated prices. When, because of Dickins' ill health, this lucrative business came to an end, another man was hired to make the personal acquaintance of Dickins on the pretext of being a fellow art-collector. He persuaded the latter to exchange genuine specimens bought elsewhere for spurious, and the fraud was not finally discovered until the executors' sale. Ellis had judgement given against him for £20,000 (equivalent to about £120,000 in 1963), but the original instigators of the fraud escaped. Perusal of some of the expert evidence given in this case recalls the epigram of Mr Justice Hawkins: There are three kinds of liars—liars, damned liars, and expert witnesses. Much of it suggests, however, that by the standards of scholarship today they were no more than deficient in knowledge. Ellis was later indicted for fraud, but escaped on a technicality.

On the Continent the official position of experts in some countries causes the police to take an active part in the suppression of such frauds. In England the law appears to be far less adequate to deal with the problem, and those charged with its enforcement seem disinclined to risk unsuccessful prosecutions. The textbook already mentioned,[1] which devotes some space to art-forgeries in a chapter dealing with cheating and fraud, may be regarded as a statement of the official viewpoint. It points out that the principal reason why frauds are not more stringently prosecuted is that reliable experts are difficult to find, and few members of police forces are qualified to express an opinion. It might well have added that those who have been deceived are, for various reasons, reluctant to prosecute. Most collectors of works likely to tempt the forger to try his skill are affluent enough to write off the loss to experience.

Like criminals operating in similar fields, such as the confidence trickster, the forger usually tries to take advantage of the man who wants a spectacular bargain. The reputable dealer has been trained by

[1] Richard Leofric Jackson, C.B.E. (editor): *Criminal Investigation*, 5th Edition. London, 1962.

experience and the possibility of financial loss to detect forgeries, and those which are deceptive enough to pass his searching eye are very few. Attempts are constantly being made to suppress the traffic by such bodies as the British Antique Dealers' Association by precept and the dissemination of knowledge, and the Goldsmiths' Company (helped by the Association) is extremely active in detecting forgeries of antique silver. It possesses powers to confiscate spurious objects, and it has succeeded in reducing very considerably the amount of fraudulent silver in circulation.

Despite the difficulties which quite obviously exist it would be a valuable service to everyone concerned with the trade in works of art if fraudulent copies could be made much more dangerous to market. The major difficulty, perhaps, is in defining the term "forgery" in borderline cases, which are extremely numerous. In the case of Van Meegeren, once the painting was established as a forgery and its authorship proved, the whole combination of circumstances could lead only to one conclusion. Many older forgeries have been made by men now dead. Others have been fabricated abroad, outside the jurisdiction of the Courts of the country in which they are sold. It is also sometimes difficult to say where a description stops being a problem of authenticity and becomes a problem of attribution. Some older works, replicas made to order centuries ago, now have considerable antique value, whilst Michelangelo's copy of the Roman marble mentioned on page 101 would, today, be worth far more in terms of money than the original.

A solution might, perhaps, be found in the establishment of a voluntary committee drawn from the art-trade, similar to that which inspects objects for inclusion in the Antique Dealers' Fair at Grosvenor House, or to those committees comprising members of the British Antique Dealers' Association which operate a scheme, in co-operation with certain Commonwealth Governments, whereby objects intended for export are examined and certified. A certificate of provenance, age, and condition given by specialists could provide a pedigree which would reassure the buyer and relieve the individual dealer of responsibility in the case of important works. Frauds could thus be detected at an early stage when the matter might be worth passing to the police for further investigation.

These remarks, however, do not apply to objects purchased from members of the British Antique Dealers' Association, which takes special precautions, within the limits of human fallibility, to protect the collector. It is a condition of membership that the business shall be controlled by a person of integrity who has been approved by the Council. He must have the necessary knowledge to buy, sell, and accurately to describe the kind of thing in which he deals. Members are required to give a purchaser an accurate descriptive invoice, in default of which an object is assumed to have been sold as purporting to be of its apparent nature. Additionally, members are required to segregate antique objects from modern in their showrooms and to make a clear distinction between them. They agree to submit any disagreements to the arbitration of the Council. For this reason English dealers have achieved an enviable reputation in their profession.

A good case can also be made out for giving a degree of legal protection to artists' signatures, old porcelain marks, and so forth, just as old silver marks are protected at present. In this way it could be made illegal to import porcelain with the Chelsea gold anchor mark. Obviously the place to stop commercially-made forgeries and deceptive copies from entering the market is at the port of arrival.

There is yet another kind of fraud for which forgeries are sometimes used, particularly forged paintings. This is represented by false insurance claims, which are probably more numerous than the number of cases coming before the Courts seems to suggest. It would hardly be doing the insurance companies a service to enumerate all the possibilities; they range from simulated housebreaking to arson. Since, under English law, criminal prosecutions in cases of this kind are hazardous, such claims are not contested as often as they ought to be. Usually companies refuse to pay when they suspect fraud, and leave the claimant to pursue his claim in the Courts. This he rarely does. There is little incentive for insurance companies to take the matter further since the sum involved is relatively small in relation to the total amount of genuine claims, and a fractional increase in premiums serves to cover losses from this cause. It is, therefore, hardly likely that the subject will be treated very seriously.

It would be a desirable addition if photographs of objects of more than an agreed value were attached to insurance inventories. Apart from assisting to prevent fraud, they would help in the recovery and identification of stolen property. It is noticeable that police circulars referring to thefts of works of art are rarely accompanied by illustrations, as they ought to be if they are to serve their purpose, and verbal descriptions are often deficient in precisely those details which would be most helpful.

*Chapter I*

# *Antiquity*

> It is far from my intention to criticize real critics; by real critics I mean those who begin with facts.
>
> MR JUSTICE BLACK: *Hahn v. Duveen*

The earliest period to attract the attention of the forger is undoubtedly that to which the Piltdown skull was attributed. This is hardly a work of art, but some of the recent literature of the subject is listed in the Bibliography because the methods used to detect the fraud are unusually interesting, and capable of extension to other things. It is impossible to say when the earliest forgery for commercial purposes was made, but certainly such things were common in the days of the Roman Empire, and must date back to the time when works of art were first freely offered for sale.

A forger who was unusually successful in his day was Edward Simpson,[1] also known by the soubriquet of "Flint Jack", who was born near Whitby in 1815. At the age of fourteen he was employed by a local geologist, Dr Young, and accompanied his master on the fossil-hunting expeditions which were then a popular pastime. Later, he collected fossils and sold them to dealers, and eventually he was attracted to the fabrication of flint implements, starting with comparatively simple things such as arrow-heads. Finding that these sold readily he turned his attention to pottery urns, which would be regarded merely as curiosities today, but which passed easily enough at the time. Before

[1] Llewellyn Jewitt: *The Reliquary Quarterly Archaeological Journal*, October 1867. Also reprinted as a pamphlet.

the end of his life "Flint Jack" himself realized how poor these copies were, and few of them could have been sold by the middle of the nineteenth century.

Then he made a Roman breast-plate from an old tea-tray, following this with a Roman milestone. Subsequently he worked in association with a dealer in Colchester, and together the two men sold large numbers of forged objects to London dealers. Some according to Jack were sold to the British Museum. To an inquiry on the point, he replied: "Of course I did! They have lots of my things—and very good they are too."

Increasing knowledge made his task more difficult, and he found it less easy to sell his work. Eventually he was requested to talk about his strange profession before the Geologists' Association, which he did successfully in 1862, demonstrating his skill in the making of flint-weapons on the spot and selling arrow-heads as souvenirs for sixpence each to the members.

"Flint Jack", an eccentric character whose small peccadilloes it is not difficult to forgive, made a bare subsistence from his work, and even his flints would hardly pass expert examination today.

Something may be learned both from the Piltdown skull and the exploits of "Flint Jack". The skull was successful at the time because a discovery of the kind was hoped for. Experts, who might otherwise have been sceptical, were deceived because it tended to confirm preconceived theories. The same attitude of mind can be seen in the reply of Bernhard Berenson to a question from counsel during the course of Hahn *v.* Duveen in February 1929:

"It is extremely difficult, exceedingly difficult, because, you see, it is very largely a question of accumulated experience upon which your spirit sets unconsciously. . . . When I see a picture in most cases I recognize it at once as being or not being by the master it is ascribed to; the rest is merely a question of how to fish out the evidence that will make the conviction as plain to others as it is to me."

This deserves to be read twice to extract the full flavour. The problem for Berenson was merely to "fish out" evidence which could prove his assumption to others. He did not need it for himself. This is the intuitive method of attribution which is a direct invitation to the forger to try his luck or skill. The same statement (with minor alterations) could have come from Dr Smith Woodward, who was deceived by the Piltdown skull for precisely the same reasons. The conclusion had been reached; it was only necessary to find the evidence to support it. The grave dangers which arise from the almost inevitable and unconscious distortions of fact to fit preconceived opinion are not recognized. In a consideration of the kind in which we are engaged it is vitally important first to observe and seek facts, and then to draw whatever inferences may be justified afterwards. In this way fewer mistakes are made, and when they are made the error is less reprehensible.

So far as "Flint Jack" is concerned, hardly any of his work would pass muster today. Knowledge has accumulated rapidly, and scientific techniques and methods of examination have become so exact, that very few forgeries need go undetected. Indeed, it is probable that long before his death "Flint Jack's" profession had become untenable. His success at the time emphasizes that especial wariness is required when approaching objects purporting to come from an artist, a people, or a period about which little is known. For this reason he has been mentioned here.

Men have always collected works of art. The tombs of the Egyptian Pharaohs were storehouses of art, the largest and most valuable so far discovered being that of Tutankhamun. This tomb included objects which were, even then, antique, and some came from other countries. Royal collections of works of art have been found at various sites in Mesopotamia.

Until there was an established trade in works of art there can have been few forgeries, but just as the Phoenicians were the first merchants in the modern sense of the term, importing and exporting goods to all parts of the known world, so were they the first art-forgers. At least, it is difficult to understand otherwise a bowl found at Praeneste in Italy. This was decorated with badly misunderstood Egyptian *motifs*, including a Pharaoh slaying his enemies probably adapted from a temple mural, and provided with a completely meaningless hieroglyphic inscription. It also bore its owner's name, added later in Phoenician characters. Another bowl from the same source was decorated with pseudo-Mesopotamian *motifs*. No doubt we have here the work of a seventh-century Rouchomowsky (page 76), and many surviving specimens of Phoenician art were close derivations of this kind, often discovered in countries other than those in which the *motifs* had their origin. Did some Italian collector want an Egyptian silver bowl? If he did, one could expect the resourceful Phoenician art-dealer to find ways to supply him.

Although records of art-forgery have not commonly survived from antiquity, there are many instances of art-frauds, such as the provision of false signatures. Archimedes, by discovering a method of determining the gold content of the crown of his kinsman, King Hiero of Syracuse, became the first man to expose a fraud by scientific means.

It was not until the days of Imperial Rome that there is evidence of a large and flourishing art-market, but by this time art-dealers and booksellers clustered around the Villa Publica. Forgery was also on a considerable scale. Caligula acquired a large collection of dubious objects by injudicious buying. These, according to Suetonius, were sold by auction to members of the Court, and the Emperor directed the auctioneer to take bids from the nodding head of Aponius Saturninus, a sleepy spectator. The unfortunate man awoke to find himself the possessor at inflated prices of a large part of the Imperial collection.

The Roman art-market seems to have been subject to the kind of rapid fluctuations of taste to be seen in modern times. At one time, like the fashion for Sèvres porcelain sixty years ago, murrhine vases would be the vogue, at another wrought silver, or furniture of rare woods. As in modern times, forgeries of paintings and sculpture, replete with false signatures, were to be had, probably in far greater numbers because little attempt appears to have been made to suppress the traffic. Collectors of small knowledge bought poor-quality works which had been supplied with sham histories even more improbable than those of today, and works of art said to have been in the possession of mythological personages were freely sold. Typical of the *parvenu* art-collector is Trimalchio, drawn from life by Petronius in the *Satyricon*. His conversation at the banqueting table on the subject of his possessions is characterized by absurd errors and childish boasting. Collectors of this kind, who rely upon ignorance, have always been fair game for the forger and the faker as well as for the satirist, and the dubious antique shop was no less a part of the Roman scene than it is in some countries today, although, due to the activities of various professional associations, it is beginning to disappear. It is amusing to recall the words of Martial about a Roman antique dealer: "Rare stuffs, chiselled silver, togas, precious stones—you sell everything, Milo, and your clients take their purchases away with them. But your wife is the best article in your shop, always bought, and never taken away."

Even though the *nouveau riche* collector was a fair target for the satirist and the moralist, there were others whose collecting was more scholarly. Among them must be numbered Julius Caesar and Marcus Agrippa. There were also restorers of works of art, and although, more often than not, they damaged paintings by cleaning them, they were more successful in supplying missing parts for damaged statuary of bronze and marble. Roman copies and forgeries, and even restored works, have their own not inconsiderable value, and these aspects are hardly to be taken into account in estimating their desirability today. It does raise the interesting question of how old a forgery has to be before it loses its fraudulent character and becomes acceptable in its own right, although the answer is more appropriate to a study of the art-market.

Extensive restorations to classical works were made to the order of the collector Giovanni Pietro Campana, Marchese di Cavelli, in the middle of the nineteenth century. Broken statues and reliefs were repaired and patched by the sculptor, Filippo Gnaccarini, who covered the surface of the work with a dull white paste to disguise his intervention. The Campana collection, of which the *maiolica* was acquired by Napoleon III for the Louvre in 1861, contained not a few forgeries and doubtful objects. The restorer, Pinelli, who was also a forger, repaired much pottery for Campana, making up incomplete specimens from fragmentary parts of others. Campana also owned a pottery at which it may be assumed that some of the enormous quantity of *terracottas* appearing in his inventories started life. He was eventually condemned to the galleys for fraudulent conversion of money which he used to add to his collection. Tanagra and similar *terracottas* are discussed on page 129.[1]

Pinelli was one of the makers, in 1863, of the "Etruscan" sarcophagus in the British Museum reproduced on Plate 1. It is worth analysing at this point because its many defects, which have since become obvious, are similar to those of other objects later discussed. It is said that Pinelli made this sarcophagus after restoring a sixth-century specimen for the Louvre, but the differences between this and the Pinelli forgery are

[1] *Cataloghi del Museo Campana*. Rome, 1850. This private museum contained a number of large Etruscan sarcophagi.

profound. The latter was illustrated by Walters (Vol. II, Fig. 183),[1] who quoted Sir Charles Newton's description of the style as "archaic, the treatment throughout very naturalistic, in which a curious striving for truth in anatomical detail gives animation to the group, in spite of the extreme ungainliness of form and ungraceful composition". Walters goes on to remark, "the contrast with the Hellenic style of the reliefs round the lower part is very marked". Both these remarks are perceptive, and both are attempts to explain away to the writer's own satisfaction his intuitive doubts, which yet remained unrecognized for what they were.

Sir Charles Newton referred to "very naturalistic treatment" and a "curious striving for truth in the anatomical detail". Neither of these things were compatible with the period. They do not appear in the modelling of the Louvre sarcophagus. The modelling of the reclining figures on the latter is only superficially naturalistic. It obeys a recognized and recognizable formal convention, the pectoral muscles of the man, for example, being forms of almost geometric accuracy. The drapery falls into certain geometrically-disposed folds and patterns which also follow the bodily contours. The hair is disposed in symmetrical braids. The headdress of the woman has a severe and formal shape which is an integral part of the composition. Regarding the whole, the conception gives an immediate impression of a work which is homogeneous and the product of coherent inspiration. The formal relationships are not an intellectual construction. Looked at in conjunction with archaic Greek sculpture one finds nothing disturbing, because the circumstances which brought each of them to birth were not dissimilar.

If we turn to the forgery, however, we find it informed by a very different spirit. We notice at once Newton's "curious striving for truth in anatomical detail" in the torso of the man, particularly in the pectoral muscles and those of the abdomen. Obviously the sculptor was striving for a close approximation to the natural flesh. The drapery is also an attempt to reproduce the natural fall of a soft material. The woman's hat has no parallel in the formal treatment to be seen in the Louvre example. It looks like a bath-cap, or one worn to protect the hair. The shape of the hands and feet is grotesque; the length of the toes and fingers is exaggerated beyond anything to be seen in genuine

[1] H. B. Walters: *History of Ancient Pottery*. London, 1905.

work. The feet seem better adapted to clinging to tree-branches.

By comparison the faces are a travesty of ancient work. The slight "smile" which appears on the face of the man of the Louvre example has become a leer. The shape of the eyes is wrong, and those of the forgery have been slanted in consequence to an extent which suggests deformity. The composition is certainly ungainly, and, with minor alterations to the drapery, it could well be labelled "Amorous Trippers on Brighton Beach". It passed muster at the time, like the latter forgeries of the Etruscan warriors described on page 129, because little was known of the Etruscans as a people, and their art was neither well known nor understood.[1]

As an epithet "Wog" sounds discourteous and uncomplimentary. Set out in full, however, it means "wily oriental gentleman", and it can be applied to the Egyptian dealer in forged antiquities with good reason. The manufacture of Egyptian "antiquities" for the gullible tourist has provided a good living for many of those who might otherwise have been condemned to a life of semi-starvation, relieved perhaps by an affluent spell as labourers in the tomb-excavations of the archaeologists. It is not surprising, therefore, that much of their work is deceptive and highly ingenious. On several occasions the Egyptian Government has legislated against the export of antiquities, imposing stringent conditions on the small amount which it is prepared to allow out of the country. The vendor of forgeries has taken full advantage of this, offering his wares under clandestine conditions which have precluded recourse to the authorities when the fraud has been finally discovered. Many of them have acquired knowledge and experience from their work with European excavators; enough to fabricate objects which will pass the enthusiastic novice, if not the expert. For these reasons there are in existence a large number of imitations of ancient Egyptian objects most of which are not particularly deceptive, but some require great skill to distinguish them from genuine examples.

The most profitable field is probably the manufacture of spurious gold ornaments, some of them made in Athens and sent back to Egypt for sale. Jewellery, such as necklaces, is sometimes partly genuine—old beads with new gold settings, for instance—and the gold is "aged" by

[1] Large sarcophagi were not very saleable in 1850. Dennis (*Cities and Cemeteries of Etruria*) estimates the value of a good specimen at £100 delivered to London—say about £1,500 in today's money.

covering it with lacquer. Rings are also copied, often those with some particularly desirable ornament. In one instance recorded by Wakeling[1] gold-foil was laid over plaster of Paris. The weight, of course, would differ from that of solid gold, which always feels extremely heavy in the hand. Generally, when handling objects purporting to be of gold it is advisable to pay some attention to weight. Silver-gilt, and gold on a copper base, both give an impression of lightness. Appearances can be deceptive. I once examined a medal given to jurors at an American Exhibition early this century. The surface was undoubtedly gold, and the usual tests gave a positive result. A small cut, however, penetrated through the gold to a lead core underneath. In this particular case the weight by estimation was approximately correct for solid gold. Gold-foil, even on ancient objects, is usually thin, and a small scratch in an inconspicuous place can be used to verify its nature.

Pure gold is soft and easily scratched, and a red patina is usually evidence of age.[2] Wakeling appears to be in error in stating that Egyptian gold is always of 24-carat standard, i.e. pure gold. Other authorities are agreed that silver, copper, and even iron are to be found as alloys, and these cause surface discoloration. Thin gold-foil was used in early times to cover articles of silver, probably with the intention of preventing tarnish. Sheet-gold was also used on mummy-cases over a *gesso* foundation.[3]

Old Egyptian silver, usually alloyed with copper, is not often forged because the effects of age are difficult to counterfeit successfully. A few objects have survived in reasonably good condition, apart from surface tarnish, but many are fragile and corroded to a marked degree.

Copies of Egyptian bronzes were produced in Europe in the seventeenth and eighteenth centuries, but these have rarely deceived anyone well versed in the styles of Egyptian sculpture. Many of the early European imitations were taken from the *Antiquité Expliquée* of B. de Montfaucon, published in 1719,[4] which itself illustrated many

[1] T. G. Wakeling: *Forged Egyptian Antiquities*. London, 1912.

[2] The word *patina* is hardly correct, but long-buried objects of gold often develop this peculiar red, which should remain in places not exposed to rubbing and handling.

[3] *Gesso* is whiting and size which is often used in the preparation of wooden surfaces for painting or gilding.

[4] Also editions of 1722-4 and 1791. English translations by D. Humphreys, London, 1721-5.

doubtful objects. A bronze figure, probably made in Italy, was detected because the Egyptian dealer to whom it was sent as an excavated object already had another in his stock which was precisely similar.

Bronze corrodes easily. The effect of this corrosion is discussed in Appendix 2, but a common product of the process in Egypt is the green copper oxychloride which is due to the prevalent salt. Even cleaned bronzes will show the effect of time, and this is extremely difficult to reproduce deceptively.

Perhaps more deceptive than bronzes are close copies of ancient stone sculpture which are made in Egypt. The realistic style of the period of Akhnaton has been particularly abused as more likely to appeal to contemporary European taste. In this the forger has guessed correctly. The unusual realism of the head of Akhnaton's Queen, Nefertiti, now in the Berlin Museum, has caused it to become one of the best-known and most widely illustrated examples of ancient Egyptian portraiture. Akhnaton's own portrait has been forged repeatedly, probably because his features are distinctive, and known even to the amateur collector of Egyptian antiquities. The peculiar malformation of his thighs, however, was overlooked on one such imitation shown to me. The discovery of the tomb of his son, Tutankhamun, has provided inspiration for some recent forgeries, and, in general, ambitious works tend to copy the idiosyncrasies of a few easily recognized periods. The chances are that any well-publicized discovery in future will be followed by forgeries based on the objects found.

The *ushabti*, a tomb-figure intended to act as a kind of *Doppelgänger* for the dead man in the world of spirits, has been copied in such large numbers that it has assumed the proportions of a thriving industry. It is also seen in many different materials. The *ushabti* is comparatively easy to simulate, and there is less opportunity for mistakes in style. Even the use of dried Nile mud blackened over a charcoal fire has been recorded by Wakeling, who recalled seeing many examples in the houses near Gurna and Deir-al-Bahari just as they came from the mould, awaiting processing.

The softer stones such as serpentine and alabaster are frequently used; the harder stones (basalt, granite and so forth) but rarely because of the time and labour needed to shape them. Modern machinery, however, has been adapted to working some of the harder stones, and the ancient vases have been imitated in a fraction of the time needed to do so manually. Signs of age are not so easy to counterfeit successfully. Some Italians working on the Aswan barrage early this century were adept at cutting the harder stones, and may have been responsible for granite bowls which appeared on the market at the time. These were accused by an unusual regularity of shape, and by suspiciously good condition, with none of the usual signs of age or burial. Granite bowls in fragmentary condition are frequently made up from pieces of others, sometimes with wax to fill out the missing parts. When this has been done well it is often difficult to detect. The contempt exhibited by the oriental dealer for the intelligence of the tourist (in which, as often as not, he is quite justified) is proved by the manufacture of simulated basalt *ushabti* figures in plaster of Paris with a lump of metal embedded to give them the correct weight. Plaster can be scratched with the thumb-nail; basalt is an igneous rock.

Forgeries in wood are not always easy to detect. After carving they are often dipped in plaster of Paris or *gesso* and polychrome painting added. This effectively prevents an examination of the surface of the wood, which will differ significantly in genuine work. Pigments need close examination. Although the brownish-red derived from iron oxide is correct, Prussian blue, a relatively modern colour, suggests at best a fake and at worst completely new work. Wakeling states that the smell of new wood is different from that of old, a test which I have not had an opportunity of making on a forgery. Amusing is his story of an Egyptian forger who learned of this method of discrimination and boiled down a mummy, coating his imitations with the evil-smelling liquid which resulted. The tombs contained many objects of wood which represented those of everyday life, such as ships, farmyards, and so forth, as well as models of funerary chambers and portraits of the gods. Ships are especially sought, and need careful examination. It should be remembered that such objects have only been found in the tombs of important persons, and were originally carved with care and skill. Slovenly work, therefore, is a cause for suspicion. If the wood of a forgery is cut, it will be found that all the signs of age are on the surface. This has usually been covered with size or weak glue and smothered with dust. In some cases microscopic examination of this dust might prove interesting, particularly if the object was made in a different place from that in which it is said to

7. An angel in marble by Dossena. The pose is clumsy and the drapery badly arranged; on the left leg it actually defies the force of gravity. [*Ullstein*

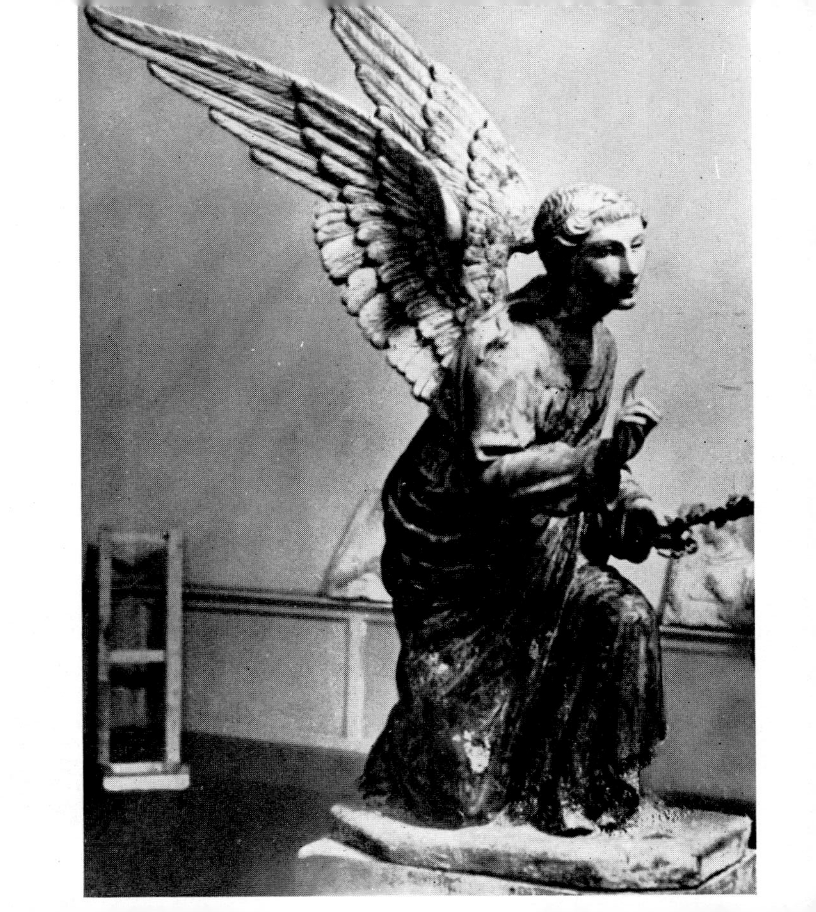

8. (*Right*) Angel by Dossena based on the work of the Sienese painter, Simone Martini (c. 1283–d. 1344). [*Ullstein*

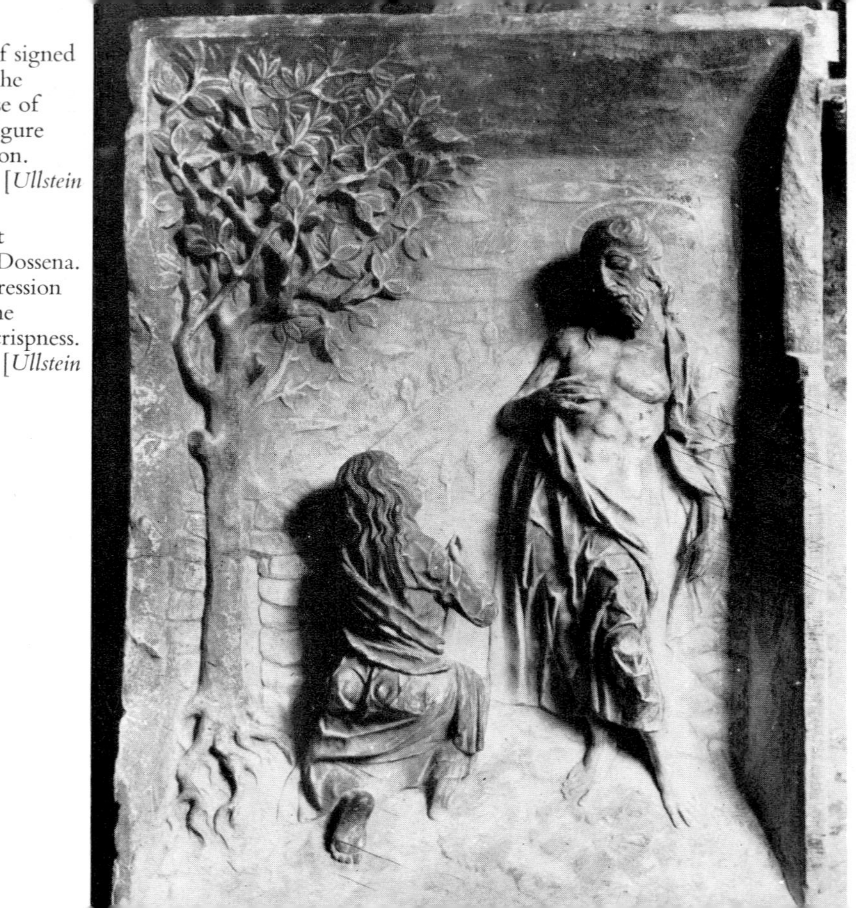

9. (*Left*) Relief signed by Dossena. The ungraceful pose of the kneeling figure arouses suspicion. [*Ullstein*

10. (*Right*) "St Bernard", by Dossena. The facial expression is revealing; the drapery lacks crispness. [*Ullstein*

have been discovered. The dusts of the Mediterranean seaboard, for instance, contain fragments of shells; those of Aswan are rich in granite particles; river sand contains much silica, whilst desert sand usually contains lime, and so on. Of course to employ any such test effectively presupposes that some kind of history has been supplied.

It is certain that the use of glass for glazing stone and *faïence* beads preceded the making of vessels. Coloured glass is an early development, however, and was the result of the accidental inclusion of some kind of impurity which was later identified. Some Egyptian colours are opaque—blue and green from copper, yellow, violet, white, and black. Transparent colours were introduced later, probably in Alexandria, and include brown, violet, and blue. Red, always a most difficult colour to attain in either glass or enamels, which are closely related to glass, appears to have been known in Alexandria about the first century B.C. Forgeries of Egyptian glass are not numerous, and some general remarks on the imitations of early glass will be found on page 195. Old glass, however, is much softer and more prone to decomposition than modern glass, and the effects of time are exceedingly difficult to imitate convincingly.

Egyptian glazed *faïence* is not *faïence* at all. It is a siliceous body coated with a glaze which is usually either blue or green. The glaze is liable to disintegration, falling from the surface and leaving bare patches. It is also likely to change colour. Green changes to brown, and blue to green or white. This, of course, is most difficult to reproduce convincingly.

*Faïence* (sometimes called "porcelain" in older works) was commonly used for the making of *ushabti* figures, and these have been copied in large numbers in a material which seems to be compounded from sand and lime. Less often seen are genuine amulets, small figures of animals (for instance, the hippopotamus with papyrus reeds painted on its flanks), and vessels such as vases, small and large.

Amulets and scarabs, as well as vases, have been copied, although I have not yet seen a hippopotamus. Imitation vases with a piece of genuine mummy-cloth inside have been noticed, as though it were possible to confer age by association. These things are especially popular as a bait for the unsuspecting tourist, to whom the romantic associations of a piece of genuine mummy-wrapping are irresistible.

Hieroglyphic inscriptions are sometimes painted on the *ushabti* figures in black.

Mummy-cases have been made up from fragments, whilst completely new work is not unknown. Genuine but plain mummy-cloth, the warp of which is more pronounced than the woof, has been decorated with figures painted on with a brush instead of a reed. In one such case the dirt in the cloth showed signs of being wetted by the water used as a vehicle for the pigment.

The predynastic tombs of Nubia, complete with sun-dried body and the usual array of vessels in pottery, have been faked. Of these Wakeling tells a story which will bear repeating. In one case it was said that the victim of the sacrifice on the altar of commercial gain was a rival dealer in forgeries, and that the culprits afterwards boasted that they had sold old Aboutig to a museum for £450. He adds that it is much more likely that the corpse came from a local graveyard, where the same conditions prevail as in predynastic times and bodies are likely to dry out completely before decomposition has time to make serious progress.

Of course, the salting of genuine but empty tombs has commonly taken place in Egypt, as it has elsewhere. Almost the only kind of antiquity which the forger has not attempted is the reproduction of an embalmed mummy, although unrelated bones wrapped in mummy-cloth have been sold.

The skilled Egyptologist is often able to condemn an inscribed specimen because of mistakes. The hieroglyphs are sometimes meaningless, or have been copied from another inscription totally unrelated to the object. This is a difficulty which often faces the modern forger of antiquities, and it is usually worth having an inscription checked, whether it be Egyptian, cuneiform, or ancient Chinese.

The discovery of the inscribed stone of Mesha, King of Moab, was made by Charles Clermont-Ganneau, who sent it to the Louvre in 1870. This stone, in 1872, inspired a Jewish forger, Shapira of Jerusalem, to create an entirely new type of pottery figure intended to represent the art of the Moabites. They were unusually crude, and bore no relation to anything else existing from this or any other region. Most had the addition of seven dots, usually arranged in a single line but sometimes in other simple patterns. Meaningless inscriptions appeared on one or two. The heads were mere blobs, the bodies usually roughly cylindrical or pear-shaped with no arms or legs, and the material used was clay so lightly baked that it could not have withstood burial. Although these things would hardly deceive an intelligent child today, enthusiasm for Biblical archaeology at the time was such that they found limited acceptance, and were bought by the Berlin Museum for a large sum. Clermont-Ganneau was able to bribe a workman to reveal the source, and he discovered that Shapira employed an Arab, Selim-el-Gari, who had previously been engaged to copy the inscription on the Mesha stone, to make them. For a time the authenticity of these curious objects was hotly defended by the Museum in question, but eventually they were withdrawn from exhibition. Shapira later tried to sell a manuscript of Deuteronomy on strips of leather to the British Museum, but this had previously been seen by Clermont-Ganneau, who condemned it as a forgery. Shapira committed suicide in Rotterdam in consequence of the discovery.

Forgeries of Babylonian objects exist, especially sculptures. Some are reputed to have been made by an Arab who lived in Baghdad about fifty years ago. Most specimens of this kind will not bear comparison with genuine Mesopotamian work. The man referred to also made moulds of cuneiform tablets from genuine originals, although he sharpened the casts and deepened the incisions by hand. Subsequently he became more ambitious, and covered tablets with meaningless wedge-shaped markings copied haphazardly from genuine tablets. This emphasizes the advisability of submitting early writings on objects which have no ascertainable history for expert examination. A report of the founding of a temple inextricably mixed up with accounts for beer and bread, for instance, is not a surrealist joke of the second millennium B.C., but the result of a forger's ignorance. This is not unknown on genuine objects. The Moors of Spain made the earliest and most prized examples of Hispano-Moresque pottery, sometimes with Arabic calligraphy used decoratively. The tradition was continued by Spanish potters after the expulsion, but the Arabic motifs became progressively degenerate and meaningless because they were not understood and were merely something to be copied.

Luristan bronzes of the first millennium B.C. have certainly been forged. From an unimpeachable source I have an account of a visit in the early 1930s to what was almost a factory about six miles outside Hamadan, where bronzes of this kind were sold as excavated specimens. These seem to have been offered in Persia to tourists for thirty-five years or so at least, in fact ever since they became popular among Western collectors of antiquities. The forgeries include standard-heads and horse-bits, but apart from an obviously false patination they lack the liveliness of originals. One sees specimens occasionally which are obviously not genuine, and they have probably come from this source, although much copying of the kind also seems to have been done in Paris.

Forgeries of pre-Columbian antiquities from the Americas have been made in large quantities for more than a century, and more recent specimens have been unusually deceptive. It is worth remembering that there are stringent laws controlling the export of ancient works of art from Mexico, and an object of importance should either have a history of inclusion in a known collection or documentary evidence of its legitimate export. These things help; but inclusion even in a good collection is not a guarantee of authenticity, and a smuggled object may none the less be impeccable. If neither of these things are present, however, anything purporting to come from Mexico, Colombia, and the Central American states particularly, needs especially careful examination. Forgeries exist in jade, rock-crystal, and gold which are exceedingly dangerous. The bullion value of gold in such things is trivial beside their worth as antiquities.

Reproductions of American pottery are also to be seen, and modern Indian work is a colourable reproduction of old types in some instances. In general, these are not deceptive to anyone well versed in the characteristics of genuine wares. Older forgeries—those made in the nineteenth century—are not usually hard to detect, but the field is not an easy one for the modern European collector. Like Chinese art, it demands a long apprenticeship before judgements are reasonably trustworthy.

Forgeries of ethnographical objects are becoming more frequent to meet an increasing demand from collectors. Benin bronzes, African wooden masks, New Zealand wood-carvings, and similar objects are all reproduced, either deliberately as forgeries, or with less attention to detail as tourists' souvenirs. Recent negro work has been classified in two categories—"airport" art and "Christian Mission school" art. Neither justifies the serious attention of the collector.

Forgeries of negro art, for the most part, are masks and wooden statuettes. They are frequently made by native craftsmen with the assistance of someone acquainted with the requirements of the European market, and are sometimes accused by the marks of modern imported tools. Others were made in Germany when these things first became popular about forty years or so ago. The wood, stained and smoked, was not even from Africa in many cases, the makers relying on the surface treatment to disguise the use of European wood. It has been suggested that forgeries of Congolese carvings were at one time made in Belgium—likely enough, in view of the relationship between the two countries.

In general, the use of steel knives and chisels imported from Europe will have an effect on the style of the carving, and the difference will be especially notable in the case of engraved ornament. This may not, in some cases, seriously detract from the value of a specimen honestly made for purposes natural to primitive art, but it does mean that it is of fairly recent manufacture. It is difficult to detect the methods used without a close acquaintance with genuine work. A poor forgery will certainly not survive expert examination by someone well versed in the type of work in question. It is not difficult, however, to deceive someone whose knowledge is superficial because ordinary methods of judgement are difficult to apply.

*Chapter II*

# *Furniture*

> The basic error lies in the idea that a forgery which has deceived many people looks exactly like the authentic work.
>
> HANS TIETZE

Old furniture is faked and reproduced more often than any other class of object appearing on the art-market. Good forgeries are uncommon.

Any piece of furniture must fall into one or other of the following categories:

(*a*) completely genuine, in untouched condition, or with very minor repairs.
(*b*) repaired more or less extensively.
(*c*) more replacement than original work.
(*d*) faked by the addition of ornament to make it more desirable (often seen in conjunction with (*c*)).
(*e*) an honest commercial reproduction.[1]
(*f*) a reproduction faked with the signs of age.
(*g*) completely new work; a forgery made either from old wood or from wood given the signs of age artificially.

Of these classes, the serious collector of antique furniture is interested in (*a*) and (*b*) and in avoiding the remainder. The buyer who wants

[1] Many such reproductions of English mahogany and satinwood furniture were made in the 1870s by several London manufacturers, especially by Wright and Mansfield. These now have many of the signs of age, although few of them would deceive anyone with experience.

interior decoration can make use of any of these classes, including (*g*) if the price is related to its value, which it seldom is. Work of good craftsmanship, including forgeries, must necessarily be paid for, and it is never cheap. Much genuine furniture is, in fact, undervalued in relation to the manufacturing cost of similar objects.

The antique furniture market is by no means an easy one, since anything, genuine or not, can be used for a practical purpose. The collector who is interested in old furniture as such, and in the investment value of his purchases, needs a working knowledge of furniture styles, enough information about old methods of work and of the tools used to be able to form a judgement on quality and workmanship, an acquaintance with the effects of time on furniture, and profound scepticism. Buying old furniture is made much less easy by the difficulty of examining it properly, and a good deal of experience is needed to detect the signs of tampering from cursory inspection. It is, therefore, better to buy from reliable sources. This chapter will be mainly devoted to detailing some of the more suspicious features exhibited by doubtful specimens.

The most important asset the collector can acquire is an eye for patina, which is the observable effects of time on surface appearance. This cannot be reproduced although it can be imitated, and it is to be seen alike on important and humble specimens. Good patination can lift the value of even a plain example enormously; defective patination will often depress the price of an otherwise genuine object of good quality.

The best examples of old furniture have been polished throughout their life with beeswax and turpentine. This polish needs time and energy to apply, but it ultimately confers an effect which cannot be obtained with modern commercial polishes.

With the passing of time wood hardens and gradually changes colour. This is partly due to exposure to the air, and partly to dust-particles which are forced into the interstices of the wood during cleaning. The surface, therefore, darkens in places. But exposure to light, particularly bright sunlight, has a bleaching effect on the colour which modifies the gradual transition from red to brown seen in old mahogany, for instance, or the increasingly golden shade of old walnut. The result of all these influences is a variegated surface which defies exact imitation, and the collector should study the patination of genuine untouched specimens in places such as the Victoria and Albert Museum until he is reasonably proof against the fake.

There are, however, cases in which genuine patination has later been destroyed. About the middle of the nineteenth century French polish was introduced. This is a kind of varnish made from shellac and spirit which gives a highly-polished, completely characterless surface. It protects the surface of the wood from the actions of time, and much well-patinated old furniture was stripped and smothered with this varnish in Victorian times. This vandalism, typical of the period, not only destroyed a great deal of the charm of old furniture, but it makes it much more difficult to be certain of its character. For the discriminating collector French polish makes a specimen undesirable, and the price will depreciate in consequence.

Until comparatively recent times French polish offered an ever-present temptation to the dealer, because the affluent collector is inclined to regard shiny surfaces and a high finish, in furniture as well as in pictures, as desirable in itself. The quotation which follows is an example of the attitude of mind which led to this ignorant tampering: "An outstanding difference between a product of an uncivilized race and of modern society lies in the finishing touches. Furniture veneered with valuable wood is often preferred to solid furniture of cheaper wood . . . man strives towards perfection and precision which means a removal of rough edges."[1] There can be no doubt that this is the attitude which the forger prefers, and which is most conducive to the production of deceptive work of all kinds. It is, fortunately, an attitude which is gradually being discarded.

The difficulty of reproducing patina has led to the development of a large trade in old wood. It is here that the powers of observation of the collector can be put to good use. The complete history of any work of art can be deduced from its appearance if one knows the language. For instance, if wood has once served another purpose before being made into a piece of furniture, traces of that purpose will almost inevitably remain. The patina of an old table-top will be different from that of the sides of a commode. If an effect appropriate to the first appears on the second, an explanation must be sought. It may be a repair; equally it is possible that the whole piece is a forgery. Scratches and similar marks which are difficult to account for in one

[1] *Made of Earth*. Cornell University pamphlet, 1935.

position may be perfectly natural in another, showing that the wood is not being used for its original purpose. Nail-holes appear in the wrong place, and need to be "stopped". This can usually be seen on careful examination. Such things sometimes occur in oak table-tops made from old floor-boards.

Cut edges will have a different colour from the old surface, and will have been stained to match. But staining will not reproduce the old colour exactly. Take, for example, an old table-top which has been cut down and given fresh carving to the edges. Staining will produce an even colour which is approximately similar to the original, but the wood is now older and harder than when it was made, and even the same stain as that used originally to give the wood its final colour would yield a different result. The forger, therefore, has to use something else, and it is hardly surprising that this is only an approximation. The wax mixed with dirt which, in an old specimen, collects and hardens in the angles of the carving will have been added, and if this has been done fairly recently it will still be soft. Wax, like oil-paint, takes a long time to *harden*, although it appears to dry fairly quickly.

The more complicated the carving, the more difficult it is to reproduce the effects of time satisfactorily, and this aspect should always be the first to which attention is directed. In any elaborate carving some parts will be lower than others, and protected from the cloth used for polishing. These will remain sharp and detailed. The highest parts ought to be softened and rounded. The duster is not the only cause of this kind of wear; human hands also play a part. A chair, the arms of which have carved finials, is often so made that the hands fall naturally on the carving. It is a common habit to rub the polished wood finials of a chair with the palms of the hands, and in two hundred years or so this can cause an appreciable amount of wear.

Forgers, of course, know all about wear and patina, and close and intelligent observation is often needed to detect the fraud. The cleverest fakes are those to which the greatest care has been given to simulate this aspect convincingly. For instance, one observer records seeing a workman walking past some newly-made stools to find out where the leg would naturally brush them in passing, so that signs of wear and polish could be put in the right places.

It is especially important to examine the unpolished wood to be found in those parts which are not exposed. New wood is difficult to disguise, and staining and attempts to give it the signs of age are much more easily detected. In some cases polish is applied to parts which would not normally be polished in a genuine specimen, simply because it would be too dangerous to leave the raw surface exposed.

Pieces fresh from the workshop are battered with heavy sticks to simulate bruising from natural wear and accident. Often a piece will be damaged and repaired in a clumsy and obvious way with the intention of distracting the eye from making a close examination of the remainder, and the seller will offer to have the part repaired skilfully as part of the bargain. This is usually cause for suspicion. A reputable dealer having a fine piece to sell will obviously have any essential repairs done before he offers it, not only from natural pride in his stock, but because an object in good condition will be easier to sell. Of course some discretion needs to be exercised. A dealer may put a mediocre piece in his basement to await repair and will show it if he gets an inquiry for something of the kind.

Minor pieces of a suitable type (for example, imitations of small antique tables) are sometimes lent to restaurants, where in a few months they receive the wear and tear of many years in normal circumstances, as well as stains and polish in the right places.

The forger is often a specialist, decorating a cabinet made by someone else to a pattern provided. The old craftsman was usually capable of carrying the job through to its conclusion, and the *motifs* were traditional. He had grown up with them during his apprenticeship. Fakes which have been decorated later with carving can often be detected by the shallowness and skimped appearance of the work. The old craftsman, who had a clear vision of the ultimate form his furniture was to take, be it a cabinet or a chair, allowed himself plenty of wood to cut away. Because he worked without continually referring to a pattern his carving is much more free and less mechanical in appearance. The collector should take every opportunity of studying genuine carving until he is completely familiar with it.

English furniture, particularly that of the eighteenth century, is remarkable for the quality of its design and workmanship, and even plain specimens have this kind of excellence. It has been well said that craftsmen of this period decorated a construction rather than constructed a decoration, and this is worth bearing in mind when examining suspected specimens. In the Victorian period the craftsman responsible for carved decoration usually did not know where to stop. Every conceivable plain surface received its share of ornament. Eighteenth-century cabinet-makers, however, used carved work with discrimination, balancing it against plain surfaces which depended for their effect on the figure of the wood.

A method of reproducing carved walnut panels of which I have no direct knowledge, but which is vouched for by Nobili,[1] is the application of a matrix of hot iron cast from a mould taken from genuine carving. This is pressed, whilst very hot, on to the wood, burning the pattern into it. The burnt surface, when the desired depth has been attained, is said to provide a good foundation for further treatment. There is nothing inherently impossible in Nobili's description, although it seems doubtful if it could be adapted to deep carving. It is doubtful, also, if panels made in this way could succeed in deceiving a skilled observer, no matter how cleverly the subsequent surface were faked. In any case such panels would form only part of a spurious piece, and the remainder ought to provide sufficient evidence of fraud.

Beware of elaborate decoration, and treat any such objects with more than usual care. The forger knows that the simplest things are the most difficult to forge successfully, and these he avoids. The revealing characteristics of the fake and the forgery can often be hidden beneath a mass of ornament, and may then escape the unwary eye. An object of any kind which carries a greater amount of ornament than its purpose warrants, or in which the ornament appears to be excessively complicated, is nearly always a worthy target of suspicion. Exuberant ornament is quite usual on genuine pieces, but it is rarely incoherent. Nineteenth-century imitations particularly suffer in this way especially, because the purchaser demanded an excess of ornament for its own sake.

Worm-holes are sometimes regarded as a sign of genuineness, but their value for this purpose is very doubtful. They are made by the larvae of the furniture-beetle (*Anolium punctatum*), which also attacks structural timbers and panelling. In a genuine piece of furniture their presence, either now or in the past, will be revealed by a small circular entrance hole. The track is governed to some extent by variations in the structure of the wood, since the larva prefers its food to be as soft as possible. The track, for this reason, is sometimes straight, and some-

[1] Ricardo Nobili: *The Gentle Art of Faking*. London, 1922.

times curved. Faked worm-holes, done with a drill, will be straight. The legend that these holes were made with a shot-gun is apocryphal, but if anyone in the past had been misguided enough to try it, a probe would immediately detect lead at the bottom of the hole.[1] A forger who is compelled to use worm-eaten wood can hardly help cutting through some of these tunnels, and a few are sliced longitudinally, appearing on the surface as half-tunnels visible throughout their length. Attempts are made to fill them with wax or some kind of stopping, but they can usually be seen on close examination, and the stopping invariably falls out after a few months. Worm which is still active can be detected by tapping the wood sharply, when a fine sawdust will be emitted from the holes. Generally, the worm avoids the harder woods and the heart-wood. He prefers soft wood and sap-wood. Walnut is particularly liable to attack by worm; oak and mahogany much less so.

Much early English furniture especially, and a great deal of eighteenth-century provincial furniture, was made from oak. Oak is a hard wood of exceptional strength which was formerly much used for constructional work, including the floor-boards mentioned, as well as panelling and structural timber. The grain is well-marked and easily recognized. Old oak used in furniture-making is now dark brown, and the use of oil turns it to a rich dark colour which is almost black. Some early specimens have been given a coat of thin varnish, probably at a slightly later date, which is not to be confused with French polish.

Walnut has been much used for furniture-making, especially at the end of the seventeenth century and during the first decades of the eighteenth. English walnut is now rare; timber was felled in large quantities and no systematic planting undertaken to replace it. At present walnut is usually imported from a number of sources, and these woods differ from the English variety in colour and figure. The forger, therefore, finds supplies of suitable wood particularly difficult. Walnut is hard, but not as hard as oak. Slight pressure will dent it, whereas oak resists a test of this kind. Walnut is excellent for carving, and rarely warps or twists during seasoning. It has the defect of being particularly prone to attack by woodworm. Walnut is much valued for its decorative figure (the name applied to the appearance of the

[1] The characteristic pattern of a shot-gun is not difficult to recognize. One can easily be made by firing at a paper target.

grain on the surface), and it usually develops an increasingly rich, deep tone with age, the dark striations of the figure becoming more marked. When it is exposed to the sun this wood develops a pleasing greyish shade, and this, like the sun-fading of other woods, is usually found on the top of a piece which has been stood in a window where sunlight is strongest. Fading on the front as well as on the top suggests some other part of the room, and fading on opposite sides demands much closer inspection. There are few rooms where a strong light can fall on both sides of a cabinet, for instance. Old walnut was sometimes given a coat of varnish, but solid work in particular was often oiled and waxed.

Mahogany has always been the preferred hardwood for decorative purposes since its introduction. Because of its close texture a long period of seasoning is necessary, and the colour mellows in consequence. Mahogany does not twist or warp, and it is an excellent wood for carving, allowing the work to be crisp and detailed. Although known in England during Elizabethan times, it was not imported before 1730, and did not come into general use before 1750. It owes its popularity to the fact that it was a favourite with Thomas Chippendale. The first imports came from San Domingo, and this variety is hard, has a close grain, is dark brown in colour with a slight figure, and is heavier than the varieties which were imported later. It was generally treated with linseed oil.

The new sources of supply (Cuba, Jamaica, and the South American mainland) produced a wood which was lighter in weight and colour, with a more obvious figure. Figure is probably more handsome, and more easily seen, in mahogany than in almost any other furniture wood in general use.

A yellowish or reddish tone in mahogany is often found on forgeries, and on old pieces which have been stripped and polished. The effect of stripping may be judged from the methods used. Solvents are employed to remove or soften any adherent wax or varnish. Caustic soda and liquid ammonia are both recommended for this purpose in handbooks. Softened varnish is removed with a scraper of metal, and the surface "finished", in more senses than one, with glass-paper. Holes and dents are stopped, and the wood is stained and French polished. There is, of course, no reason why old furniture which has already been treated in this way should not be repolished by the same methods.

The damage has already been done. Repolishing may improve the appearance, and can hardly worsen it.

Satinwood, which probably arrived in England about 1765, was in general use about ten years later, and it soon became popular, particularly for furniture in the neo-classical style. It was especially used by Hepplewhite and Sheraton. It was at first scarce and expensive, and used for inlays in conjunction with mahogany. Later it was more extensively employed, generally in the form of veneers. There are two principal varieties—East Indian and West Indian. Satinwood used for furniture during the eighteenth century and early in the nineteenth came from the East Indies. This resembles the West Indian wood except that the colour is yellowish-brown instead of the paler yellow of the latter, which has a more open grain and was not used for furniture-making until the nineteenth century. Satinwood was usually given a thin coat of varnish.

Woods were stained for decorative purposes and to improve the colour during the eighteenth century. The colours mentioned in eighteenth-century works[1] include reds of various shades, blue, green, purple and black, whilst white woods were stained yellow with turmeric. Mahogany was stained to improve the colour before the wood was finally treated, and a thin varnish employed at the time of manufacture was seed lac dissolved in alcohol.

If the patination of old wood is difficult to simulate deceptively, gilt furniture presents fewer problems to the forger, although detection in most cases is not difficult. Dossie has much to say on the subject. Gilding was of two kinds—the laying on of gold in the form of finely-beaten leaves or in the form of powder. The principal methods used were oil-gilding, varnish-gilding, and japanner's gilding or gilding with gold-size. Leaf-gold could be bought in a number of shades and grades of quality. Both copper and silver were used as alloys in the inferior qualities, the former giving a greenish hue, the latter being pale in colour. The full yellow appealed to the more exacting taste of the period, but a fashion for reddish-gold was to be seen shortly before 1750. Dossie recommended that a specimen of perfect colour be kept with which any new parcel could be compared. The so-called "Dutch gold" was employed for cheaper work. This was nothing more than

[1] Robert Dossie, *The Handmaid to the Arts* (London, 1765) is a mine of information on contemporary methods employed in the decorative arts.

copper-leaf, which had the disadvantage of changing colour and developing green spots unless covered by a lacquer or varnish to exclude air. It was recommended for large pieces, and for theatrical work.

Oil-gilding was executed by cementing the leaf to the surface with fat oil, prepared from purified linseed oil. It was mixed with a little yellow ochre, to which vermilion was sometimes added. Japanner's gilding was done with gold powder, or with imitations of it, cemented to the ground by gold-size, which is similar to drying oil. The powder was prepared from leaf-gold by grinding it in honey. The mixture was then put in water to dissolve the honey, leaving the gold to sink to the bottom of the vessel. A similar powder was prepared from "Dutch gold". Bronze powders were sometimes used for colouring plaster busts and figures in imitation of bronze, and this, incidentally, is often done today.

Silvering was executed by the same methods, using either leaf or powder, but immediate varnishing was essential to prevent oxidation and tarnishing.

In the making of furniture and picture-frames the wood was first covered, or primed, with *gesso*. In the middle of the eighteenth century this was commonly made by mixing whiting with a size of parchment scraps or cuttings of glovers' leather boiled to a jelly in water. The *gesso* was laid on the surface of the wood, which had been prepared by rubbing down with coarse and then fine abrasive. Seven or eight coats were applied with a brush and allowed to dry, and the surface was rubbed until it was perfectly even. The work was then gone over with gilder's size to which a little vermilion had been added, and sometimes yellow pigment was used to give the appearance of gold in the deeper parts of the carving where it would be difficult to add the leaf. Finally, the work was damped with water and the gold-leaf laid on and burnished with a dog's tooth or polished with agate burnishers.

The *gesso* was laid on to the wooden carcass of furniture which was of comparatively recent manufacture. The carcass was usually of deal, and this has shrunk in course of time, leaving minute cracks in the gilded surface. The gold is also considerably darker on surfaces which face upwards, since the falling dust of two centuries or more has altered the colour of the gold. This point is usually missed by fakers, who give the surface too even a tone. In the case of tall mirror-frames, the gilding often shows signs of wear at the bottom because this is more accessible to the duster than the upper parts, which were cleaned less frequently. Some old pieces have been regilded, and exhibit an even, harsh brightness which often obscures fine detail. Others have been refurbished with so-called gold-paint, which is usually made from powdered brass. A few have been painted with black or brown oil-paint, and this can often be removed with solvents.

Silvering belongs to the last thirty years or so of the seventeenth century, and is rarely to be seen later. It almost always appears on elaborately carved stands for painted lacquer cabinets. Surface cracks are even more obvious than on gilded work, and the silver has a yellowish tinge. These characteristics have not been successfully imitated, although attempts have been made.

During the seventeenth century and the early part of the eighteenth Oriental lacquer was extensively imported into Europe and used for the manufacture of furniture and similar objects. Although Oriental lacquer does not appear to have been the subject of recent forgeries, probably because the materials and methods of working defy close simulation, many copies were made at the time which are now collectors' items in their own right. This work was known as "japanning", and the term is correctly used to describe the covering of various woods with a varnish mixed with opaque colours, the surface afterwards being decorated with painting and gilding.[1] Although this was, at one time, extremely popular as a method of ornamenting furniture, it had declined by the middle of the eighteenth century and was then limited principally to the decoration of sedan-chairs and such things as snuff-boxes and screens. At this time similar work was being done in France in the so-called *vernis Martin*, a type of japanner's varnish invented by the brothers Martin. Most japanning was done on a wood foundation, although metal and even leather were both used to a small extent. Paper, converted into *papier mâché*, was also employed.

Priming of the surface, as well as veneering, was commonly used as a foundation on the older English work, and on that done in France. Much unprimed work was done in Birmingham, and this was due to the tendency for priming to crack and peel off. Dossie noted that Birmingham snuff-boxes never peeled or cracked, whilst those of Paris were easily damaged.

[1] John Stalker and George Parker: *A Treatise of Japanning and Varnishing* Oxford, 1688. Reprinted 1960.

11. "Madonna" by Dossena—a wood-carving based on the work of Simone Martini. The pose and the drapery both give cause for suspicion. [*Ullstein*

12. "Lucrezia Donati", marble carving by Bastianini. This is in a completely different class from the other objects illustrated here. The features are, perhaps, the most revealing point. Their nineteenth-century origin can be seen, although with some difficulty. [*Victoria and Albert Museum*

When it was used, priming was of *gesso*, and the addition of isinglass reduced the tendency to crack. Two coats were given and smoothed. Without priming, the ground was prepared by varnishing with shellac dissolved in alcohol (spirits of wine). The ground itself was flake-white (white lead) mixed with shellac varnish, and other pigments were used in the same way for coloured grounds. Pigments in general use included Prussian blue, King's yellow, and vermilion; a green from Prussian blue and King's yellow; orange from vermilion and King's yellow; purple from vermilion and Prussian blue; and black from either carbonized ivory or lamp-black. A tortoiseshell ground for such small items as snuff-boxes was achieved by brushing vermilion over with black, a simulation mentioned by Stalker and Parker in 1688.

Painting was carried out in pigments mixed with varnish and the final operation was the laying on of several coats of clear varnish, polished when dry with a very mild abrasive, such as tripoli or rotten-stone (pumice-stone) mixed with a little oil. Colours were sometimes laid on with water instead of varnish, but this was unsatisfactory. It was, however, recommended for the amateur decoration of furniture because of the ease with which such colours could be applied. Inferior surviving work is usually attributable to the efforts of the amateur.

Coloured or transparent varnishes were also laid on to metals either to vary the colour or to preserve them from the atmosphere. The lacquering of brass clock-dials and spandrels is an example. Silvered picture-frames were sometimes lacquered with coloured varnishes, but this had fallen into disuse by the middle of the eighteenth century.

The most characteristic specimens of seventeenth-century japanning are the large cabinets on elaborately carved stands made during the reign of Charles II. Later English work includes small tables, chests, corner-cupboards, small bookcases and bureaux, chests of drawers, and clock-cases. These are usually in the style of Queen Anne or George I. After about 1730 only clock-cases were commonly made.[1]

Many specimens of lacquer work have been damaged and restored. Japanning was particularly vulnerable as a form of surface finish, and few examples today are in good condition. Some, too, have been

[1] The reader interested in pursuing the study of the art of japanning should consult Dossie, as well as Stalker and Parker. The former is to be found in the larger reference libraries; the work of the latter has been reprinted. For Oriental lacquer see page 117.

repainted and varnished afresh, and the nature of the original work makes this difficult and tiresome to remove.

Forgeries exist of the elaborate seventeenth-century cabinets on stands. Those with grounds of different colours inside and outside should be seriously questioned. This was not a contemporary practice. Surface appearance should be examined carefully. Wear from cleaning may even have reached the *gesso* foundation, and will be seen where dusting has been most frequent. It is useful to ask someone (preferably a woman accustomed to such work who, of course, is not told the reason for the request) to dust an object and observe the sequence of operations. This gives some indication of the points at which wear is most likely to have occurred. Another place to be observed is the region of the keyhole, where there ought to be scratches surrounding the escutcheon-plate. This can frequently be seen on furniture generally when it is in original condition, particularly on bureaux and similar pieces where it has been customary to use the locks provided. The clear varnish used as a finishing coat on old lacquer pieces will have mellowed and changed its colour with time, and this has a noticeable effect on the colours underneath, particularly on any gilding present.

There follows a description of a seventeenth-century cabinet shown by the Burlington Fine Arts Club in their exhibition of forgeries in 1924.[1] This cabinet was partly genuine but extensively faked, and it forms an excellent guide to the examination of this kind of work. Three drawers had been added to the interior. They were made from old drawer-liners and dovetailed; the others were nailed. On a completely genuine specimen all would have been made in the same way. Lacquer was applied directly to the carcass instead of over a veneer of fruitwood, which was used to prevent the serious cracking and peeling resulting from shrinkage of the carcass wood. (Another reason is that the soft carcass wood, usually pine, left the harder annular rings of its grain in slight relief as it shrank.) In genuine cabinets the colour of the lacquer on the *inside* of a door, for example, will be brighter than that on the outside because it is less exposed to the effects of light and atmosphere. In the case of the object under discussion the colour was the same on both sides. Large cracks on the exterior surface did not resemble genuine cracks, which usually form a minute network. The

[1] *Catalogue of an Exhibition of Counterfeits, Imitations, and Copies*. Burlington Fine Arts Club, 1924.

colour of the lacquer *behind* the escutcheon-plate covering the keyhole, where it had been protected from the light, was the same as that of the remainder—incontrovertible evidence of recent manufacture. The metal mounts were tarnished. Old mounts were protected either by varnish or by gilding.

On a clock-case which had been completely relacquered, probably because it was too extensively damaged to be worth restoration, the green ground was the wrong shade, and the surface had been cracked artificially by applying quick-drying plaster to the newly-varnished surfaces. Plaster contracts as it sets, and this would have the effect of crazing all but a hard varnish. The effect was quite different from the cracks resulting from the contraction of carcass wood. In this particular case the forger made a ludicrous mistake. Old clock-cases are always damaged to some extent at the bottom by brooms, and by impact from the feet during winding. The latter usually passes unnoticed, but observation will prove how frequently it happens. A protective strip of wood is often added to the bottom of the case, and this is sometimes called, significantly, a "kick-plate". In the case of the specimen under discussion the bottom was almost as perfect as the remainder. Finally, the artificial patina had been much too evenly applied. The sides of genuine specimens are usually darker than the front. All these points are comparatively trivial, but they add up to an irrevocable condemnation.

The next aspect requiring consideration is the skill displayed in craftsmanship. The forger may, in some cases, equal the old craftsman in skill; his work is rarely so competently produced. Some objects are rare today; in former times they were made in relatively large quantities. In this way the old craftsman developed a remarkable degree of manual dexterity. The forger, however, does not usually make any particular class of object in large quantities; he devotes his attention to important-looking specimens likely to command a high price on the art-market, which for this reason are notable also for their rarity. To make rare objects in quantity would be to defeat his purpose and facilitate detection. It is possible that one rarity might have been overlooked, or even two, but if such things begin to appear in threes, fours, and more, even though they are marketed in different places, suspicion is certain to be aroused. Many of these things, therefore, are betrayed by the forger's inexperience.

The old craftsmen served a long apprenticeship to the use of the kind of hand-tools which are now obsolete, and they frequently employed techniques which are not ordinarily taught today. The forger cannot afford the time to learn to use old tools, and he employs those which are ready to hand. He is, for this reason, vulnerable. The marks left by a circular-saw are unmistakable. Unless wood has subsequently been planed or sanded an ordinary saw leaves slight parallel ridges. The circular saw leaves curved ridges, which can often be felt with the finger-tips even when they cannot be seen. Of course, this can only be done on such things as drawer-bottoms which were not brought to a high finish, but the forger has to choose between sanding them smooth (unusual on all but later specimens of genuine furniture) or leaving the saw marks. His choice either way tells the same story to the collector who knows the language.

Old furniture will show a progressive improvement in minor details of finish and in refinements of design. Much oak furniture is primitive in construction, and early cabinet-work generally often made insufficient allowance for "movement" in the wood. All furniture woods alter slightly in their dimensions as a result of changes in humidity. When moisture is absorbed a slight expansion takes place, often enough to jam a door or a drawer; when drying occurs there is a corresponding shrinkage. This factor has to be taken into account in all structural work. Joints in a concrete road, for example, are expansion joints to allow for increases in the size of the slab on a hot day; they are filled with a plastic substance like bitumen, which forms ridges standing above the surface when a considerable degree of expansion has taken place. In some early cabinet work insufficient allowance was made for shrinkage, and the panel has cracked in consequence. These cracked panels are often unsightly, and the result of incompetent designing. They are also a sign of age in many cases. Much the same thing has happened with table-tops and flaps. Trouble arose when veneers with a different shrinkage rate from the carcass wood were used.

An excellent test of age which can be used for chairs, and sometimes for other small items of furniture, is to rock them firmly to see whether the joints are loose. New work will be immovable; old work often yields to some extent unless it has been taken apart and reglued. The reason is that there is a slight shrinkage at the joints in genuine specimens, whereas in new wood there is no shrinkage and the glue will also be holding firmly. The test is, of course, inappropriate for cabinets and large objects generally.

Nails and screws are sometimes suggested as a test of authenticity, but it is very uneven in value. The presence of old nails is probably of greater significance than that of screws of the correct design, especially if they do not appear to have been disturbed. Nails do not fall out easily, and nearly always they have to be drawn. Until about 1790 nails were hand-cut, but the demolition of old houses provides a small but constant supply. Screws were introduced about 1675, and therefore will not be found in anything made earlier than this unless they have been added subsequently in the course of repair or addition. The earliest have hand-filed threads with a shallow spiral, practically no taper, and no point. The slots are nearly always slightly off-centre. The tapering gimlet-pointed screw with a more pronounced spiral in the thread was not introduced until 1851. Modern screws in furniture suggest either replacement or that the piece was manufactured subsequently to 1851 at the earliest. If the screws securing a lock or a hinge are in question, replacement is quite likely. Elsewhere, replacement is not impossible but much less probable. The chance that a screw which has been in place for a century or so will come loose, fall out, and need to be replaced by a modern product is fairly remote unless there is some kind of movement at the part in question.

Chairs need close examination when they occur in matching sets, particularly if the set is unusually large and complete because this is extremely rare. Small sets of six are sometimes expanded to twelve by using old parts in conjunction with new. This can be very deceptive if it has been well done, because even though the new parts are detected (and this is not unduly difficult) they may be mistaken for repairs. Close examination of each chair in a set is essential.

A revealing point is to be found where the central splat meets the bottom rail of the back and rests on a shaped piece sometimes termed the "shoe". This shoe in a genuine chair was invariably made separately from the straight bottom rail, and the joint between the two will be apparent. Forgers usually make the two parts in one piece, although they sometimes try to imitate the appearance of a joint if they are unusually knowledgeable.

Early settees have much in common with the chair, the design of those of the early part of the eighteenth century being based on two or three chairs joined side by side. Those designed on a two-chair principle will have one leg in the centre, a three-chair settee will have two. Any other arrangement should be viewed with grave suspicion. Stools with upholstered seats, instead of the old drop-in seat, also need careful examination. They have sometimes been fabricated from cabriole chair-legs, although the underframing will usually reveal when this has been done.

Most imitations of chairs are based on the Chippendale period, but the later satinwood chairs have also been copied. Symonds[1] points out that the modern copy is generally much lighter in weight than a genuine chair. Most reproductions were made in the 1870s, and variations in design from that of the eighteenth-century originals will be noticed.

By far the greater amount of forged English furniture, and nineteenth-century reproductions, are in mahogany, and it is essential to be able to recognize the types of wood employed at various periods. The forger often has to make do with such things as mahogany counters, a feature of some older shops, or Victorian table-tops, but these were all made from a variety of mahogany not in use in the eighteenth century. The reasonably expert observer usually finds little difficulty in separating the various woods, and the best safeguard is a close study of genuine examples, such as those to be seen in the Victoria and Albert Museum.

Less easy to detect are those specimens which have been "improved" by later carving. Particularly in demand for this kind of work by fakers are the mid-eighteenth-century English commodes to designs based on those of France. Some have plain canted corners which can be ornamented to make something more desirable. The French faker finds his task a little easier, because he can add gilt-bronze mounts to plain provincial commodes, and this is more difficult to detect if it has been well done. The slightly later English half-circular commodes of satinwood have painted and inlaid decoration added. The half-circular types are rarely entirely new, although the straight-sided commode presents fewer difficulties in manufacture. In general, every specimen of cabinet work should be carefully examined for "improvements" of one kind or another, especially of those features likely to enhance the value, such as a pediment top to bookcases.

[1] R. W. Symonds: *The Present State of English Furniture*. London, 1921.

Tables are always in demand, and the small inlaid walnut table of the end of the seventeenth century has been commonly forged. Most spurious specimens will be relatively new constructions (i.e. made within the last hundred years or so), and a description of the points to be observed in one such table exhibited at the Burlington Fine Arts Club exhibition will provide some valuable hints on how furniture ought to be examined.

This particular example had scroll-legs and a serpentine stretcher, and was ornamented with panels of seaweed marquetry. The carcass-work and drawer-linings were made from old deal and oak, and care was taken to preserve the old surface wherever it was exposed to view. The originals were designed as side-tables; the forgery was a centre-table and therefore had marquetry panels on all four sides instead of only on the front and at the sides. The inside surfaces of both legs and stretcher were veneered to disguise freshly cut wood. There were no cracks of the kind commonly found in old veneered work. The background of the marquetry panels was darker than the borders because the former were of holly and the latter of boxwood. Holly is a relatively soft and absorbent wood, whereas box is close-grained and much harder. The holly, therefore, absorbed more of the stain needed to finish the surface. A genuine example, however, would not have been stained at all, but allowed to mellow with time, and the inlay would therefore have been approximately of the same colour. When the drawer-handles were removed the colour of the surface behind them was found to be the same as the remainder, whereas it ought to have been lighter in colour as a result of the protection afforded by the covering metal. The removal of handles from a suspected specimen is an excellent test.

The most common forgery is undoubtedly the old tripod table with a circular top. These are often made from discarded pole-screens or damaged *torchères* cut down, with a circular top added. Very rarely the top is as old as the tripod, and attention should then be directed to the way in which the two are joined together. New work is usually fairly obvious. Circular tops of this kind are sometimes taken from a damaged dumb-waiter. Nearly always, however, the top is newly-turned from old mahogany, and a useful test is to measure it with callipers. A genuine circular top is always very slightly oval due to shrinkage across the grain. This shrinkage is, of course, very slight, one specimen showing $26\frac{7}{8}$ ins. *with* the grain and $26\frac{5}{8}$ ins. *across* it, but this is enough to say that the wood had not been freshly turned. An antique-dealer of my acquaintance recalls that his introduction to the trade as a boy many years ago was in making tables of this kind by joining trays and circular tops to tripod bases.

Genuine tripod tables do not often have carved legs, although the toes are sometimes carved, but carving is added to plain specimens when there is enough wood to cut away. The table with a plain top is enhanced by a carved rim, or by adding a fret-cut gallery. In the latter case it is often difficult for the forger to disguise the signs of recent work to the inner surface of the fretted pattern at every point.

Satinwood tables need to be examined first to see that the mellow colour of the old wood is present. Painted decoration is frequently added, and covered with varnish. This should be inspected very carefully, remembering that the style should be compatible with the neo-classical designs then fashionable. Bastard *rococo* motifs mark the work immediately as spurious or as a much later reproduction. That an old table was not originally decorated with painting may be deduced from such points as a cross-banded edge, inlay at the top of the legs, and so forth. Inlaid decoration is usually a sign that painting was not originally intended. Generally, the colour is poor and dull, and the painting rarely shows those signs of wear which are inevitable in an old specimen. Most such fakes are French-polished.

Inlay is added to genuine plain examples, and is not only accused by an unwonted profusion of ornament, but by irregularities of surface. Over-decoration is a common habit of the forger with which he hopes to distract the eye from those points likely to reveal his handiwork. Pembroke tables, because of their popularity, need careful examination, and it is worth remembering that genuine satinwood veneered tables are almost invariably cracked. This is especially noticeable in Pembroke tables and in such large expanses as the sides of cabinets.

Much of the value of a mirror often depends on whether the glass is original or a replacement. In the chapter devoted to glass I have referred to the methods whereby genuinely old mirror-glass may be recognized. I am here concerned with frames. It is not always realized that mirrors of all kinds were exceedingly expensive throughout the eighteenth century, partly due to the cost of making large sheets of glass of a quality suitable for the purpose, and partly for fiscal reasons.

When the duty on glass was repealed the price dropped at once, but an examination of some of the early catalogues still preserved in the archives of Christie's, the auctioneers, reveals that mirrors were often the most expensive items in a furniture sale, and only rarely did prices for bureaux, and cabinet-work generally, even approach those for large wall-mirrors.

Much more common are the swing-mirrors intended to be stood on dressing-tables. These can be examined for new work or tampering in the manner already suggested. The appearance of the mirror ought to tally with the remainder. Gilt wall-mirrors are much in demand, and were always made in pairs. Matched pairs, however, are now very rare, and there is always the possibility of one being a reproduction. The *chinoiserie* mirrors of the Chippendale period are especially sought after, and need to be examined with care. Variations in the colour of the gilding suggests restoration, and wear in a genuine specimen will always be near the bottom within reach of the duster. A good-quality mirror will be gilded over a thin *gesso* ground laid on carved wood. Forgeries, and the cheaper-quality eighteenth-century mirrors, are often made from composition usually over a supporting core of thick, soft iron wire. Sometimes a genuine mirror will be part-carved and part-composition. This can usually be detected by the difference in sharpness between carved work and modelled; but the wooden mirror-frames are comparatively soft to a sharp point, the composition is much more resistant.

Generally, the collector would do well to make a careful survey of small pieces. Rooms were formerly much larger, and those specimens most in demand today were rarely made. The risk of buying a large specimen which later proves to be spurious is comparatively small. A careful study of the dates on which new designs, decorative *motifs*, and materials were introduced is also essential. Anachronisms are fairly common in spurious furniture of all kinds. Due consideration ought to be given to whether the type of furniture was popular at the time, or even made at all. Cabinets for the display of china were rarely made before the reign of George I, but are now much in demand. The forger is, therefore, tempted to supply the deficiency.

Careful watch should be kept for objects which have been "married". Lacquer chests, for instance, are supplied with spurious stands, or joined to genuine but unrelated stands. Bookcase-tops are supplied to writing-bureaux, and so on. Two original parts do not amount in value to a genuinely complete object.

French furniture has been a prolific field for the faker and the forger, and it has been manufactured on a very large scale for the antique market. Even legitimate reproductions, if they are of a quality comparable with that of the originals, will always realize high prices, as much as £2,000 having been paid for a mid-nineteenth-century table by Dasson which was properly catalogued. Paris furniture of the eighteenth century was made with craftsmanship which has yet to be matched, and a good reproduction (or even a forgery) is not cheap to make. The value, nevertheless, will still be much below that of a genuine specimen of comparable quality. The very elaborate brass and tortoiseshell marquetry of André-Charles Boulle was reproduced fairly extensively in London in the early part of the nineteenth century by Louis le Gaigneur of the Buhl Manufactory, Queen Street, Edgware Road, London, and by others.

It is comparatively easy to add gilt-bronze mounts to plain provincial furniture, supplying the *cachet* of the Paris *ébéniste*, and shops exist on the Left Bank who deal in mounts of all kinds. Some, legitimately enough, are used in restoration to replace those which are missing; others must go for less honest purposes.

It is important to the collector to know how to estimate the age of mounts of this kind, and the ability to recognize quality is essential. Eighteenth-century castings were very carefully finished, the detail being sharpened by chiselling. This was less often done in the nineteenth century and later, even on the best examples.[1] On the other hand, the interior of the woodwork—the parts which are not normally seen—was often finished with less care in genuine specimens than in reproductions. The stamps of important *ébénistes* need to be examined with care, and compared with those known to be genuine. Minor mistakes occur in fraudulent stamps—for instance, *RIESNER* appears on one example, perhaps made in the eighteenth century, which is not the work of J. H. Riesener. It is said, and it is probably mainly correct, that spurious stamps were not used before 1882 despite this solitary example, but they could, of course, have been added subsequently. The position is complicated by the fact that an English firm, Edwards and Roberts, who made reproductions in London during

[1] See also page 65.

the early part of the nineteenth century, not only added a stamp to their own work, but they sometimes used it on furniture sent for repair. The presence of their stamp, therefore, does not necessarily condemn a specimen which otherwise appears to be genuine.

Generally, French furniture is very much a field for the expert, and the inexperienced collector would do well to rely on the services of a reputable dealer.

*Chapter III*

# *Metalwork*

"It is a capital mistake to theorize before one has data. Insensibly one begins to twist facts to suit theories, instead of theories to suit facts."
Sherlock Holmes in *A Scandal in Bohemia* by A. CONAN DOYLE

Bronze was a favourite metal in ancient times because of its versatility. It melts at a comparatively low temperature, within reach of simple furnaces. The proportion of copper to tin affects its properties. If, for instance, the tin represented less than 5 per cent of the whole the metal could be shaped and tempered by cold hammering; if about 10 per cent it was suitable for tools, and could be hardened and consolidated by hammering; and if about 15 per cent it became brittle and more suitable for casting. The melting-point dropped progressively with the increase in the amount of tin. Zinc was first added to bronze as an alloying metal in Roman times, and it then becomes a kind of brass, although the metals are often confused in ancient writings. Lead was occasionally added deliberately to Italian statuary bronzes, and silver occurs as an alloying metal in late Roman times.

Lead was an early discovery. It was occasionally used by the Egyptians for roofing, and by the Romans for casting small works of little importance. The employment of lead for food- and liquor-containing vessels may have been the cause of the prevalence of lead-poisoning in Imperial Rome.

Most ways of shaping metals are extremely ancient and did not change in essentials until comparatively recent times, although they were improved and refined. The ductility of gold was exploited by the Egyptians, who beat it into leaves and used it for gilding. On wood gold-leaf was sometimes laid over a coat of wax to which it adhered, and in some cases *gesso* was employed as a foundation. Other metals, copper especially, were hammered into sheets, and both these and gold were shaped by hammering into *intaglio* moulds of wood or stone. Hollow cups were embossed (*repoussé*) by first drawing the outline of the design and then raising it with punches and a hammer from the back. Subsequently the vessel was filled with wax and chased from the front. Wire dates from the third millennium, when it appears in Egypt, and it was often stranded. Stamping was employed for such things as coins and medallions, and to decorate metalwork of all kinds. Engraving was done with tools not dissimilar from those used for the same work today, and metals were joined by riveting, soldering, and welding. Soft-solder was made from tin and lead; hard-solder from copper or brass. A high degree of skill was attained in making joints of this kind. The forging of metals, and the manufacture of objects from wrought iron, was well understood and frequently practised. Iron was tempered by quenching in water or oil by the Romans, and case-hardening was known.

So far as art objects are concerned, casting was the most usual method of fabrication, although it is uncertain whether or not iron was ever cast. The earliest bronze casts are solid, and in Egypt may also have been made with the aid of founders' sand. The methods commonly employed are described in more detail on page 69, but the use of stone-moulds appears to have been superseded by the "lost wax" method at a comparatively early date. The metal-workers of ancient times were superb casters. Many of their statues are much thinner, and therefore much lighter, than those of today. They also excelled in the representation of detail. The secret may have been that these things were modelled in wax over a clay core which closely followed the form of the final cast. Both exterior mould and core were, apparently, made from either a refractory clay or a mixture of clay and brickdust, and a support in the form of a containing box to keep the mould surrounded by hard-packed sand during pouring must have been essential; otherwise warping would have been likely. The modern use of plaster of Paris and brickdust to make a rigid outer case tempts the caster to use more metal, which has the effect of making the operation quicker and more certain.

The art of colouring metals was well known, bronze in particular being treated to give the fashionable colour. Less honest practices sometimes resorted to include the treatment of copper with mercury to simulate silver, and the colouring of silver with arsenic trisulphide (orpiment) to give it the appearance of gold. Other methods of imitating desired colours were known. Plating with molten tin was done in Gaul to imitate silver, and methods of gilding and silvering were used in Roman times, especially mercuric gilding, which consists in first applying mercury to copper, and then overlaying this with gold which has been dissolved in mercury, driving off the latter by heating. This is similar to the eighteenth- and nineteenth-century method of applying gold to porcelain glazes.

By far the most common proportion of copper to tin used in the making of bronze was nine to one, but this varied with the purpose for which the metal was intended, and these variations affected the colour. The most usual was golden brown, but bronze of a more golden colour was probably the result of adding zinc. This was much sought by Roman connoisseurs. "Pickling" in solutions of one kind or another was undoubtedly known, but such surface applications are now no longer perceptible.

Bronze was the first of the metals to be used extensively for making tools and weapons, and although preceded by gold in the fabrication of ornaments and works of art, it was employed for this purpose also from very early times. Bronze was an excellent general-purpose metal. Poured into a mould it made sharp casts; it could be shaped and tempered by hammering; it was ductile as well as malleable, and could be hammered into thin sheets or sawn into wire. Sheets could be handled without much risk of either breaking or tearing.

The Greek methods of finishing their casts remained more or less unchanged for many centuries. Indeed, some of their tools bear a striking resemblance to those in use today. A newly-cast bronze has surface imperfections which need to be eradicated with various metalworking tools, such as the rasp. The Greeks used saws. These were not unlike the modern hacksaw, although they did not have the hardness of the tempered steel blades. Nevertheless, tools of bronze or copper were much harder than the cast metal, and such blades, inefficient though they were, served the purpose. Drills, similar to the bow-drill, appear on ancient vases. The nature of the bit is not clear, but it was probably employed in conjunction with certain hard abrasives, the process of drilling resembling the use of grinding-paste in refurbishing the valves of the automobile engine. Rasps were employed for removing surface blemishes, and special varieties of this tool were made for burnishing the surface. Hammers much resembled the engineer's ball-peine hammer of today. Engraving was done with the burin, similar to that still in use, which cut the same triangular groove, and the characteristic marks of the multiple burin—a flat chisel with a cutting edge formed from several triangular teeth, similar to the stonecarver's claw chisel—can be traced, particularly in the rendering of hair. Punches and chisels of the same kind as those employed by contemporary goldsmiths no doubt found their place among the tools of the bronze-worker.

The student ought to make himself familiar with the marks left by these and similar tools in the cutting and finishing of metalwork. They are as applicable to Greek and Renaissance bronzes as to the gilt-bronze mounts of French furniture and *objets d'art*. Early bronzes were always carefully finished, and signs of careless and slovenly work are a cause for suspicion, and suggest special vigilance. These remarks are equally applicable to much later work, and one always takes into account the care and skill with which the cast has been finished. This is not, however, entirely reliable because some late work of the kind has been finished with a degree of care and skill equalling that of the earlier. Large quantities of mounts have been made both in Paris and London, and in a few cases the quality is deceptively good. It is advisable to look at the surface. Later mounts are usually made from brass of a colour resembling gilded bronze, or they have been gilded electrically. Earlier mounts were often gilded with mercury, which sometimes overlaps and washes over on to the part of the mount which is not exposed. There is nothing difficult about mercuric gilding, which can be done as easily today as in the eighteenth century, but it has the drawback of being extremely dangerous, and early gilders often had a relatively short life. Few craftsmen today would be willing to do it as a matter of course; a special assignment, highly paid, is another matter. Probably style is as good a guide as any in the case of a carefully finished mount gilded with mercury, and this makes a close acquaintance with genuine mounts essential.

Bronze which has been buried for long periods, or exposed to air and the weather, develops a corrosion of the surface which is termed *patina*. Some remarks about patina in connection with other objects have already been made. The term was originally applied to these surface changes of bronze, and subsequently, by extension, to other things.

Primarily bronze is an alloy of copper and tin, although silver, lead, zinc, and other metals were sometimes added. It would be impossible in a book of this nature to discuss the subject of early metallurgy with the slightest pretence to adequacy, but it can be studied in detail in the book noted below.[1]

Bronzes which are noted for a particularly handsome and variegated patina are those made in China during the Shang dynasty (*c.* 1766-1122 B.C.), and those of the Chou dynasty (1122-249 B.C.). These colourful types of patination arise usually as a result of chemical interaction between the metal and various substances in the soil in the presence of oxygen. Damp soil induces considerable degrees of corrosion; drier soil does not attack the metal to the same extent. Variations in the constituents of the soil in different parts of the world lead to marked differences in the kind of corrosion to be observed on excavated bronze. Air-patination, which results from exposure to air and weather, is not so well-marked, and corrosion does not normally proceed to the same lengths. Much work has been done on this subject, particularly by Dr Plenderleith, whose paper on the subject should be studied by collectors of old bronzes from any source.[2] This defines patina as a form of incrustation which is stable under normal conditions of temperature and humidity. Irreversible changes in the structure of the metal have taken place, and these products of corrosion are difficult to remove, even if it were desirable, without damaging the object. If patina can be removed easily with a pen-knife, or by softening with benzol, pyridine, or alcohol, it has been faked.

The finest colouring is the result of the formation of green malachite and blue azurite, and the red or deep brown cuprite. A smooth and hard green patina is the result of burial in water-logged soil; a polished black, especially on old Chinese bronze mirrors, is probably due to the inclusion of more tin than usual.

[1] R. J. Forbes: *Metallurgy in Antiquity*. Leiden, 1950.
[2] *Trans. Oriental Ceramic Society*, 1938-1939.

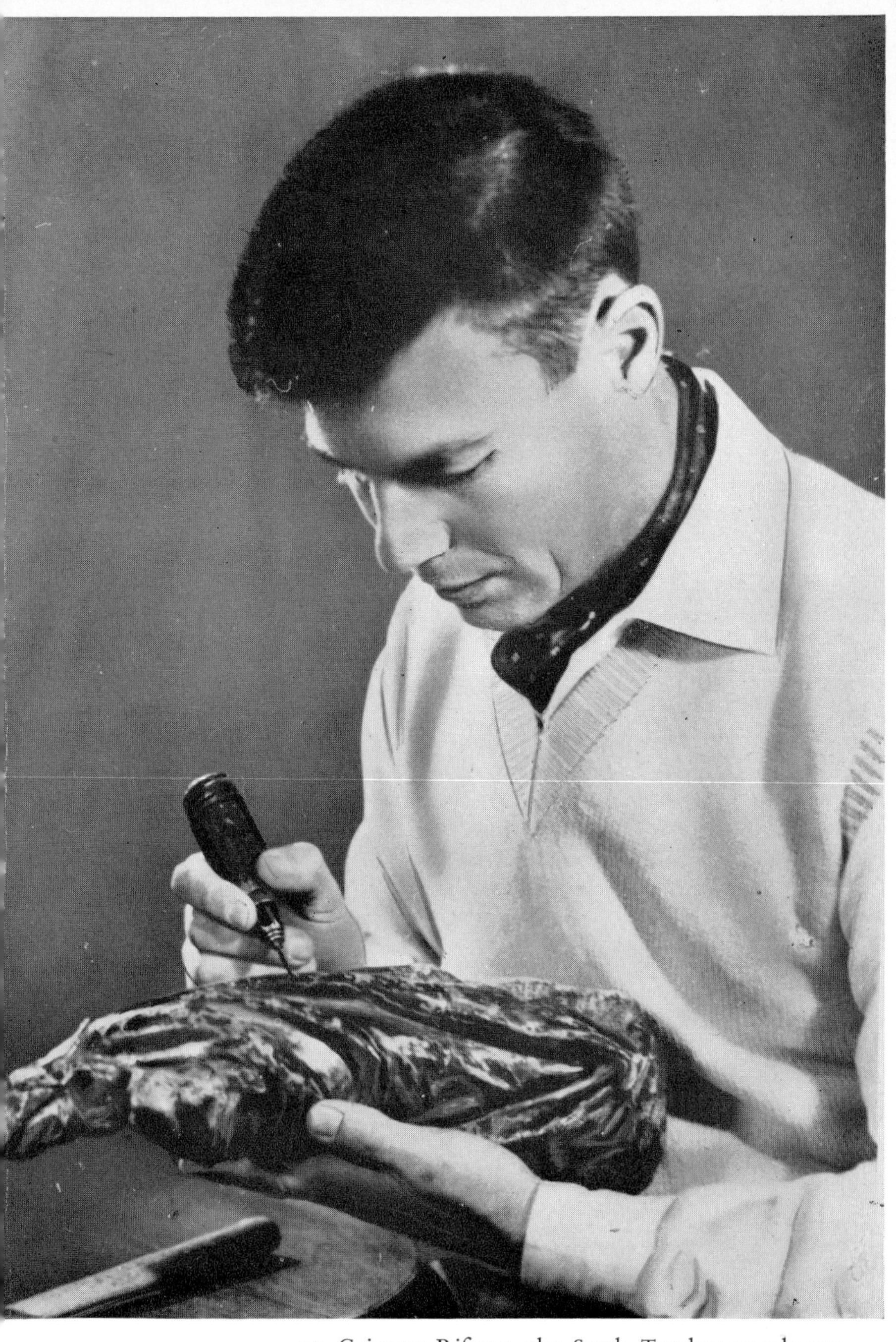

13. Guiseppe Rifesser, the South Tyrolese woodcarver working on a Madonna. c. 1958. [*Ullstein*

14. Gothic sculpture —a "Madonna" by Rifesser. Pose, features, and drapery, all combine to suggest that the work is spurious. See Chapter IV. [*Ullstein*

Dr Plenderleith has pointed out that green patination without signs of the underlying presence of cuprite is almost certainly spurious, since this formation seems always to precede the green and blue copper carbonates. It is, therefore, evidence in favour of the genuineness of patination if removal of a small part of the green layer discloses a reddish foundation underneath. This, however, is only evidence of a certain degree of antiquity. It is an indication of *how* the patination has been formed, but it does not necessarily favour a Shang or a Chou dynasty dating in the case of Chinese bronzes. A specimen on this evidence could as well belong to the Han dynasty, or even later. Some remarks on the use of ultra-violet radiation in examining patination will be found in Appendix 3, and the corrosion of metals is further discussed in Appendix 2.

It is impossible to reproduce this kind of corrosion successfully by chemical means. The surface of bronze which has been buried for a long period will be attacked to varying degrees and by different substances; corrosion by immersion in chemical solutions is usually evenly disposed over the whole surface. It is also very difficult to induce the smooth green patination which results from exposure to air and weather in a deceptive manner. A number of methods have been employed with varying degrees of success. Usually these have taken the form of treating the surface with acid. It would be doing the reader no service to list the substances employed in greater detail, and it might save the dishonest recruit to the art of faking the labour of experimenting to find those acids which are the most effective. Faked patination, particularly on Chinese bronzes, sometimes takes the form of copper carbonates in lacquer or shellac varnish painted on, but this can only be superficially deceptive, and detection with solvents or a knife-blade is swift and easy. The accretions can be flaked away, leaving clean bronze underneath.

Bronzes which have been cleaned present problems, because some of the evidence of age, and often the best evidence, has been removed. Cleaning is undertaken by museums in a few cases, usually when the presence of underlying engraved or inlaid ornament is suspected, but the history of such objects is known, and, in these days at least, the kind of patination originally present has been recorded. In other instances of the removal of the products of corrosion, style and workmanship are the best guides, and it becomes essential to know something of the ways in which objects of bronze are made.

There are two principal ways of shaping this metal—by hammering into shape and by casting—and the method employed will be reflected in the appearance of the finished work. It is essential to remember that, unlike stone-carvings, cast bronzes are essentially an exact copy of a pre-existing work in another medium. Those wrought by hammering may be inspired by a design in another material; they do not reproduce it faithfully.

Every cast bronze starts as a *modelled* work in clay or wax, or as a wood-carving. From all of these moulds can be taken. Bronze imposes on the artist few of the limitations which have to be observed by the sculptor in stone, about which more will be said in its place. Briefly, at this point, it should be remembered that legs and thighs, for instance, are insufficient to support a head and torso carved in stone unless some kind of additional support be added. This usually takes the form of drapery from the waist downwards, or a tree-trunk suitably disposed. The Venus de Milo was not carved with drapery covering the legs for reasons of pudency, but because she could not have stood safely upright otherwise. A bronze statue, however, may even be posed on its toes without undue risk, provided it is properly made and balanced. Outstretched arms are difficult in stone, and when they exist they usually point downwards. In bronze they can be modelled in almost any attitude, since it is always possible to support the clay model internally. The differences between the two techniques are obvious; equally obvious is it that bronze lends itself to a style impossible in stone. Original artists naturally adopt the design and technique most suited to their selected medium. Forgers who are adapting designs from something other than bronze may well betray themselves by their attempts to interpret one medium in terms of another.

There are several methods of casting in bronze. The best work has usually been done by the *cire perdue* (lost-wax) method, which is especially suitable for fine and intricate work. Although a clay model can be used, the work is often first cast in plaster as a safeguard against damage. Either clay or plaster is coated with shellac to prevent subsequent adherence during the process which follows. This is to take a plaster piece-mould, or, quite often today, a gelatine mould, and from this a wax cast is made of variable thickness, usually at least one-quarter of an inch. This will be the thickness of the bronze cast. The hollow interior is next filled with a mixture of plaster and brick-dust, or some other fire-proof substance of the same kind, to form a core which supports the bronze during cooling. The outer mould can now be removed, exposing a wax copy over a fire-proof core, and the founder inserts metal pins to support the outer case still to be cast, and arranges ducts to release trapped air which would otherwise cause an explosion. The outer case, which faithfully copies the wax surface, is now cast, and when this has set the wax is melted out. The model now consists of an outer case, an empty space which will shortly be occupied by the metal, and a core. The outer case and the core are held into their correct relative positions by the pins. The metal is poured in and left to cool, after which case and core are removed, and the cast cleaned up with metalworking tools. This is the best and most accurate method of casting, and one which allows facsimiles to be made.

An alternative method of making simple objects is to cast them in founders' sand. This is close and clinging, and when packed tightly round the matrix will take a fairly sharp imprint. Objects which were originally cast by the *cire perdue* method have sometimes been reproduced later in founders' sand. Generally, sand-casts are thicker and heavier than originals. Ancient Chinese bronzes were much copied during the Sung dynasty (960-1279), when this technique appears to have been adopted. Although there are observable discrepancies in some instances, it is often exceedingly difficult to differentiate between a Shang or Chou bronze and a good Sung copy, especially if marked patination has developed. Most of the copies are now a thousand years old, and this is ample time for corrosive effects to appear which are to some extent comparable with those to be seen on earlier specimens, but, since they were not made to be buried, this has not usually occurred. Blurring of the outlines, to be looked for especially in the linear background (the *lei wên* fret) which is present on many of the ancient bronzes is, perhaps, a good guide. The earliest vessels appear to have been cast by a "lost-wax" method, although this is controversial, but the *lei wên* fret when it is not eroded by corrosion is usually clear and sharp. Fine detail of this kind is rarely reproduced convincingly by sand-casting. Reproductions of ancient bronzes using the *cire perdue* method are a problem of a different order, and must be judged from the style and patination.

Very early bronzes were sometimes cast in stone moulds, at first a single mould which formed only the outline and one side, and later two moulds bound together, with a pouring-hole for the metal and a smaller hole for the escape of air. Few of these interest the collector, and the archaeologist is well equipped to take care of himself if he is offered spurious works of this character.

The modern process of electrotyping needs to be mentioned. This can give a perfect facsimile, down to the smallest surface blemish, but from the forger's viewpoint it has one serious drawback—it can only do so in pure copper. A mould is taken from an original. If more than one copy is to be made a piece-mould will be used.[1] The surface of the mould is coated with plumbago (black lead), and the whole immersed in a bath of a suitable electrolytic solution. It is connected to an electrode, and at the opposite pole is a bar of copper. When current flows between the two poles, particles of copper are detached from the bar and deposited on the surface of the mould. In this way an exact duplicate of the mould surface can be obtained, the metal varying in thickness with the amount of time that the process is allowed to continue. Electrotyping is often used legitimately. It can be detected not only from the composition of the metal, but from the surface, which is closed-grained and unlike that of cast bronze, since the metal has been deposited particle by particle. Objects of this kind will not have the same "ring" that can be heard if hollow bronze sculpture is tapped. Careful examination, bearing the method of manufacture in mind, will usually reveal an electrotype, even in the absence of analysis.

The Greeks used bronze extensively for decorative work of all kinds. Statues are usually of athletes and figures in motion, the freedom of the material lending itself to the suggestion of movement. At first bronze plates were beaten into the shape and size desired over wooden formers. Embossed or *repoussé* decoration was hammered in from the back, the object resting on some yielding substance like the pitch-

[1] A piece-mould is one which is made with a large number of interlocking parts, each of which will "draw" from the surface. Moulds of this kind can be used for making repetitive casts. They are employed by porcelain factories for figure-making and other intricate work. The only limit imposed is the ingenuity of the maker.

block of the silversmith. Statues, especially those of large size, were built up from such prefabricated sections.

The earliest castings were small and solid, the diminutive horses which have often acquired a magnificent patina being made in this way. A form of *cire perdue* casting was almost certainly in use by the sixth century B.C. Such *tours de force* as the Colossus of Rhodes, which was 105 feet in height and took twelve years to make, may have been cast in sections and assembled, much in the same way as the Statue of Liberty was erected more than two thousand years later, but by tradition it was cast *in situ* from the feet upwards, the exterior being buttressed by mounds of earth and the core filled with blocks of stone. The point is academic, since the statue no longer exists, but in this case tradition may reasonably be doubted.

Detail to bronze statues was incised into the metal with the burin, and surface casting irregularities smoothed with rasps and abrasives. The eyes were inlaid in a variety of materials, and inlaying of the surface with other metals—silver eyebrows, for instance—was practised. Roman bronze techniques followed the same paths as later Greek work.

There is little that can be said in a general work such as this on the positive aspects of attribution by style. Only if a close preliminary study of all aspects of classical decorative art and its cultural background has been undertaken can style be employed with even a reasonable degree of assurance. The examination of later bronzes particularly demands an intuition, acquired from long acquaintance with genuine objects, which will reject anything out of keeping with the spirit of the period. Properly understood, patina and the techniques of decoration may point the way to the detection of forgeries, but anachronisms and the misunderstanding of mythological *motifs* have proved the undoing of many forgers.

The Renaissance was a revival of the mature Greek and Roman styles, and it is hardly surprising that antique bronzes were imitated and forged from the beginning. The collector began to flourish again for the first time since the days of ancient Rome, and especially important is the assemblage of works of art made by the Medici family of Florence. Lorenzo de Medici, named the Magnificent, spent vast sums on works of art of all kinds, and was an especially large buyer of Greek and Roman objects, as well as providing encouragement for the artists of his day—Leonardo da Vinci, Filippino Lippi, and Sansovino, to name only three. Forgeries of all kinds were rife, some unusually stupid. There is, for instance, a copy of an antique bronze modelled and cast without arms because the original was found in this condition. It is, perhaps, natural that at a time when bronzes were in such demand, and the art of casting them had reached so high a degree of excellence, that they should be especial favourites with imitators, and artists of note did not scruple to do work of the kind. Verrocchio is an example, and he turned his hand to making copies of ancient bronzes.

Spurious cast bronzes begin at this time to fall into three main categories:

(*a*) completely new, inspired by antique sources
(*b*) casts from moulds taken from a genuine bronze
(*c*) casts from an original work in some other material.

Completely new work, even that inspired by old sources, is comparatively rare in modern times, and such things are not unduly difficult to detect, either from the style or from surface appearance. Renaissance copies offer problems of far greater complexity, although they now have a considerable value of their own as works of art. It is not that they have acquired respectability with time, but because the line of demarcation between classical and Renaissance works regarded solely as objects of art tends to become less well defined as time passes. For the most part Renaissance copies, although they were made for gain, were not brought into existence because they had a greatly enhanced value on the art-market of the time. The problem is, therefore, principally one of attribution. They are often unwittingly included in modern collections among classical bronzes, and that these things were intended to pass for ancient work at the time is proved by the fact that some have been deliberately damaged after fabrication. An amusing instance recorded by Otto Kurz[1] concerns a torso taken from a faulty repetitive cast of Giovanni da Bologna's well-known "Mercury" which, with a little additional damage and some artificial patination, became a faked fragment of antiquity.

Casts taken from genuine originals need no little skill to detect them. In nearly all cases, however, the moulds have been taken from objects

[1] Otto Kurz: *Fakes*. London, 1948.

of considerable age which already had some signs of wear, and possibly of damage. Attention, therefore, ought to be directed to both these points, and much may be learned from a careful study of damaged parts. Obviously there will be a difference between the appearance of injury inflicted on an original bronze and a cast of that injury. Quality should be carefully observed. Old craftsmen sharpened the detail of decorative bronze-work by chiselling. The difference in appearance of chisel marks made directly into the metal and those which have been reproduced by casting is usually discernible.

The manifold dangers which beset the creation of completely new work, and the likelihood of discovery which attends the copying of important existing works in bronze, have led the forger to use works in other media as sources of inspiration. Particularly if these are reasonably faithful copies is it possible to see the original material in the style. As an obvious example of this kind of blunder, a bronze standing figure with a tree-trunk support, or with drapery from the waist downwards, is obviously copied from stone, and therefore not original. Neither classical nor Renaissance sculptors would have been guilty of this solecism.

Fakes are not numerous in bronze, although a soldered line at the neck of a statue purporting to be the portrait of a well-known personality ought to give rise to the suspicion that it has been provided with a new head. Inscriptions engraved later on European bronzes are known. The obliteration of the signature of a Renaissance sculptor so that the work could pass for an antique bronze has also been recorded.[1] Fake inscriptions are rather more frequent on Chinese bronzes, which need to be examined with special care. The act of cutting these into old metal leaves traces which are visible under a reasonably powerful glass, the outline being ragged and the characters too angular. Translations of inscriptions are less likely to be helpful since they will probably have been copied from a genuine specimen. Most will record details of the presentation of the vessel, with the addition of some such pious hope as "may it be treasured and used for a thousand years". Engraving has frequently been added to classical European bronzes, especially mirrors.

Extensively repaired bronzes are occasionally offered on the art-market, and here the ultra-violet lamp can be extremely useful. They

[1] Otto Kurz, op. cit.

are often largely genuine, with, perhaps, a missing part imitated and soldered into position, the whole being disguised with a false patina. If the work is important in an unrepaired condition it is worth acquiring at an appropriate price.

Modern forgeries of Renaissance bronzes belong, for the most part, to the latter years of the nineteenth century and the first decade of the twentieth, when these things were much in demand, and high prices were being paid. Some of the more elaborate were even offered, with more than the customary amount of impudence, as the work of Cellini. The modelling is usually weak and poor, and their fraudulent nature begins to be apparent if they are compared with genuine works. Perhaps the most stringent test which can be applied is to put a suspected bronze in the company of a few genuine examples for a day or two. A spurious specimen will soon become all too obvious.

It is, perhaps, essential to close these remarks on a note of caution. The attitude to patina at the present time is very different from what it was seventy years or so ago. Collectors today regard untouched condition as important, and cleaning is only undertaken when some more than usually interesting inlaid or engraved ornament is thought to exist. Towards the end of the nineteenth century, however, a patina which displeased the owner was often removed and replaced with a chemically-induced substitute which was more to his liking. In cases where this apparently proved difficult green varnish was used, as well as a dark brown application which quite often scaled off, leaving the lighter bronze underneath. Even the most scholarly of works on this subject at the time did not hesitate to give favourite recipes for pickling to provide the bronze surfaces with a "truly antique effect".[1] Later bronzes, therefore, particularly those of the Renaissance, with what appears to be faked patination, should not be condemned on this evidence alone without a hearing, although the value has suffered to some extent.

Forgers who have gone to the trouble of making a complicated piece-mould are rarely content with taking one copy from it. Identical bronzes purporting to belong to classical antiquity are spurious, although one of them may be original. It is not possible to be quite so certain about later work, but the chances are greatly in favour of fraud.

[1] I forbear to record either the publication or the author's name, but both were of surprising eminence.

Modern bronzes of importance are sometimes issued in limited editions, and when this has been completed the moulds ought to be destroyed. Value obviously depends on how many casts have been taken, and the buyer must be able to rely on the honesty of the artist and the bronze-founder to limit the edition to the prescribed number. There is no reason to suspect the good faith of the greater number of artists, but in a few cases it is difficult to be certain whether or not the collector's confidence has been misplaced.

Spurious works in gold would be exceptionally difficult to detect were it not for hall-marks of one kind or another, because this metal does not show the signs of age in the same way as bronze. Ancient silver is hardly in the same case. Corrosion varies in extent, and can sometimes be extensive. In those examples which are furthest advanced little metallic silver remains, and it is impossible to remove the corrosion without severely damaging the specimen.

The modern forger does not use base metal. He would hardly exercise his skill on anything but an object likely to be highly valued for rarity and craftsmanship. For this reason it would be distinctly unwise to court detection by using inferior materials. In some circumstances, therefore, style may assume considerable importance in deciding whether or not any particular specimen is genuine.

For the most part the forger does not possess the degree of craftsmanship which was usual in former times. Neither is he continually engaged on the production of important works, since they can only be marketed as single items or, at best, in extremely small numbers. His hand, therefore, is likely to betray itself by sheer inexperience in handling both tools and material. The old craftsman was using decorative *motifs* which were almost as natural to him as the air he breathed. The forger is either copying a pre-existing work, when he is at his most dangerous, or creating something entirely spurious based on *motifs* taken from contemporary sources which need to be related and adapted. To do this he first has to design a viable composition by joining together several hitherto unrelated parts which may not be of the same date as each other. Then, in transferring his design to the metal, he must imitate closely the way in which the old craftsman handled his tools and material. He must take care to see that he is not betrayed by his own unconscious assimilation of later styles of which the original craftsman knew nothing. He must, therefore, concentrate on far more aspects than the original relatively simple one of using manual skill and knowledge to create a work necessarily in keeping with all other works of the period.

An excellent illustration of these difficulties may be found in the notorious tiara of Saitaphernes which once deceived some of the experts of the Louvre. This tiara, in the form of a headdress similar to that of the Popes, purported once to have belonged to one of the Scythian kings. It was first offered in 1896, with other objects by the same hand, to the Imperial Court Museum of Vienna by a Russian dealer. Accompanying them was a spurious history of excavation at Olbia, on the Black Sea coast. The date suggested was in the region of the third-second century B.C. The tiara was of gold, and the workmanship excellent in quality. The lower part consisted of a narrow band of *repoussé* ornament, surmounted by a wider band with figures, which was later found to be inspired by a silver dish of the fourth century A.D. in the Bibliothèque Nationale in Paris.

The offer to the Viennese Museum was rejected. The Director considered that the disposition of the damage, which avoided all important parts, was highly suspicious. If he had any other reasons, they have not been recorded, but his observations were sound enough, and the situation certainly demanded close investigation. An offer to the British Museum met with no better fortune.

The reception in Paris was much less hostile, and the tiara was at once purchased for the Louvre. Criticism was almost immediate, and grew in volume. Reputable archaeologists in Russia and Germany condemned it as a forgery. It was attacked in detail by Adolf Furtwängler of Munich, whose criticisms later proved remarkably accurate. It was he who drew attention to the existence of the silver dish, as well as to numerous other anachronisms and misunderstandings of ancient *motifs*. Then, the names of Schapschelli Hochman, a Russian dealer, and a silversmith of Odessa, Isaac Rouchomowsky, began to be mentioned.

There can be no doubt that Rouchomowsky was a silversmith of uncommon skill; the tiara and some other work from his hand are sufficient testimony to this. Paris experts were still publishing articles defending the tiara's authenticity when a sensational letter in *Le Matin* on 23 March 1903, written by a Russian dealer in Paris, gave details of the whole transaction. The writer claimed that he had watched his friend Rouchomowsky at work on it. Still it found defenders, who took the ludicrous position that it must be genuine because no living artist was capable of producing it—an attitude of mind which has started more forgers on their nefarious careers than any other.

Rouchomowsky arrived in Paris on 5 April 1903, and was hailed in some quarters as the greatest goldsmith since Cellini. As in the case of Van Meegeren and his paintings, no one would believe Rouchomowsky's claim to have made the tiara without a demonstration of his ability in producing a test-piece. When this had been completed there could no longer be any doubt. Now Rouchomowsky was referred to in scathing terms as a forger and a criminal. Made wiser by his experience, he returned to Russia, to disappear into obscurity. Before he went he confirmed that Furtwängler had been correct in tracing the origin of part of the decoration to the silver dish. The remainder had been copied from illustrations to various books on classical antiquities. The inscription, *The Senate and People of Olbia to the Great Invincible Saitaphernes*, had been adapted from a genuine inscription referring to the walls of Olbia as a protection against the Scythian chief, Saitaphernes.

Renaissance and ancient gold and silver ornaments have been imitated in Italy for centuries, and the tradition has continued since the end of the Second World War, an American museum being swindled in 1954 by a Neapolitan dealer who gave his objects a spurious history of having been excavated from volcanic lava just outside Naples. The museum in this case could blame only its own enthusiasm, since it is common knowledge that export of objects of this kind from Italy is illegal.

An amusing portrait of an Italian forger was drawn from life by Norman Douglas in his novel, *South Wind*. Count Caloveglia, it will be remembered, was in the habit of forging classical sculpture, which he "dug up" in his little vineyard in the hills. Part of one of the Count's soliloquies is worth quoting: "These experts—what a crowd of fools they were! Especially the honest ones."

An expert does not need to be personally dishonest if he is to detect forgeries, but he needs to be able to think himself into a dishonest frame of mind, just as a good policeman is able to think like a criminal. If he could not, he would be a poor thief-taker. An expert in the field of the arts can only be successful in detecting forgeries if he is constantly alert to find out as much as possible about methods of fabrication and distribution. He must also try to invent new methods for himself. He may be assured that anything he devises will either have been used already, or will be at some future time. To have considered all the possibilities means that he will be that much more difficult to deceive. It is not a task for the naïve, the unsophisticated, or the unworldly.

The buyer of gold and silver, unlike the collector of most other things, enjoys a certain amount of protection from the law, probably because these metals are intrinsically valuable and have been used in the past for coinage.

It is easy to see why protection is needed. At the time this was written pure gold, for instance, was worth about £12 an ounce troy. A cup weighing 5 oz., therefore, would be worth about £60 in metal alone, irrespective of workmanship, rarity, age, or any of the other factors which increase the value. If there were no check on quality there would be nothing to prevent a dishonest maker from adding base metal in the form of an alloy. An ounce of alloying metal worth a few pence would thus bring an additional profit of £12. Proportionately, of course, silver is worth much less, but in 1962 the price rose to about 8s. an ounce.[1] Moreover, both these metals in the past have been scarce in the sense that it has been difficult to buy them on the market, even when the purchaser was prepared to pay the price. The temptation to extend them by adding alloying metal has, for this reason, been strong.

From early times it has been compulsory for the goldsmith and silversmith in England to submit his work to an Assay Office which tests the quality of the metal. If this is found to reach the required standard, a series of punch-marks are added which form the purchaser's guarantee of quality.

Every collector of old silver needs a book of pocketable size which

[1] At the time of writing (1963) the silver in a half-crown minted before 1920 is worth 3s. 6d; those struck between 1920 and 1946 are worth 1s. 11d., and the price of silver is rising. The current half-crown is worth about 8d. in pre-war money. It has no intrinsic value because it is made of cupro-nickel. No doubt intelligent anticipation of the inflation to come was the cause of the withdrawal of the English silver coinage in 1947.

gives lists of such marks and their meaning so that they can be identified and interpreted. The best is Frederick Bradbury's *British and Irish Silver and Assay Office Marks*, which also gives the marks commonly found on old Sheffield plate. The symbols indicate the name of the Assay Office, acknowledge the standard of the metal, give the date of assay, and in most cases identify the maker by means of his symbol or initials.[1]

These hall-marks provide a point of difficulty for the forger. If he reproduces an old piece it must, to pass current, bear the old marks. There are to be found occasional specimens of genuine old silver which are not marked, or which bear only the maker's mark, but these are very rare. They are not forgeries, but they need expert knowledge to be certain of their character. Antique foreign plate, Continental and Oriental, is also exempt from marking, but the former will often bear a guild mark of the country of origin which will help to identify it.

It is illegal to add metal to marked wares unless they are again submitted for examination, when the additions will probably be given current marks. This hardly applies to metal added in the course of a legitimate repair, but only to that which alters the character of a specimen. For example, it is not illegal to add a cover to a mug, making it a tankard, if the piece is submitted to the Goldsmiths' Company and the new cover marked with the year of assay; to do so otherwise is contravening the law. The faker, however, cannot afford to have such additions marked, since it would make his work unsaleable at the price of the original mug, leave alone that of a covered tankard which would be considerably higher.

If an illegal piece of silver is possessed *knowingly*, and the owner does not report it to the Goldsmiths' Company, it is an offence, and if he attempts to sell it he is guilty of the crime of "uttering". If, however, the owner does not know that his piece is a forgery, then upon discovery he is required to co-operate with the authorities concerned in trying to trace the origin.

It is not, however, an offence to decorate plain silver, although it ought to be, provided this requires no substantial addition or subtraction of metal. During the Victorian period the revived *rococo* style then current caused much plain silver to be redecorated with *repoussé*

[1] For these the reader will need to consult Sir Charles Jackson: *English Goldsmiths and Their Marks*, 2nd edition, London, 1921.

ornament which almost completely destroys its antique value. Attempts are sometimes made to restore the original form by hammering out the embossed work, usually with disastrous results. Marks should be carefully watched when later embossing is suspected. Assay Offices in the past often added the marks over the ornament, and they are for this reason difficult to see. A faker will usually take pains to avoid spoiling the clarity of the marks in this way. Victorian decoration of this kind is inferior to eighteenth-century *rococo* ornament, and, to anyone versed in the original style, a nineteenth-century hand is not difficult to detect. The amount of embossing is also nearly always grossly excessive, the surface being literally smothered with it. It must be remembered that some plain silver was embossed during the currency of the eighteenth-century version of the *rococo* style, and these pieces are not easy to detect except from the date, since this may be perhaps twenty years earlier than the ornament suggests. Things of this kind do not lose their value to the same extent as those embossed in the nineteenth century.

Most frequently to be seen is an alteration in the character of the piece, and this takes many different forms. Naturally, some forms are more in demand than others, and consequently sell for higher prices. The faker, therefore, looks for objects which can be altered, since if this is done successfully a good profit can be made with something which has a genuine set of hall-marks. For example, a triangular piece can be cut from a mug and a pouring-lip inserted; the result is the much rarer jug. An oval teapot robbed of its spout and handle can be made into a tea-caddy; a caster which has lost its top can be reshaped into a cream-jug. Early saucepans become posset-pots and caudle-cups, or, if they are straight-sided, tankards. Mugs are converted into tankards by adding a lid, and small mugs, with a cover added, become mustard-pots. Small objects such as spoons can be converted into the rarer forks, and early, valuable spoons can be cast from moulds in which the genuine hall-mark is reproduced. The latter type of fake is fairly easy to detect from the general appearance. Plates have been re-fashioned into baskets and bowls, and pap-boats turned into sauce-boats with a few minor additions such as feet and handles. All these will bear genuine marks, although they may not always be in the right place.

It must be remembered that both silver and gold are malleable and ductile. Skilful use of the hammer, therefore, can do much to alter the character. Hammering, however, can only make the metal thinner, and therefore will extend it. It can never be contracted. There is insufficient space in a book of this kind to discuss the methods of the silversmith, but the serious collector would do well to study them carefully, perhaps spending a little time at an art-school where the subject is taught, even though he only watches students at work. Collectors of other things, apart from silver, can do the same. To watch a good cabinet-maker or repairer of antique furniture is a valuable lesson in the detection of fakes and forgeries, and some of the more important pottery and porcelain factories welcome visitors. Forgery, like politics, is the art of the possible, and unless one knows how things are made, and what a skilled craftsman can do with his material, the detection of spurious work will never be easy.

The legal penalties for tampering with the hall-marks on English silver are severe, but this has not deterred a few hardy spirits, probably because they are rarely enforced with the full rigour of the law. Perhaps the most usual form of fraud, apart from reshaping, is to cut the marks from a piece of genuine silver in bad condition and incorporate them in a newly-made piece. This form of fraud was also practised in the eighteenth century for a different reason. In 1784 a tax was placed on silver, receipt of which was acknowledged by the addition of an extra punch-mark—the sovereign's head. Some silversmiths with enlightened ideas on the subject of tax evasion cut the marks from inexpensive pieces made before the imposition of the tax, and added these to their own work. This obviated the necessity for presenting it to the Assay Office for marking, and therefore for payment of the tax. Cases have also been noticed in which the only mark to be added by the silversmith—his maker's mark—has been used once clearly, and four times in such a way as to be indecipherable, the piece passing for a badly-marked specimen. This, incidentally, does not normally exist, although some marks are now indistinct as a result of constant cleaning or wear. This kind of fraud means either an attempt at tax evasion or the use of sub-standard metal.

Occasionally the circular bottom of a suitable object is cut out and soldered over that of a newly-made piece, thus providing it with a false bottom bearing genuine marks. The size can be extended by hammering if this is necessary. As an example, a damaged eighteenth-century mug with a full set of marks on the bottom would be of the utmost value to a forger who wanted to make a coffee-pot of the same period.

The usual position of the marks is given below, with the caution that the position is not invariable. Marks out of position mean that the object must be inspected with more than the usual care.

| SIDE-MARKS (NEAR TOP): | BOTTOM MARKS: |
|---|---|
| Early tankards | Tankards (later) |
| Porringers | Trencher salts |
| Caudle-cups | Jugs |
| Coffee-pots | Dishes |
| Teapots (rarely) | Punch-bowls |
| Chocolate-pots | Coffee-pots |
| Sauceboats | Teapots (usually) |
| | Chocolate-pots |
| | Sauceboats |
| | Casters |
| | Tea-caddies |

Generally, early pieces are likely to be marked on the side, whereas later specimens usually have bottom marks. The latter may be in line, or arranged radially. The maker's mark may appear at the beginning or the end of a line, but not in the middle, since it was added by the silversmith himself, the others were punched by the Assay Office. Candlesticks are usually marked on the side, near the bottom, and early spoons on the bowl or the stem, but, from the last decades of the seventeenth century, only on the stem. Separate parts bear a separate mark, and these should agree with the marks on the rest of the object.

Punch-marks were added one at a time, and they are, therefore, not likely to be evenly spaced or exactly in line, although the deviation may be very slight. One ingenious fraud was detected because the forger made a single stamp of the four punch-marks, and several pieces all with marks in precisely the same position by exact measurement came on to the market. The inference was obvious. New punches are apt to give a much sharper impression than that of a genuinely old mark which, even at best, will have some wear from cleaning. It is exceedingly difficult to simulate wear convincingly.

Although it is a serious offence in the United Kingdom to possess false punches, it is not even a misdemeanour in the United States. Many falsely marked pieces purporting to be English silver are therefore in circulation in that country, which may account for the lower prices ruling even for genuine examples in the American sale-rooms. Silver from American collections bearing the makers' marks of John Wakelin and William Taylor need especially careful examination. It is said that an American factory employing twenty men was, at one time producing forgeries of English silver, and attempts have been made by the American authorities to prosecute on charges of fraud.

Another form of fraud is to have newly-made ware in the old style properly marked at the Assay Office and then to give the marks signs of wear artificially, leaving that of the Assay Office fairly clear and heavily blurring the others. This has been done with silver of the Britannia standard (i.e. 11 oz. 10 dwt. of pure silver in 12 oz. troy). The presence of the Britannia mark makes a specimen purporting to belong to the early years of the eighteenth century more convincing, since it is now rarely used. Silver purporting to belong to the years between 1697 and 1718 with blurred marks needs careful examination, although worn marks certainly appear on silver which is absolutely genuine. The remedy is to examine the other characteristics already noted with more than usual care.

Transposed marks are not always easy to detect; some, in fact, are exceedingly difficult. Breathing on the surface may reveal the fraud. Silver mists over; solder does not. Although metals do not fluoresce, it is possible that ultra-violet radiation might be effective in particular cases. Results obtained from the examination of other metals in similar circumstances (see Appendix 3) suggest that the outline of the inserted part might become visible, although I have not yet had an opportunity of making the test. A microscope would undoubtedly reveal the line of insertion in most cases. The type of mark may be incorrect for the place in which it appears, and the nature of wear from cleaning which it received in its original position may not compare with that to be seen on genuine marks of the new form. A silversmith can melt the solder essential to the insertion of the mark, when the addition can be detached.

As a rule fraudulent trading in silver is either done privately or by dealers on the fringe of the market. The penalties attached to the possession of forged silver are such that no reputable dealer would take the risk, even if he were actuated by no higher motives. In silver, as in most other things, the established dealer is the most active in stamping out the distribution of forgeries, and in this the British Antique Dealers' Association as a body co-operates with the Goldsmiths' Company.

Reference must be made to the repair of old silver; to restoration which sometimes comes perilously close to fraud; and to refurbishing of one kind or another which, if it passes unnoticed, is calculated to give the specimen an enhanced value. As with most other things, the faker's activities are made lucrative by too great an insistence on perfection by the buyer, who often looks askance at an engraved coat-of-arms or a monogram, although it is understandable that a presentation inscription to a nonentity with a comparatively recent date should affect desirability. Inscriptions and similar engraving are often removed, which not only causes the metal to be unduly thin at this point, but alters the colour which all antique silver acquires with the passing of time by removing the surface of the metal. If erasure of an inscription is suspected gentle manipulation of the metal between the thumb and finger will often reveal the fact, especially if the gauge has been seriously altered. Patches will usually show quite plainly if the surface is breathed upon, or if it is tarnished. Ultra-violet light can also be used.

Both electro-plating and gilding are employed to disguise patches, thin places, and repairs generally. Genuine silver is an alloy, and the small addition of base metal alters the colour slightly. Electro-plating can only be done with pure silver, since it is impossible to deposit an alloy, and the difference in colour is fairly obvious if an electro-plated specimen is placed with genuine objects. An overbright surface, without gradations of colour, is a danger-signal. Electro-plated silver is better left alone. Gilding, of course, can be done by old methods. It is easy to distinguish from gold, because the colour of the metal is modified by that of the silver under it, and in any case the object will be much too light in weight. Nevertheless, much silver-gilt is perfectly genuine, and important specimens were often gilded. The interior of salts was also gilded when no glass liner was provided, because salt attacks unprotected silver seriously. Generally, specimens gilded at a later date are virtually indetectable, but silver-gilt was not often used for ordinary domestic silver in the past, rather for show-pieces.

Most difficult to detect are certain repairs to plain silver. Repairs to embossed and engraved specimens are much more difficult to execute successfully, and they can usually be detected by the inevitable clumsiness of new work, especially where it connects with old.

Although false punch-marks are comparatively rare on English silver, they are rather more common on that of the Continent. The various guilds devised stratagems to preserve the quality of the metal, but forgery flourished. It is, of course, difficult to regard early things of this kind as fraudulent today. The market for antique works of art in the Middle Ages, and even during the early years of the Renaissance, was relatively small, and copies were usually of contemporary works made for reasons other than the one which is the common cause of forgeries today. It might be that a prince or a church wanted a replica of an admired work which belonged to someone else, or the imitation might be in a heavily alloyed metal. During the Renaissance, of course, forgeries became much more common.

In general, Dutch silver demands close examination, since the number of spurious works is fairly high and the marks are by no means reliable. Silver purporting to belong to the reign of Louis Quatorze of France also needs to be looked at with a sceptical eye. Workmanship is usually poorer in quality, and such *motifs* as the baroque strapwork of the period often diverges sufficiently from genuine work as to make forgeries apparent. Wine-tasters of silver-gilt with a gold coin of Louis Treize inset are to be seen occasionally, and some have been made in Paris within the last century or so.

The plating of base metal as an early fraudulent practice is mentioned on page 64. It led, eventually, to the system of hall-marking and other means of regulating the trade. Plating of this kind, however, was done after the object had been made, and it was not until 1742 that a substitute for sheet-silver was devised by Thomas Bolsover. A few years later manufacture was established by Joseph Hancock at Sheffield, and this new manufacture became known as Sheffield plate.

Sheffield plate is a sandwich. Two relatively thin ingots of silver were fused by heat to either side of an ingot of copper, and the whole rolled into a sheet. The earliest examples were silvered on one side only, the reverse sometimes being tinned, but this was soon developed to include silver on both sides, when the appearance became distinctly deceptive. The nature of the metal can always be seen if it is possible to examine a sheared edge, when the colour of the copper lying between two thin sheets of silver will be obvious, but it was customary at the time to disguise this edge with silver wire soldered over it. It was, of course, impossible to form elaborate articles from Sheffield plate; embossed decoration was difficult, and engraving impossible because this would have cut through the silver into the copper. Decoration was usually cast or stamped in silver, backed by a lead alloy and soldered on. Engraving was replaced by flat-chasing, which is produced by hammering along a line with a fine punch. An engraved line is formed by the removal of metal; a flat chased line is indented, and can be seen faintly on the reverse in slight relief. The same method was sometimes used to decorate silver. Manufacture of Sheffield plate ceased about 1850 with the invention of electroplating, introduced by Elkington's of Birmingham in 1840.

Much Sheffield plate was broken up towards the end of the nineteenth century for its silver content. At this time the metal was worth about 5s. an ounce (about £2 in today's money). Specimens for this reason have now acquired a scarcity value. Wear and cleaning in the course of nearly two centuries has succeeded in getting through the silver to the copper beneath in many cases. Dealers sometimes send such specimens to be electro-plated, but this ruins the appearance. Electro-plating deposits pure silver; the silver used for the outer foil of Sheffield plate was alloyed with brass and has a colour of its own.

The market of fifty years ago was flooded with Continental copies and electro-plated reproductions. It must be remembered that all genuine Sheffield plate was made by methods appropriate to the silversmith—the shears, hammer, and soldering iron. Such things as coffee-pots, therefore, will exhibit seams, similar to silver coffee-pots of the period. Later copies are often spun, without seams—a technique introduced in the nineteenth century. There is also a marked difference between silver deposited electrically and the foil-like nature of silver on genuine specimens. Since Sheffield plate was originally intended to deceive, although not fraudulently so, hall-marks were sometimes closely imitated by the original makers, but they were careful never to do so exactly. This is not unknown today, as may be seen from the marks appearing on some electro-plated tableware.

Manufacturers were not, in fact, permitted to use other than workmen's marks before 1784, and they had then to register the mark they proposed with the Assay Office. It was, however, legitimate to sell completely unmarked ware, and in many cases marks were put in inconspicuous positions.

Careful examination and a good magnifying glass is all that is usually required to identify a genuine piece of Sheffield plate, and the commonest marks are listed in the handbook of silver marks already recommended.

British plate (so-called) was a deceptive alloy, somewhat akin to German silver, which was made between 1830 and about 1855, after which it was superseded by electro-plate. It was finished by plating with silver, and is very similar in colour. Since it was an alloy and not a sandwich it did not suffer from many of the disadvantages of Sheffield plate in course of manufacture, and could be made to resemble silver fairly closely. It was, indeed, used for precisely this purpose, furnishing forth the tables of the emerging *bourgeoisie* with fairly close imitations of the table silver of the influential and the affluent. Its principal danger lies in the exceedingly deceptive imitations of genuine hallmarks. They come as closely as possible to genuine marks without actually being counterfeits, and often the only difference is that individual punches are used in impossible combinations. For instance, the leopard's head crowned appears, but this was not used after 1822. The sovereign's head also appears, but the profile is reversed in its direction. The remedy is to examine marks with great care, and to see that they bear the correct relationship to each other. It seems that no specimen of British plate was ever manufactured with counterfeit marks which, of course, would have brought severe penalties upon the makers. This kind of imitation is also accused to the experienced eye by divergences in form, ornament, and general appearance.

Pewter, another silver substitute made from early times, is an alloy of tin and lead. Old specimens are sought by collectors, but only unusually fine examples are highly priced. Forgeries are not especially common, but the metal is soft, malleable, and easily worked. For this reason there has been a certain amount of faking, aimed at making a nondescript specimen more saleable. A ewer, for instance, has been noticed refashioned with a spout and handle added. There is no shortage of old metal for additions, because minor pieces, such as plates, hardly fetch more than a pound or two. There are also several alloys, such as Britannia metal, used for commercial imitations which are not deceptive to anyone acquainted with old silver.

Coins and medals are made from bronze, gold, and silver. Two methods have been generally used—casting, and stamping the design on a blank with the aid of a die. These two kinds of medals are referred to as cast and struck, and both types of forgery can be seen. The former are made in plaster moulds and taken from a genuine original. Struck reproductions necessitate a forged die. The latter is the more difficult operation, and it is mainly used by skilled counterfeiters of current coinage. It would not be very profitable to make half-crowns in moulds because the time needed for the operation would be considerably greater than that needed to make money by honest work.

Cast coins and medals if well made can be extremely deceptive, because a good mould is a completely faithful reproduction of the original. Two points of difference occur, however, The first arises from the removal of the thin rod of metal attached to the cast at a point where the metal was poured into the mould. This has to be cut off and the defect cleaned up with a file, and if examination is sufficiently close traces will usually be found. It is also difficult to eliminate minute air-bubbles in the casting, and these often appear as slight pitting on the surface, visible under a good glass or even to keen eyesight. Of course, in some cases, medals were cast in the first place, but if a cast specimen of which struck versions are known is in question, the conclusion that the former is a forgery is virtually inescapable.

Careful comparison of struck forgeries will inevitably reveal divergences from genuine specimens, proving the use of a die which has been copied from an original. It is impossible to make a die which will be exactly the same in every minor detail, but the possibility that more than one genuine die existed should not be overlooked. This would apply particularly to coinage. Because of the pressure exerted, metal used for struck coins and medals is consolidated, and the impression under magnification often appears sharper than the details of a cast specimen. It is common practice among forgers, however, to add the signs of wear which will help to mask these slight differences. Excessive wear of coins is to be expected; medals were designed for a different purpose, and wear is normally less well marked. Specimens which have been cast from a worn original, a piece of chicanery which can be detected with a little practice, are obvious frauds.

Generally, it is usually possible to detect a forged medal if it can be compared with an original; counterfeit coins, however, are very difficult to separate from genuine. Certain coins, the Maria Theresa dollar for instance, have been officially reproduced in modern times for circulation in more primitive parts of the world because the originals were still current, and regarded with greater confidence than contemporary coinage. This suggests that the term "primitive" may be misapplied.

The work of Billie and Charlie demands passing reference, although it is, today, merely a curiosity which could hardly deceive a novice. These two were London workmen who excavated a genuine object which they were able to sell for a relatively large sum. This excited their cupidity, and, since no more discoveries came their way, they started to make antiquities on their own account from "cock metal", an alloy of copper and lead. Their productions included medallions (very common), daggers, vases, and a miscellany of objects. An example is illustrated (Plate 4), from which the reader may see the kind of ludicrous mistake that the illiterate forger commonly makes. The date (always 1,000, 1001 or 1002) is in Arabic numerals instead of Roman, which would have been used at the period; the figure, vaguely indicated, is an entire figment of an untutored imagination; the knights are wearing body armour of large overlapping scales, reminiscent of fish-scales; and the helmets resemble no type in use at the date in question. The inscription is nonsense. The ornament on the reverse is equally obscure and spurious. These things did succeed in deceiving a few collectors in the middle of the nineteenth century, and some have since been excavated, suggesting that suitable places were "salted". They still exist in fairly large numbers.

Enamelling—the fusion of powdered, coloured glass to a metal background—was practised in Europe and the Near East from very early times, although few examples in a good state of preservation exist. Generally, some at least of the enamel has fallen from its setting. The early things form a field so specialized that there is small point in discussing forgeries in a general work of this kind, although I do not intend to imply that forgeries are non-existent.

Enamels are divisible into three main categories:

(*a*) *Champlevé*, in which cells are cut into the metal with chisels and engraving tools to receive the glass-powder.
(*b*) *Cloisonné*, in which the containing cells are formed by soldering or attaching wires to the background. The wires may be permanent or, as in the case of some rare classes of Oriental enamels, they may subsequently be removed (wireless *cloisonné*).
(*c*) *Painted enamels* which resemble enamelling on a porcelain glaze (see page 125), except that the base (equivalent to the glaze) is rendered opaque with tin oxide and laid on to copper instead of porcelain.

Some examples of early European *cloisonné* and *champlevé* enamel have been the subject of forgeries, which are usually clumsy and not difficult to detect. The best however, particularly spurious altar-pieces, are very deceptive. Modern forgeries are not particularly likely at present because the market is not great, and they demand a high degree of skill to make, but a notable nineteenth-century practitioner of the art was the Viennese, Solomon Weininger, who succeeded in duping some of the connoisseurs of his day. His honest work, which sometimes appears in the modern sale-room, is good enough to fetch high prices as decoration. Eventually he served a term of imprisonment for making a spurious copy of a genuine altar-piece sent to him for restoration, returning the copy instead of the original.

His work is represented here by Plate 3, side by side with a genuine original by Tiziano Aspetti. Careful comparison will show that these two are alike in every particular, and so close a resemblance could only have been attained by taking moulds from the original bronze. There is, in fact, little difference between the two objects, but Weininger has obviously been alive to the fact that he was reproducing the wear of centuries, and appears to have heightened the effects of time a little on his own copy. Certainly I would infinitely prefer to be confronted with a forgery of the calibre of a Van Meegeren painting than to give an opinion on chicanery of this kind, and this plate lends point to what has already been said on page 72.

Old *champlevé* enamels have been forged in Düsseldorf and aged artificially, and most such things purport to be of the twelfth and thirteenth centuries, much work of the kind then being done at

Limoges and in the Rhineland. An attempt was made to revive the craft towards the end of the nineteenth century, when the sale-room prices for good specimens were also high, and most such forgeries belong to this period.

The principal problems to be met in the case of Chinese *cloisonné* enamel are those of dating. Deliberate forgeries are rare; work in earlier styles more common. Marks are sometimes incised, and sometimes cast or in enamel. Incised marks can be cut long after manufacture. Marks in enamel are less easily added, because the heat needed to fuse them is likely to have some effect on the remainder. Both these and cast marks could be added in the form of a separate base subsequently let in, similar in its effect to the method already described for adding spurious silver marks. Chinese marks, however, are notoriously unreliable, and they should not be given undue weight in the face of other indications, such as decoration and technique. Sir Harry Garner[1] notes that the mark of the Ming Emperor Ching-t'ai (1450-7) never appears on enamels made before the seventeenth century. There seems, in fact, little reason to give any greater credence to marks on enamels than to those on porcelain—they may be of the period, but they are equally likely to have been used at a later date as a mark of appreciation for the work of an earlier reign.

Sir Harry Garner has observed that split wires (that is, wires with longitudinal cracks for part or the whole of their length) can only be seen on enamels manufactured during the Ming period, and this is a useful indication of date.

Although the possibility of an object being a Japanese copy of an earlier Chinese object should not be overlooked, the problem presented by Chinese *cloisonné* enamel is principally one of attribution. Probably because of the amount of highly-skilled work necessary, attempts to forge important objects do not appear to have been made, although some poor-quality work on unambitious shapes may have come either from China or Japan.

Painted enamels of Canton made during the eighteenth century do not appear to have been copied deliberately with the intention of deceiving Western collectors as to their date, but some examples are obviously of more recent manufacture. Again, the problem is one of dating, and the experienced collector should not be deceived. If he is,

[1] *Chinese and Japanese Cloisonné Enamels*. London, 1962.

he will probably get good value for his money, since those things which seem to be modern Chinese manufacture are excellent in quality. Perhaps the best safeguard is to avoid specimens of poor quality. The rise in prices for this kind of work, however, obviously presents a temptation against which the buyer would do well to be on guard.

European painted enamels are especially popular among collectors and have frequently been simulated by Edmé Samson of Paris (see page 144 for more information about Samson) as well as by other Continental manufacturers. Recently excellent copies of small boxes of one kind or another have been offered to antique dealers and others as honest reproductions. They appear to have been made in Czechoslovakia. They are principally accused by their brand new appearance, but a few chips and hair-cracks, and some of the signs of age at the corners, would make them much more deceptive. The price at which they are offered is less than a sixth of the current price of a genuine box of similar quality. Style of painting and workmanship, and the quality of the metal mounts, is generally a good guide, and the collector reasonably well acquainted with old work is unlikely to be deceived. Many small pieces of old enamel pass in England under the name of "Battersea" which were really made elsewhere. Battersea was a small factory working from about 1753 to 1756, and it used transfer-printing[1] extensively. Indeed, it is highly probable that the process was originally invented here. Anything in the neo-classical style was made elsewhere, probably at Birmingham or Bilston in Staffordshire. The problem is one of attribution, but since higher prices are usually asked for "Battersea" enamel it is worth taking a little trouble to establish the facts.

Sixteenth-century Limoges enamel especially, now out of favour in the sale-room, realized exceedingly high prices during the nineteenth century and immediately afterwards. Forgeries exist, some initialled *IP* for Jean Penicaud. In general, forgeries are—piece for piece—heavier than comparable genuine specimens, and the black ground is usually defective, lacking intensity. The blue is inclined to be over-bright, and the white is usually poor. The drawing is weak in comparison with genuine examples. This by no means exhausts the defects which may occur, but indicates some of the aspects which need to be compared.

[1] See page 163.

The best course is to submit a suspected example to a museum which has a collection of genuine work, such as the Wallace Collection or the Victoria and Albert Museum, for an opinion.

Imitations of precious stones for jewellery and other objects of *vertu* were especially fashionable during the eighteenth century, and social custom encouraged their use. The prevalence of bandits and highwaymen made them popular among travellers, but imitations of this kind are much older. Cheap glass substitutes with a backing of coloured foil were common in the days of the Roman Empire, and are mentioned by Pliny. Counterfeits of precious stones were made in medieval times, and fourteenth-century goldsmiths were prohibited from mounting them in gold settings. Many of these cannot be regarded as forgeries; neither have they the value of genuine stones, and care should be taken to distinguish the genuine from the artificial. Rock-crystal and suitable varieties of quartz were much used to simulate diamonds, and it is of little use testing them by trying to scratch glass. Both rock-crystal and quartz are harder than glass and will cut it, although not so easily or so deeply as a diamond. Incidentally, both will be scratched by a genuine diamond.

A German named Strass, who had a workshop on the Quai des Orfèvres in 1758, made imitation diamonds from hard and glittering glass cut in the same way as the genuine stone. They were mounted with a backing of foil to increase light-reflection. These stones, also known as "paste", were generally set in silver, sometimes in pewter, and coloured pastes (simulating emeralds, rubies, and sapphires) were used in conjunction with gold or silver-gilt. Such copies are quite legitimate, and only become fraudulent if they are offered as genuine stones. Old paste has a superiority of colour generally lacking in modern manufacture, but the foil backing tends to discolour with age. Other imitations of diamonds such as marcasite, which is a crystalline form of iron pyrites cut in facets like diamonds and highly polished, are not in the least deceptive. Steel was sometimes treated in much the same way.

Artificial stones have usually been made of glass, and most can be scratched with a steel file (see Appendix 10). This test may fail with a few types of glass made specially for scientific purposes, but these have not been adapted, to my knowledge, to the manufacture of fake stones. Usually old imitations made of glass will exhibit multiple scratches from wear, and are sometimes so badly scratched that reflection is poor. Under a magnifier small bubbles and flaws, similar to those to be seen in old glass, will be found, whilst if such a stone is held to the lips, paste feels appreciably warmer than a genuine stone because the latter is a better heat conductor, and draws warmth from the surface of the skin more rapidly. The test is of little use if jewellery has been worn recently.

Doublets and triplets are very deceptive frauds which need an expert to detect. A doublet is a genuine stone cemented to a base of glass or rock-crystal; a triplet is a sandwich, with glass or crystal in the middle. The settings are devised in such a way as to obviate the possibility of detection under a magnifier. It is obvious that such stones will scratch glass and much harder materials. Removed from their settings they can be soaked in a solvent (chloroform, acetone, or alcohol) which will dissolve the cement and thus reveal the fraud, since the stone will fall into two or three pieces. An expert, of course, has other means at his disposal, and it is best to get advice of this kind on all purchases of considerable value from an unknown source.

The application of heat temporarily changes the colour of some stones for the better. Some varieties of yellow topaz, for instance, become the more highly valued pink if treated in this way. Some kinds of zircon not only increase in lustre with heating, but become colourless, and zircon has been used for the fraudulent imitation of diamond. Heating also develops a blue or golden colour occasionally. Quartz is sometimes heated fairly strongly, and develops cracks. It is then put into a bath of dye which percolates along the line of the cracks, adding a distinctive colouring. This can be detected with a reasonably powerful glass from the way in which the colour is distributed.

A few stones have been made artificially, and small rubies have been fused together to make a large single stone. Rubies are also prepared from alumina and chromium oxide under intense heat, but so far diamonds suitable for ornamental purposes have not been synthesized. Sapphire, spinel, and emerald have been produced artificially, and both ruby and sapphire thus made can hardly be distinguished from natural stones except under a microscope. Two comparatively new stones are those made from titanium dioxide and strontium titanate.

Blue-white diamonds, a much-valued variety, are simulated with the more usual yellow-white stones by adding a small amount of blue wax or varnish to the back. Immersion in a solvent such as alcohol is a quick method of detecting this kind of fraud.

Gem-stones of all kinds, including synthetics, may be studied in the London Geological Museum, which also publishes an excellent guide to the subject.[1]

Imitation pearls are not particularly new. They first appeared in France towards the end of the sixteenth century, and by the eighteenth century the imitations were close enough to interfere with the market for genuine pearls, which, in consequence, were returned to their place of origin in the East, where the market still flourished. They are made in a number of ways, perhaps the most common being to coat the interior of thin glass globes with fish-scales digested in ammonia. Wax or gum is injected to give the required weight, and in some cases, for imitations of high quality, the glass is then dissolved in hydrofluoric acid.[2] Black pearls have been simulated in haematite, which is much heavier, and pink coral has been used to imitate pink pearls. The pearl is the end-product of a grain of sand or similar irritant finding its way into the oyster, which covers it with a nacreous substance to form the true pearl. Natural pearls are the result of the irritant finding its way into the shell fortuitously; the Japanese, however, have built up a flourishing industry by adding the irritant artificially. These, known as cultured pearls, are difficult to detect for anyone but the expert.

During the Middle Ages frauds were perpetrated by passing off brass which had been silvered or gilded, and even tin, lead, and pewter which were plated for the same purpose. Various cheap alloys for the manufacture of jewellery and objects of *vertu* were introduced in the eighteenth century, perhaps the best known being the alloy of copper and zinc devised by Christopher Pinchbeck (1670-1732), who was succeeded by his son, Edward. This metal was sometimes given a wash of gold to increase its deceptive appearance. A similar alloy was made in France, but an inferior metal invented by a Lille jeweller tarnished rapidly until it was improved by Leblanc of Paris.

Deliberate forgeries of old jewellery and personal ornaments are comparatively recent, and started when things of the kind began to

[1] McLintock and Sabine: *Guide to the Collection of Gem-stones*. Geological Museum, London, 1951.

[2] A useful but not certain test is to draw the pearls across the teeth. Genuine pearls feel rough; artificial pearls are smooth.

attract the attention of collectors. Etruscan and Greek jewellery has been especially copied because of the high prices it has always realized. Italy has been the principal source of these copies, and the work of Fortunato Pio Castellani (1793-1865) is especially noted for its quality, and for the revival of a granular surface of globular grains of gold which he copied from early Etruscan work. He was followed by his son, Augusto, and by others. A member of the same family, Torquato Castellani, copied Italian *maiolica*. Other copyists of this early work were Melillo and Giuliano and Isaac Rouchomowsky of Odessa. The ancient goldsmiths were masters of granulated work, each distinct grain being soldered accurately side by side. The work of the copyists mentioned certainly did not approach it for quality and delicacy, although Rouchomowsky's imitations were exceptionally skilful.

Medieval jewellery has been reproduced in Paris and Frankfort, and Renaissance pendants have been forged, although the quality of workmanship is nearly always much poorer, and hardly deceptive. Usually the metal employed is silver-gilt and not the more expensive gold.

Eighteenth-century styles in jewellery have been frequently copied, and diamonds have the old rose-cutting. Frauds such as the removal of genuine stones and the substitution of paste during the course of repair are not unknown, and the remedy is to send work of this kind to a reputable firm. Old shagreen cases have sometimes had jewellery especially made to fit, the old case being intended to divert attention from the contents.

Cut and engraved cameos in hardstone, and similar small objects for mounting in jewellery, have been copied from early times (page 115). There is, for instance, little doubt that the Egyptian *faïence* scarabs were first made as a substitute for those in harder and more expensive materials. Carved gems have also been imitated in glass, which could be worked more easily; some were cast in moulds taken from genuine specimens, and afterwards finished by the lapidary. Old gems of all kinds were frequently copied in glass during the Renaissance and in the eighteenth century, sometimes with a backing of genuine hardstone to forestall possible tests. In nearly all cases the workmanship is inferior to the genuine object, even when a specimen is not accused by the material (see also page 115).

Early watches are similar in their decorative qualities to jewellery, and the cases were at first intended to be worn outside the clothing as ornaments. Good forgeries need skill and experience to separate them from genuine specimens. Generally, it is important to see that all the details of case and movement are in keeping with the supposed provenance. This requires a careful study of the characteristics of manufacture at various periods. Most difficult to detect, if it has been well done, is the old movement in a new case. Many forgeries exist of work by such makers as Tompion, George Graham, Le Roy, and Breguet, but few are calculated to deceive the collector with reasonably adequate knowledge. Most of them are limited to the use of the name. As an example of the absurdities which sometimes occur, I once saw a grandmother clock in a lacquer case, obviously fairly new, which had a nineteenth-century movement and a rocking ship in the arch of the dial. It bore the name of "Tompion" engraved on the dial. This could hardly be called a forgery. G. H. Baillie in his book, *Watches; their history, decoration, and mechanism* (London, 1929) includes a useful chronological survey of innovations and modifications in watchmaking.

Among the forgeries which have been noted in the past is a watch bearing the name of George Graham in a silver case signed *D. Cochin fecit*, which was probably a contemporary Dutch forgery. English watches had earned an excellent reputation at the time, and they were, therefore, a tempting target for the Continental faker, who added the names of better-known English makers. These are curiosities with a certain amount of antique value.

The faked clock-movement is much more common than the deceptive forgery. To make a movement by hand, which would be essential, could hardly be profitable, because the amount of highly-skilled labour needed would be excessive. It is not usually difficult to detect machine-made parts if one is acquainted with the appearance of hand-work.

Certain parts of the clock-mechanism are subject to a good deal of wear and tear, especially the escapement. Some renewals, therefore, are inevitable. It is, however, important that the new parts should be limited to the escapement and to other parts on which wear is likely to be unduly heavy. Study of genuine examples will make it evident that makers like Tompion and Quare had their own methods of handling mechanical and decorative details, and these provide a useful test of genuineness. It is also essential to see that the style of engraving and added cast ornament, such as the spandrels, is correct for the period and the type of movement. The quality of the pierced hands is a useful indication of the nature of a movement, but it is unreliable by itself because hands sometimes need to be replaced.

Although it is desirable that a clock, regarded strictly as a collector's item, should be as nearly as possible in original condition, it must be remembered that movements were modified in the seventeenth and eighteenth centuries for purely practical reasons. The verge escapement was frequently replaced by the later anchor because this was more accurate. Such clocks can be allowed to remain in the condition in which they were found, or the original type of escapement can be replaced. A clock which still has the escapement with which it started life is very unusual, and certain to be a bad timekeeper.

Forged movements are almost as old as the genuine specimens they copy. Most emanated from Holland, and may, indeed, be comparable in quality. Cases need careful examination to be certain that they are of the same period as the movement. For instance, no specimen of Tompion's work is known in a marquetry case. He preferred those veneered with walnut or ebony. The original case, however, might at some time or another have been damaged beyond repair and a contemporary case substituted. This would undoubtedly reduce the value, but the extent of the reduction might not be excessive if both case and movement were otherwise in good condition.

15. (*Left*) A Bow figure modelled by Mr Tebo, c. 1760. (*Right*) The same model bearing the red anchor mark of Chelsea copied by Samson of Paris. The Continental hand in the modelling of the reproduction is obvious, the colouring is inaccurate, and the treatment of the hair differs from that of the Bow painters.
[*Victoria and Albert Museum*

16. Unmarked Samson copy of a Bristol mug which may have been marked originally. The differences in the style of painting are obvious to the experienced eye. The colouring is also inaccurate. [*Victoria and Albert Museum*

*Chapter IV*

## *Carvings and Modelling in Various Materials*

> You will be wary in accepting the conclusions of experts. Because a man says he is an expert it does not make him one. An expert is no better than his knowledge.
>
> MR JUSTICE BLACK: *Hahn v. Duveen*

Sculpture in wood and bone has been discovered among the earliest of man's artifacts. They are, in fact, the only two materials which could be carved with stone tools, although stone-carvings are to be found before the introduction of metal tools in places where natural deposits of abrasives occur. Wood-sculpture, often elaborately inlaid with ivory and gold, was made by the Greeks, but nothing has survived. Egyptian wood-carvings, however, because of the more favourable conditions under which they have been preserved, are much more numerous. These have been mentioned in Chapter I.

Stone used for sculpture in antiquity is of two kinds—soft, represented principally by sedimentary marbles, limestone, and alabaster, and the harder stones, such as the igneous granite and basalt. Obviously it is to be expected that there will be great differences in technique in the carving of the two categories. Marble, for instance, can be worked with punches, chisels, and drills, whereas the harder stones were shaped to a much greater extent by abrasives, such as emery (corundum) from Naxos. The natural deposits here were widely known throughout the Mediterranean world. (See Appendix 10.)

The most skilled carvers of such stones as granite were the Egyptians, who devised methods of sawing and drilling, using the Naxos emery and jewel-dust. The saws were probably without teeth, although Flinders Petrie mentions the discovery of a saw-blade at Tiryns set with particles of emery. The Egyptian use of the tube-drill may be observed in the cylindrical holes of early stone vases.

The stone sculpture was first roughly shaped by sawing, followed by hammering to remove the larger surface irregularities and to bring the material to something approaching the final form. Abrasives were then employed to smooth and polish the surface and to round off the forms. Inscriptions were cut with a tool pointed with emery. The tube-drill may have been made from either bronze or wood. The Chinese jade-carvers sometimes use wooden tools in which the abrasive becomes embedded, and this occurs also with those of bronze.

This may usefully be contrasted with Greek and Roman methods of working the softer stones. To judge from the unfinished specimens which have come down to us, statues were probably first outlined on the front and sides of a squared block and the sculptor then shaped it roughly with punches and a hammer, probably clearing large amounts of waste material with a pointed hammer, and, occasionally, with one having a striking surface studded with points, similar to the modern *boucharde*. This, also known to the Egyptians, crushed the surface and enabled it to be removed easily with relatively soft bronze chisels and punches. Few mechanical aids to accuracy were used, and certainly nothing equivalent to the modern pointing-machine which enables accurate replicas of a clay or plaster model to be made.

When this first stage had been completed, the chisel and the gouge were brought into use, and drills were employed for shaping the deeper parts such as the hair. The claw-chisel, still a favourite tool today, was much used. This is similar in appearance to an ordinary chisel, but the blade is cut into triangular teeth. It leaves a characteristic mark which can often be identified.

The collector of stone sculpture of any kind will find it extremely valuable to study the methods of the modern stone-carver. There has been little change in the fundamental technique over the centuries, and a working knowledge of the marks left by various tools is necessary to a complete understanding of the way in which early sculpture was fashioned. The most useful work known to me is that of Stanley Casson,[1] which will provide the reader with a great deal of information

[1] Stanley Casson: *The Technique of Early Greek Sculpture*. Oxford, 1933.

which can profitably be employed in the study of work from other countries and periods. The illustrations of tool-marks are clear and valuable. Much, also, may be learned from watching a sculptor or a skilled mason at work, and from a discussion of the techniques of the craft.

Forgeries of stone sculpture are nearly always limited to classical or medieval work. Few examples of forgeries of Egyptian work in the harder stones are known, and these are not usually very deceptive. Those in limestone are more frequent, and are often panels carved in low relief with figure subjects which were probably derived in the first place from tomb-paintings.

The first forgers of Greek sculpture of the fifth century B.C. were the Greeks themselves, working for Imperial Roman masters. These things, of course, have to be attributed on grounds of style, and require both knowledge and experience to do so with a reasonable degree of certainty. Style, in fact, is almost the only guide. Greek and Roman sculpture greatly influenced the sculptors of the Renaissance, and fine reproductions were then in demand among collectors. Many such forgeries of early work exist, although these now have considerable value. Well-known from contemporary records is the "Cupid Asleep" of Michelangelo which no longer exists. To this he attempted to give a false patina by burying it, and it was then sold by the art-dealer, Baldassare de Milanese, at a high price. Like more recent forgeries, however, it did not succeed in deceiving everyone, and it was subsequently returned as spurious. Today, if it could be offered for sale, it would be the subject of fierce competition from the world's wealthiest buyers. Renaissance copies of classical sculptures are, perhaps, the most dangerous of the more recent work, not only because the sculptor could enter more easily into the spirit of earlier times, but because what he made then now has many of the signs of age.

Most forgeries of the so-called classical period, whenever they were made, are much more deceptive than those purporting to belong to the archaic period. The latter were first attempted during Roman times, and again more recently. It is almost axiomatic that the expression of the lips, the so-called "smile", of these sixth-century faces cannot be reproduced convincingly, and certainly I have never seen an instance of it being done, not even by Alceo Dossena who several times attempted it. His so-called Etruscan objects, especially the "Diana" sold to the St Louis Museum, are conspicuous failures in this respect.

Even a perfectly genuine history of excavation (and excavated objects are always a risky purchase unless the work has been properly supervised) is not, by itself, a good and sufficient reason why sculpture in the classical style should be dated to Greek and Roman times. Statues have always been favourite garden ornaments, and several hundredweight of stone, perhaps tipped from its pedestal in the course of some of the interminable wars which have plagued Europe since the beginning of the present era, can, if left undisturbed, sink into the earth in a few decades.

Modern forgers sometimes start by making a clay model, which is then cast in plaster and transferred to stone with the aid of a pointing-machine. This can be used by a reasonably skilled mason to make almost perfect facsimiles. Although a clever modeller who is fully conversant with the techniques and problems of stone-carving can make provision in his design for the difference between the two materials, the method is completely at variance with that used by early sculptors, and forms are apt to be softer and more rounded, lacking the strength of genuine work.[1]

The appearance of age—the patina—is difficult to imitate successfully, particularly if exact methods are used to examine the surface. The tricks adopted, however, can be superficially deceptive. Abrasives are used to disguise the marks of the chisel, pitting of the surface is quite easily imitated, and the chisel supplies the damage of centuries, although rarely in a part likely to affect the value. Those who are principally acquainted with old sculpture through the medium of the museum and the art gallery often do not realize how much of the work they admire is restoration. A couple of examples are worth recording. The "Venus de Medici", rediscovered in the Forum of Octavia about

[1] Since these lines were written a newspaper report suggests that a pointing-machine that can be used in conjunction with a kind of stereoscopic photography developed during World War II by the Royal Air Force has been devised. In the hands of its inventor it is being honestly used for portraiture. The possibility of a machine based on these principles being used by a forger to reproduce old sculpture must not be overlooked. Detection would be by the appearance of induced damage, by surface changes and their imitation, by the nature of the stone or metal, and the absence of normal tool-marks.

1680, was first placed in the gardens of the Medici family at Florence in the sixteenth century. It was discovered in thirteen pieces, although most of the fractures were fairly clean. The right arm and hand, and the left arm from the elbow downwards, are replacements by Bernini, and the plinth is also modern, the inscription having been recopied. The "Venus Callipygous" of Naples was restored by the sculptor Albaccini, who added the head, the right leg and hand, part of the left arm, the left hand, and the breast. By contrast the "Venus de Milo" is relatively well-preserved, only the nose, the left foot, and part of the plinth being later additions. These remarks are not intended as a denigration of these works, but to warn the reader against objects which exhibit an unusual degree of preservation.

The surface of forgeries is treated to modify the crudity of newly-carved stone. Among the Greeks and Romans the best statuary marble came from Mount Pentelicus (Pentelic). This is white and sparkling when freshly-cut, but changes to a warm ivory tone with exposure. Parian marble from the Island of Paros, which has a fine grain, is creamy-white in colour. The Carrara marble quarry, near Florence, is one of the principal sources of supply at present. This stone is pure white in colour, and is apt to suffer from blemishes and dark veins. One authority records the use of a wash of green vitriol to give the requisite ivory colour to the surface. This is said to penetrate and be difficult to detect. Silver nitrate has been used for the same purpose. The colouring of marble to imitate the ancient practice is also undertaken, and, generally, marble takes stain fairly well. The fact that ancient marbles have been buried, and that Renaissance copies have been preserved above ground, usually results in a noticeable difference in surface colour best learned from a comparison of genuine works of both periods (see also page 266).

Drapery should always be examined with great care. Apart from the face, and the treatment of hair, this is the place where most spurious copies are likely to fail. Goethe called drapery "the thousand-fold echo of the form", and early Greek sculptors, before the art began to decay towards the end of the pre-Christian era, lavished great care and skill on this aspect. The rendering of drapery is, perhaps, one of the greatest tests of the ability of a sculptor.

The selection of the folds appropriate to the subject should be carefully examined. Art is a process of selecting and arranging the forms to be seen in nature, and the forger is inclined to use an excessive number of trivial folds which are not essential to the design. Generally, genuine drapery has perpendicular folds which fall naturally, depending on the weight of the material. It should fit the form loosely, and this should, in later works, be revealed by it. Drapery is sometimes drawn together by being gathered in the hand. It falls diagonally between the knees of seated figures. Especially in bas-reliefs it may appear to float behind the figure, and to follow its movement.

The purpose of the folds of genuine drapery is clearly evident; they are well-defined and logical. When drapery is carelessly rendered or unnecessarily complex, the work is likely to be spurious. The forger sometimes simplifies drapery, and often misunderstands its nature. Not only does his work lack the authenticity of folds carved by a good craftsman working in his own period, but in some cases gross and obvious errors are made. The fall of drapery on a spurious Tanagra *terracotta* figure, for instance, actually defied gravity by falling at an angle to the ground. Where three-dimensional carvings have been adapted from two-dimensional originals, such as a Greek marble from a vase-painting, there is an even greater margin for error. Folds which exist for no apparent reason should be noted. The remarks of the sculptor, Flaxman, on the movement of drapery may be read with profit.[1]

Inscriptions need careful examination by an expert. Occasionally one meets specimens of little merit with inscriptions so blatantly false that they do not need the eye of the specialist to detect them. Forgers are rarely Greek scholars, and either copy from a genuine inscription or fabricate something which will pass superficial examination.

It is worth devoting a little space to Alceo Dossena who enjoyed a certain amount of success in this field in the 1920s, although, as in other equally notorious instances, the reason is not particularly apparent. Dossena was a Cremonese stone-mason who came from a family of artists and craftsmen, and his career seems to have started in 1916, when he carved and sold a "Madonna" to an art-dealer in Rome, Alfredo Fasoli, to supplement his meagre army pay. In the circumstances this was, no doubt, blameless enough, but Fasoli saw profit in the deceptive appearance of the carving after he had sold it as an antique at a handsome profit, and he commissioned more of the same

[1] John Flaxman: *Lectures on Sculpture* (various editions).

kind. When the war ended saleable subjects were suggested to Dossena, and he soon had as much work as he could handle in stone, wood, and *terracotta*. The subjects he portrayed became increasingly ambitious, and he found he could work with almost equal facility in any antique style—classical, Gothic, or Renaissance. Dossena succeeded in devising a deceptive artificial patina by immersing his stonework in what may have been some kind of acid, although the nature is unknown.

Apologists for Dossena, who appears to have been an engaging rogue, have made much of the fact that he did not receive more for his work than would have been paid for it as contemporary sculpture, and that he did not know for what purposes it was being used. This may have been so at first, and certainly when he had reason to suspect that large sums were being paid for his work he consulted a lawyer, which resulted in the exposure of the fraud. It is, however, difficult to accept the contention that he was an innocent party. Not only did he supply an imitation patina, but he damaged his work to give it a spurious appearance of antiquity. When certain experts refused to believe that he was the author of a particularly deceptive piece of pseudo-classical carving, he produced parts which he had knocked off, and these fitted so exactly that there was no further reason for doubt. It is inconceivable that anyone could be so naïve as to fake both damage and patination without knowing that there was an intention to defraud, and knowledge of the intention would make him a party to it.

As in the case of Van Meegeren, Rouchomowsky, and others who have deceived some of the experts, Dossena was hailed as a master-forger, and his work (correctly attributed) exhibited in New York, Naples, and Berlin. It soon became apparent that it was not so deceptive as had been claimed. Once such work becomes generally known those who previously accepted it, even honestly, are in an extremely embarrassing position; either their good faith or their judgement must be impugned. Naturally they prefer to have it thought that the deficiency was one of judgement, and it then becomes better to have been deceived by a master-forger than by a lesser man. This is the reason why successful forgers are glamourized, and it is always essential to accept these after-valuations of their work with reserve. Dossena was an excellent craftsman; he was little else.

Dossena may well be considered with another sculptor whose work was even more deceptive, and who better deserves the laudatory descriptions awarded to others. This was Giovanni Bastianini of Fiesole, who was responsible for the *terracotta* portrait bust of the Florentine philosopher, Benivieni (1453-1542), which was bought by a Paris collector in 1864 from an Italian dealer for 700 francs. This caused a furore as soon as it was publicly exhibited, and attributions to such sculptors as Verrocchio and Donatello were freely canvassed. In 1866 it was the subject of keen competition when it appeared at the Salle Drouot in Paris, ultimately being purchased for the Louvre for about 14,000 francs—an exceedingly high price at the time. The dealer who had handled the original sale, in an article in the *Chronique des Arts* in December 1867, gave an account of the fabrication of this bust by Bastianini which galvanized Paris art-circles. At first the article was regarded as no more than a malicious attempt to cast doubt on a great work of art by a dealer disappointed at selling it too cheaply, but details supplied by Bastianini left no room for doubt.

Bastianini's skill in imitating works of the *quattrocento* has never been approached, but they were not originally intended as forgeries. Nor were they marketed deceptively at first. The Benivieni portrait was described to the original purchaser in a way which laid no claim to antiquity, and what followed was purely self-deception on the part of a few experts. Like other things of the kind which start life honestly, however, some of these imitations were sold after Bastianini's death as antique for large sums.

In general outright forgeries of medieval stone sculpture are comparatively few; those of wood-carvings are more frequent. Fakes of the softer stone-carvings, however, are relatively common. In this field damage is often fairly severe. Works have fallen or been prised from architectural settings. External sculpture has weathered until much of the detail is blurred. It is, therefore, to be expected that a Virgin and Child surviving from the fourteenth century will lack one head, or even two, and medieval statues which lack heads are not in demand among collectors. The faker, by an adroit piece of surgery, provides heads, hands, or any other amputated part. Badly-chipped and weathered drapery, which affects the desirability of the object in the international art-market, is tactfully improved. Folds which seem skimped and shallow, therefore, always need special attention, as do those which appear soft and clinging. As in archaic Greek sculpture curves which are softly feminine are also a warning which it would be well not to ignore. Tool-marks are unusual on genuine works, which were finished with abrasives, particularly in the exposed parts of the flesh. It is, perhaps, easiest to detect the replacement of a head from style than that of any other part. Like the Greek "smile", the austere facial expression of genuine medieval carving is difficult to counterfeit, particularly that of female figures, and the forgery is usually too expressive. The representation of hair, too, seems to have given most forgers especial difficulty. Invaluable to the student of the characteristics of medieval sculpture is the *Encyclopédie Photographique de l'art* (*Sculptures du Moyen Age*) which contains 179 large photogravure plates of objects in the Louvre dating from the eleventh to the sixteenth century.

Many of these early statues—those intended for interiors—were painted, just as much earlier Greek sculpture was also coloured, the classical white marble being a figment of the eighteenth-century neoclassicist's imagination. Traces of this paint, often in considerable quantities, have survived on genuine medieval work. To reproduce the effect of damaged paint the forger has first to apply colour to his work and then to remove it in convincing places in a manner which will not be obvious. Paint can, of course, be examined by methods similar to those used for old paintings but, in any case, new work lacks the rich colour of old, and can usually be recognized from this alone.

Dangerous forgeries have been made from plaster-casts of genuine objects which have been used as models, perhaps in conjunction with a pointing-machine. This calls into question the advisability of allowing the reproduction of objects in public collections, except those which are too well-known to matter. It is difficult for any but the specialist to recognize work taken from a cast from an obscure provincial museum; if someone could be found to buy as genuine a forgery based on the Berlin head of Nefertiti (a frequent subject of reproductions) he would deserve to lose his money.

Dossena was responsible for some very deceptive forgeries of medieval and Renaissance sculpture, examples of which are shown on Plates 7, 8, and 10. He selected as inspiration for some of them the painting of Simone Martini (1285-1344) of Siena, and he almost succeeded in convincing some of the experts of the time that Martini had been a sculptor as well as a painter, even though Vasari had not heard of this extension of his activities.

Most other medieval sculptures appear to come from Paris, many being made between 1900 and 1930 when demand was at its greatest and high prices were being paid. The name of Boutron has been connected with some of the cleverest, but little is known about him. His name appears in some police investigations made just before the last war, but hostilities probably prevented his identification. Nothing further seems to have come to light since 1945. Forgeries of Renaissance sculpture have come principally from Italy.

When we come to consider later forgeries of Renaissance work we find that, although many are fairly close to the originals, the forger is often betrayed by sentimentality in the facial expression which was foreign to the period. The Renaissance was a time of remarkable intellectual activity; it was neither sentimental nor compassionate. This is particularly to be seen in genuine child portraits. It must be remembered that the attitude to children has undergone a remarkable change during the last century or so. Previously they were regarded as small adults whose business it was to grow up and accept responsibility as quickly as possible. Their essentially amoral nature was recognized and accepted. It was not even deplored. Modern times have seen not only a notable tendency to sentimentalize about children, but they have come to be regarded almost as a race apart, living in an unreal world of anthropomorphic rabbits. The forger can hardly avoid the atmosphere of the time in which he lives. He will either drift unconsciously into a sentimental approach to the subject, or, far less often, he will adopt the more realistic attitude of a Giles. In either case he will produce an improbability. Even so skilled a craftsman as Bastianini could not avoid sentimental passages, as may be seen from the bust of Lucrezia Donati in the Victoria and Albert Museum (Plate 12).

Portrait-reliefs are copied from medallions. They are at several removes from the wax or clay original, which first had to be converted into bronze. The medallist, of course, designed his work for miniature bronze-casting or stamping, and if one is considering a suspected work of this kind, it is a useful exercise to try to envisage it as a circular composition in bronze, greatly reduced in size.

The catalogue of the British Museum Exhibition of Forgeries and Deceptive Copies held in 1961 quoted the remark of a well-known museum official, who once said "every director has a bust of Flora waiting for him at the end of the corridor". This bust, attributed to Leonardo, was the centre of a sensational controversy at the beginning of the present century when it was bought, in 1909, for the Kaiser Friedrich Museum in Berlin by the noted Wilhelm Bode, director of the Prussian Art Collections. It represents the half-length portrait of a young woman, naked except for light drapery at the waist and shoulder. *The face is in excellent condition*; the neck and bosom are extensively cracked, and the forearms completely missing. That they once existed, however, is proved by the discovery of part of a hand at a later date. The back is unfinished because the work was intended for an architectural setting. In pose it is virtually the same as an existing painting of Flora, a Leonardo schoolpiece, but by itself this proves little. The painting might well have been inspired by the bust had it been genuine. The material is wax, and the final details and modelling, as well as the colouring, were added in thin layers over a preliminary cast.

Flora is said to have been sold in a London auction for a few pounds, and at one time to have been in the possession of the art-dealer, Durlacher, who paid £150 for it (say, £900 in today's money). Bode bought it for 160,000 marks—about £8,000 at the time, and close to £50,000 today. Soon afterwards a Southampton auctioneer stated that the bust had been made in 1846 by Richard Cockle Lucas for an art-dealer named Buchanan, and that the schoolpiece mentioned above had been lent to Lucas to copy. The sculptor's son, who rejoiced in the name of Albert Dürer Lucas, was still alive at the venerable age of eighty-one, and he joined in the controversy, not only confirming the story but adding that he had helped with the work. Other eye-witnesses gave similar testimony, one attributing the poor condition to the fact that the bust had been left unprotected in the garden. This hardly seems likely, however, because the hair and the face would undoubtedly have suffered much more from this treatment than is apparent. It is, of course, possible that the bust was deliberately aged in this way, with the head suitably protected.

No doubt little more would have been thought of the matter, but Bode's position tempted the radical newspapers and parties to try to make political capital from it, forcing the unfortunate director to defend his purchase. His position was seriously undermined when nineteenth-century rags and paper were found embedded in the interior, and he shifted his ground, admitting that the bust had been restored by Lucas. The battle raged until 1914 when the director was given a title of nobility, emerging as von Bode. After the war internecine hostilities were renewed, the last shot being fired in 1935.

The standpoint of Wilhelm von Bode and his supporters is more firmly based than in most other instances of the kind, and although there can be little doubt that this bust was not by Leonardo's hand, the kind of evidence needed to stigmatize it as an undoubted forgery is lacking.

Originally it may have been the property of Lord Palmerston, although it certainly cannot be traced any further back. It is suggested that the bust was damaged whilst in his possession and given to Lucas to restore, with the proviso that if it proved beyond restoration he could keep it. This is not so unlikely as it appears at first sight, because it was not, perhaps, regarded as worth anything in its damaged condition—a viewpoint which was probably right at the time. The work of Lucas, as it is illustrated in a book of photographs presented to the British Museum in 1859, does not suggest that he possessed the skill needed to forge a work of this character. In a second volume containing miscellaneous works of art by other artists a photograph of the bust appears, under which is written in the hand of Lucas *The Flora of Leonardo*. The appearance of the surface suggests that Lucas was a restorer rather than its maker, and it may have been at this time that the rags mentioned by his son were added to the interior for greater strength. Lucas, it is suggested, found the work of restoration both risky and troublesome, Lord Palmerston did not want it back in its damaged condition, and it was put on one side until the death of Lucas. This, too, is likely. Those well acquainted with restorers know that difficult work of uncertain merit is often put on one side, and gradually finds its way to the back of the shelf unless owners make a point of the repair being carried out. The auctioneer of the property of the deceased Lucas was doubtful about selling it, since the ownership was not clear. Chemical analysis has not brought out anything definitely against its fabrication during the period of Leonardo's lifetime which cannot be otherwise explained. For example, pigments which are obviously of later manufacture could have been added in course of restoration.

There is a certain amount of force in the contention that nothing exists which would irrevocably stigmatize the bust as being of nineteenth-century manufacture, and it would, perhaps, be reasonable to regard it as a schoolpiece.

*Terracotta* has been a favourite with the imitator and the forger in the past because the materials are cheap and ready to hand. The clever imitations by Bastianini are an example. Little work of this kind appears to be done at present, probably because Renaissance works are fetching relatively low prices in the art-market, but also because craftsmen with the requisite degree of skill are becoming fewer. *Terracottas* are made in a kind of red-burning clay which is widely distributed. Although they are fired in a kiln, they differ from pottery for the most part in the fact that they are larger and more ambitious in scope, and only one copy is usually made. It is, however, quite possible to make plaster piece-moulds from which "squeezes" can be taken. The skilled workman can also vary poses—the position of the arms, the tilt of the head, the fall of drapery, and so forth—on duplicated pieces by cutting and remodelling the clay while it is still plastic. Forgeries exist both in the round and in the form of reliefs (usually with minor variations and additions that serve to differentiate them from the original source of inspiration) which may be taken from illustrations of existing works, or even from moulds of little-known stone or bronze statuary. Generally, copies of Renaissance *terracottas* are limited to portrait-busts and reliefs, which were afterwards coloured to give them the appearance of age, the absorbent surface bring treated with wax. Detection of a good forgery is singularly difficult, and appraisal must be principally on grounds of style.

Not only early Renaissance work has been forged in this way, but also that of the eighteenth-century French sculptors, Falconet and Clodion. The *terracottas* of Clodion have particularly suffered, one such group apparently having been faked from a damaged original, since it was held that the part bearing Clodion's name was genuine, although no certain conclusion was reached. The reliefs of the della Robbias are essentially *terracotta*, although they were covered with a tin-enamel glaze and are therefore related to Italian *maiolica* (see page 134). These have been imitated extensively, but rarely well enough to trouble the sceptic.

Wood sculpture may be either an outright forgery or a fake. An example of the latter is the well-known instance of the fifteenth-century Tyrolese carving of God the Father, who lost his beard and became Rudolf I of Germany. This did not entirely remove its antiquarian interest because the remainder was perfectly genuine, and fifteenth-century carvings are very rare, but its value was seriously depreciated by these alterations. Ultra-violet light could undoubtedly help in a case of this kind because newly-cut wood is inclined to show some differences in fluorescence from old. The new surfaces also had to be matched with the original, not a particularly easy task and one which may have required tampering with the whole.

Wood-sculpture is aged in various ways, of which treatment with potassium permanganate or various alkalis[1] are probably the most frequently used. Robert Dossie[2] gives a comprehensive list of dyes in use for colouring wood during the eighteenth century. Polychrome statuary is first coated with *gesso*, and the colours laid on this ground. The surface is finished in various ways to give the appearance of age. New gilding is sometimes dulled with liquorice juice, or even with a type of carbon black made from burnt paper. The appearance of old *gesso* surfaces is discussed on page 49.

That new work can also be deceptive is proved by the recent Austrian case of Giuseppe Rifesser, a wood-carver from the Southern Tyrol, who deceived Viennese experts with carefully "aged" copies of Gothic sculpture. *Gotische skulptur* is a popular item in the Vienna sale-room, and forgeries of wood-carvings at present are likely to come from Austria, not only because the tradition persists in the Tyrol, but because prices for good specimens are relatively higher than in Western sale-rooms. Anything sufficiently deceptive to pass muster in Vienna is likely to be even more deceptive further west where these things are not so well known.

The case of Rifesser seems to be one of genuine naïvety, in which a talented wood-carver made copies of old work without definite fraudulent intent, although he was incautious enough to imitate the signs of age. Recognizing a "fourteenth-century" Madonna in the State auction room as his own work he consulted a lawyer, who communicated the information to the authorities. Once again we find

[1] "Mould" on the surface of wood suggests comparatively recent staining in which soda has been used, the excess coming to the surface and remaining as a white powdery deposit.

[2] *The Handmaid to the Arts*. London, 1758.

doubts being expressed, especially by dealers, as soon as a disputed work comes on to the market, and it is noticeable that the dealer of repute is always to the forefront in exposing frauds of all kinds. This, of course, is only to be expected. He sees much more that is doubtful than most museum officials, and if he makes a mistake he has to bear the loss. The prospect of losing one's own money sharpens the wits to a remarkable degree.

One of the dealers reported the matter to the police, and Continental police take a much more serious view of art-forgery than those of England. Inquiries resulted in the arrest of a dealer who had sent the carving for sale, and his subsequent confession brought another case to light. His defence was the not unusual one of "revenge on the experts" for some imagined slight. The feelings of art-forgers are unusually tender, but, like a certain well-known entertainer, they are always prepared to "cry all the way to the Bank".

The auction-room officials were difficult to convince, and once again we see the familiar pattern emerging of experts defending an untenable position because it would be too embarrassing to accept the alternative. Rifesser was asked to make a similar carving under supervision, but before he could do so the Madonna in question was found to be of chestnut and not cedar, and there was no further room for doubt. The dealer, Josef Auer, was imprisoned for twelve months, and it was stated that he had already acquired twenty-five previous convictions.

This case once again raises the question of the culpability of the author of these objects—Beppi Rifesser. Whilst it is true that he consulted a lawyer (as did Dossena before him) it was only after the first questionings had been heard, and he took the trouble to "age" his productions in a deceptive manner. He can, therefore, hardly have been ignorant of the fact that his reproductions could be sold as antique.

In this case I have only been able to study photographs, one to which is reproduced on Plate 14, but I find it extremely difficult to understand why this work was accepted. The resemblance between the style of this and a genuine Gothic carving is slight. The drapery is singularly unconvincing, the folds lacking the crispness and certainty of Gothic carving. The medieval face was, making due allowance for differences in provenance, much the same throughout Western Europe. It obeyed certain conventions which will be obvious enough if several genuine specimens are examined. Nor do they vary very much between wood-carving and stone-carving. The specimen of Rifesser's work shown here leaves no doubt whatever that we cannot be looking at a work of the thirteenth or early fourteenth century, but something entirely modern. It is to be seen in the sentimental expression of both the faces, and in the pose of the child which is outside the medieval convention. Sentimentality of this kind is common from the middle of the nineteenth century onwards, and is still to be seen today in imitations of antique work.

This, however, is a modern instance; the greater number of existing forgeries were done in the nineteenth century, and some of the appearances of age must already be genuine. The comparative ease with which wood may be carved suggests that spurious works ought to be numerous. Completely new work, however, is not often seen: fakes are much more common, and the collector should be especially alert for signs of recarving.

Hardstone carvings which should be approached with caution include such diverse objects as ancient engraved gems and Chinese jade. Works of art in rock-crystal from various periods have been imitated in suitable types of glass, but the crystalline structure (the peculiar striations to be seen in the interior of most hardstones) is missing, or replaced with those more appropriate to glass. The difference between the two is easy to tell; rock-crystal is always harder than glass, and the surface of glass can be scratched by any stone of the quartz classification, to which rock-crystal belongs (see Appendix 10). Elaborate forgeries of European rock-crystal carvings are not likely to be modern, but to belong to the nineteenth century. The manufacture of such an object costed on a "time and materials" basis and then compared with modern sale-room prices suggests that it could only be done at a loss, even if it were accepted. This is a useful indication, although it is sometimes dangerous. It can best be employed by someone well-versed in the history of art-prices, who can usually say when, in the past, an object would have been most worth imitating.

Hardstones have been carved at Oberstein-Idar, in the Rhineland, and they include rock-crystal, rose quartz, jadeite, and nephrite. The objects imitated are European, Chinese, and even the old Maori *tiki*, for which genuine New Zealand greenstone has been used. These copies have not been made for fraudulent purposes but as decoration.

17. (*Left*) A Samson tea-jar imitating Chinese export porcelain of mid-eighteenth century. (*Below*) The mark on the base. The letter "S" is incorporated.
[*Victoria and Albert Museum*

18. Chinese export plate in true porcelain with an almost contemporary copy from Caughley in soft porcelain. Both second-half of the eighteenth century.
[*Victoria and Albert Museum*

19. A "skinned" vase (see Chapter V) with decoration in the *famille noire* palette purporting to belong to the reign of K'ang Hsi. The porcelain is Chinese of approximately the correct period, the redecoration European. By comparison with genuine specimens the drawing is obviously not Chinese, and the *motifs* at the base have been misunderstood. The tone of the aubergine enamel is too pink. Nevertheless, this is an extremely clever forgery of a type which, when genuine, can still realise £2,000 or more for a good specimen, and once sold for much more.

[*Private Collection*

20. Persian vase apparently copied from a damaged va in the Victoria and Albert Museum. Originally in glaz earthenware, this reproduction by Samson of Paris (it bea his mark) is in hard porcelain. The neck is wrongly forme the arabesques in blue surrounding the central *cartouc* differ noticeably from genuine drawing, as do the flor sprays in red enamel (which vary in colour from genui work) inside it. The *motifs* on the base follow a Persia original, but are unconvincing. It also bears a mark i blue in Arabic script.

[*Private Collecti*

There can be little doubt, however, that they could be marketed as genuine work in unscrupulous hands.

Forgeries of engraved gems in hardstones are not only common, but they are difficult to detect. At one time they were much in demand, but their value today is less and they are consequently no longer imitated. Renaissance copies now have their own value which, at present, is not high, although it is consistent. Those which need to be identified are copies made in the nineteenth century.

Most antique gems are irregular at the back. Later imitations have a flat back, but both Renaissance and nineteenth-century jewellers flattened the back of antique specimens for the purpose of setting them. Repolishing old gems, which are inclined to have dull patches on the surface, was done in Renaissance times. The material is so hard that signs of wear are not very perceptible, and they were, in any case, kept with care. Ancient *intaglio* gems are nearly always small; those decorated in relief may be much larger. The diamond was used for carving in ancient times, and in more recent times by Natter and Sirletti, the latter especially doing some very deceptive work of this kind. Forgers have usually avoided the full-face portrait because this was, technically, the most difficult. These are, therefore, more likely to be genuine.

It is, in fact, a most difficult field, even for the specialist, who can rarely be completely certain that a particular specimen is as old as it purports to be. Style, and the quality of the carving, are probably the safest guides. Work of poor quality and definition is nearly always relatively modern.

Jade is also a difficult subject to discuss because problems of attribution loom much larger than those of fraudulent copying in most cases. Jade is a hardstone which normally changes very little as a result of the passage of time, although some degenerative changes are to be noticed as a result of burial, including colour changes and a softening of the surface.

Some specimens purporting to belong to the early Han dynasty exist, particularly stylized human figures, which are of doubtful authenticity, and pseudo-archaeological specimens apparently belonging to the early periods are always to be looked for. In general, however, this is a small and specialized market in which potential buyers are alert to the possibility of forgery, and able to exercise skilled judgement on anything presented to them. This kind of fraud, therefore, is likely to be rare. Anything of the kind will be of recent manufacture, because it is only within the last few decades that a market has existed.

Those best acquainted with the decorative *motifs* of Chinese art generally will be able to make the soundest judgements on the age of objects made from jade, but this material has always been used for ritual and religious purposes, and the archaizing tendencies to be noticed in Chinese art are probably stronger here than in many other fields. Unlike the speed and flexibility of the brush in painting on silk or on porcelain, the decoration of jade can only be abraded slowly and with infinite patience. For this reason it is not susceptible to examination by the same methods.

The most recent observations on the situation in China itself appear to be those of Karlbeck[1] who saw in Jade Street, Pekin, large vases, urns, and bowls "all brand new, very expensive and attractive to tourists". He also saw several instances of jades faked with the signs of burial, "white as bone, with green flecks". This should act as a warning to anyone optimistic enough to accept the apparent effects of burial as an undoubted sign of age.

Later jades, of course, are easier to classify. "Jade" is a generic term for several stones which differ slightly one from the other. The two employed in China which commonly pass under this name are nephrite and jadeite. The main source of supply of nephrite was Chinese Turkestan, and Chinese literature refers to jade from here as early as the Han dynasty. Jadeite, on the other hand, comes from Upper Burma, and although suggestions have been made that it was imported into China as early as the thirteenth century, there is no reliable evidence that it was known there before the eighteenth century.

The distinction is not a difficult one to make. Nephrite appears to be denser; it is normally less translucent than jadeite, and it has an "oily" surface. Jadeite is highly translucent, and in thin sections it is almost transparent. Its colouring is usually brighter and more vivid than that of nephrite. Both stones show wide variations in colour, many of which are known by such distinctively Chinese names as "mutton fat". The *fei ts'ui* jade of the auctioneer and the art-dealer is jadeite.

[1] Orvar Karlbeck: *Treasure Seeker in China*. London, 1957.

Jades of all kinds are fashioned by abrasives, and occasionally by the diamond-pointed drill, because the surface is harder than all but the specially hardened steels of the modern metallurgist. The tools used are comparatively soft and the abrasives are embedded in them. The commonest abrasives used are quartz sand (in conjunction with a wooden polishing wheel), corundum, or emery. A saw made from a single strand of wire in an open bamboo frame, similar in form to a fret-saw without teeth, is today used for cutting in conjunction with emery, and must be similar to that used for sawing blocks of granite by the Egyptians. Drills were used in early times, but the lathe is a later development, perhaps suggested by the potter's wheel.

A full account of the methods used in carving jade is provided by Howard Hansford.[1] These are applicable in principle to all kinds of hardstone carving.

Two stones in which carvings in the style of jade have frequently been made are steatite and serpentine. The former is well known, particularly for its soapy surface which has also caused it to be known as soapstone. Methods of differentiating between these and jades are described in Appendix 10, but it may briefly be said that neither nephrite nor jadeite can be scratched with a pen-knife blade, whereas serpentine and steatite cut quite easily.

Inscriptions need to be regarded with care. Frequently they are a later addition, although they may still be of genuine interest. A jade of the Ming period with an inscription of the Emperor Ch'ien Lung, for instance, would have an enhanced value. A modern addition, however, would fall into quite another category.

Undoubtedly eighteenth-century jades were copied in the nineteenth century, and the manufacture goes on today. In general, the carving is shallower, and lacks the crispness of earlier work.

Lacquer work, particularly the so-called Coromandel lacquer, was imitated in Europe during the seventeenth and eighteenth centuries, but not deceptively. Work of this kind often has a high antique value of its own. It is, however, useful to be able to separate genuine Oriental work from European, and even the novice can do this by observing the differences in the style of the ornament. As in the case of the porcelain described on page 5, the work of a Chinese hand is always obvious.

[1] S. Howard Hansford: *Chinese Jade Carving*. London, 1950.

Genuine old Chinese carved lacquer has not been imitated in the West. Indeed, the European forger is hardly likely to be able to develop the necessary skill to do so, even if the materials were available. On the other hand, fairly deceptive copies have been made in China by other methods. Lacquer for carving is made from the sap of the *Rhus vernicifera*, and is prepared by painting successive coats over a thin wooden body, usually of pine, each of which is rubbed down. When the desired thickness has been attained, intricate designs are carved with small knives. The sap is dyed to the desired colour with various pigments. The earliest imitations were made not later than the Ming dynasty, and there is reference to them in the *Ko ku yao lun*, published in 1387. The design was modelled in a kind of lime-putty, and painted over with a thin coat of lacquer. These objects appear always to be small in size, principally perfume-cases ornamented with flowers, and the material was called by the Chinese *chao hung* (plastered red). They were being made as late as the reign of Ch'ien Lung, and perhaps later. If the demand for old red lacquer became sufficiently strong, the manufacture might well be revived. Another type of deceptive imitation was made from carved wood over which had been painted a thick coat of lacquer, and these have also been made in Japan. The best, and almost the only, way of differentiating between carved lacquer and a good imitation with certainty is to make a slight cut in an inconspicuous position and observe the result. Old lacquer is solid throughout; it will not be difficult to penetrate a single coating to wood or lime-putty if these are the foundation. There ought also to be noticeable differences between modelled and carved work, and the blunting of carved wood ornament by a superimposed coating of lacquer should also be obvious.

The term "ivory" does not necessarily refer to the tusk of the elephant. The hippopotamus and the walrus are surviving animals which are a source of this material. Mammoth-ivory, however, has been much used, particularly that from deposits in Siberia where some carcasses have been found preserved in a kind of natural deep-freeze. Siberian mammoth-ivory is worth a digression. These carcasses, the meat fresh enough to be used as food for sledge-dogs, are found preserved in the ice in parts of Siberia, in the region of the River Lena. Skeletal remains are found in even larger quantities. The carcasses, about 8,000 years old, have the remains of vegetation belonging to a much more temperate zone in their stomachs which obviously formed their last meal. The inference must be either that they were killed and frozen within the space of a day or two, which presupposes a drastic and permanent drop in temperature, or that the carcasses were deposited by a vast flood which swept them rapidly from a temperate climate to the regions of the permafrost.

Mammoth-tusks are usually much heavier and longer than those of the elephant, one specimen recorded being 2 ft. in diameter at the root. Hippopotamus-ivory is denser than elephant-ivory, but can only be used for small objects. Walrus-ivory was used fairly extensively in the east but less often in the west, although such things as early Swedish chessmen were made from it.

Ivory has always been valued as a material for carving because it lends itself to the rendering of fine detail, and some exceptionally good engraved work appears on prehistoric specimens. It has also been much used for inlaying, although this aspect hardly concerns us here.

Ivory-carvings of all kinds have been forged, faked, and restored. Nevertheless, outright forgeries are probably less common than is sometimes supposed. Those current during the nineteenth century, when high prices were being paid for early examples of this kind of work, have mostly been recognized, and present-day prices are not high enough to attract the more skilful forgers. Most of the nineteenth-century copies came from France, and from Geislingen and Erbach in Germany.

Close acquaintance with genuine work is the best safeguard. To attempt the collection of old and valuable ivories without considerable experience of the styles of the period selected, or without specialist advice, would be unwise. The specialist would, for instance, if on no other ground, immediately detect the spurious nature of a consular diptych from which the recess necessary to contain the wax was missing. These diptychs were writing-tablets made to commemorate special events. They were usually carved in relief with a portrait of the Consul and scenes from the circus games. In the instance mentioned, a diptych of this kind was sold already framed to a museum. Care is needed with objects of any kind which are framed or mounted in a way which effectively conceals a part, especially if the frame has been elaborately sealed to make it difficult to remove. Plaques of enamel or porcelain, for instance, will often have some revealing mark on the reverse which can be hidden by a closely-sealed frame.

Medieval forgeries of ecclesiastical subjects are often condemned by faulty iconography, or by the inclusion of detail which is meaningless or inaccurate in the particular context. It must be remembered that when such ivories were especially fashionable, and forgeries likely to produce the highest profit, scholarship was much less exact than it is today, and in this way fraudulent specimens found their way into museums and private collections. A rising market for ivories of this kind in the future may bring some of these forgeries back into circulation. We must also take account of the fact that copies might have been made for honest purposes in monasteries in late medieval times, and that the iconography could have been drawn from more than one much earlier original. These might give an impression of fraud which would not be justified, since the problem is rather one of attribution.

A note of warning must be sounded on the subject of such well-known forgeries as the *vierge ouvrante*, a figure of the Virgin hinged at the back, and opening on either side of the central line to reveal miniature carvings inside. Maskell illustrates a forgery of this kind which deceived the Louvre in the nineteenth century.[1] Most of the existing examples of this kind appear to be forgeries, and they have been followed by such secular figures as knights and kings which are obviously suspect. Since these, and most forged medieval ivories, were done in the nineteenth century the sentimental flavour of the period can usually be noticed in the carving. Apart from some kinds of later Greek art, sentimentality is not seen in European work of any kind before the late eighteenth century, and certainly not in its more saccharine form until the nineteenth.

Egyptian ivories have been forged, usually without much success. Forgeries of classical ivories from Greece and Italy, and those of Hispano-Moresque work done by Francesco Pallás y Puig (1859–1926), are discussed in greater detail by Kurz.[2]

Unusual, and showing a degree of impudence, are forgeries of the Chinese "oracle bones" discovered in Honan belonging to the Shang dynasty (1766–1122 B.C.). These will not be difficult to distinguish for the specialist acquainted with ancient calligraphy, which is well known and has been studied in detail on bronzes of this period and of

[1] A. Maskell: *Ivories*. London, 1905. Plate 84.

[2] Kurz: *Fakes*. London, 1948.

the later Chou dynasty (1122-249 B.C.). Forgeries of prehistoric bone objects said to have been found in the Dordogne have long been discredited, and attempts to market these, or anything similar, are hardly likely.

Ivory has been stained and coloured at all periods, and gilding has sometimes been added. The Japanese, especially, were adept at staining carvings of this kind. The patination of old ivory has also been imitated in various ways which are discussed at greater length on page 267. Ivories have been restored very cleverly by the addition of newly-carved replacements for missing parts. This is legitimate because collectors demand perfect specimens, but the altering and recarving of existing work to make a more saleable specimen can only be regarded as fraudulent. If the recarving is recent it should be obvious under ultra-violet radiation. Ivory can be bleached. Dipping in turpentine and exposing to the sun has been suggested. This might have some effect on its subsequent appearance under ultra-violet radiation, but I think it unlikely to prove deceptive. Cracks in ivory are simulated by first putting the new carving into boiling water and then drying it quickly before a hot fire, whilst the manure-heap is sometimes used to supply artificial patination.

Finally, it remains to mention certain kinds of artificial ivory or substitutes for it. Synthetic ivory is usually employed for such things as billiard balls and piano keyboards. These lack the striations of genuine ivory, and will not deceive anyone acquainted with the natural substance. A type of palm-nut with a hard white kernel was occasionally used by the Japanese for carving such small objects as *netsuké* and resembles ivory fairly closely. This, properly described, is quite legitimate, and these things can hardly be termed forgeries. It has been said that a substitute for ivory can be made by boiling potatoes in sulphuric acid, but I have not seen anything which could be identified as having been made in this way.

*Chapter V*

# *Ceramics*

Enthusiasm is not a method of judgement.
GIOVANNI MORELLI

The examination of specimens of pottery and porcelain falls under three main headings—body, glaze, and decoration. All three must agree with the same features in other specimens known to be genuine, or some good and sufficient reason must be apparent for any divergence. Although reproductions, fakes, and forgeries abound in this field, very few (especially of European wares) are really dangerous to the informed collector who is acquainted with genuine wares, and for this reason it is one of the safest forms of collecting. Here, however, as in other fields, enthusiasm must be tempered by scepticism during the examination of objects which show discrepancies of any kind.

Not all beds of clay and of the fusible materials used in the making of ceramics are equally suitable. Manufacturers, therefore, established their kilns near to reliable sources, or they transported their materials from the place where they were found. They tended to use established formulae, and raw materials which had been tested by practical use, because methods of purifying such substances were primitive and empirical. The behaviour of the materials during manufacture was known, and more or less predictable results could be obtained. This applies equally to materials used for glazing and decoration. It will be seen, therefore, that wares from a particular source will be likely to resemble one another in their physical appearance fairly closely, and that any perceptible difference ought to be the subject of close inquiry.

In some cases the history of the factory or centre is fairly complete; changes in the source from which raw materials were drawn have been recorded, and the effect may be seen in the wares.

We are not here concerned with problems of attribution, and of the copying of the wares of one factory or centre of production by another. These are not forgeries, and can only be regarded as reproductions when there is a considerable time-lapse between them. The potters of Corinth, for example, copied the work of the Athenians, even to the extent of washing the body of their wares with a slip containing red ochre to simulate the Athenian body-colour, but as the wares are more or less contemporary, both are equally interesting to the collector of Greek pottery.

Before proceeding to a consideration of forgeries and deceptive copies of pottery and porcelain, it is essential to make a brief classification of the wares themselves. They fall into three principal categories—earthenware, stoneware, and porcelain.

Earthenware is lightly fired. At this temperature only point-to-point attachment of the clay particles occurs, and the material is therefore porous. It varies in hardness. Such soft wares as the Greek figures of Tanagra and certain kinds of T'ang pottery from China can be scratched with the finger-nail, but in other varieties particles of flint, feldspar, or some other vitrifiable material occur as impurities or are added to the clay, and it then becomes much harder whilst retaining its porosity.

Stoneware is clay mixed with some kind of fusible rock which has been fired to a point where vitrification of the latter occurs. It is hard, non-porous, and usually gives a noticeable ringing tone if gently tapped.

Clay is refractory, and will only fuse under much greater heat than that needed to vitrify the fusible materials. For this reason it is not only used for its plastic qualities in the manufacture of both stoneware and porcelain, but for its refractory qualities which help to hold the object in shape in the kiln. Stonewares vary considerably in their physical appearance and properties according to the nature of the fusible substances employed.

True porcelain is made from white burning clay mixed with fusible rock (generally a type of feldspar), and is fired to a point where translucency occurs when it is held to the light. Although this is a useful test for the porcellaneous nature of a specimen, translucency may occur to a slight degree in wares which are more correctly classified as stoneware if a higher firing than usual has been given to a thinly-potted vessel. Porcelain vessels and dishes which are very thick—i.e. over about 5 mm. for the coarser wares and 8 mm. for the finer varieties—lose their translucency and become opaque. Underfired wares which are not sufficiently vitrified also tend to be opaque, and sometimes retain a measure of porosity.

True porcelain is so called because it is made from materials obtained from natural sources. For reasons presently to be described it is also commonly called hard porcelain. It is not difficult to reproduce with a varying degree of fidelity to the original, and these reproductions sometimes approach fairly closely the appearance and properties of the older wares. Until about 1800 in parts of Europe, and particularly in France and England, an imitation of true porcelain was made artificially, using clay as the refractory material and ground glass, or some closely similar substance, for the fusible part. This is termed artificial or "soft" porcelain, and it is exceedingly difficult to reproduce. The differences to be observed between the two varieties are later set out in detail, and it is essential that the porcelain collector should be able to separate the two kinds since the earlier wares are often forged in a hard porcelain body.

Three principal types of glaze occur. The first, used on certain kinds of stoneware and true porcelain, is derived from powdered feldspathic rock similar to that employed in the porcelain body. It is deposited on the surface in various ways—usually by dipping the object in a suspension of powdered glaze in water. The subsequent firing melts the particles of rock and allows them to spread over the surface in a glass-like layer which is transparent. It is sometimes possible to judge whether it was applied before the first firing, or whether the vessel was fired first and the glaze applied subsequently at a lower temperature. In the first case the surface of the glaze will be even; in the second a slight pitting occurs which the Chinese well describe as "chicken-skin". Some wares, particularly Japanese porcelain of the seventeenth and eighteenth centuries, show the effect to a fairly well-marked degree, whereas Chinese porcelain of the same period has a much more even glaze.

The second type of glaze is akin to a transparent glass; in fact, it is virtually indistinguishable from it. The two principal kinds of glass are soda-glass and lead-glass, and one or other of these two varieties is to be observed on most old pottery. The lead glaze is to be seen commonly on early Chinese pottery of the Han and T'ang dynasties and on European wares; the soda-glass variety mainly occurs on Middle Eastern wares.

The third variety is glass made white and opaque by the addition of oxide of tin, and glazes of this kind appear on a large body of wares which are termed tin-enamelled, and sometimes subdivided into *faïence*, *delft*, or *maiolica*. The white glaze is used in conjunction with an earthenware body which burns to a colour varying from pale biscuit to light reddish-brown.

There are many ways of decorating pottery and porcelain, and most of them utilize the oxides of either iron, copper, cobalt, or manganese. These substances were added to transparent glazes of all kinds to colour them. The colours yielded by these oxides were varied by altering the atmosphere of the kiln. In a kiln containing plenty of free oxygen (an oxidizing kiln) copper, as an example, yielded green and a turquoise blue, but when carbon monoxide was present in sufficient quantity (a "reducing" atmosphere) the same substance yielded a purplish-red. It is essential for the collector to be able to recognize colours derived from these oxides (which are fairly distinctive) because forgers often try to reproduce them with colours developed after 1800, whereas nearly all the wares important to the collector belong to an earlier date than this.

Not all the metallic oxides used could withstand the full heat of the kiln. This led to a mixture of the colours with glaze material to enable them to be painted on to the glaze after the high-temperature firing. The addition of fluxes to lower the melting-point made it possible for them to be fixed in an enamelling or "muffle" kiln at a lower temperature than that of the glaze firing. They are then termed enamels or "muffle" colours, and are over the glaze.

Oxides which could withstand the full temperature—cobalt blue and manganese—were used *under* the glaze. The Chinese also used a copper red in the same way, but this is an exceedingly rare colour. These are termed underglaze colours.

The tin-enamel glaze melts at a lower temperature than porcelain and stoneware glazes, and a wider variety of colours are suitable for decorating wares of this kind. They were painted on to the raw glaze before firing, and glaze and decoration were fired in one operation. These are usually termed high-temperature or *faïence* colours. Enamel colours are also found on later *faïence*.

Slip is clay mixed with water to the consistency of cream. It was used as a wash to rectify faults of colour in the body and minor irregularities of surface arising from the use of a coarse clay. Slip of a different colour from the body was employed as decoration, particularly in conjunction with ornament incised through it to the body beneath, giving a decoration of two colours. Slip is also "trailed" and "dotted" like icing on a cake. These techniques can all be seen on wares of different kinds from various centres of production.

This brief description of the methods of making and decorating pottery is essential to an appreciation of the discussion of forgeries and deceptive copies which follows, but some acquaintance with the history and development of the wares mentioned is also essential. Reference to the Bibliography will enable the reader to select appropriate works.

It is essential to remember that pottery-makers have always copied each other's wares. Ceramics (the general term for all kinds of pottery and porcelain) have been an article of trade between countries for thousands of years, and popular imported forms and patterns naturally attracted the attention of those who wanted to meet a local demand. This can be seen very early in the history of the art, and the use of Mesopotamian and Egyptian *motifs* on Greek pottery of the seventh century B.C. is an example. Much better known, of course, are the numerous copies of Chinese wares, porcelain especially, made by European potters. But this is not a history of the art, and most such things are collectors' items in their own right. I am not here concerned with wares made for trading purposes, but with copies made to deceive the collector.

Forgeries of classical pottery are not new. In a sale at Christie's in March 1805 of the property of a gentleman of fashion there is an entry under lot 46, *Two Campana vases, spurious*, and fairly close copies of "black-figure" vases, sometimes of large size, were being made early in the nineteenth century. These vases, and others made since, could not reproduce successfully the pigment used in classical times, which was a kind of black slip mixed with sour wine or urine to make it flow easily from the brush. It is replaced in reproductions by black enamel. The two principal kinds of decoration are termed "red-figure" and "black-figure". Of the two, the black-figure wares are earlier, and the decoration, usually of mythological scenes, was painted in black slip on a red earthenware body. Red-figure decoration is the same in reverse. The figures were first outlined in black slip, and then the whole of the remaining surface was painted with black slip, leaving the figures themselves in red. The practice of outlining the figures leaves a slightly raised contour round them. Undecorated vases completely covered in black slip were also made.

The earliest reproductions of Greek and Italian red-figure vases were made by Josiah Wedgwood in the 1770s. Wedgwood used the collection of Sir William Hamilton as models, but the body he used was the black *basaltes*, a kind of stoneware, and the decoration was painted in red enamel. Moreover, they were impressed with the name "Wedgwood", and there was no deceptive intention.

Most genuine Greek and Italian vases have been restored, and in some cases missing parts have been replaced by fragments from other vases. The decoration in such cases has been completed with paint. Red-figure decoration has sometimes been added with paint to a black undecorated vase, but this cannot survive close examination. Apart from the lack of the raised outline round the contour of the figures, the physical appearance of paint is different from that of the red earthenware of the original ornament. More deceptive, when done with sufficient skill, is the faking of genuine vases covered with black slip by scraping away the colouring to reveal the red body beneath. Both red- and black-figure decoration can be faked in this way. Although red-figure is the more usual since it involves less work, the decoration in any case is either slightly above or slightly below the original surface.

The black slip of ancient times has proved to be an insurmountable obstacle to the forger, and the only really dangerous copies are of vessels painted in a linear style on a white ground. This appears to be a kind of limewash on ancient vessels, and is usually powdery. Genuine drawing is free and spontaneous; that of the forger laboured. Like archaic sculpture, ancient drawing is very difficult to imitate convincingly, and will rarely deceive the expert who is able to examine a specimen in favourable circumstances. Anachronisms, such as the incorrect relationship of the form and the decoration, is a trap into which the forger frequently falls, and it is a point to which great attention should always be directed in examining antiquities.

The white-ground vases have been principally imitated in Athens. Many of the best forgeries of other types of classical pottery were done in Naples during the nineteenth century. Since then the market has not been sufficiently rewarding to tempt the really skilled craftsman. Makers of such copies mentioned by Hannover[1] include Gargiuto of Naples, Giustiniani, also of Naples, Touchard of Paris, Desfourneaux of Melun, and Sältzer of Eisenach. To this list may be added the Cambrian pottery at Swansea, whilst painting *à l'étrusque* was done at Gotha in Thuringia. Apart from the last-named, all produced work in the nineteenth century. The imitations of Gotha were contemporary with those of Wedgwood in the eighteenth century and may have been inspired by him.

To the restorer we owe repainted vases, generally varnished to disguise new work. This is usually fairly obvious and will yield to such solvents as alcohol or acetone, although neither of these substances will affect a genuine example. Ultra-violet radiation is also useful for detecting fakes of this kind. Varnish usually fluoresces with a characteristic yellowish colour.

The most ambitious forgeries, and those which have been accepted for the longest period, have been of large Etruscan figures and sarcophagi. It was, perhaps, natural that Etruscan pottery should have been selected because knowledge of this civilization is incomplete, and errors were less likely to be noticed. Until the middle of the eighteenth century most Greek and Italian vases were indiscriminately termed "Etruscan", and Wedgwood, who extensively imitated classical models, called the factory which he opened in 1769 "Etruria", and his copies of red-figure vases "The Art of Etruria reborn". There was a revival of what has been well called "Etruscomania" in 1828, and the provenance of the vases was hotly debated for years afterwards. The large sarcophagus in the British Museum (see page 29), included in the Exhibition of Forgeries and Deceptive Copies, in 1961,[2] was made about 1860 by the brothers Pinelli, who had restored the example in

[1] Emil Hannover: *Pottery and Porcelain*. London, 1925.

[2] *Catalogue of an Exhibition of Forgeries*, etc. British Museum, 1961.

the Louvre. The British Museum version has two figures—a man and his wife engaged in animated discussion—reclining on the lid, and it is no more than an amusing *pastiche*. It would certainly not pass muster today when much more is known of the Etruscans and their art.

The two warriors of the Metropolitan Museum are more recent. Nearly seven feet in height, they were the production of Alfredo Fioravanti and his associates, and were made at Orvieto, notable Renaissance pottery-making centre, about 1920. Harold W. Parsons[1] points out that, by an oversight, the forgers balanced a relatively massive body on two outspread legs which were certainly insufficient to support the weight of the head and torso. This, in itself, was suspicious. If the design had been suggested to an Etruscan potter he would have seen at once that it could not be made in pottery without the addition of supports, and these would have been provided as part of the design of the figure. The forgers were much more concerned with the problem of making something which would pass as a classical antiquity. If they thought of the problem of supports at all, they probably dismissed it with the comforting thought that the resources of modern technology could provide them in another material. In considering things of this nature, it is always useful to look at the problem from the viewpoint of a craftsman of the time at which an object purports to have been made. The approach of the craftsman and that of the forger is completely different, and it would be surprising if the difference did not reveal itself somewhere.

Parsons suggests that these figures were broken before firing, and the pieces fired separately. In this case the design supports a suggestion which might otherwise have seemed very unlikely, but the risk of the separate pieces warping and spoiling the complete figure must have been very high. Fioravanti is said to have produced other large *terracottas* of this kind, but no information exists as to their present whereabouts.

These figures are special instances. Much more common are forgeries of small Greek *terracotta* figures, especially those made at Tanagra in Boeotia. The genuine specimens are made from clay lightly fired, which is very soft and fragile. The material varies in colour from light biscuit to light reddish-brown, due to a varying amount of iron present as an impurity. This inclusion, incidentally, is almost invariable

[1] H. W. Parsons: "The Art of Fake Etruscan Art", *Art News*, 1962.

in pottery clay. The earliest Greek figures are hand-modelled, often crudely; the later Tanagra and Myrina figures are moulded. The first moulds are of the front only, the modelling being shallow to enable the cast to be removed from the mould without damage. The back is flat, or slightly rounded, and lightly modelled. These figures are solid. Then comes the two-piece mould, front and back, filled with solid clay, the interior being pierced and the head added separately before firing. Next come two-piece moulds, each half of which was filled with a layer of clay about one-quarter of an inch thick. These two casts were subsequently joined edge to edge, and a vent for kiln-gases in the form of a square hole was cut in the back. This method of manufacture was commonly used at Tanagra. Lastly, where arms, legs, wings, etc., are free-floating (i.e. attached at one end only) the clay model must have been dissected into components which were separately moulded, the parts being assembled before firing. Precisely the same method was used by porcelain-makers in the eighteenth century, and it is used even today for expensive figures.

Like Greek sculpture, the *terracottas* were coloured, although only traces now remain. The figure was first covered with a white pigment, probably some kind of limewash, to seal the pores of the earthenware body, and the colours were then painted on. Since the painting was unfired, there was a wide choice of pigments. Green and gold are exceedingly rare, but yellow and carmine are more common. Blue, red, brownish-red, and black are usual, the black being slightly brownish in colour.

This is a brief outline of how the small Greek *terracottas* were made. They were extremely fashionable and expensive during the nineteenth century, although their popularity, except for the earliest and finest examples, has declined. Arnau[1] records that Count Gregor Stroganoff paid 40,000 gold francs for twelve in the 1850s which were later condemned as fakes.

The origin of these frauds is uncertain, but they troubled collectors of the period. Some which appear to be of German origin are easy to detect, and are heavier than the much lighter Greek examples. Most such forgeries are not so difficult to detect as the writings of some nineteenth-century commentators suggest. The contemporary sentimental flavour can also be seen in the kind of late Greek work, both

[1] Frank Arnau: *Three Thousand Years of Deception*. London, 1961.

21. Van Meegeren painting "Jesus Among the Doctors" for the Dutch Field Security. The face of Jesus is completely modern in conception. [*Ullstein*

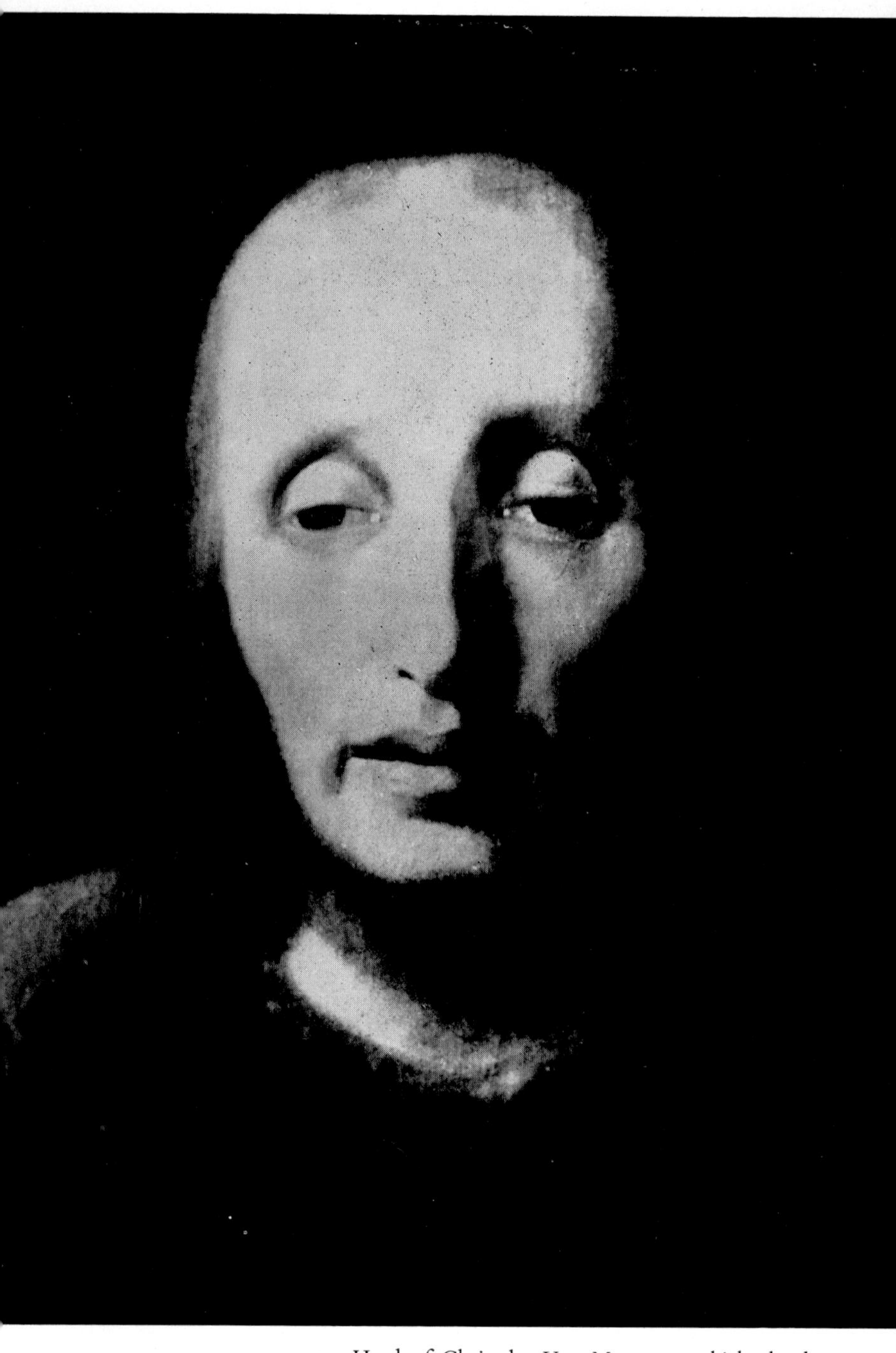

22. Head of Christ by Van Meegeren which closely resembles that of Christ in the "Disciples at Emmaus". It bears no relation to any extant work by Vermeer, but hardly differs from some of Van Meegeren's genuine work. [*Ullstein*

figures and vase-painting, which was then in favour, and it was precisely these that the nineteenth-century collectors chose. This correspondence made it much more difficult then to detect faked drawing and modelling.

It is far from easy, even for the most accomplished forger, to produce an entirely new work in the style of classical antiquity, and this aspect has defied the most skilled of them. Most such works, therefore, are *pastiches* (page 229) of existing models, and small but significant mistakes of detail are common. Close scrutiny is often needed to detect these subtle differences, and the most frequent source of inspiration for models which are not copied from genuine specimens has been vase-painting. The translation of a two-dimensional design into a three-dimensional medium has frequently proved the Achilles' heel of the forger.

Nearly all genuine figures have been excavated, and will have the signs of burial, unmistakable to the experienced eye. A few such figures have the marks of plant-roots with which they have been in contact. Originals, if of good quality, will have signs of retouching by hand after moulding. This will also be seen on forgeries, but it provides another opportunity for mistakes to be made. The Greek figure-maker knew what he wanted to do; the forger can only guess it. The joints between the moulded components have sometimes parted as a result of burial, an effect not easy to reproduce convincingly. If the unbroken *terracotta* figure exists, I have never seen it. Forgeries, too, are broken, but care is taken to avoid damage which would spoil the appearance. If a part which is relatively strong, such as the base, has been damaged, while the more fragile parts in which the interest resides are in good condition, the inference is obvious. The black pigment used in early times appears to have been the same as the black slip which decorates the vases. A deep black in place of the old brownish black is cause for suspicion.

Restorers have been responsible for some clever fakes. They add heads and arms to torsos, and often assemble a single figure from a series of unrelated pieces. Since virtually all the genuine specimens found have been in fragments, it is difficult to tell, in some cases, whether restoration is legitimate, or whether a figure is no more than a clever fake, but careful examination with a powerful magnifying glass and by ultra-violet radiation will usually reveal the fraud.

The Roman oil-lamp is a frequent target for the forger, and deceptive copies have been made since the beginning of the eighteenth century. The more ambitious require careful examination, especially those bearing early Christian symbols such as the fish, and gladiatorial combats. The forgery is usually heavier than the genuine lamp, but detection is not particularly easy. Since they have been excavated, attention should be directed towards the effects of time on the material, which are difficult to counterfeit convincingly, and to the style of the decoration. The more ordinary specimens have never been especially valuable, and little attention was lavished on these fine points in the copies. Samian ware has not attracted the forger to any great extent because only exceptional pieces have ever been highly valued, but moulds have been excavated in extremely good condition and legitimate casts taken from them. The possibility of moulds of this kind falling into unscrupulous hands should be remembered.

Turning to medieval pottery, although one or two comparatively clumsy attempts have been made to copy late Roman and Byzantine pottery with decoration of exceptional interest, the more ordinary wares have been free from this sort of chicanery. The next in point of time to claim our attention must be *Henri Deux* ware, sometimes called *faïence d'Oiron*, and more properly St Porchaire. Specimens of this exceedingly rare pottery were the goal of affluent collectors in the nineteenth century, and the copies by Minton and others at this time should not deceive anyone who has examined a genuine example, since the technique was completely different although they aimed at the same superficial appearance. Those made by Rondel are closer and more skilful. The genuine St Porchaire earthenware is very thinly potted, ivory-white in colour, and decorated by impressing bookbinders' stamps into the plastic clay, the impressions being subsequently coloured by filling them with black, brown, or red slip, with the occasional addition of blue, purple, and green glazes on later examples. The whole is covered with a transparent lead glaze. The body is unusually soft and fragile. Sixty-four pieces are known to exist, of which the majority are in public collections, and anything offered on the art-market without a history would need extremely careful examination before acceptance.

Most copies of Hispano-Moresque pottery are not very dangerous. The colour of the ground is wrong, being either too yellow or too pink. Modern wares have a bright coppery lustre, quite unlike the paler colour of early specimens, and they are usually shiny and finished with a slickness which ought to give immediate rise to misgiving. Many such copies have been made by the firm of Cantagalli of Florence, who also imitated *maiolica*, and who used the rebus of a cock as their mark.

The wares of Bernard Palissy were frequently copied during the nineteenth century when the vogue among collectors was at its height and high prices were being realized. Those of Minton are avowed commercial copies which are not deceptive, whilst the imitations of Mafra at Caldas, in Portugal, are hardly more than crude derivations, although provincial auctioneers sometimes give them a qualified "Palissy". Much more dangerous are the copies of Georges Pull of Paris, a naturalist who commenced to imitate Palissy in 1856. These were marked, in some instances at least, but there is one record of the sale of a dish by this man which had the mark covered by a collector's label. Deceptive copies were made by a restorer, Alfred Corplet, and a factory at Tours was established in 1842 by Charles Avisseau for the imitation of Palissy ware. Specimens are fairly close to the originals in appearance, and the same firm were awarded a medal for the reproduction of *Henri Deux* ware in the International Exhibition of 1862. Avisseau's nephew, M. Landais, also of Tours, imitated Palissy, and this became a thriving nineteenth-century industry which has not been without its effect on subsequent sale-room prices. It is pleasing to be able to record that none are really dangerous to anyone reasonably well acquainted with Palissy's work, and most deceptive of all is the early work of the Avon Pottery. This, however, was one of the contemporary followers of Palissy's technique, and the problem, in so far as it exists, is one of attribution.

Two methods have been suggested for identifying the genuine work of Palissy. The first is that the marbled or mottled effect of the coloured glazes on the reverse of his dishes is different from that of any of his imitators; and the second, that if an unglazed part be touched with a spot of hydrochloric acid it will effervesce. Of the two, I prefer the first as the most likely to be useful. Any of his imitators could easily have used an effervescing clay unwittingly, since this property is by no means unusual. It occurs, for instance, in some kinds of Dutch delft.

The tin-enamelled pottery of Renaissance Italy, known as *maiolica*, is extremely important, and from the middle of the nineteenth century onwards exceptionally high prices have been paid for important specimens. It is hardly surprising, therefore, that forgeries are numerous and that some of them are deceptive. Most forgeries of pottery and porcelain are not good enough to deceive anyone possessing an experienced eye, but it would be rash to make the same assumption in the case of *maiolica*, since the process is not difficult to counterfeit technically, and much more dependence must be placed upon style. One nineteenth-century authority in this field was tempted to make the statement that no forgery of Italian *maiolica* had ever deceived an expert, and accompanied it with an illustration of a fairly obvious one. Nevertheless, most copies and reproductions were made commercially, and are not especially deceptive. The occasional large and ornate vase with writhing handles, decorated with grotesques a long way after Raphael (which he derived in turn from frescoes in the Golden House of Nero) hardly needs a caution. They are sometimes seen adding prestige to the window-displays of second-hand furniture shops.

How soon these forgeries began to be made is uncertain. Pazaurek[1] mentions a *faïence* dish made in the eighteenth century in the Stuttgart Museum which is dated 1546, but this was probably a Nuremberg replacement for a broken dish.

The earliest Italian *maiolica* takes the form of wares decorated in green and manganese purple on a tin-enamel ground, which were themselves copied from the wares of Paterna in Spain. They were made at Orvieto and elsewhere, but at one time were all indiscriminately labelled "Orvieto". Clever copies of these began to appear before the end of the nineteenth century. Most of them are accused by poor form. The genuine wares often exist only in fragmentary form, and the forgeries were reconstructions of fragments, or were copied from illustrations. Also among the early wares to be forged are the Florentine jars decorated with oak-leaves in a thick dark blue, which are also clumsy in form with a poor glaze which adheres badly.

The reliefs of Luca della Robbia, his nephew, and the latter's sons, are hardly in the true *maiolica* tradition. They are *terracottas* covered with a tin-enamel glaze. These were copied by Angelo Minghetti at Bologna about 1850, and the same man copied the sixteenth-century wares of Urbino. Cantagalli of Florence produced copies of della

[1] G. E. Pazaurek: *Deutsche Fayence und Porzellan Hausmaler*. Leipzig, 1927.

Robbia sculpture, as well as the wares of Urbino, Faenza, Deruta, and Gubbio, which they displayed at the Paris Exhibition of 1900. It is evident that the attitude towards work of this kind was less severe a century or so ago. The Doccia factory, which began to imitate sixteenth-century *maiolica* in the 1840s, particularly the metallic lustre pigments to be seen on the wares of Deruta and Gubbio, received awards in the Great Exhibition of 1851, and in Paris in 1855. They also reproduced the work of della Robbia, as well as Chinese and Japanese porcelain. Gubbio ruby and yellow lustres were imitated by Carocci, Fabbri and Co., who were represented at the International Exhibition of 1862. A factory at the early centre of Pesaro belonging to Magrini was in existence in the 1870s and copying early wares, and also at Pesaro was Feruccio Mengaroni, the victim of retributive justice, who was killed by the fall of a large forgery of a della Robbia head of *Medusa* which he had hung on the wall.

A copyist of more than usual skill was Torquato Castellani, son of Alessandro Castellani, the art-dealer, whose collection of *maiolica* and specimens of Medici porcelain was dispersed in Paris in May 1878. Some of the son's work was signed, but unsigned specimens have passed into collections as genuine. In 1913 a number of forgeries which were closer than usual were placed on the market by a dealer in Rome. These deceived several collectors at the time. Their present whereabouts are unknown.

Many of the copies mentioned were not made primarily to deceive the affluent collector, but as interior decoration to accompany the kind of fake Renaissance sideboard produced by the Victorian furniture manufacturer. Subsequently, existing marks were sometimes erased (when they existed in the first place) and signs of wear and minor damage added. They were then ready to pass in a poor light as antique. The effectiveness of such copies today has been greatly reduced by the passing of time. It is a truism to say that the most difficult forgery to detect is the contemporary copy, and it is now comparatively easy to separate nineteenth-century drawing and design from that of the Renaissance. Many forgeries which are obvious now, however, were far more deceptive when they were made. Seasoned drivers know that the most potent cause of traffic accidents is the comparative newcomer who has had enough experience to handle his vehicle well, and too little to know his limitations. This is equally applicable to forgeries of works of art. Flushed with the detection of a few nineteenth-century forgeries the collector of a few years' experience may conclude that it is easy, and fall victim to something made far more recently.

Nearly all forgeries of *maiolica* betray themselves by inaccurate interpretation of ornament. Most such things are not copied from existing specimens, but combine a number of decorative elements. Exact copies would be too easily recognized.

In the early part of the nineteenth century *maiolica* was termed "Rafaelle ware", because Raphael was supposed to have painted some of it, and the subjects were often derived from his works by way of engravings by Marcantonio Raimondi, a sixteenth-century forger of Dürer engravings. It is not surprising, therefore, that the earliest forgeries were in this style, which is termed *istoriato*. It was followed by a vogue for portrait heads, and particularly of women of the period who were, if the inscriptions are to be believed, invariably beautiful. The terse *Silvia bella* appears on a Castel Durante dish of the type known as *coppe amatorie* painted by Nicola Pellipario about 1520 which is in the Victoria and Albert Museum. *Angela bella* is in the Musée de Cluny. The forger, however, provides a bevy of beauties with a variety of Christian names.[1] The *albarello* is a form commonly used for portrait heads by the copyist, but these were primarily apothecary jars, not ornaments, and although they were gaily decorated the portrait is exceptional and an inscription more usual.

Among the fakes may be mentioned a dish in the Victoria and Albert Museum which is of genuine Deruta *maiolica*, but with the glaze removed from the middle of the dish and subsequently reglazed and painted with a portrait of Perugino. Although traces of refiring are discernible, the result was good enough to pass muster for a number of years. The existence of one such example suggests a search for others.

The Italian porcelain of Capo-di-Monte, a royal factory near Naples working between 1743 and 1759, has caused confusion. Attributed to it in the past has been a decoration of figures raised in relief, often derived from Renaissance bronze plaques. These were actually made at Doccia, near Florence, and the accusation that Doccia forged these

[1] Similar inscriptions appear on derivations made by the Victorian potter, William de Morgan.

reliefs at a later date is, therefore, incorrect—they were merely copying their old wares, apparently using the original moulds in some cases. The Doccia factory has already been mentioned for its copies of Italian *maiolica*, and it is reputed to have attempted copies of Medici porcelain. Copies of the Doccia relief decoration have also been made in Italy and Germany. Acquaintance with genuine ware is the only reliable safeguard. Copies, which exist in large quantities, are not deceptively close to the originals.

Dutch delft has been widely reproduced in Holland, in Paris, and in northern France. Samson's copies are particularly good. By the turn of the present century factories existed for the sole purpose of making such reproductions. They were sold to wholesalers who supplied the antique trade. These things are still being made today, although no longer for the same market. Recently reproductions of old blue-and-white delft, hardly deceptive, have been offered as an inducement to buy Dutch bulbs. The effect of this flood of reproductions has been to depress prices for genuine specimens which, in turn, has limited the profits to be made from manufacturing first-class copies. Forgers have, in fact, killed their own market so far as the more common types of old delft-ware are concerned, and collectors are now far more interested in English delft which is extremely difficult to reproduce successfully. J. Putten and Co. of Delft made good copies until 1850 which can be regarded as no more than the use of traditional styles by a factory which started a good deal earlier. Joost Thooft and Labouchère, who employed 200 people in their works in 1890, reproduced old designs, but only in a kind of earthenware covered with a transparent lead glaze which can hardly be mistaken for old ware. Other makers of reproductions include Tichelaar of Makkum and Tjallingii of Harlingen. Among the types which need special care are objects with the mark of such important potters as Adriaen Pijnacker and Albrecht Keiser, the more highly-decorated wares such as those with black grounds (*delft noir*), and plates in sets. The notorious series of plates illustrating the tobacco industry in the seventeenth century, considered important enough for the Museum which owned them to publish a special handbook, were later found to be forgeries.[1] A set of plates is unlikely to have survived unbroken except in special

[1] *A Series of Twelve Delft Plates presented by J. H. Fitzhenry, Esq., to the Victoria and Albert Museum*. London, 1907.

circumstances, and ought to have some kind of history which would help to establish their authenticity.

Generally, most of the wares described are not particularly deceptive, but other examples, especially those made by Samson and in northern France, are dangerous. The latter sometimes suffer from a crazing of the glaze which is seen only very rarely on genuine examples, and they are apt to feel heavier. The property of effervescence already mentioned certainly applies to a good many genuine Dutch wares, but it is difficult to say whether it applies to all. Apparently an excess of lime in the body was essential to the production of a tin-enamel glaze of fine quality. The body of genuine wares is soft enough to be cut with a knife.

No forgeries of Medici porcelain close enough to be worth recording have been noticed. About one hundred specimens still remain, and most of them are in national museums. Anything appearing on the art-market without a satisfactory history would need to be checked carefully against surviving specimens, but the processes of manufacture were such that really deceptive imitations are exceedingly unlikely. There are no recorded forgeries of early St Cloud porcelain, although there is room for confusion between some of the wares of St Cloud and those of Mennecy, which is a problem of attribution. It is possible that *blanc-de-chine* might be offered as St Cloud. Indeed, I have known this to be done unwittingly, but since one is Chinese hard porcelain and the other is French soft-paste such an error would not survive critical examination. The porcelain of Mennecy has been reproduced in hard-paste, with the mark *D.V.* incised. This, quite obviously, is a forgery. Similarly, the porcelain of Chantilly has been forged, and a later factory here used the old hunting-horn mark. The mark was also added to forgeries made in Paris. Some are good, but those I have seen fail to reproduce the unusual combination of a soft porcelain body with the tin-enamel glaze successfully. They could hardly deceive the experienced eye.

Most fakes and forgeries of French porcelain were directed towards the products of Vincennes-Sèvres, especially the soft-paste porcelain of these factories. Many of them belong to the eighteenth or early nineteenth century, and the best safeguard is a close study of genuine specimens and a knowledge of their characteristics.

The earliest porcelain used both at Vincennes and Sèvres was extremely glassy. Soft-soap was added to the body to increase plasticity, but it was still difficult to work, and the scrolls, volutes, and highly-modelled decoration of Meissen and the German factories had, perforce, to be executed in gilt-bronze which was added in the form of mounts. The question of forged mounts is discussed in the chapter on metalwork (page 65). The glaze employed was extremely soft and fusible, and it remelted in the enamelling kiln in a way which is unmistakable. The overglaze enamels and ground colours sank into the glaze until they were level with the surface, and appear to be *in* it rather than *on* it. Gilding was thick and rich, the colour of the gold dull instead of brassy and metallic, and it was almost invariably engraved and tooled with great skill. Refiring of a genuine specimen of Sèvres porcelain, perhaps to add a coloured ground, will also cause the original gilding to sink into the glaze to some extent, as well as the painting. Gilding was the last operation to be performed, and it was used to cover the ragged edges of the ground colour. It should, therefore, lie over the ground, a point also worth remembering when examining suspected ground-colours on the work of other factories.

Sèvres porcelain, as befitted the products of the King's factory, was always of the finest quality. Imperfect pieces were not ordinarily sold, but those well-acquainted with the work of early porcelain factories will realize that a proportion of "seconds" would undoubtedly find their way into the market in one way or another at all times, although the proportion from Sèvres was always exceedingly small until the sales of white ware in the nineteenth century. Genuine examples, therefore, will always show superb painting meticulously executed, fine ground-laying, and gilding of careful and skilful workmanship. Obvious imperfections inevitably give rise to suspicion which is not usually ill-founded.

A word could well be said at this point on eighteenth-century gilding in general. Size-gilding, which has mostly yielded to time, is the earliest variety, and it appears on such pottery as *maiolica* and *faïence*, and on some early English provincial porcelain. It is gold-leaf laid on a foundation of gold-size. The same process is sometimes used by restorers. Lacquer-gilding, to be seen on early Meissen stoneware and porcelain particularly, was made from gold-leaf and the same kind of varnish as that used in the manufacture of imitations of Oriental lacquer. Honey-gold, used by Sèvres, was a combination of gold-leaf ground in honey and lightly fired. This could be tooled and engraved. Mercury-gilding was gold dissolved in mercury and painted on. The mercury was driven off by a light firing leaving the gold, which was subsequently burnished. This appears late in the eighteenth century, although the process itself was known to the Romans and used for gilding copper. Nineteenth-century gilding is an extremely thin film of colloidal gold[1] which did not require burnishing. The types are easily distinguishable with a little practice.

Deceptive reproductions of the wares of Sèvres in soft-paste porcelain were made at such factories as Tournai, St Amand-les-Eaux, and elsewhere, including the Coalport and Madeley factories in England. Minton's copies were in a body which closely resembled the old soft-paste but distinguishable from it, although in unscrupulous hands with marks removed they have been fraudulently used.[2]

The porcelain of Nantgarw in South Wales, always marked, was undoubtedly developed as an imitation of Sèvres soft-paste, but this was not the original intention of the maker. It was bought by London decorators and china-dealers, such as Baldock, Mortlock of Oxford Street, and Robins and Randall, when supplies of the old white ware, acquired earlier in the nineteenth century from Sèvres, were exhausted. In 1825 Randall, who could no longer obtain either old Sèvres white ware or the porcelain of Nantgarw, started his Madeley factory to supply the deficiency. This survived until 1840. The Sèvres factory itself, under the directorship of M. Deck, revived its old soft-paste in 1887 in a slightly modified form, but the difference is plain enough to the discerning eye. This type was often given a turquoise ground. The figures after Watteau which commonly appear in the white panels are notable for the sentimental flavour common to most nineteenth-century official art. The gilding, compared with that of the eighteenth century, is poor in quality.

There are two kinds of fake normally found on old Sèvres porcelain. In the first type sparse decoration has been cleaned off with hydrofluoric acid. In some cases, where this proved impossible, a grindstone was used, the subsequent refiring melting the remainder of the glaze and spreading it afresh. This leads to an uneven glaze surface, probably more apparent to the finger-tips than to the eye. The later discussion

[1] i.e. divided into particles too small to sink in the liquid of suspension.

[2] For instance, in the case of Dickins v. Ellis, page 21.

of fakes of English porcelain describes some of the effects of refiring a soft porcelain glaze, but generally a "burst bubble" appearance in the glaze, with or without accompanying black specks, is significant, since a piece showing such defects would not have been sold originally. The second type is later painting on early genuine ware, and the same defects are sometimes to be noted, although usually in a lesser degree.

Attention should be directed to the colours used, particularly the ground colours. The genuine *rose Pompadour*, always in demand in the art-market, is opaque in appearance. Faked *rose Pompadour* grounds are often much more transparent, and the original shade is rarely approached. The colour was discontinued after the death of Mme de Pompadour. A specimen should, therefore, be examined in conjunction with any date-mark present, and if the latter indicates manufacture after about 1764 it should be regarded with grave suspicion. It is, however, impossible to be certain that *nothing* with this colour was manufactured after 1764 (although nothing has yet been observed), and it would be unwise to reject a specimen dated within a few years without a proper consideration of its other characteristics. The colour of this ground varies significantly in the case of English copies, and it may have been this difference, and the necessity for justifying its use in conjunction with decoration and forms unknown at the death of the Marquise in 1764, which caused it to be renamed *rose du Barry*, which is completely meaningless. There were, in fact, no colours named after Mme du Barry, although, like her predecessor, she patronized the factory. The first imitations of this ground, incidentally, are contemporary, and were done at Chelsea, where the colour was termed "claret". Turquoise grounds, often used on later fakes, are usually too green in shade. *Gros bleu* grounds, the Mazarine blue of Chelsea contemporary wares, are almost certain to be genuine, although it is said that such grounds have been successfully melted through the glaze. I have not seen a likely specimen, and consider that it could not be done skilfully enough to deceive anyone acquainted with genuine *gros bleu*. Usually, if this ground is not genuine then the porcelain is also a forgery. The genuine *gros bleu* grounds are an exceptionally rich underglaze blue obtained from cobalt oxide, and were sponged on, giving a slightly mottled appearance.

*Bleu de roi* was a ground-colour much imitated in the eighteenth century, Meissen even sending spies to the Sèvres factory for the purpose of discovering the formula. It also appears on such English copies as those of Coalport. This, of course, is an enamel blue, added overglaze, and could be used for redecorating genuine porcelain.

These fakes are not unusually difficult to distinguish, even with little knowledge and experience. Anyone buying them would be likely to "buy" the Eiffel Tower, and, if this seems unlikely, it has been "sold" twice, each time by the same man—Count Lustig, a notorious confidence trickster.

Much more dangerous are fakes on genuine white ware. A small quantity was sold in 1753, and again in 1756 when the factory removed from Vincennes to Sèvres. It was bought by the factory's own artists and painted at home. Catrice, an important flower-painter, was arrested and charged with using the royal monogram on work of this kind. Such a specimen, if one still exists, could hardly be regarded as a fake, but must be classed with the work of the German *Hausmaler* (see p. 150). After 1756 the "seconds" were allowed to accumulate, although dishonest workmen probably purloined small items of service-ware. Just after the Revolution, starting in 1804, these "seconds" were offered at several sales by the new director, Alexandre Brongniart, as part of his plan to use only the hard-paste body, the last sale of the kind being in 1815, immediately after Waterloo. Much of it was bought by the Paris dealers, Peres et Ireland, and a good deal of it found its way to London, where Sèvres porcelain was in demand. Peres et Ireland employed a decorator named Soiron who had worked at Sèvres at the beginning of the nineteenth century. About 1813 he did a certain amount of work in the expensive early styles, and imitated the method of applying drops of translucent enamels to simulate jewels which had been invented by Cotteau in 1780. He also did cups and saucers with portrait medallions of the King, Mme du Barry, and so forth—a kind of decoration which had not been used at any time in the eighteenth century. Their spurious nature, therefore, is obvious. Soiron exhibited the kind of ignorance which has been the downfall of many forgers, adding the date letter for 1761 to one such specimen. Some of his work is also signed.

In London Sèvres white porcelain was painted by Richard Robins, formerly of Pinxton, and his partner, T. M. Randall. Their studios were in Spa Fields, in London. The porcelain was provided by the importer, Baldock of Bond Street, who employed a number of artists to decorate it. Mortlock sent Coalport, Nantgarw, and Swansea porcelain to Robins and Randall to be painted in the styles of Sèvres, but it is uncertain whether he bought any of the genuine white ware. Of course, "seconds" of this kind must have been limited principally to cups and saucers, plates, and items of service-ware generally. It is exceedingly unlikely that any of the important vases would have survived in this form. Those which did not reach the required standard were probably smashed, which is the custom today in factories making decorative porcelain of fine quality.

Randall appears to have been an unusual person. When he was working in London his copies of Sèvres porcelain were held by his contemporaries to be exceedingly deceptive, and he undoubtedly worked both on genuine white ware and on porcelain from which decoration had been removed with acid. Specimens of Sèvres porcelain with this kind of painting were, according to Litchfield,[1] known in the trade as "Quakers"—an allusion to Randall's religious persuasion. Chaffers[2] quotes a dealer as saying in 1859, the year of Randall's death: "The old Quaker stands first, at the top of the tree, but he will not put the French mark on his ware or I could sell any quantity of it at the tip-top price old Sèvres sells for." The fallacy of using a mark to identify old porcelain could not be more clearly expressed than in this remark. Few were as scrupulous as Randall, and even he must have known that his work was being sold as Sèvres whenever the opportunity occurred.

True porcelain was introduced at Sèvres in 1770, and it was at first only used for *biscuit* figures (i.e. those in unglazed porcelain). Such figures were a factory speciality. This kind of porcelain was not employed for glazed wares for some years afterwards, due apparently to the difficulty of devising a suitable glaze. Apart from the physical appearance of the body, the glaze of wares of this kind is thinner and harder, and the enamels no longer sink into it. The reproductions of Samson are in a hard-paste body, and are properly marked at the time of manufacture. The factory of Herend in Hungary, owned by Moritz Fischer, made copies of this kind, including the famous *vaisseau à mât*,[3] which sometimes bear the Royal monogram of Sèvres, although this

[1] W. Chaffers: *Marks and Monograms on Pottery and Porcelain*, edited and revised by Frederick Litchfield. London, 1912. [2] Ibid.

[3] The *vaisseau à mât* was also reproduced by Minton.

may have been added later. The factory, however, is notable for extremely accurate copies of certain kinds of Chinese porcelain, as well as that of Sèvres.

The factory of Edmé Samson et Cie, of the rue Béranger, Paris, requires special mention. It is one of the first enterprises of its kind which is likely to be brought to the attention of the novice, and the many excellent reproductions made by them are commonly to be seen in the shops of small antique dealers. The firm was founded in 1845 as the result of an accidental meeting between the founder and one of the Grand Dukes of Russia, who wanted replacements for an important porcelain service. Samson's work was so well received that he extended it to the copying of Chinese, Meissen, and English porcelain, and subsequently to the *faïence* of Strasbourg and other important wares, as well as to enamels. We have the firm's assurance that their copies are always fully marked, and there is no reason to suppose otherwise. It is, of course, possible for an unscrupulous dealer to remove the "S" which often accompanies a representation of the original factory mark, and this has obviously been done in some cases. Marks in enamel can easily be removed with hydrofluoric acid, although those underglaze need a grindstone. Samson's work is only dangerous to collectors of certain kinds of Chinese porcelain, principally that with Armorial decoration, Continental true porcelains, and *faïence*. His hard-paste reproductions of figures which were originally made in soft-paste porcelain are especially easy to detect even if the mark has been removed. Suspected pieces should be examined carefully for signs of the use of hydrofluoric acid which leaves a small patch of glaze that is mat and not shiny. The grindstone removes the glaze completely, and any specimen where this is seen to have occurred should obviously be regarded with suspicion. Samson is credited with many more reproductions than he actually makes. The name has, in fact, become almost a household word among collectors for copies which are reasonably accurate.

A word needs to be said on the subject of value. Fine reproductions are not cheap to make, and are valuable as decoration, although in most cases their price will not approach that of genuine specimens. It is also true that some kinds of old porcelain not much in demand are sold at a price equivalent to, or even less than, the cost of making a modern reproduction.

Forgeries of the true porcelain of Sèvres are not particularly common, because these later wares have never realized the same high prices as the old soft-paste in the art-market. *Vieux Sèvres* has always been synonomous with *pâte tendre*, and from about the middle of the nineteenth century until 1914, the prices given for important specimens, particularly such things as the *vaisseau à mât*, were higher than anything paid for porcelain since, especially when adjustments have been made for the devaluation which has taken place in modern currency.

Sèvres *biscuit* figures in the old soft-paste are not so highly valued as they were, but an important specimen can still reach £2,000 or so (1962). The old figures and groups were rarely marked in any way. An incised mark might have tempted contemporary fakers to glaze and paint them, and this temptation remains.

The factory did, in fact, make a very small quantity of glazed and coloured figures, the surviving number of which is not known, but it must be comparable to that of existing Medici specimens. Figures of this kind purporting to come from Sèvres need exceptionally careful examination, although every fake of the kind which I have seen has been a conspicuous failure, with all the signs of refiring. White glazed figures made at Vincennes before the removal to Sèvres in 1756 survive in greater numbers, although they are still very rare. Some genuine Sèvres glazed and painted figures were marked with the Royal monogram.

Unmarked *biscuit* figures came from contemporary French factories, but these are not deceptive, differing particularly in the body used, although subjects and styles were copied. These copies were clandestine, *biscuit* being reserved to Sèvres by various Royal edicts.

This lengthy examination is not intended to suggest that fakes and forgeries of old Sèvres porcelain are especially difficult to detect. A few are dangerous, but of the vast number existing most are only superficial copies which would not pass even reasonably expert examination. The study of genuine specimens in the Victoria and Albert Museum, the Wallace Collection, and the Sèvres Museum is the collector's greatest safeguard.

It is appropriate at this point to say something of the difference between true porcelain and the artificial variety, because every collector needs to know this much before he can safely acquire specimens from anything but a reputable and expert source. The term "hard" porcelain usually applied to true porcelain did not originally refer to the hardness of the ware, but to the "hard" or high-temperature firing necessary to make it. Nevertheless, the material is distinctly harder than soft porcelain, which can be scratched with a file. If a file cuts into hard porcelain at all it will only be with difficulty, and there will remain traces of a black powdery substance which is actually metal abraded from the file. This test is best carried out with a small file of triangular section used for sharpening saw-teeth, and only a slight abrasion is necessary. If the file cuts easily, the porcelain is soft, and no further test is required. A steel pen-knife blade will often scratch soft porcelain. The relative hardness of materials is a useful test for a variety of purposes, and it is further discussed elsewhere (Appendix 10).

To make a test of this kind is not always possible. The specimen may be too valuable, or the seller may object. It then becomes necessary to judge from physical appearance. The first point to be examined is the translucency, for which purpose the porcelain should be held to a reasonably powerful light. Some soft-pastes have small cavities inside the body, especially plates and dishes, and these appear as specks or patches of bright light. When they are fairly large—$\frac{1}{4}$ in. or so in diameter—they are often called "moons". The specks are sometimes called "pinholes". These are signs of an early porcelain, but not invariably of a soft porcelain. The same thing can occasionally be observed in a few early specimens from Meissen. The cause is not certainly known, although a number of theories have been advanced. I am inclined to regard them as arising from a combination of a body lacking plasticity and formation by a jolley—a profile used to fashion the reverse side of a dish whilst revolving on a wheel—which tends to leave small cavities in the interior of the body.

Firecracks—sometimes erroneously called "age-cracks"—are commonly seen in early soft-paste porcelains, and occasionally in later examples. They are due to an unequal contraction of the body in cooling, and are usually the result of faulty design, although in some cases the fault seems to be inherent in the porcelain. These, too, may appear in badly-designed specimens of true porcelain, but they are far less frequent. At Sèvres such things were rejected out of hand, but small factories occasionally sold wares of the kind. Firecracks are not, in themselves, cause for a specimen to be rejected, because much depends on the origin. From one of the larger factories, however, they

23. Pieter de Hoogh (c. 1632–c. 1683) "The Card Players". This obviously inspired Van Meegeren's forgery opposite.
[*Reproduced by gracious permission of Her Majesty the Queen*

24. *Pastiche* by Van Meegeren purporting to be an "Interior with Drinkers" by Pieter de Hoogh. The position of the glass in the woman's hand is discussed on page 213.
[*Ullstein*

25. The Seven-hundredth Anniversary celebrations of the founding of the Marienkirche of Lübeck. The Federal Chancellor, Dr Konrad Adenauer, is on the right with Lothar Malskat. Left centre: Minister President Lübke and

suggest that a close look at the decoration might be desirable in case it should be a "second" painted outside the factory at a late date. No porcelain develops cracks in the body merely as a result of age, although it can develop cracks in the glaze from this cause. The true firecrack often begins and ends within the limits of the porcelain, and, if it leads out to an edge, will often be wider at the edge than at the beginning. A crack which is virtually the same width throughout, and does not separate at an edge, is usually the result of damage.

Soft porcelain is nearly always slightly porous. Dirt on an unglazed part will never be easy to remove, and it may be impossible to wash it off. Some underfired soft-pastes (such as that of Bow) will absorb ink like blotting-paper, and this effect will be accompanied by poor translucency, and even by complete opacity, since firing has not proceeded to the point of complete vitrification. Porcelain plates from Bow which are virtually opaque are not uncommon. A little stain, such as writing-ink, applied to the unglazed surface of soft porcelain will often be difficult to remove. Dirt or stain on hard porcelain can be washed off without the slightest trouble.

Soft-porcelain glazes, applied after a preliminary firing of the body, are altogether thicker and more glassy than the thinner, glittering glazes of hard porcelain. Sometimes these glazes have run into pools, and even form drops near the base. They are then greenish or yellowish in colour. Often the glaze collected under the base of a figure or under the footring of dishes, which were then ground on an abrasive wheel to remove it. The flat, even, and close-grained base to be seen on some figures (Chelsea figures are an example) is the result of grinding for this purpose. These glazes are also soft, and scratches from normal wear and tear are common in appropriate places. Forgers, of course, know this, and sometimes supply the deficiency to new manufacture, but this is usually easy to detect under a powerful glass. Similar scratches are added artificially to bases of old glass vessels, but it is impossible to do the work of decades and centuries in an hour. The old scratches were acquired one at a time, and no two will have precisely the same direction. The feldspathic glazes employed on hard porcelain are much less liable to damage of this kind, although scratched glazes and enamels on certain kinds of old Chinese porcelain have sometimes resulted from careless cleaning with sand.

Enamel colours used on a soft porcelain glaze often sink into it to an extent which is dependent on the fusibility of the glaze. Hard-porcelain glazes do not allow enamels to sink in this way, and they always appear to be very much more on the surface. Particularly is this to be seen on Chinese porcelain, where they are often raised above the surface and can be felt by the finger-tips.[1] Enamels vary in surface appearance. Most European enamels are opaque and mat; Chinese enamels in particular are often translucent, although the *rose* and the *white*, used on later wares, are opaque. The Chinese also copied the effect of European enamels on wares made for export.

Lastly, chips and breakages should be examined with great care. The process of vitrification was not carried to the same lengths in soft porcelain, and the body will still have a granular texture, whereas chips from hard porcelain look like a chip from a thick glass bottle—a type of fracture referred to as *conchoidal*.

These notes will enable the collector to differentiate between hard and soft porcelain, but before the knowledge can be put to practical use it is essential to know which the various factories used. To do this means giving time to the study of some of the books listed in the Bibliography. Briefly, the German factories used true porcelain from the beginning, and still use it today; the French factories used a soft porcelain until 1770, when the hard porcelain body was increasingly adopted, and became universal by the end of the eighteenth century; English factories used a soft porcelain throughout the eighteenth century, and in some cases into the nineteenth, with the sole exception of factories at Plymouth and Bristol (Champion's factory) which made a small quantity of true porcelain between 1768 and 1780. Since the beginning of the nineteenth century English porcelain manufacturers have increasingly used Spode's bone-china body for decorative ware, whereas the Continental factories, including nearly all makers of reproductions, have relied on true porcelain. The ability to tell the difference is, therefore, an asset of the first importance.

Long before the nineteenth-century manufacturer began to reproduce Italian *maiolica* of the sixteenth century it was being copied in France, Germany, Holland, and even in England. These early reproductions are contemporary, or nearly so, and are now sought by collectors. Early French tin-enamelled wares are often copied, one of

[1] Not invariably: the rare Chinese *tou ts'ai* (soft enamels) will not have this characteristic effect.

the chief sources being Samson of Paris. Recently, perhaps as a result of good prices for genuine specimens in the sale-room, slick copies of large oval Strasbourg dishes have been offered for sale decorated with characteristic flower-sprays including the typical carmine pigment, but much whiter in appearance than the greyish glaze of the originals. The *faïence* of Nevers was being imitated in the nineteenth century by Montagon, who manufactured a wide variety of commercial pottery, as well as reproductions of the old deep blue Nevers ground (*bleu Persan*) with white enamel decoration. A common type of forgery is the so-called *faïence patriotique*, decorated with such crudely delineated Revolutionary subjects as the Tree of Liberty, the Bastille, and so forth, generally with inscriptions of which "*à la liberté ou la morte*" is an example. Of course, figures with Phrygian caps are the rule.

The *faïence* of Rouen, particularly the type decorated with swags, pendant drapes, and so forth which are termed *lambrequins*, was much imitated at the beginning of the eighteenth century by *faïence*-makers and by the porcelain factory at St Cloud. These contemporary copies are the most deceptive, although the problem is entirely one of attribution. Some modern circular dishes have been given a footring, which never appears on the genuine Rouen wares of the same kind, the bottom being flat. The wares of Moustiers, the gilded *faïence* of the Veuve Perrin at Marseilles, or that of Honoré Savy decorated with the well-known copper-green, are all copied and given appropriate marks. The mark of Lille appears frequently on snuff-boxes and other things which could hardly have come from the factory.

Perhaps the *faïence* of Strasbourg is the most frequent target. It was copied avidly at the time of its first production, and no doubt the decorative effect of its floral subjects has attracted both collector and forger alike. A misunderstanding of the purpose of the numerals which appear on the later wares of Joseph Hannong has led to a large number of copies being marked *39*. The vivid carmine used on many genuine Strasbourg dishes has never been reproduced successfully, either in the eighteenth century or later, and to judge by the most recent attempts I have seen, it still baffles the forger.

The well-known figures from Niderviller not far away, and at Bellevue, which were modelled by Paul-Louis Cyfflé were being produced in the nineteenth century, and early in this century, at Bellevue. The old moulds were used, although these had become blunted with time, and the later versions are much poorer in quality and lack the sharpness of modelling of those made in the eighteenth century. The effect of taking new moulds from old figures is later discussed.

A factory at Nevers, founded in 1850 by the Italian sculptor Ristori, made copies of French *faïence*, including those of Rouen ware, which bear their own mark. The manufacture of *faïence* was revived at Aprey from 1806 to 1885, and after about 1860, under Girard, forgeries were made of the eighteenth-century wares using old moulds. Mugs painted with an Oriental horseman and a palm-tree in blue, with a greyish crackled *faïence* glaze, probably came from here. Samson has also copied old Aprey *faïence*. At Quimper, in Finistère, a factory established early in the eighteenth century was taken over by a Rouen potter in 1743 and imitated the old wares. The factory passed to a new owner in 1872, and eighteenth-century wares were then extensively imitated.

Old German porcelain has always been an especial favourite with collectors, and forgeries are in the same true porcelain as the original manufacture. It is, therefore, much more important to develop an eye for contemporary styles in decoration. The study of this is complicated to some extent by the existence of the *Hausmaler*, considered at length in Pazaurek's monograph, *Deutsche Fayence und Porzellan Hausmaler*. These men bought white porcelain and *faïence* and decorated it at home, and they were working from the middle of the seventeenth century. Some of the German factories also still copy their old models, and, if we can accept the statements of one writer of about fifty years ago, the Meissen factory itself was then prepared to make figures from those original moulds which it still possessed.

Meissen porcelain, of course, has been the principal inspiration of the forger from the beginning, and the notes on marks (page 187) should also be consulted. Particularly frequent is the gross misuse of the *AR* monogram of Augustus the Strong and Augustus III. This usually appeared originally on specimens decorated with Oriental flowers (*indianische Blumen*) and *chinoiseries*, and colourable imitations of the old wares thus marked undoubtedly exist, although they are uncommon. Much more frequently seen are cups and saucers and vases decorated alternately with Watteau subjects by a nineteenth-century hand, and with panels of flowers, usually painted on a yellow or turquoise ground. This is a kind of decoration seen on genuine porcelain of the 1740s, but not with the *AR* monogram. The imitations were made by Mme Helena Wolfsohn, proprietor of a private establishment at Dresden in the 1870s, who started as a decorator of genuine Meissen porcelain of the period. As a result of litigation with the Royal factory (now the State factory) she changed her mark to a crown with "Dresden" immediately underneath. This is the "Crown Dresden" of the provincial auctioneer. Another Dresden factory, Meyer und Sohn, used the Meissen crossed-swords mark with the addition of the letter *M* between the hilts.

Many of the wares of Karle Thieme of Potschappel are not especially dangerous, but this firm later became the Sächsische Porzellanfabrik and copied the Kändler crinoline figures and groups which before the First World War were highly valued by collectors. The chief figure amongst those made was once thought to represent one of Augustus the Strong's mistresses, the Countess Kösel.[1] Deceptive forgeries of Meissen figures also came from Weise of Dresden. Samson of Paris has copied the Kändler birds but without the distinctive colouring of the originals. A new palette introduced by J. G. Höroldt soon after his arrival in 1721 is easy to recognize, and the collector of old Meissen ought to be well acquainted with its strong, bright colours especially to be seen on wares made between about 1721 and 1756. Paler colours usually denote manufacture after 1763, outside decoration (*Hausmalerei*), or a reproduction.

The Passau factory of Dressel, Kister and Co. made dangerous copies, not only of Meissen, but of Ludwigsburg, Frankenthal, and Höchst figures, during the nineteenth century and into the twentieth. The Höchst figures made here were replete with the "wheel" mark. Poor copies of Meissen figures were made by the Voigt Brothers of Sitzendorf, in Thuringia, after about 1850. As might be expected Samson has a large *repertoire*, and his copies are excellent.

Dressel, Kister of Passau may have had the old Höchst moulds. These were certainly in the possession of the firm of Müller at Damm, near Aschaffenburg, earlier in the nineteenth century and they used them to make earthenware copies. Müller used the "wheel" mark, with the addition of the letter *D*. Earthenware copies can easily be detected by the difference between this and porcelain. Most copies seem to be limited to the models of Johann Peter Melchior who was

[1] See page 21. Dickins v. Ellis.

the best-known and most sought Höchst modeller until a few years ago. Like the other factories which closed at the end of the eighteenth century, during the Napoleonic Wars, it is probable that white ware was sold to decorators at the time. Genuine Höchst figures usually show passages of a distinctive pink enamel of fine quality which has not been successfully reproduced.

Forgeries of Nymphenburg porcelain seem to have been limited to painting the old white ware, much of which was sold to *Hausmaler* in 1792. Some of the older figures and groups were reproduced at Munich during the nineteenth century, including perhaps Bustelli figures. The Nymphenburg factory also became the owners of the Frankenthal undertaking at the end of the eighteenth century, and they started to reproduce some of the old figures and groups at the beginning of the present century, using the original mark of Carl Theodor. These differ from genuine Frankenthal groups in the quality of modelling and decoration, but are otherwise deceptive.

Old Ludwigsburg moulds were used at Amberg in Bavaria for the reproduction of figures, whilst the more recent factory of the Württembergische Porzellanfabrik at Schorndorf has used all the old marks with the addition of *WPM*. At Fürstenberg the old mark has been used for reproductions taken from old moulds, and the mark *A.a.M* (*aus altem Modell*)[1] has been added.

A word must be said of the Greiner family, who owned several porcelain factories in Thuringia during the eighteenth century. To them copying the wares of other factories seems almost to have assumed the proportions of a sacred trust, to be handed down from one generation to another. They had numerous disputes with Meissen on the subject of pseudo and deceptive marks in the 1770s. At the end of the nineteenth century they began to reproduce their own eighteenth-century work, also with deceptive marks. The blue jasper of Wedgwood was copied in Thuringia in the eighteenth century, and occasional unmarked reproductions have been produced in this part of the world since.

Old German porcelain figures are not difficult to counterfeit convincingly enough to deceive a buyer without expert knowledge. Methods of detection fall under several headings. The first is the colour and appearance of the body which, to be on the safe side, should in

[1] From an old model.

cases of doubt be compared with genuine specimens. The figures of Weise for instance are not so white as eighteenth-century Meissen figures. The true porcelain bodies of the eighteenth century were made from materials taken from a variety of sources which could not be completely freed from impurities. They were, therefore, by no means as standardized as they have since become, and many of them developed useful idiosyncrasies during firing. The true safeguard is to learn these by a close study of eighteenth-century work.

Except where the old moulds have been available some differences in modelling are likely, even when a figure has been closely copied. It is often possible to compare dubious examples of important figures with undoubted specimens, and in this the pottery and porcelain collector is more fortunate than those in other fields where strictly similar versions ought not to exist. Photographs are, however, less reliable as a means of comparison than with some other things. It is important to remember that the original clay model from which the moulds were made was first dissected, the moulds being of the parts and not the whole, and these moulded components were put together before firing by an assembler, sometimes known in England as a "repairer" and in Germany as a *Bossierer*. The intervention of the "repairer" between the original design and the finished model leaves room for small variations, especially with eighteenth-century specimens, since precautions were not then taken to ensure complete fidelity. Also, it must be remembered that Meissen figures especially were copied by contemporary factories, when the question becomes one of attribution. Kändler's well-known group of *Lovers*, produced about 1745, exists also in a version from Ludwigsburg made about twenty years later. The difference in the two porcelain bodies and the colouring, as well as variations in modelling, are quite easily seen.

Colouring often approaches that of the original; it rarely duplicates it. The nineteenth-century forger often used pigments not in existence in the eighteenth century, such as those derived from chromium oxide which yields an opaque yellowish green and a rather unpleasant heavy and opaque maroon introduced at Meissen in 1815. Both of these have only to be seen to be recognized thereafter. Eighteenth-century decoration is usually finished with meticulous care. Slovenliness may be the mark of a minor contemporary factory; it is equally likely to be the sign of a poor commercial reproduction. Eighteenth-century figures are said invariably to have brown eyes, and the nineteenth-century copies blue eyes. This is a rule to which I have not yet found an exception, but it cannot be regarded as certain. Blue as a pigment was certainly known in the eighteenth century, although in forms which were probably unsuitable for this purpose. It would be unwise to say, however, that this point of difference, known to so many, has entirely escaped the notice of the forger. It is likely, nevertheless, that only comparatively modern forgeries will follow the eighteenth-century originals in this respect.

Forgeries are often given chips and scratches, and some have been deliberately broken and restored. The forger believes, with good reason, that a buyer occupied by the assessment of the extent of a restoration, and its effect on the value of a figure, will be less inclined to give close attention to the remaining defects of colouring, modelling, and so forth.

The Meissen factory sold "seconds" throughout the eighteenth century, and since the glaze did not give trouble when redecorated to the extent which was common with soft porcelain, they were eagerly bought, at first by the *Hausmaler* and later for less honest purposes. The factory production was divided into *gut, mittel, und ausschuß* (good, middle, and rubbish). About 1763 the practice of scoring across the glaze covering the underglaze mark of service-ware was begun. The incision was about one-third of an inch in length, and made with a glass-engraver's wheel. The precise meaning of this cancellation is not known, but one cut appears to denote sale in an uncoloured state, and two cuts defective ware decorated at the factory. Three cuts are sometimes seen, but not on factory-decorated ware. The system was also applied to figures which have the mark underglaze, and a cut of this kind across the mark means decoration outside the factory. Another mark incised with a diamond in the glaze of Meissen and Oriental porcelain is the Johanneum inventory mark, of which the following is a specimen:

N-294
W

Several sales took place of unwanted duplicates from this collection shortly after the First World War, and specimens thus marked, coming from so distinguished a source, are likely to command higher prices. This has not escaped the attention of the faker who has scratched it in more or less convincingly on genuine wares, both German and Oriental. Dishes with a patch bare of glaze inside the footring have had a mark removed by the grinding-wheel. If someone has preferred a bare patch, which proclaims the reason for its existence, to the original mark, then the mark in question must have provided information which greatly reduced its value as a collectors' item. Occasionally attempts are made to cover this patch with varnish, but they are never particularly successful. They should, however, be watched for.

The cuts mentioned do not appear on wares sold to the early *Hausmaler*, whose work is much sought, but sales of this sort were discontinued at Meissen during the 1730s. So far as later wares of the kind are concerned, whatever merit they possess is entirely a matter of the quality of the painting, which is usually poor.

Of the porcelain made at Vienna it has been said that a letter *A* signifies a factory reject, and *X* that it was sold undecorated. These marks, however, certainly do not appear on white porcelain bought after the closing of the factory in 1864 by Ludwig Riedl and others. This was elaborately, and sometimes badly, decorated, usually with figure subjects calculated to appeal to the taste of the period, sometimes with such signatures as that of Angelica Kauffmann, whose work also inspired the late eighteenth-century painters.

Fakes are not numerous on German porcelain. Superficially the true porcelain body is not difficult to reproduce fairly successfully, and there has not been the same temptation to tamper with genuine decoration as with French and English wares. The feldspathic glaze of German porcelain, however, does not reveal subsequent decoration in the same way as the softer glazes of artificial porcelain. Most such work was done in the nineteenth century, and the artistic idiom of the period is so strong and persistent that little difficulty ought to be experienced with figures after Watteau and the like. The coloured *chinoiseries* of Höroldt have not been counterfeited successfully, but those in gilt silhouette have been added recently to genuine old Meissen porcelain in Berlin. The porcelain selected has been of the correct period, and these are extremely dangerous.

Most forgeries and reproductions are of fairly well-known types, the larger proportion being of subjects fashionable among collectors between about 1870 and 1914, especially the large crinoline groups of Kändler. Generally, forgers avoid unusual themes in porcelain, just as they seek them in some other things. A subject which is not mentioned or illustrated in the various handbooks is likely to send the collector to an expert dealer or a museum in search of information. He is less likely to do so if it seems to be illustrated in his favourite handbook.

The porcelain "toys" of Meissen (small scent-flasks, *bonbonnières*, and miniature figures, often with gold mounts), which are popular collectors' items at present, have been deceptively forged, the small size contributing to the difficulty of detecting them. A seated pug, the head forming a stopper and the body a scent-flask, and a *bonbonnière* in the form of a pug's head, have both been reproduced in this way, and are probably the commonest examples of a deceptive type.

The case of Dickins v. Ellis already cited (page 21), which was heard in the London High Court before the First World War, is evidence that the closest of these forgeries of German porcelain can be difficult to recognize, although Mr Dickins seems to have been singularly deficient in knowledge and to have bought from doubtful sources. The expert evidence, a fair measure of the standard of knowledge in the trade at that time, engendered more heat than light, and the criteria of judgement would not be accepted seriously today. Such cases are, in fact, a measure of how far the standards of scholarship in these and related matters have risen during the past half-century.

German *faïence* and stoneware forgeries have been said to include such early things as the owl jugs attributed to Paul Preuning, but suspected specimens may, in fact, belong to the seventeenth century, and are therefore early derivations. Much more frequent are forgeries and reproductions of early Rhenish stoneware (*Steinzeug*), some of which were made with clay from the original beds. By far the most common are nineteenth-century commercial reproductions of the grey stoneware vessels with intricately moulded ornament touched with blue pigment which were made in the Rhineland during the sixteenth and seventeenth centuries. These have a serial number of obviously recent design stamped in the base. It is impossible to grind out these numbers without leaving obvious traces. The most deceptive copies are probably those of Hubert Schiffer of Raeren, who used both the brown and grey clay. Careful comparison of the base with that of a genuine specimen will usually reveal a copy by Schiffer. The difference is not otherwise easily discernible. The important drab white stoneware of Siegburg was copied by Peter Löwenich in the nineteenth century, some of his copies, particularly spouted jugs and tankards, being very successful. Other such makers include P. Dümler of Höhr, Merkelbach und Wick at Grenzhausen, and Villeroy und Boch at Mettlach. Some genuine Rhenish stoneware vessels bear dates in the latter part of the sixteenth century when many of them were made, and copies were being produced in England at the end of the seventeenth century by John Dwight of Fulham and others. They became unfashionable before the eighteenth century was much advanced, and only returned to favour with the vogue for medieval styles in the nineteenth century.

Böttger's red stoneware, first produced in 1709, was itself a copy of the Chinese red stoneware of Yi-Hsing. Other contemporary copies of the same wares were made in Holland by Lambertus Kleffius and Ary de Milde, and in England by John Dwight and the Elers brothers. The copies of Plaue-an-der-Havel (sometimes called "Brandenburg porcelain") were first made a few years after the earliest Meissen production by a former employee, and reproductions have been made at various Continental factories during the nineteenth century and in modern times. Böttger's stoneware is much harder than any of the copies known to me, which is a useful test of genuineness, although reproductions made at Kamenz, in Saxony, are reputed to be deceptively hard. Black-glazed stoneware painted in gold with lacquer is a rare early Böttger type, and this has been imitated in Bohemia. Some of the eighteenth-century wares were decorated by lapidaries and glass-engravers with such incised ornament as coats-of-arms, and these have usually been sought by collectors. Suitable plain examples have been decorated in this way in modern times, and are often difficult to distinguish. Close attention should be paid to the arms, and to the style in which the work has been executed. Errors of detail are not unknown, and the styles differ subtly but perceptibly.

The more familiar types of German *faïence* have been reproduced, particularly the work of Hanau, Frankfurt, Nuremberg, and Bayreuth, although they are rarely deceptive. German *faïence* is, generally, more difficult than that of France to counterfeit successfully. The *Vögleinkrüge* (the *Enghalskrug*, or narrow-necked jug with plaited handle, painted with scattered flower-sprigs and birds in blue, commonly produced at Hanau, Nuremberg, Frankfurt, and Ansbach) have been imitated but will hardly deceive anyone acquainted with genuine examples. The *Eulenkrüge* (owl jugs) are said to have been reproduced by Fleischman of Nuremberg, and whilst this is uncertain, the report is worth remembering. The works of the seventeenth-century *Hausmaler*—Johann Schaper, Abraham Helmhack, and Johann Ludwig Faber—have been forged. Jugs and tankards from Augsburg and Nuremberg were usually selected for decoration by these artists, and the forger finds it difficult to get white *faïence* which will pass muster. Counterfeits of bird-tureens in the Höchst style are known, and those of the wares of the Holitsch factory in Hungary, which also made tureens of this kind, have been recorded. Holitsch tureens in the form of fruit, vegetables, and such things were originally copied from the wares of contemporary factories.

Deceptive objects purporting to be old English pottery and porcelain fall into several distinct categories. Apart from the porcelain factories of Plymouth and Bristol, all the eighteenth-century manufacturers used a soft porcelain. Generally, the soft porcelain body is exceedingly difficult to counterfeit successfully. This is not to say that it cannot be done, but such things rarely deceive anyone who has passed his novitiate. A soft-paste was, for instance, made at the factory of St Amand-les-Eaux. Lady Schreiber describes a visit to this factory in her *Journals*, and it is probable that, in addition to outright forgeries, they redecorated such old white ware as they could acquire from Chantilly, Tournai, Sceaux, and other early factories. Whilst they were principally content to specialize in copies of the old Sèvres *pâte tendre*, there is no doubt that some soft-paste copies of Chelsea porcelain, usually those decorated with exotic birds in a late red anchor style, come from here. Those which I am inclined to regard as from St Amand-les-Eaux lack the "stilt" marks which are almost invariably present as three points of defective glaze within the footring of genuine Chelsea dishes. It is, however, both amusing and confusing to the novice to recall that similar "stilt" marks appear on Japanese porcelain made at Arita towards the end of the seventeenth century and decorated in the manner of Kakiemon. These dishes were cleverly imitated by Chelsea during the early period, and the Chelsea version has been known to deceive experts in Oriental wares until they have been able to examine them closely.[1] The use of a gold anchor mark on plates purporting to be of the red anchor period has been noticed and is probably the result of ignorance on the part of the maker, who still accepted the erroneous idea, current in the nineteenth century, that the colour of the anchor denoted quality rather than period.

Much more dangerous are some soft-paste figures of birds usually purporting to be Chelsea of about 1752, which made their appearance about ten years ago. I viewed the first of them in company with a noted authority on the early wares of Chelsea and Derby. We were unanimous in rejecting the catalogue description of Chelsea, but, at the time, we did not consider the possibility of a modern fake. We were inclined to regard it rather as one of the disagreements on points of attribution common among those interested in these things, and to award it to Derby in the early period, principally by process of elimination, since it seemed an obvious *incunabula* and we were obliged to reject Bow as a possible origin. Later, I was given an opportunity to make a test of another bird which appeared to come from the same source, and found that a phosphatic body had been used. Phosphates indicate the presence of bone-ash, a well-known ingredient of Bow porcelain, and of that of Chelsea after about 1755, which became more widely used after 1770. I have referred to these birds at some length because they illustrate an important point. Since they appeared to be fairly primitive, the possibility of a later origin was not suspected. It illustrates, also, the weakness of using the eliminative process in such cases. Although it did not strictly resemble a Derby production of the first period, we were willing to regard it as coming from here simply because less is known about these wares than any others of the period, and therefore unusual objects were more possible. It suggests that considerable caution is necessary in considering figures of any kind which depart from normal. Every type of forgery has to appear on the market for the first time, and it is then that it is most likely to deceive.

A factory in the West of England has made some not very deceptive copies of certain types of English porcelain, although they at first deceived some provincial dealers in general antiques. The manufacture includes a girl dancing and holding out her skirt with either hand, a

[1] They were also imitated at many other eighteenth-century European factories.

well-known model of the "Girl in a Swing" type of about 1752. The first of these was shown to me by the late William King of the British Museum, and, amusingly enough, it had been painted in the manner of a perfectly genuine example which had received later enamelled decoration. This is an example of a reproduction made by a maker with insufficient knowledge which perpetuates an earlier fake. From the same source have come some *rococo* vases, decorated with applied flowers, of the kind made at Longton Hall and Derby.

Chelsea porcelain was also copied at Coalport in a bone-china body, and at Tournai (which was associated with St Amand-les-Eaux in the nineteenth century) in a type of soft porcelain. There were eighteenth-century connections between Chelsea and Tournai which may account for the later copies. Believed to have come from Coalport is a chocolate cup imitating the Chelsea "claret" ground, sometimes called *rose du Barry* in the nineteenth century, which is discussed on page 141. A copy of a "Derby" figure of about 1760 on which the characteristic "dirty" turquoise was well imitated has been tentatively ascribed to this factory. Usually attributed to Coalport are the well-known forgeries of the early Chelsea jugs modelled in the form of goats facing opposing ways which also have an applied bee (the "Goat and Bee" jugs). The original jugs were based on a silver-pattern, but, to my knowledge, those silver versions which exist are themselves forgeries, probably inspired by the porcelain jugs. I have failed to discover direct evidence of the manufacture of the porcelain forgeries at Coalport, but they would have been well within the technical competence of the factory in the early part of the nineteenth century. The most puzzling aspect is that demand for such *incunabula* was very slight at the time, and the project hardly seems to have been worth while. It is not, in fact, difficult to distinguish between thin Chelsea potting and the glassy paste, which has a translucency plentifully be-sprinkled with bright points of light known as "pinholes", and the harder paste and thicker, often slightly clumsy potting of the copies. The horns of the goats on the latter are also long and moulded in low relief. They probably did not bear the incised triangle mark in the first place, but most of them do now. This has been scratched in after firing with varying degrees of persuasiveness. Usually it is much larger than a genuine mark; evidently the forger wanted to be sure that no one would overlook it. This piece of chicanery is also to be noted on some perfectly genuine examples of the early period which were originally issued unmarked. Collectors have been inclined to pay higher prices for marked specimens, and it does not require much effort to supply a mark. The genuine mark, however, was incised into unfired clay, and this had a distinct effect on its edges. The easiest way to see the difference is to scratch a triangle in a piece of smooth clay with a point and observe the rough, slightly ploughed-up edges which result. The same effect to a greater or lesser degree will be exhibited by a genuine mark, although it may need a glass to see it.

It has been suggested that unmarked reproductions of the very rare bird-tureens of Chelsea belonging to the red anchor period were made by Randall at the factory he established at Madeley, although neither Jewitt[1] nor Chaffers refer to work of this kind. There is little to prevent a red anchor mark being added to such specimens. The possibility that reproductions of the "Goat and Bee" jugs were made here rather than at Coalport should not be overlooked. The cabbage tureens of Chelsea certainly exist in a later version usually attributed to Coalport. The latter factory, however, was much more interested in revived *rococo* styles and the work of Sèvres.

Among the less usual examples of forgery quoted by Wallace Elliot[2] is a "Lowestoft" mug in underfired porcelain inscribed *Abr. Moore August 29th 1765* which even has the smudged underglaze blue decoration often seen on genuine specimens. It had, however, the unusual feature of a crazed glaze which is extremely unusual on genuine Lowestoft. A number of these mugs seem to be in existence.

It is essential to notice a rare type of forgery which deceived at least one expert dealer fifty years or so ago. Porcelain shrinks during the firing process by approximately one-sixth. In the early years of the present century the collector who gave me this story sent what is still a unique Chelsea figure to London for repair. The restorer was unscrupulous enough to take from it a series of moulds, and subsequently made several forgeries in a porcellaneous body which have since appeared from time to time on the art-market, the first occasion being shortly before the First World War. All of them are instantly recognizable because they are smaller by about one-sixth than the genuine figure, measuring about 9½ ins. instead of 11½ ins. This, of course,

[1] Llewellyn Jewitt: *The Ceramic Art of Great Britain*. London, 1878.
[2] *Transactions of the English Ceramic Circle*. No. 7, Vol. 2.

applies equally to all remoulds, but care is needed because the Derby factory, for instance, usually issued their figures in three sizes. The method, however, is hardly likely to be used for anything but a unique example, or for something so rare that the chance of the difference being noticed is fairly remote. The genuine figure in the case discussed was purchased by an American collector, and confirmation was obtained later by his purchase of one of the forgeries for purposes of comparison.

Reproductions of eighteenth-century English figures in true porcelain are common and hardly dangerous, since the nature of the body instantly reveals the difference. This can equally well be seen in the decoration, because the effect of using enamel colours on a hard-porcelain glaze is not the same. Idiosyncrasies of manufacture noticeable on genuine specimens, such as the three patches bare of glaze on the base of Derby figures (the so-called "thumbprints") are missing. Marks are commonly added, the most usual being a large and prominent gold anchor in imitation of Chelsea, nearly always on the base. The Chelsea gold anchor is always small and placed low down on the back in an inconspicuous place. Most of the figures to be seen are of the gold anchor period, since red anchor figures have only achieved their present popularity since the 1920s.

The forger's lack of knowledge once again traps him into inconsistencies. Until the 1920s the large group of unmarked Derby figures made about 1765, usually with a bocage of flowers at the back, were often attributed to Chelsea, particularly the finer examples. The separation was made when the "thumbprints" mentioned were correctly interpreted by Bernard Rackham. The addition of a gold anchor mark to such copies immediately exposes the deception without further examination. Bow figures are copied by Samson, but the colouring is inaccurate, and no one with an elementary knowledge of the wares in question could be deceived. So little has been known of English pottery and porcelain on the Continent that the reproductions have been a fruitful field for sometimes ludicrous errors.

Worcester porcelain has been imitated since the eighteenth century. Lowestoft porcelain with a pirated crescent mark is not unusual, and the Caughley factory not only made close copies of Worcester blue-and-white wares but adopted a letter "C" as a mark, which was drawn deceptively as often as not. Although the problem is one of attribution, it must be remembered that the Worcester engraver and one-time partner, Robert Hancock, not only went to Caughley, but took some of his engraved plates with him which were used for transfer-printing. The factory at Liverpool of Chaffers and Christian not only used a similar porcelain body containing soaprock, but undoubtedly copied Worcester decorations, and this has led to confusion in attribution.

Although few wares have escaped this kind of attention, the Worcester decoration of a scale-blue ground with bird-painting in panels has suffered most. Flowers in panels are to be seen occasionally on copies, but bird-painting has always been more in demand. Many forgeries of this kind come from the Continent, and are in hard-paste porcelain with inferior gilding. They are usually badly potted, the shapes being poor and the porcelain thicker. Copies in fine earthenware by Booth of Tunstall are superficially much closer, but will not withstand the test of holding them to the light, since they are completely opaque. The scale-blue ground is also *printed* and not painted; the regularity of printed scales can easily be seen. The original ground was done by hand. Other forgeries of Worcester scale-blue were made at Coalport, and some were given the seal mark. Blue-and-white copies have been made in Staffordshire, and a type which needs careful examination is the cabbage-leaf jug with a mask spout which was not only imitated in the eighteenth century, but also at a much later date in a whiter, thicker body, perhaps by Chamberlain. A few transfer-printed forgeries exist, but are principally accused by bad printing and worse plates. Lilac overglaze prints sometimes belong to this class.

Most genuine old Worcester has a narrow unglazed area immediately inside the footring which is almost invariably present. No forgery or copy will have this idiosyncrasy. It is easily tested by running a pencil round the inside of the footring. This will mark the unglazed body, but will slide over glaze in a manner which is quite unmistakable. Worcester have reproduced some of their older wares, principally scale-blue and birds, but these are always properly marked. Some of the later Barr, Flight and Barr copies, however, done towards the end of the eighteenth century, are either not marked at all or bear the normal factory mark. As often as not these were replacements.

Exotic birds of a slightly different kind from those hitherto discussed, without an accompanying ground but with slight landscape painting, were done in the eighteenth century in the manner of the Sèvres painters, Evans and Aloncle, by a certain M. Soqui who worked at both Plymouth and Worcester. These were imitated during the nineteenth century at Tournai and in Paris, as well as at Worcester during the early years of the nineteenth century.

Samson has made some copies of Bristol porcelain, and others may have been made elsewhere. The copies are in the same hard porcelain as the factory used originally, and are therefore inclined to be dangerous. Many Bristol wares, however, have a spiral "wreathing" in the body, especially when they were thrown on the wheel. It is to be seen on cups, bowls, and so forth as slight spiral ridges, and appears to have emanated from the tendency of the body to "unwind" slightly during firing. This led to the handles of cups and mugs being slightly askew—a defect which is almost invariable. If a specimen purporting to be Bristol lacks either of these two idiosyncrasies then it needs careful examination, although they are not invariably present.

Poor reproductions of English porcelain figures were made at Sitzendorf in Thuringia during the nineteenth century, and sometimes bear a gold anchor mark. But for this, they would hardly be worth mentioning. They are not deceptive, and appear to have been made as cheap chimney-piece ornaments or fair-ground prizes.

Hitherto we have discussed forgeries and reproductions of English porcelain. It is now essential to turn to the study of fakes—genuine specimens, altered and added to for the purpose of obtaining a high price on the art-market.

These are principally white and sparsely decorated wares which have been painted with rare, much sought-after decorations. It is quite possible to remove slight enamel decoration with hydrofluoric acid, the only acid which will seriously attack glass and allied products containing silica. Slight decoration in underglaze blue can often be hidden by an opaque ground-colour laid overglaze, although if the specimen be held to the light the original decoration can usually be traced. Painting which diverges from the normal factory types ought, therefore, to be regarded with a questioning eye.

Before stigmatizing a piece of this kind as a fraud, however, it is essential to consider the possibility that it may be the work of the outside decorator (analogous to the German *Hausmaler*) who was a legitimate and established adjunct to the porcelain factories in the eighteenth century. They bought white wares and decorated them in their own studios, and Worcester supplied James Giles of Clerkenwell both with porcelain in white and with the scale-blue ground already laid, white panels being left for him to fill in with flowers or birds. The white wares were sometimes decorated by Giles with scale-grounds in enamel colours. I have seen several specimens of scale-blue porcelain in blank, that is, wanting the enamel decoration, and this was obviously the form in which it was supplied to the decorator.

Eventually Worcester engaged London painters and became less willing to supply Giles with his needs. He then bought porcelain transfer-printed in black at auction and coloured it with enamels. In my opinion some of the sparsely decorated blue-painted wares subsequently covered with an opaque enamel ground are the work of Giles at this time. Painting in his style is also to be found on the porcelain of Chelsea and Bow, and at least one example of his hand on that of Plymouth exists. Giles's painting on Chinese porcelain is not infrequent.

Decoration can only be added by a faker if the specimen is put back into the enamelling-kiln, and this often leaves signs in the form of sputtering of the glaze and black specks, with occasionally an uneven surface. The defect, however, is also present on some eighteenth-century wares, and it is difficult to be certain what length of time has to lapse between manufacture and decoration before the risk of such defects appearing becomes almost inescapable. The problem was the subject of correspondence between Josiah Wedgwood and Sadler and Green in the 1760s, when these defects appeared on creamware sent to Liverpool for transfer-printing. Sadler and Green suggested that the trouble might be caused by damp which aggravated the fact that the plain ware had been in stock for a longer period than was safe. Certainly after the lapse of a considerable period the glaze seems to have absorbed substances which cause a deleterious reaction in the enamelling-kiln. Experiments with a type of cement which needs the application of a moderate degree of heat to mature it caused me to subject fragments of various kinds of old English porcelain to controlled temperatures which did not rise above 300 degrees Fahrenheit. Most of them discoloured to some extent before this was reached.

These signs of redecoration, therefore, should not necessarily be considered proof of a fake, although anything which exhibits them needs to be regarded with a considerable degree of suspicion. Overglaze inscriptions and signatures, or unusual marks, need to be examined carefully. Enamel colours can be fired on at comparatively low temperatures if a suitable flux is added.

Worcester porcelain has undoubtedly been the subject of more fakes than the other varieties, partly because it has always commanded excellent prices among collectors, but perhaps because the glaze was a little more tolerant of refiring than that of Chelsea, which now discolours rapidly after a relatively slight degree of heat has been applied. It is probable, too, that only from Worcester has white ware been available in worth-while quantities, a sale of this kind being held in 1841 when the original factory amalgamated with the later enterprise of Humphrey Chamberlain. No doubt it was at this time that the scale-blue "blanks" found their way on to the market, and some of them must have been redecorated.

The principal signs of refiring have already been discussed, but an iridescent stain round the edges of the enamels, to be seen if the painting is examined in a light falling on to the surface at an angle, is a danger signal on specimens purporting to be old Worcester, although on Nantgarw porcelain it is no more than a useful test for whether the porcelain was decorated in London. Here, too, the lapse of time between manufacture and decoration is unknown, and may sometimes have been a matter of a few years. A defective blue ground on old Worcester suggests tampering. Grinding of the footring is also suspicious. This was rarely done on genuine wares, but it has been necessary occasionally to remove some of the traces of refiring.

The green enamel should be examined carefully. The old colour differs from that of the yellowish, opaque chrome green introduced in 1802. Old Worcester gilding is always of fine quality, carefully executed, often in a variety of elaborate patterns. Poor gilding is a cause for suspicion.

The substitution of green or yellowish-brown enamel for gold suggests either a fake or the work of James Giles. The "Quail" pattern, a comparatively rare example of the Worcester use of Kakiemon styles, sometimes has the gilding replaced by the yellow-brown mentioned, and can be attributed to Giles with a certain amount of confidence. He also did excellent gilding which rivalled factory work.

The brassy mercuric gilding appears to have been introduced about 1780 when the factory was bought by Thomas Flight.

The removal or overpainting of sparse decoration on old Worcester porcelain was the speciality of an Italian, one-time *chef* to the Italian Minister in London, during the 1870s. The decoration is poor in quality, usually of fruit or flowers, and the ground-colours dense and opaque. This was at one time generally known among collectors and dealers as "Cavallo's Worcester". His work is generally to be found on old tea and coffee services. Claret grounds with Watteau figures in reserves need specially careful examination.

Forgeries of nineteenth-century English porcelain are uncommon; the factories were preoccupied with copying early things. Nantgarw and Swansea productions, however, are much sought by collectors. It must be remembered that the Coalport factory took over the remaining stock and formulae of the Nantgarw enterprise, as well as some of the artists, although it is very doubtful whether they used the porcelain body since this was exceptionally difficult to fire successfully. Hard-paste copies of Swansea porcelain are fairly numerous, and may be connected with the fact that the same hand has been observed decorating genuine Swansea porcelain and that of Nast of Paris. Quite possibly he was the de Junic recorded as working at Swansea, and most such copies have an unmistakable Parisian air. Rockingham styles in service-ware were copied by other contemporary factories, and occasionally appear in hard porcelain. The decorative porcelain cottages have also been reproduced in hard porcelain and are usually unmarked.

Forgeries of most kinds of English pottery exist, and some imitations of Lambeth delft posset-pots, an expensive type, are known. Imitations of early slipware, however, are rarely dangerous to anyone acquainted with the technique of seventeenth-century manufacture.

Saltglaze wares have been in demand among collectors for many years, and forgeries undoubtedly exist. Wallace Elliot[1] illustrates a cat of solid agate-ware which is an obvious fraud. Agate-ware is made by superimposing layers of coloured clay one on the other, subsequently "wedging" them together to produce a marbled effect. In the case of the reproduction mentioned this effect was achieved by painting on the exterior, and part of the interior. The difference between the two

[1] op. cit.

techniques is obvious. The modelling is also poor, and the total effect hardly deceptive. The same authority refers to a poor imitation of the standing figure of a man.

Much more dangerous are some forgeries of Astbury-Whieldon figures of which a number have appeared on the art-market. One I might have passed had it not been a genuine experimental attempt on the part of a studio-potter who showed it to me as a curiosity. The technique of those which have appeared on the art-market is a close simulation of eighteenth-century work, and the only important difference is the softness of the body used. A few deceptive copies of Whieldon figures decorated with the characteristic coloured glazes have been noted. Wallace Elliot suggested that the putty-coloured body of the reproductions, which differs from the primrose-yellow of most genuine specimens, might be used as a way of differentiating between the two, but the body colour of both genuine and false is variable, and I am inclined to think that the collector's eye for form is probably a safer guide.

The same authority illustrated a copy of the well-known Fitzwilliam Museum saltglaze "Pew" group representing Adam and Eve in lead-glazed earthenware with the impressed mark of "Wedgwood"—an example of a forger's attempt to create a puzzle for the collector in the absence of an ability to reproduce the original. Pottery and porcelain are especially open to this kind of fraud, since the factories copied each other, and a forger short of a subject can confidently reproduce a model from elsewhere with the assurance that his selection might conceivably have been made by an eighteenth-century manufacturer. In the case of the subject under discussion, however, the subject and its treatment was too much at variance with the remainder of Josiah Wedgwood's production to pass muster, and it ought to have aroused more scepticism on its first appearance than it did. Another figure obviously modelled by the same hand appeared later in the style of Astbury with the mark of Ralph Wood. It is probable that others from this source exist, and may find their way on to the market in future.

Cream-coloured saltglaze ware, popular in the eighteenth century as an inexpensive substitute for porcelain, exists in fairly large quantities in an uncoloured state. Some specimens have been enamelled subsequently, and the thin glaze is not so much affected as the thicker lead glazes by refiring. Some enamel painting has been done on moulded surfaces obviously not intended for such decoration, but enamelling on saltglaze was done in Holland during the eighteenth century, much of it on ware which was not made specially for the purpose in the first place. Differentiation between eighteenth-century work and later enamelling needs skill and experience in doubtful cases. There are no short-cuts. Painting with Jacobite significance requires careful examination.

Creamware of the kind made by Wedgwood was reproduced in the eighteenth century at Leeds. Both varieties have been copied later, and plain specimens have been decorated. Since the more ordinary examples are not especially valuable, work of this kind will have subjects calculated to attract the collector, and are therefore likely to be unusual. Creamware was extensively manufactured on the Continent, in France under the name of *faïence-fine* and in Germany as *Steingut*, from the eighteenth century onwards. Usually the body colour is yellower than English creamware and the glaze thicker, but not invariably so.

Wedgwood's productions were frequently reproduced, which is not surprising since the factory was the most influential in Europe during the latter part of the eighteenth century. Some of the early copyists are worth noting here. Ralph Wedgwood, a cousin of Josiah, was associated with a factory at Ferrybridge, near Pontefract, in 1792, which stamped its wares "Wedgwood & Co." The addition of "& Co." reveals the difference. In 1848 J. Smith and Co. of the Stockton Potteries marked imitations of Wedgwood's products "Wedgewood". The intrusive median "e" should be noted. There are, of course, such contemporary copies of the jasper ware as those of Neale and Palmer, and Adams, but imitations from the Continent are almost as numerous. The Sèvres factory made the familiar white reliefs on blue in *biscuit* porcelain; Meissen introduced "Wedgwood-Arbeit"; the black *basaltes* ware was made at such northern factories as Ulfsunda and Königsberg; whilst the factories of Thuringia—accomplished copyists all, with an existing reputation for pirating the Meissen mark—made unmarked reproductions of jasper. Gotha, towards the end of the century, listed vases "*à l'étrusque*" which may have been copied from Wedgwood's own imitations of red-figure Greek vases, or they may have been taken directly from the originals.

None of these reproductions, however, need be mistaken for genuine Wedgwood productions. I have seen no example of the use of the Wedgwood impressed mark, which was invariably added to genuine wares. Wedgwood are at present reproducing some of their old wares in the jasper body, but these are always plainly marked.

In the nineteenth century many of the established English factories turned to the manufacture of reproductions of wares made from classical times onwards, and they eagerly used the technical advances of the time to make these as close to the originals as possible. Minton's copied the work of Sèvres extensively in a type of soft-paste, and their turquoise ground is principally accused by its technical perfection of application rather than by the shade. It was, perhaps, less of an achievement to copy the old forms, since they worked in a more tractable porcelain body, but copies of the famous *vaisseau à mât* were made for Mortlock, the china-dealer, from an original lent to them for the purpose. An imitation of the "Duplessis" vase with elephant heads reproduced the old apple-green ground. At Coalport imitations were many and varied. The most competent were those of Sèvres, and if old stories are to be believed, a vase of this kind even succeeded in duping one of the factory's directors into paying £600 for it at auction under the conviction that it was Sèvres *pâte tendre*. The flower-encrusted Meissen vases and cups and saucers, a type not now in much demand, were copied, but with less success. Coalport also made many replacements for broken pieces of services of old Sèvres porcelain. Copeland Spode introduced Parian porcelain for the manufacture of figures, which was obviously copied from Sèvres *biscuit*, and some of the models were derived from this source. *Biscuit* figures had first been made in England by the Derby factory soon after 1770, and were extensively manufactured for many years afterwards, some being fairly close repetitions of Sèvres designs.

It is more difficult to draw a strict line of demarcation between fakes, forgeries, and reproductions in pottery and porcelain than in some other things. Original work in the arts generally is scarce; derivative work is common. This is especially true of ceramics. The principal sources of inspiration in eighteenth-century manufacture were the factories of Meissen, Sèvres, and Wedgwood in that order of date. Most of the others copied the work of these factories because they were either unwilling or unable to supply the demand. Some of

26. "Madonna" in the medieval style painted by Lothar Malskat in Schleswig Cathedral from a photograph of the film actress, Hansi Knoteck. [*Ullstein*

27. Head from the Schleswig frescoes by Lothar Malskat modelled on his sister, Frieda. [*Ullstein*

28. "Madonna and Child" by Lothar Malskat in the Lübeck Marienkirche. [*Ullstein*

29. The scene in Court in October 1954 when the forged easel-paintings by Malskat were first discussed publicly. The picture in the foreground appears to be a forgery of the work of Chagall. [*Ullstein*

the decoration of Meissen is derivative, because they attempted to augment the supply of Japanese porcelain decorated by Kakiemon. A number of their figures can be traced to existing ivory-carvings. Wedgwood took classical subjects as his main source of inspiration.[1] The porcelain of Sèvres was slightly more original because it owed little to the inspiration of other porcelain factories, but it drew heavily on the work of contemporary painters. Some of the factories which sprang up in Germany, France, and England did original work of no little merit, some of which is important—the *rococo* figures of Bustelli at Nymphenburg for example. The position of the nineteenth-century factories was peculiar, inasmuch as they were supplying a market for wares in the style of medieval and Renaissance times which were much in demand as decoration.

Few of these nineteenth-century imitations are deceptive today, although many found them so when they were made. This is natural enough for reasons discussed elsewhere. Today, when the general level of scholarship is much higher, these things can be instantly recognized for what they are, and the number of deceptive copies is much fewer than formerly. Forgeries of English porcelain can at once be recognized if the body is analysed chemically, since genuine wares fall into well-marked categories which cannot be imitated. Little work of this kind has been done on Continental porcelain, however, whilst the various types of pottery and stoneware have been left almost untouched. Some notes on this aspect are included in Appendix 6. Ultra-violet radiation (see Appendix 3) has also been extensively used in the investigation of English porcelain, but hardly at all outside this field. Generally, English porcelain is the safest for the beginner because of the difficulties of making a counterfeit which is good enough to pass even an inexperienced eye.

Forgeries of Chinese wares usually need a considerable amount of skill and experience to detect them, and even the expert is sometimes deceived. It is also difficult to agree on precisely what is meant by the term "forgery". For instance, some of the classic wares of the Sung dynasty (960-1279) were copied during the reign of Yung Chêng (1723-1735) because the earlier wares were much revered at the time. These copies were not necessarily intended to deceive, and the reign

[1] The Wedgwood "Portland" vase is, of course, an excellent example of a fine reproduction made for completely honest purposes.

mark of the Emperor appeared on some of them, although this has, in some cases, since been removed to allow the object to pass as Sung. Nevertheless, this does not alter the original intention.

Many specimens of Chinese porcelain bear a series of characters, of the kind illustrated below:

| | | | | |
|---|---|---|---|---|
| (4) Hua | 化 | Great | (1) | 大 |
| (5) in the | 年 | Ming | (2) | 明 |
| (6) reign of | 製 | Ch'êng | (3) | 成 |

This, as may be seen, records the dynasty and the name of the Emperor Ch'êng Hua (1465-1487). Books on marks (see Bibliography) give a complete list.

It became the custom to mark porcelain with the name of a former Emperor as a mark of reverence and commendation. A mark, therefore, may belong to the period indicated or to a later period, and much eighteenth-century porcelain, especially that painted in blue, was given the marks of the Ming dynasty, that of Ch'êng Hua being particularly frequent. In fact, the mark of this Emperor probably appears on more blue-and-white porcelain of all periods than that of any other. This is not to say that forged reign marks are unknown. These occur fairly frequently, and most porcelain bearing the mark of K'ang Hsi (1662-1722) was actually made later, sometimes very much later.

The Neolithic pottery urns of the type found in the Pan Shan cemetery do not seem to have been copied, although I have seen one specimen with decoration which I thought might have been added to create a unique object likely to ensnare an unwary collector.[1] Generally, however, there are no forgeries of pottery purporting to be any earlier than the Han dynasty (206 B.C.-A.D. 220). Copies of the glazed wares of this period have undoubtedly been made to deceive the Western collector, but they are not very convincing, and attempts to imitate the glaze iridescence which results from burial have ended in failure. The unglazed wares painted with unfired ("cold") pigments are sometimes forged, but more often only the painting is new. Like

[1] Karlbeck (*Treasure Seeker in China*, London, 1957) also refers to attempts by villagers in the An-yang region to make ancient pottery jars more valuable by scratching pseudo-Shang dynasty designs on them, presumably taken from the "oracle bones" excavated in this region, which have, themselves, sometimes been forged (page 120).

the European forger of ancient Greek drawing, his modern Chinese counterpart finds it difficult to reproduce the styles of a period as early as Han. Purporting to be slightly later are some vases, also decorated in "cold" pigments, with figure-subjects which are accused as much by the modern idiom in drawing as by anything else, and the subjects selected from the Han repertoire are precisely those likely to appeal to modern taste.

Forgeries of T'ang tomb figures are by far the most numerous among the early wares, and fall into two classes. The first are made as honest reproductions, and sold as such by the importers. The forms are wrong, and the glaze colours vary considerably from those of genuine specimens. They look, and are, hot from the kiln. They are sold as objects of modern manufacture in the first place; what may happen afterwards is anybody's guess, but a collector buying one and believing it to be old, had better give up collecting for some safer pursuit. These have been made in China, but some even less deceptive copies appear to have emanated from San Francisco. The latter are rarely seen in England, but I identified one specimen of this kind in the shop of a provincial dealer.

The second variety has been made to meet the Western demand for tomb-figures, and is exceedingly dangerous. These are unglazed, and since they have been made from moulds taken from genuine figures, they are almost indetectable. They have also been made in such quantities that unimpeachable observers[1] have recorded seeing them laid out in rows in the factories responsible.

Orvar Karlbeck[2] gives an interesting description of a visit to a factory making early funerary figures which was situated in caves near Lo-yang. Genuine figures excavated locally were used as models, and the periods copied were those of the Wei, Sui, and T'ang dynasties. Dancing-girls and women musicians were popular models, and Karlbeck considers that the bodies were a little too long and slim, in contrast with the dumpiness of genuine T'ang figures of women. Glazed horses, camels, and fabulous monsters (presumably temple-guardians and Lokopalas) could be bought for a hundred dollars, and the very popular mounted women polo-players, unglazed, were to be had for the same amount. The remarks of an experienced observer as

[1] For instance, Gerald Reitlinger and the late Professor Yetts.

[2] Orvar Karlbeck, op. cit.

to the differences between these and genuine specimens are especially valuable. At this particular factory only off-white and reddish-brown clays appear to have been used, and no grey clay was evident. The glaze, to Karlbeck, appeared to be a close simulation of a genuine glaze, except that it was present in excessive amounts. The figures, on the instructions of Pekin dealers, were broken and then buried in soil which was full of mineral salts, and more salt was added, the place of burial being watered frequently. When the figures were dug up and repaired some months later they were already covered with a thin layer of salt which resembled the iridescence of a genuine glaze, except that it would wash off with a little trouble whilst genuine iridescence is virtually irremovable, although it can be subdued with a smear of Vaseline. An interesting observation is that adherent earth had a pitted appearance owing to the frequent watering, whereas this effect was absent on genuine figures.

Figures which have been modelled by the forger, and not moulded from original specimens, are much easier to detect by departure from the old styles, and these are sufficient to give rise to suspicion, although they are often slight.

Forgeries probably began with the high prices paid for the impressive T'ang fighting horses, with hoof upraised and mouth open in a snarl. When these first arrived in Europe collectors realized that here was an important art-form which was almost unknown. They soon became much more widely known, however, and were sought as interior decoration in the 1930s. Some of these later arrivals are an example of the warning given by Honey against the danger-signal provided by objects in pairs, or by the same type of object appearing in several places at about the same time. Genuine unglazed T'ang figures are usually made of soft, lightly-fired earthenware which is either almost white, pinkish-buff, or light grey. Before painting they were given a wash of white slip to seal the pores and to provide a background for the cold pigments used. As a result of burial much of this colouring has now disappeared in most cases. Earlier figures, such as those of the Wei dynasty, were usually made from a dark-grey material, or occasionally from a dark-red body similar to that of Han pottery. Both were washed with white slip and coloured.

It is difficult to formulate rules for the detection of forgeries which would be applicable even to most cases, but it is useful to remember that forgeries are generally in a slightly harder material, which is less absorbent. A little saliva touched on to the surface of a genuine figure with the finger will usually be absorbed at once, and the mark will disappear rapidly. The "cold" pigments are likely to be of the wrong shade (too bright a red, for instance) but this demands close acquaintance with the appearance of undoubtedly genuine specimens such as those excavated by a reputable European archaeologist. Moulds sometimes leave seam-marks, but these may also appear in those old wares which were moulded.

T'ang figures decorated with the typical coloured glazes are much more difficult to forge deceptively. The effects of time on the glaze are not easy to counterfeit. The absorbent nature of the body is evident in the fall of the glaze, which is similar to that of jars and bowls of the period. The glaze is minutely crazed and iridescence is occasionally present to a marked degree.

Generally, the other characteristic T'ang wares do not appear to have been copied to the same extent, and those which have been are not excessively difficult to detect. Forgers have also tried to create new T'ang types which have passed current for a time in some quarters, but they have usually had a relatively short life before someone has disputed them. Forms are clumsy, and the harder body employed has not been without its effect on the glaze. The fall of the genuine glaze of the period undoubtedly owes something to the absorbent nature of the soft earthenware used, and the employment of a harder material will affect the appearance of any glaze covering it.

Care needs to be exercised in the examination of repaired examples. Chinese restorers are extremely skilful. Some degree of restoration in figures which are so soft and fragile is inevitable, but this should be limited in extent. Some exhibit more restoration than original material. The Chinese restorer often makes an obvious job of an unimportant part to divert attention from much more extensive and skilful repairs elsewhere. The ultra-violet lamp is useful in examinations of this kind.

This is, perhaps, an appropriate place to refer to the exceedingly rare Japanese tomb-figures known as *haniwa* (A.D. 300–645). Forgeries began to appear on the market in 1950. Information received from Japan suggests that the body is harder than that of genuine specimens, being compounded of genuine fragments ground to powder, with new clay added to make the mixture plastic and fired in a closed kiln. The body is harder than the soft and friable earthenware used for the originals, which were trench-fired. So little is known about these figures in the West that caution is needed in acquiring a specimen from any but an expert and reputable source.

Copies of Sung wares abound, but the majority are not likely to deceive anyone well versed in the characteristics of genuine objects. The celadon glaze, which varies on different varieties from a putty colour to sea-green, has always been especially sought. The Sung glaze was used on a stoneware body which burned to a deep reddish brown where the glaze did not cover it. This will enable most eighteenth-century copies to be detected, since the body is often white porcelain. The unglazed footring was washed over with brown to disguise the whiteness of the body, but this can be seen under the glaze, and at the edges, in the form of a distinct lightening of the colour where a Sung specimen would be brown. These eighteenth-century glazes, and those made later, were coloured with iron to which a little cobalt was added, but the shade is a trifle too blue in comparison with that of early wares. The brownish areas to be seen in the glaze of many genuine specimens are also missing. A bluish celadon glaze of the Sung period is called "kinuta" in reference to the shape of the vase on which it is often found. These wares, of course, are quite genuine, and glaze should always be considered in conjunction with the body and the physical appearance generally. Later copies often bore the incised mark of Yung Chêng or Ch'ien Lung which has since been ground off, although the effect is sometimes explained as the result of the removal of a Palace mark from a stolen piece.

Celadons continued to be made at those centres operating during Sung times at least until the eighteenth century, and the Jesuit missionary, Père d'Entrecolles, describes the eighteenth-century imitation of Sung celadons at what appears to have been the notable Sung centre of Lung Ch'üan.[1]

Decoration in painted slip replaced the old carved ornament at this time, and the styles not only of the Sung period but also of the following Yüan and Ming were copied. It is difficult to say when these old kilns ceased to work. It may have been well into the twentieth century, and they may even be functioning today, although nothing so recent

[1] Père d'Entrecolles: *Lettres édifiantes et curieuses.* 1717 and 1724.

as an undoubted post-war specimen has been recorded. These very late dishes are usually heavy and clumsy, poorly decorated, and badly potted. The early Yüeh celadons with a putty-coloured glaze have recently been the subject of copies with an inferior greenish-brown glaze, which like that of so many imitations is too shiny. A characteristic of most Sung glazes is their obvious treacly consistency, and they usually finish towards the bottom of a pot in a thick roll, as though too viscid to flow any further. They are also cloudy, which is caused by the presence of large quantities of bubbles and minute solid particles. This effect is imitated to some extent on the best copies, but few do so with any degree of real similarity. The collector of Sung wares will find Hetherington's work on this subject indispensable.[1] Later developments are discussed in Appendix 1.

Japanese copies of celadons are sometimes close, particularly those of the Lung Ch'üan and *kinuta* celadons, but the "musliny" appearance of the glaze surface, also to be noticed on Japanese porcelain, helps to separate them from genuine wares. The *mishima*[2] decoration of Korea has been copied by Japanese potters, and a Korean factory has reproduced both this and the characteristic Northern celadons.

The showy Chün ware, with its lavender-blue glaze and purple splashes, has been a favourite with Western collectors since the first Sung wares found their way to Europe at the end of the nineteenth century. There were a number of early copies, such as the so-called "soft" Chün which has a buff body and a waxy appearance to the glaze as well as distinct variations in the colours, the splashes being usually more crimson than purple. Imitations were made at Yi-Hsing and in Kuangtung during Ming times, and manufacture has probably continued to the present day. "Fatshan Chün" came from Shekwan, near Fatshan, sometimes known as the "Birmingham of Canton", where the kilns may still be working, and glazes closely resembling Chün types have come from Japan. Copies in white porcelain, treated similarly to the celadons to disguise the colour of the body, were made in the eighteenth century at Ching-tê Chên, and just before the Second World War deceptive copies were reaching the West from Yü-chou.

[1] A. L. Hetherington: *Chinese Ceramic Glazes*. South Pasadena, 1948.

[2] *Mishima* is an incised decoration heightened by slip much in the same way as the decoration of *Henri Deux* ware already mentioned.

The tea-bowls of the *temmoku* type, called Chien *yao* in China, were always popular in Japan for use in the Tea Ceremony, and have been freely copied there. Certain underfired specimens with a deeply fissured glaze, termed *lizard skin*, are sometimes refired at the correct temperature, producing a curious variant of the more usual glaze. I have known the same thing to be done with an underfired Chün bowl of typical form, but the glaze did not assume the characteristic appearance.

The finer Ting wares have a close-grained greyish-white body and, unlike most other Sung wares, are translucent, yielding an orange tinge when viewed by transmitted light. They are therefore porcellaneous rather than stoneware. The glaze is ivory-white in colour, and on the exterior drops of glaze are likely to form, which are often called "tear-drops" and regarded as a sign of genuineness. The rim is usually unglazed, and often bound with metal. These bowls were fired either upside down or standing on edge. The best have carved and incised designs; moulded ornament is commoner and less valuable. Ting *yao* has been much copied later, but never convincingly. The moulded designs become increasingly crowded, such incised decoration as exists being no longer of Sung quality. The rising porcelain centre of Ching-tê Chên made imitations of Ting ware during the Yüan dynasty, whilst the original kilns appear to have been working at this time and later in the Ming period. A potter named Chou T'an-chüan is reputed to have copied the old ware indetectably towards the end of the Ming dynasty, but since nothing can be attributed to him we are not in a position to judge the truth of the statement—unless, of course, his reputation was justified. Good imitations were made of the old Ting *yao* during the seventeenth and eighteenth centuries, and new forms were developed which were not intended to represent Sung types.[1] The Ch'ing copies are chalk-white instead of the ivory-white of the original wares.

The wares of Tz'ŭ Chou in Chihli are of buff-grey stoneware covered with white slip and then with a transparent glaze—a type made in Sung times, and perhaps before. Sung painting in black or brown slip is the only decoration of the kind to be observed during

[1] Soame Jenyns, in his *Later Chinese Porcelain*, quotes Rücker-Embden as saying that modern Ting bowls are rubbed with the worn-out shoe-soles of rickshaw coolies to remove excessive shine.

the period. Ornament was also incised through slip to the body beneath (*sgraffiato*). During the Ming dynasty jars with flamboyant carved floral decoration, in conjunction with a glossy and viscous glaze, repeated a Sung type, but are more thinly potted. The form varies subtly but perceptibly from the earlier versions, the decoration of which is more restrained. These have been extensively forged.

Copies of Tz'ŭ Chou wares have also been made in Japan in recent times. Orvar Karlbeck (op. cit.) recalls visiting a Japanese factory at Dairen which specialized in copies of Sung wares. Their celadons differed noticeably in colour from the genuine glaze, but the imitations of Tz'ŭ Chou pottery covered with brown glaze through which floral decoration was carved appeared to be a speciality of the factory, which Karlbeck, an exceptionally experienced buyer, regarded as unusually deceptive.

*Ying ch'ing* (the name means *shadowy blue*) is a thin translucent ware, slightly reddish where unglazed, covered with a glaze which is distinctly bluish or greenish where it is thickest. *Ying ch'ing* bowls, like those of Ting *yao*, have an unglazed rim which is often metal-bound. Incised and moulded decoration are both to be seen, the former being the more desirable. Perhaps the most remarkable thing about these wares is the quantity in which they appeared on the market when they they were first brought to Europe. It is impossible to attribute them all to a definite centre of manufacture, which appears to have been widely distributed. The conclusion that many are of comparatively recent manufacture is inescapable, and it is a type which needs much care.

The rarer kinds of Sung wares, such as Ko, Ju, and Kuan, were copied during the eighteenth century in the reign of Yung Chêng but these are highly specialized and the interested collector will have approached them by way of years of experience. Most Sung types were continued during the following Yüan dynasty, and the problem is principally one of dating.

During the Ming dynasty the type of white porcelain with which we are familiar, decorated under the glaze in blue (rarely in copper red) or in overglaze enamels, become the most usual. As I have already mentioned, the potters of the Ch'ing dynasty abused the Ming reign-marks unmercifully. Ming porcelain can be divided into two kinds —heavily-potted wares for export, and more thinly potted wares of much finer quality for home-consumption. The wares of the Ming dynasty have been so misunderstood, both in China and Europe, that many later things have passed for Ming, even though the style was completely improbable, merely because they were not finished slickly in the manner of the later wares of K'ang Hsi and Yung Chêng. In the former reign a system rivalling the modern production-line came into operation; the design was split into components, figures being done by one specialist, landscape by another, diaper borders by another, and so forth. Designs, therefore, tend to lose their individual character and cohesion. As Hobson so truly says: "Ming is not a home for stray pots in which every mongrel piece which has no fixed attribution can find a refuge, nor is it a *locus penetentiae* into which anything wrongfully posing as Sung or Yüan should be degraded when found out."

Among the wares singled out by Hobson for special mention are stoneware ridge-tiles and finials in the form of figures decorated in coloured glazes, reminiscent of those of the T'ang period, which were made at least until recently in traditional forms. Some, of course, are Ming, but others are not. Then there is the class commonly called "enamel on *biscuit*" which loses nothing of its value by being dated correctly to the reign of K'ang Hsi in the Ch'ing dynasty, although a Ming label is still sometimes attached. Kuangtung stoneware figures of lions, Taoist deities, birds on rocks, etc., with a celadon glaze, or a glaze of mottled grey-blue or *flambé* red, are usually nineteenth-century products, but are almost as persistently called Ming as they were when Hobson wrote.[1]

To quote Hobson again: "Not long ago all glazed pottery figures were called Ming as a matter of course. No self-respecting merchant would have thought of stocking anything later in that line of goods; and even the little joss-stick lions with slippery blue-green glaze or patches of turquoise and yellow on a rough oatmeal stoneware, which are bought at Kowloon for a few cents, become Ming in London. The same glazes cover the same body on pottery ginger jars. Extract the ginger and place the pots on a shelf. They become Ming in a twinkling of an eye."

It is important to remember that Hobson was not referring to the expert London dealers. Their reputation is so high, in fact, that

[1] R. L. Hobson: *The Wares of the Ming Dynasty*. London, 1923.

Chinese forgers prefer to sell their wares in the Far East rather than send them to London, because they know quite well that detection would be certain. Chinese pottery and porcelain, however, has an almost fatal attraction for the small dealer whose enthusiasm outruns his knowledge, and it is here that attributions are likely to be optimistic and governed by wishful thinking.

Particularly dangerous are some copies of Ming three-colour ware in which the design is outlined by ridges of clay subsequently filled in with coloured glazes, dark blue or turquoise usually predominating. These have been copied later, in China and Japan.

The early type of stem-cup decorated with three fruits or three fishes in underglaze copper red during the reign of Hsüan-tê (1426-1435) were repeated in the reign of Yung Chêng, and perhaps in that of K'ang Hsi also. Styles of the blue-painted wares of Hsüan-tê were copied, sometimes deceptively, in the sixteenth century, and the reign mark is particularly common on blue-and-white wares of the eighteenth century when the idiosyncrasies of fifteenth-century underglaze blue painting were copied with a certain amount of skill, although a truly deceptive similarity was never achieved. The mark of the later reign of Ch'êng Hua (1465-1487) has been much abused on Ch'ing wares, and has even appeared on specimens with a *famille noir* ground, a sophisticated kind of decoration not introduced until the reign of K'ang Hsi. Some of the K'ang Hsi copies of the wares of this reign are very deceptive, but the body of the later porcelain is usually much whiter than that of the Ming period. This is a useful point of difference; Ming porcelain has a slightly bluish cast. Whatever the makers of detergents would like us to believe, pure white does not exist as a colour. It is either bluish, greyish, or yellowish, however slight the tinge may be. The colour of most K'ang Hsi porcelain shows an almost entire absence of either blue or grey, and it is therefore fairly distinctive.

The famous cups decorated with chickens in "soft" enamels (*tou ts'ai*)—the so-called "chicken" cups of the reign of Ch'êng Hua—have been frequently copied, both in the eighteenth century and in the nineteenth. Plain white bowls of the Hung Chih period (1488-1505) have been decorated in modern times with red, yellow and aubergine enamels by Chinese dealers—a risky pursuit.

Painting in the five-colour palette—enamels combined with underglaze blue—began in the reign of Chia Ching (1522-1566). Some wares with slight blue painting may have later been embellished with enamels, but genuine specimens are a deliberate combination. Japanese copies of this type are very numerous. The Ming tomato-red enamel is not only more opaque than that of the Japanese, but it often induces a slightly iridescent halo in the glaze surface surrounding it. Of course, the addition of enamels to blue-painted Chinese porcelain of all periods was especially done in Europe during the eighteenth century. This is usually termed "clobbering".

Western interest in Ming porcelain is comparatively recent. Copies made for the Western market, therefore, will be relatively modern, and of objects likely to appeal to European and American collectors. Older Chinese copies are of those things which were sought by collectors in that country, particularly the *tou ts'ai* or "soft" enamel colours which were regarded as especially desirable. Ming blue-and-white, almost the only decoration in this colour realizing high prices at present, has been copied in Japan from the nineteenth century onwards, and those of Mikawachi are deceptive although the drawing has a Japanese flavour. The ability to recognize this particular idiom in drawing is especially useful to the collector, since it can hardly be avoided by the Japanese copyist. It is as distinctive in its own way as the sentimental nineteenth-century drawing to be seen on copies of early Italian *maiolica*. The Japanese blue varies in shade from the Chinese, commonly being too grey or too violet in tone, and the musliny texture of the surface has already been mentioned. This can be seen alike on such genuine wares as those of Arita, and on those which copy Chinese porcelain.

Patterns of the period of the Emperor Wan Li (1573-1619) were used in Japan, and copied by the Chinese early in the eighteenth century for export to Europe as well as the designs of Arita which are commonly termed "Chinese Imari". This is an example of the complications which await the student of Far Eastern imitations.

Ch'ing reproductions of Sung and Ming wares have already been discussed. The reign of the Ch'ing Emperor K'ang Hsi was a period of great activity in the arts generally, and many technical developments and innovations took place in this and the following reigns of Yung Chêng and Ch'ien Lung. The nineteenth century is chiefly notable for copies of the wares of these three reigns, although they are almost always inferior.

Enormous prices were paid in Europe for certain Ch'ing wares earlier this century, especially for the flashier varieties such as the *famille noire*—large dramatic vases with a lustrous black ground and rather coarse bird- and flower-painting in brilliant enamels. The black enamel was washed over with green to add lustre. These were the goal of millionaires, and also of forgers. The difficulty facing the forger, however, was to find a porcelain on which to work. Imitations made in European factories would hardly serve for such expensive things; examination would be too close and severe. A way out was found in a few cases by "skinning" a blue-and-white vase of suitable size and shape. The glaze and decoration were ground off, and a new glaze subsequently added on which the required decoration was executed. Examined very carefully, the surface will usually show signs of grinding, and there will be a line of demarcation, not always easy to find, between old glaze and new. Colours will also show some distinct differences. These *famille noire* wares were also imitated in China during the nineteenth century, but do not reach the quality of earlier genuine vases, especially in the colour of the enamels which are "oily" in appearance. The green especially fails to imitate the tone and shade of the K'ang Hsi enamel.

This green is the basis of another large group of wares termed the *famille verte*, which was frequently exported. Although green is the predominant colour, the palette usually includes passages of an enamel blue, and this colour provides a useful but not infallible test of genuineness. On K'ang Hsi specimens the blue, in my experience, always has a slight but distinct "halo" surrounding it; the glaze immediately adjacent to it has a mat surface. This is not always easily to be seen unless the light is allowed to fall on the surface at an angle, but if the piece is turned about in the hands a position will be found where the effect can be observed.

Many forgeries of K'ang Hsi wares, especially blue-and-white, bear the reign mark. This, on genuine specimens, is exceedingly rare, and a marked piece demands more than usually careful examination. Underglaze blue in this reign was a particularly pure sapphire in colour, and, as I have mentioned, the glaze lost the bluish tinge of the earlier Ming and the later Ch'ien Lung porcelain with a consequent whitening of the body.

Particularly popular among collectors have been the wares painted with European subjects and armorial bearings made in China during the eighteenth century for export, and copied from designs provided. These are still sometimes known, quite erroneously, as "Oriental Lowestoft", and are correctly termed "Chinese export porcelain". Armorial porcelain particularly has been much copied in Europe in a hard porcelain approaching that of the original specimen by Samson of Paris, the Herend factory and many others. They can be detected by the European flavour in the drawing, although attempts are made to reproduce the Chinese style of painting European subjects. This is rarely successful, and with a little practice it is quite easy to distinguish without hesitation the hand of a Chinese painter copying a European original. They are also accused by an inaccurate footring.

The *sang de bœuf* and the *flambé* glazes of the seventeenth and eighteenth centuries have been copied both in China and in Europe. Superficially deceptive are some copies made in Staffordshire about seventy years ago by Bernard Moore, who experimented with glazes of this kind, but these are over a stoneware body, not porcelain, although the colour is often very good.

The *famille rose* pigment, the European purple of Cassius, found its way to China in the latter part of the reign of K'ang Hsi, and was much used thereafter, particularly for export wares. These have been copied in Europe, but the shade is incorrect, the starch-blue tinge of the glaze is wrong, and the drawing is weak and obviously by a European hand. European copies can also be found with the ruby-back. Copies made in China in the nineteenth century are often more deceptive, but the designs tend to be overcrowded. Here and there specimens occur which are almost impossible to separate from earlier work.

A word needs to be said on the subject of Chinese porcelain decorated in Europe during the seventeenth and eighteenth centuries, since this is apt to be confusing. *Blanc-de-chine* figures painted with enamels are invariably decorated in Europe, although enamelled *blanc-de-chine* bowls and so forth are not. The decorator was not usually particular about fine points of accuracy, and a Chinese Kuan Yin with added flowers in the Japanese style has been recorded. Some of this kind of painting was in "cold" colour and has usually flaked off, although traces sometimes remain, just as they can be seen on some early European porcelain figures. Both German and Dutch decorators added enamel colours to blue-and-white Chinese porcelain. Good specimens are highly valued, particularly if the hand of the painter is known. J. F. Ferner is an example. Poor specimens, with elaborate painting of low quality, have been awarded the derogatory description of "clobbered". Their value is small. European painting over Chinese monochrome glazes has been noticed, and Dutch painting frequently appears on Japanese porcelain.

The difference between this and Oriental decoration is not usually difficult to perceive. Oriental enamels are slightly raised from the surface of the glaze, some at least are translucent, and their surface is glossy. European enamels, on the other hand, are thin, mat, and opaque. The use of perspective and shading, both foreign to the Chinese, also betrays a European hand. All these things are, of course, collectors' pieces for which high prices are sometimes paid, but they are mentioned here because they tend to be confusing to the novice.

Among the early copies made in China and Japan must be classed the repetition of seventeenth-century European *faïence* shapes in porcelain painted with blue underglaze. Although they cannot be regarded as forgeries, and are collectors' items in their own right, they, too, cause a certain amount of confusion. Many more of them were made in Japan than is generally recognized, and the glaze should be examined for the typical musliny surface.

A discussion in detail of the observed varieties of early wares which have been copied in China would occupy the pages of this book to the exclusion of everything else. The collector soon learns to regard these not as a hazard but as a challenge to increasing powers of perception which adds to the fascination of the study in which he is engaged. If there were no problems of this kind the serious collector, as opposed to the collector of ornament, would disappear.

The inexperienced buyer can safeguard himself adequately by acquiring specimens from dealers of reputation and integrity in the West whose knowledge is usually far greater than that of Chinese dealers. The search for bargains in the Far East will meet with small reward. Oriental dealers are excellent stage-managers, but the buyer has to depend on his own knowledge. Elaborate stories of fine pieces smuggled from Communist China into Hong Kong can nearly always be discounted. Objects offered from an unknown source in the elaborately padded Chinese cases also need very careful examination.

Despite the old adage, fine feathers do not necessarily make fine birds.

It would, perhaps, be salutary to repeat a story told by an American visitor to a modern Chinese porcelain factory some years ago. The manager of the factory asked him, when he returned to the West, to request Sir Percival David, the noted collector of Chinese works of art, to reproduce both sides of his vases in future catalogues because they did not know what to put on the other side of those illustrations they were copying. This information can be put to good use when examining modern copies.

Persian pottery is not often forged, but fakes are very common. Nearly everything has been excavated in a fragmentary condition, and Armenian dealers in particular are past-masters of the art of making a complete object from a few, often unrelated fragments, supplying the deficiencies with plaster and paint. A bowl which has more than two-thirds of the original material is worth buying if the decoration is good; even lesser fragments may be desirable for one reason or another, but it is essential to know exactly what one is buying. Here the ultra-violet lamp is invaluable. Persian bowls which appear complete, or almost so, by ordinary light will sometimes be revealed as pitiful wrecks under ultra-violet light. This is discussed in Appendix 3.

The greatest care is needed in buying the more important-looking varieties, particularly those with enamel (*minai*) painting. The iridescence of the glaze, which is commonly seen on genuine specimens, is sometimes reproduced by transferring iridescent patches of glaze, fragment by fragment, from worthless shards. When it is impossible to subject a specimen to detailed examination, much may sometimes be learned from tapping the rim. The peculiarly "dead" sound of overmuch plaster soon becomes recognizable.

Persian tiles have been reproduced within the last hundred years or so for tourists by potters in Ispahan and Teheran. Particularly popular as a subject is a mounted falconer. These appear to be quite new and have no traces of adherent mortar as a rule, although this could easily be supplied.

Isnik pottery has not been deceptively forged to a great extent, probably because the characteristic red pigment is difficult to imitate. Some early copies were made in Italy. The more recent ones rarely follow the Turkish technique with any degree of exactness, and most should not prove deceptive to anyone acquainted with genuine wares.

A factory for the manufacture of Turkish pottery, then miscalled "Rhodian", was established by Emile Sanson, and continued to work from about 1875 to 1900.

It is impossible to improve upon the dictum of Emil Hannover when marks are being considered: "The surest way to get together a bad collection is to rely on marks." Yet it often happens, even now, that beginners will receive the news that they have bought a reproduction with shocked incredulity, and point to the mark in refutation. The fact is that the legal protection accorded to old marks is very slight in any country. Where a factory still exists and uses the old mark, it can, of course, take steps to put an end to forgery, but it is usually not worth doing, since they are interested in selling current production, not specimens of their old wares.

If one is not well acquainted with old pottery and porcelain, then it is unwise to acquire it other than from a reputable source, and it is better to go to a member of a recognized trade association which does its best to exclude anyone not reaching a proper standard of knowledge and integrity. These associations exist in England, America, and on the Continent.

The value of marks on Chinese porcelain has already been discussed. Those on European pottery and porcelain have been copied, simulated, and forged from the time when the first factories were established. Among the earliest examples of this kind of chicanery are the marks of the Thuringian factories, such as the crossed hayforks of Rudolstadt, the crossed L's of Limbach, and so forth, all of which were intended to deceive the casual purchaser into thinking them the crossed swords of Meissen. The use of the *AR* monogram by Helena Wolfsohn has been mentioned; Carl Thieme used the crossed swords with the letter *T* between the hilts; Meyer added a letter *M* in the same place; and Samson uses an *S*. Genuine Meissen marks included a dot between the hilts (the "Dot" period, or *die Punktzeit*), and an asterisk (the period of Count Marcolini's directorate). Very occasionally letters (of which *K* is an example[1]) appear between the *points* of early Meissen swords.

The monogram of Sèvres—the crossed *L*'s which were also the Royal monogram—appear from 1753 onwards up to the Revolution. These are accompanied by a date-letter which indicates the year of

[1] Probably denoting the work of the underglaze-blue painter, Kretschmar.

manufacture, starting with *A* in 1753, and omitting *W*. These letters were doubled in 1778, beginning with *AA* and finishing with *PP* in 1793, used until 17 July. The Royal monogram was used again during the reign of Louis XVIII (1814-1824). These date-letters, however, are not reliable. The decorator, Caille, added the letter *C* to monograms on fakes made towards the end of the nineteenth century. This would indicate 1755 on genuine specimens. The decorator Lehoujour (or perhaps Levy) used the letter *L*, and *BB* stands for Bareau et Bareau, also working at the end of the nineteenth century. The Minton factory sometimes used an approximate simulation of the Royal monogram in conjunction with the letter *M*. The painters and decorators of Sèvres porcelain signed their work with initials and symbols which are listed in the various books on marks. These are often added by fakers, but the date-letter sometimes does not agree with the period during which the artists are known to have worked, or the subjects are different from those which they were listed as painting.

English porcelain of the eighteenth century was not universally marked. The most frequently copied is the gold anchor of Chelsea. The red anchor is rarely copied, although I have examined a tea-service thus marked which had small bread-and-butter plates. These were not introduced until the 1830s. The incised triangle mark has been mentioned, but the raised anchor mark seems to have defeated the forger so far. One sometimes sees genuine specimens of the raised anchor period from which the mark (an anchor in relief raised on an oval medallion[1]) has "fled", leaving an oval patch bare of glaze. The mark might be replaced by a restorer, but this would be gilding the lily. A painted anchor is also the genuine mark of Sceaux and Venice, but it is much larger than the genuine Chelsea anchor.

Some forgeries of Derby figures bear the gold anchor of Chelsea. A crown similar to that used on later Derby production with the monogram ꞵB immediately under it has been awarded to makers of reproductions named Bell et Block, of Paris. The Derby factory was in the reproduction business until 1770, and called itself the "second Dresden". It refused to mark its wares at all for many years with the intention of passing them off as either Chelsea or Meissen.

[1] This mark was probably first adopted to prevent other manufacturers from passing off their wares as coming from Chelsea.

A number of eighteenth-century marks were imitations. Worcester used a seal-mark based on a similar mark appearing on Chinese porcelain, and some of its wares decorated with Chinese designs were not marked at all for obvious reasons. It also made use of the Meissen crossed swords with the figures "9" or "91" between the hilts. The Lowestoft factory did not adopt a mark; instead, it used those of other factories, including Worcester and Meissen. The Bow factory's best-known mark, an anchor and dagger, was obviously based on that of Chelsea.

Inscriptions on *maiolica* and *faïence* are common, and dates sometimes occur. They were also added later to genuine specimens in some cases, since dated examples are always much more in demand. Additions of this kind have to be made in an enamel suitably fluxed to lower the temperature at which it needs to be fired to a point where it will not damage the glaze. Collectors well acquainted with such things are not likely to be deceived.

Specimens of pottery and porcelain should always be attributed by the appearance of the body, glaze, and decoration. There is no other safe method. Certainly to rely on marks will make the acquisition of fakes and forgeries inevitable.

It is possible to discuss ceramic forgeries and their detection at somewhat greater length than has been possible in other fields because factory archives have not uncommonly survived, and the popularity of both pottery and porcelain among collectors, proved (if proof were needed) by the number of attempts to produce deceptive copies, has caused the subject to be studied in detail. There is, for these reasons, far less room for speculation, and judgements can often be more firmly based. Generally, much more is known about porcelain manufacture than about the various kinds of pottery. Porcelain was extremely fashionable as interior decoration from the seventeenth to the nineteenth century, whereas pottery was more utilitarian in character and intended for humbler households. Chinese porcelain, of course, has always been in great demand among European collectors and those of China. The literature in Chinese is considerable in extent, but the exact meaning of these commentaries is not always easy to decipher. The *Ch'ing-tê Chên Tao Lu* (translated by Geoffrey Sayer) has some illuminating comments on the subject of Ch'ing reproductions.

*Chapter VI*

# Glass

> Remember that all tricks are either knavish or childish.
> SAMUEL JOHNSON

The date of the discovery of glass is lost in the remote mists of antiquity. Certainly it was known in Egypt in predynastic times as a glaze for stone-beads, and its use for this purpose preceded the making of glass vessels. Glass is not, by strict definition, a solid; it is a supercooled liquid. When glass cools from a high temperature it becomes increasingly viscous and passes into a rigid state without crystallizing. Under suitable conditions it can be made to flow, even at normal temperatures. For instance, surface scratches can be removed with the aid of jeweller's rouge and a chamois leather because the surface is dragged until the scratches are filled. Plate-glass windows which have been installed for long periods are found to be slightly thicker at the bottom than at the top, proving that a slight downward flow has occurred.

Apart from manufactured glass, there are natural glasses which also result from the fusion of silica. One of these is obsidian, a volcanic glass used for the making of knives by flaking in much the same way as flint tools were made. Obsidian, however, is very dark in colour due to the presence of iron in the rocks from which it was fused. The principal source of silica in manufactured glass is sand, and the amorphous structure of glass causes it to break with what is termed a conchoidal fracture, similar in appearance to the chipped surface of a flint. True porcelain exhibits the same fracture (see page 148) because it is also a kind of glass made from natural substances.

A recipe for ordinary window-glass runs somewhat as follows:

| | |
|---|---|
| Sand (silica) | 100 parts |
| Soda | 30 parts |
| Chalk (calcium carbonate) | 35 parts |

Lead-glass (English flint-glass), much used for ornamental cutting, is made from:

| | |
|---|---|
| Sand | 100 parts |
| Potassium carbonate | 20 parts |
| Red lead (lead oxide) | 60 parts |

To both of these is normally added a variable quantity of cullet (broken glass) which assists the fusion of the other ingredients.

Glass is formed in a number of ways, one of which—the blowing process—is peculiar to this material. When glass is in its plastic state it is extremely ductile; perhaps the nearest familiar comparison is to molten toffee. This can be drawn out into threads; the same can be done with glass. I have not experimented with toffee-blowing, but it seems certain that it could be done. Glass in this state is gathered on the end of an iron blow-pipe, rolled on an iron table (called a "marver") and blown into a hollow bubble. The bubble can be shaped in various ways—by rolling on the table, by swinging, which gives it an elongated pear-shape like a retort with a straight neck, and by shaping with various iron tools. It can also be cut with shears. In this way the skilled worker can make a great variety of objects. Plasticity is regained by heating whenever necessary.

Much old glass has been formed in this way and the point of attachment to the blow-pipe can often be seen, although, in the case of wine-glasses the bowls of which are formed by the blow-pipe, the later addition of stem and foot disguises the original point of attachment. A defect, however, does appear underneath the foot of some old glasses made by hand, in the form of a roughened patch which is known as the "pontil" mark. This was sometimes smoothed by grinding, but the mark is not thereby entirely removed, remaining as an approximately circular area of polished glass immediately below the attachment of the stem to the foot.

Glass can also be formed in moulds. This needs an outer matrix and an inner core. Some early glass was shaped by wrapping it round the core (which was subsequently removed) whilst in the molten state. Very occasionally the space between matrix and core has been filled with powdered glass and fired to melt the contents into an homogeneous mass. Such things as small figures, which can neither be blown nor cast, have been made by manipulating glass softened by heating, and many examples of this kind of ingenuity survive.

Sheet-glass was made formerly in one of two ways—by blowing and rolling a cylinder which was slit down one side and opened out, or by casting on a flat bed. Plate-glass is made by the latter method today, although refinements of technique have been introduced. Plate-glass first became a commercial proposition in France about 1690.

Sheet-glass made by the process first mentioned is to be recognized by the slight irregularities of surface to be seen especially when light falls on it at an angle. It was employed in old mirrors, and as glazing for bookcases, and once its peculiarities are known it is easy to recognize whether or not old glasses have been replaced by modern. When replacement of this kind is noticed a specimen should be examined with more than usual care. It is possible that, in the course of two centuries or so, one or two panes from a door which has several panes set in glazing-bars may have been broken, but completely new glass in both doors suggests, at the least, that the specimen has been seriously damaged at some time or another in the past, and it may, of course, be entirely new.

Sheet-glass made by blowing is thinner than most modern factory-made glass, and this can also be noticed in old mirrors, where the glass is much thinner than that used for the same purpose later. To find the thickness of mirror-glass a coin should be placed on edge against the surface. The apparent distance between the edge of the coin and its reflection is the thickness of the glass. A Queen Anne mirror, for instance, which has a perfectly even surface, and a glass of a thickness equivalent to that of a modern mirror, is either completely spurious or the glass has been broken and replaced. In the latter case, of course, a good deal of the market value has been lost. Mirrors are also discussed in Chapter III.

The mirrors of the eighteenth century were "silvered" with mercury, and this will be evident if the back is examined. A new process introduced in the nineteenth century resulted in a final coating of a reddish-brown composition. If the glass is thin and the surface irregular it may be old despite a nineteenth-century appearance on the reverse, because mirrors have sometimes been resilvered. This, however, usually reduces the value considerably and is not advised. The eighteenth-century process is known, and can still be used.

The reflection of an old mirror is usually blackish and slightly hazy. Bevels on old mirror-glass are extremely shallow and much wider than those of modern glass. In some cases they may even be difficult to see. New mirror-glass is faked with the correct silvering, and the kind of spotting and damage one expects to be present. Where the colour of the clear glass can be seen, that of the eighteenth century will have a dark tinge, whereas that of the nineteenth century and later will be much whiter. The faker tries to reproduce the dark tone by modifying the "silvering". Of course, if genuinely old glass has been resilvered by the old methods it matters little whether the restoration can be detected or not.

Glass is decorated in a variety of ways. It can be coloured with metallic oxides of the same kind as those used for colouring pottery and porcelain glazes. The addition of tin oxide makes it white and opaque, like the glaze of tin-enamelled pottery. Glass opacified in this way was used during the seventeenth and eighteenth centuries as a porcelain substitute (*milch-glas*), and manufacturers have recently revived the practice for plates in "fire-proof" glass. Most glasses have a natural green colouring which has often been removed or modified, usually by means of manganese dioxide. This leaves the metal with a faint tinge of yellow or green. Colouring of this kind is due to minute traces of various substances which occur as impurities. It can be imitated, but not reproduced exactly. Modern glass of good quality is virtually colourless.

Other methods of decorating include painting with "cold" colour (lacquer colour) and true enamelling; the application of trailed threads of glass; engraving; and cutting into light-reflecting facets. Engraving was done with a diamond, and this leaves a characteristic narrow incised line, or with small wheels charged with abrasives of the kind commonly employed by lapidaries for carving hardstones and gems. These wheels leave broader and deeper incisions, and sometimes the two techniques were combined. Engraving of this kind was used to cut patterns in *intaglio* which were more or less elaborate on clear glass. It was also used in conjunction with layers or "flashings" of coloured glasses applied one over the other, the engraver cutting through the layers to the different colour beneath. This can be seen in the "Portland" or "Barberini" vase in the British Museum, and was a Roman development of the gem-engraver's technique.

Cut-glass is more broadly ground into facets like the cutting of precious stones, the facets collecting and reflecting light in a way which enhances the brilliance of the glass. Lead-glass was particularly employed for this kind of work. Cut-glass is reproduced in moulds at a fraction of the cost involved in time and labour—a practice by no means new, and it is essential to know how the two may be separated. The facets of old cut-glass are ground to a sharp edge easily perceptible to the finger-tips. Moulded reproductions have blunt edges. This can also be seen under a magnifying-glass, the appearance of the edges in a moulded specimen being unmistakable. Some modern reproductions are first moulded and the principal facets then sharpened on the abrasive wheel. This saves a certain amount of time, and is inclined to be more deceptive. Very rarely are all the facets sharpened in this way, and those which are deep and awkward to get at are left untouched. The remedy is to examine the whole of a specimen, and not the more obvious parts of it. The presence of mould-seams, of course, is an immediate condemnation. Glass cut by a craftsman on his wheel will show traces of irregularity in the pattern which will be missing from a moulded reproduction.

The colour of the metal should be carefully examined against a background of good white paper, and unless the reader is familiar with the colour of old glass it is better to do this alongside an attested specimen of similar characteristics. The bluish-green or greyish tinge of much old glass is unmistakable, even without the assistance of the background, to an experienced observer.

It is also necessary to be alert for signs of recutting. This does not mean that a specimen is spurious, but that it has been damaged. For instance, an elaborate and vulnerable scalloped rim may have been ground away altogether to disguise serious chipping. The glass-cutter's abrasive wheel is sometimes used on porcelain, particularly that from China, a badly-chipped neck, for example, being ground down to disguise the damage.

Although it is virtually impossible for a forger to imitate old glass

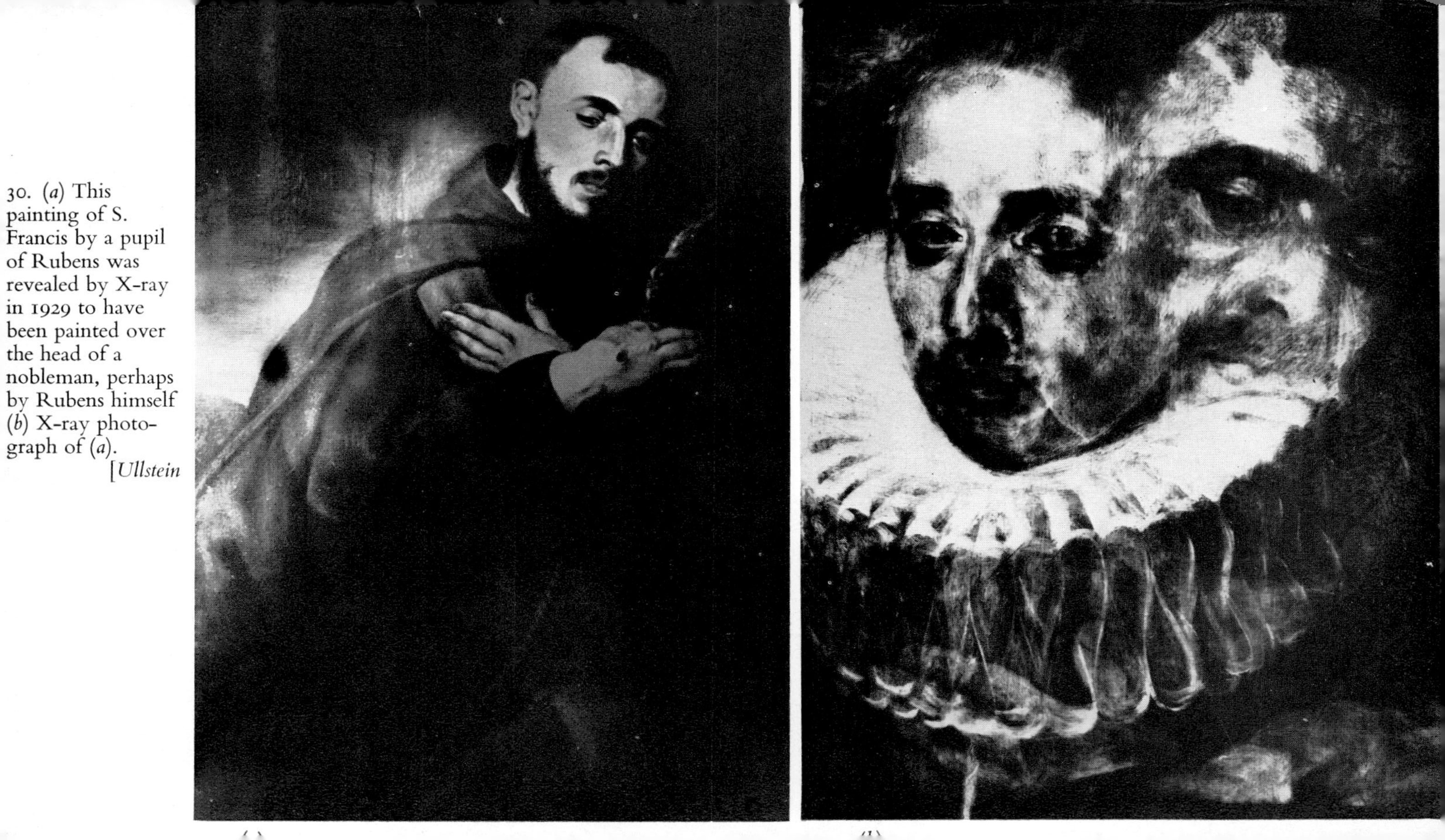

30. (*a*) This painting of S. Francis by a pupil of Rubens was revealed by X-ray in 1929 to have been painted over the head of a nobleman, perhaps by Rubens himself (*b*) X-ray photograph of (*a*).
[*Ullstein*

31. Brush-strokes seen by X-ray. (*Top*) A genuine painting showing the coherent nature of the brush-strokes and the underlying structure. (*Bottom*) A forgery of the same subject. See Chapter VII. [*Ullstein*

successfully in a way which will deceive the experienced observer, plain antique glasses worth a few pounds have had engraved decoration added which, had it been genuine, would have made them much more valuable. A common target for this kind of fraud is the Jacobite wine-glass made for the followers of the Old and Young Pretenders during the eighteenth century.

Attention should be directed towards the "frosted" areas of the design—the mat, unpolished effect which forms part of the pattern and results from the removal of the surface. In a spurious example the mat surface will be even, without variation. It may be either a dull grey or have the appearance of being lightly polished. An old specimen, however, which has been frequently handled, will have irregular patches of brightness where contact with the fingers has repolished the surface. Set beside a genuine example, spurious engraving appears obviously mechanical, and the style will vary to a more or less marked degree from eighteenth-century work.

There are always differences between old glass and reproductions. The points especially to be examined are threefold:

(1) the colour of the metal
(2) its appearance when held to the light
(3) evidence of age such as wear and scratches, and, in the case of ancient glass, of burial, to be seen in degenerative surface changes of various kinds.

Completely clear glass, without colour, is modern glass made from refined materials. The slight colouration of antique glass is, as we have seen, due to the presence of impurities, and even where this has been cleared by the addition of manganese some colour remains. The commonest impurity is iron, which is ubiquitous. It can be seen equally well in glass and in the light biscuit colour of the unglazed parts of certain porcelains, especially those from China.

In early times the sources of raw materials were selected from observation of the colour yielded, those which had the least effect being the most valued. A greenish or yellowish tinge is invariable, especially in glass manufactured before methods of decolourizing were devised. The clearest glass in antiquity was probably Alexandrian, but it usually exhibits green with a faint blue tinge; Egyptian glass is faintly purple; Syrian glass is either a faint green or a pale light yellow;

old German glass from the Rhineland was often bluish-green. These observations are not consistent enough to be used as a method of identification, but they help to establish the genuineness or otherwise of doubtful specimens.

Originally glass was made from quartz sand, quartz, siliceous pebbles, flints, or some similar source of silica. When the place of manufacture was inland it commonly included potash made from wood-ashes (potash-glass), whilst that made near the sea-coasts contained soda which came from the burning of sea-weed (soda-glass). There is a distinct difference between the two. Potash-glass needs a higher temperature to fire it, and it hardens rapidly into the rigid state on cooling. The melting-point of soda-glass is lower, and it remains longer in the plastic state. It is, therefore, more easily moulded, blown, and drawn into fine threads. Soda-glass was much used throughout the Mediterranean littoral; potash-glass, more suitable for cutting, polishing and engraving, was employed for much Continental production of ornamental glassware. The nature of the material to some extent governed the kind of decoration selected.

When old glass is held to the light, or closely examined against a sheet of good white paper, small air-bubbles will be seen, similar in many ways to those which appear in much greater profusion in Sung stoneware glazes (see Appendix 1). These are virtually unknown in modern glass, but it is extremely rare to find a metal made much earlier than 1800 which will not show at least some of them. Dark specks in the metal are impurities of one kind or another, perhaps unfused sand, and these again are not found in modern glass. Small surface defects can also be noticed on some old glass.

We have already seen that glass is peculiar in its structure, and is, in fact, a supercooled liquid. As a substance it is resistant to change which results from the passage of time but is by no means immune from it. Exposure to a humid atmosphere, or burial in damp ground, leads to the formation of an iridescence which is the result of the interaction of the surface with carbonic acid. This neutralizes the alkali in the glass, and the disintegrating surface assumes a laminated structure. The same effect can be seen on pottery glazes, notably those of Persia from the ninth to the twelfth centuries, and on those of the Han dynasty of China.

At first iridescence is merely a film on the surface which gives a metallic lustre, appearing in reflected light as a rainbow-like display of colour similar to that of petrol spilled on a wet road. This layer gradually penetrates downwards from the surface, and eventually it can be flaked off. Iridescence of this kind is especially likely to attack glass which has been decolourized with manganese dioxide, and it tends to affect least those glasses which have been coloured with metallic oxides. The predominant colour of the iridescence seems to be governed by the natural colour-tinge of the glass. If this is yellow, the iridescence will be mainly golden yellow; if green, this colour will be predominant. Coloured glasses usually develop a slight silvery glint on the surface. Iridescence also causes glass to become lighter in weight.

This deterioration is, of course, evidence of age in many cases, and it is therefore faked on new glasses, and occasionally on old ones which are deficient in this respect because it tends to increase the value. Iridescent flakes are sometimes scaled off broken pieces and specimens of small antique value, and cemented on to the surface of other, more saleable specimens. This is also done to pottery glazes. Colouring with some kind of silver paint is rarely very deceptive, but it is done; and stippling with silver and variously coloured pigments, if well executed, can be superficially deceptive at first. Natural iridescence is induced by leaving glass in a cesspool for long periods. Specimens purporting to be ancient glass which entirely lack iridescence are probably not genuine, and certainly need very careful examination.

Glass which has been coloured by the addition of metallic oxides will also show some changes as a result of the passage of time. Opaque colours are the least affected. Emerald-green retains its shade particularly well; red and brown retain their shade to a great extent; blue is perhaps the least resistant to change. All such glasses, however, will exhibit some modification or muting of shade. Faked glasses are nearly always much brighter, with more vivid colouring, which is particularly obvious if they are placed with genuine specimens.

These, of course, are general observations; the specialist in old glass knows that there are many characteristics of provenance and period which must agree before a specimen can be regarded as genuine, including the kind of metal used, the form, the decoration, and such points as the shape of a handle (when present), and the treatment of rim and base. All these must accord with the colour of the metal and the degenerative changes discussed before a specimen can be accepted.

Enamelling has been used on ancient glass as decoration, and nowhere to better effect than in certain medieval Near Eastern specimens, especially represented in European collections by the highly-valued mosque lamps—actually glass-containers for a separate oil-lamp. The demand for these, and the high prices paid, has led to a certain amount of faking, principally in the touching up of defective enamels in "cold" colours, which can be scratched with a knife. Genuine fragments can sometimes be cemented together. This, of course, is done quite legitimately. In a case known to me the fragments of an important lamp were ingeniously cemented over a perspex base, enabling a collection of fragments to be used for purposes of study. It is said that fragments have been built up into a complete object by fusing, but I have not seen an example of this kind of work, and consider it to be technically too difficult for a deceptive repair to be made in this way. It is possible that the report owes something to the writings of Theophilus (see footnote, page 206), who gives many recipes for the manufacture of glass of various kinds. He recommends the use of blue and green powdered glass with a low melting-point as a cement to repair a broken goblet, the interior being filled with ash during firing in a kiln to distribute heat and preserve the form. This is feasible, but highly dangerous even in the hands of a skilled workman, and could hardly be used for enamelled glass. Later glasses of suitable kinds are sometimes repaired by welding with the application of local heat. Broken wine-glass stems are repaired in this way.

Mosque lamps were copied very closely in the nineteenth century by a Frenchman, Joseph Brocard. A specimen of his work is in the British Museum. Another European forgery, perhaps by Brocard, was revealed by an inaccurate inscription. Islamic glass of this kind does not appear to have been systematically examined by ultra-violet light, but Rorimer's experience with Syrian glass (see page 265) suggests that something of value might emerge.

Later enamelled glasses with defective decoration have also been restored with "cold" painting. Repairs with enamels hardly seem possible, although those who have had experience of the ingenuity of the restorer would prefer not to place it entirely outside the bounds of possibility. Not only must the difficulty of matching the shade be overcome, however, but the reheating necessary to fuse the new enamels would affect those already existing, as well as the surface appearance of the glass.

"Cold" or lacquer painting must not necessarily be regarded as faked or restored. Some quite genuine glass was decorated in this way, and evaluation depends principally on style. A mixture of enamels and "cold" painting, however, especially if the design itself is an amalgam of the two techniques, is highly suspicious. The rare enamel painting of the German *Hausmaler* (see page 150) is also to be found on glass, and forgeries exist which, if executed on glass of the period, must be recognized by the style of the decoration.

When we come to examine later European glasses the question of colour will also be found to be important. As a general rule the deeper the tint the older the glass, but this is not invariable. The usual shades are bluish-green, greenish-yellow, brownish with perhaps a violet tinge suggesting the presence of manganese, and a faint yellow. Of course, all these tints are imitated, not only by fakers but by those specializing in the matching of old glass who may be required to supply missing parts. When glass is examined it is important to see that everything is right—colour, type of metal, form, and the small idiosyncrasies of manufacture common to the period.

Glass made in the seventeenth century is usually lighter in weight than most eighteenth-century glass in comparable specimens. Some seventeenth-century glass in which too much alkali was included developed a network of fine interior cracks, known as "criselling". Such glass will eventually decompose. Criselling is found in glass made in England, Germany, and the Netherlands, and can also be noticed in occasional Chinese specimens. The English glassmaker, Ravenscroft, introduced lead into his glass in an attempt to rectify this fault, and lead-glass became popular for decorative cutting and slicing.

During the Renaissance Venetian glassmakers devised a technique of embedding threads of white opaque glass in clear glass, known as *latticino*. This they developed to form elaborate lace-work patterns, and threads of other colours were used in the same way. During the eighteenth century this technique was employed in England and Holland for the decoration of wine-glass stems, made by drawing out and twisting glass containing air-bubbles. These are called air-twists.

The same thing was done with clear metal containing white and coloured glasses. Old English white-twist stems are much whiter than contemporary Dutch work. Colour-twist is usually found in conjunction with white-twist, sometimes with air-twist, and sometimes with both.[1] Forgeries more commonly utilize colour-twist decoration. It appears to be more deeply embedded in the stem than in genuine specimens, where the decoration seems much nearer the surface of the glass. Forgeries of air-twist stems, to which the same remarks apply, are much less frequent. The threads in forgeries often lack continuity, and are not symmetrically disposed.

Observation suggests that the diameter of the foot of an old wine-glass is always greater than that of the bowl, whereas the reverse is the case in modern glasses of the same kind.

The buyer should always be alert for replacements. Upon careful examination it will sometimes be found that such things as honey-jars have covers which do not belong to the base. Usually care is taken to match the parts as closely as possible, and the difference in the decoration is often slight. Whilst this is certainly not fraud unless the specimen is offered as being in original condition, and it will obviously have its own value as decoration, it has not the value of an object in perfect condition.

Scratches are an important indication. In the course of centuries glass comes into contact with a great deal of abrasive dust. In the case of a wine-glass, for instance, much dust falls into the bowl, and if this is polished with a dry duster small scratches remain behind which will accumulate and become increasingly obvious. Scratches under the foot, or under the base, are the result of dust on table-tops. Multiple scratches of this kind are acquired very slowly, and, in time, they cover the surface with a dense network at the appropriate places. A consideration of the way in which they are acquired will show it to be extremely unlikely that any two scratches will have precisely the same direction, and that, especially under a powerful glass, this will give a well-marked appearance which it will be impossible to imitate. Forgers know all about scratches, and try to reproduce them with emery-powder, but faked scratches are usually too deep, and in any case have far too great a proportion running in approximately the same

[1] This complex subject is discussed and classified by E. Barrington Haynes: *Glass*. Harmondsworth, 1947.

direction or in a noticeable pattern, simply because they have all been made mechanically at the same time. Equally suspicious, of course, is a complete absence of such marks.

Paperweights are now much in demand among collectors, and high prices are paid for rare specimens. The most valued were produced in France at Baccarat, St Louis, and Clichy during the 1840s. The initials B, SL, and C sometimes appear among the intricate decoration and are regarded as identification marks of the factories mentioned. Some specimens are dated, also among the decoration. Similar weights were made in London about the same time, and in the West of England. Production in Germany, Bohemia, and Belgium was considerable, and copies are now being produced in Czechoslovakia (formerly Bohemia) and offered to antique dealers, and dealers in decorative glass, as modern work at low prices. With scratches added they could possibly be passed off as original work, but the decoration is usually coarse and the quality poor. Since value is mainly based on quality of workmanship it is unlikely that anyone could be induced to pay a great deal for them.

The so-called old "Irish" cut-glass, much of which is English-made when it is genuine, has been reproduced in Bohemia and America, but the colour of the metal is usually incorrect and too strong, and the quality and workmanship is inferior. The collector who has an eye for quality, therefore, will not be deceived.

Candelabra and chandeliers made up from cut crystal drops are being extensively reproduced on the Continent and exported to England as interior decoration. Prices are usually low when the work is sold as modern. The trade has received a fillip recently from the increasing popularity of this kind of decoration. Missing parts of such chandeliers, of course, have always been "made up" from the stock of old drops which every dealer likes to accumulate. Some chandeliers are made entirely of matched and assembled drops which did not start life together, and they have wittily been described as "a miniature history of glass during the last one hundred and fifty years". The ability to tell the difference between old and modern drops is mainly a matter of experience in seeing and handling all kinds. It is, perhaps, more essential in the field of old glass than in most others to be able to study the difference between old and modern productions. Many forgeries can be recognized immediately from the appearance of the metal.

Problems of attribution sometimes present difficulties. In general, nineteenth-century revivals of old styles are not likely to be deceptive. Some modern Venetian glass is "bubbled" in much the same way as old glass, although the metal was exceptionally clear during the nineteenth century. Occasional specimens of modern Venetian work are especially deceptive, and could pass quite easily for those of Renaissance times.

More ambitious forgeries include those of the early German *Zwischengoldgläser*. This type needs two glasses, usually of tumbler-shape, ground to fit exactly one within the other, the outer glass being bottomless. Gold-leaf is then applied to the surface and engraved into patterns. When the two are fitted together the decoration appears on the inside, and all that is necessary to complete the job is to fuse both together and finish by grinding. Both metal and decoration should be examined closely for signs of divergence from old work.

Although the principal types of forgeries have been mentioned, it must be remembered that popular and attractive styles and techniques have been copied in subsequent periods, and these are not necessarily forgeries. Much depends on age and intention.

*Chapter VII*

## *Painting and Drawing*

> Painting is not a matter of dreaming, or being inspired. It is a handicraft, and a good craftsman is needed to do it well.
>
> PIERRE-AUGUSTE RENOIR

The subject of spurious paintings and drawings is so vast that it would need several volumes to examine it in detail. This chapter cannot do more than discuss it in outline, although the Bibliography contains a number of suggestions for those who wish to know more.

An oil-painting is a series of layers. First, there is the support, which may be canvas, wood, or metal. If it is canvas it will be nailed over a frame known as a stretcher which is adjustable in size, enabling the tension of the canvas to be altered. The support is first primed to form a foundation for the subsequent application of paint. Primings are often white or greyish-white, but other colours are sometimes employed. Next comes the oil-paint which is the actual picture, and lastly a protective film in the form of varnish.

Pigments are of various kinds. In former times they were made for the most part from minerals and earths ground to a fine powder and suspended in oil and resin (the vehicle). More recently, pigments have been synthesized chemically. Some pigments alter drastically in shade and intensity with exposure to light, and they are then termed "fugitive". Few of the early pigments altered seriously in this way, although some did so to a variable extent.

Every artist evolves his own technique for handling his materials, and this is partly governed by their nature. For example, some paints resist the action of brushing more than others (they have greater viscosity), and the surface tends to be uneven and raised here and there in slight relief. The marks of the brush can plainly be seen. Other painters (Rembrandt is an example) made deliberate use of this, and the technique is then referred to as *impasto*. The surface appearance will also be affected by the instruments used to apply the paint; the effect of the palette-knife is quite distinct from that of the brush.

The viscosity of paint can be reduced by the addition of "thinners", such as turpentine, which in turn leads to a smooth surface that often resembles enamel on copper rather than paint on canvas. This slick technique is often used by fashionable artists for highly-finished work. The work of Mengs is an example.

It will be seen from these brief remarks that much may be learned from careful observation of the surface of a picture before we even look at the subject matter and the materials used.

The forger, if his work is to pass all the tests which can be applied, must deceive on several points. The first is the stretcher, which must be made of a kind of wood in use at the time. Inventory marks and those of famous collections are sometimes burnt in on the wood, but these, of course, may be forged. The stretcher should be correctly formed, and have the signs of age, some of which may be found in Chapter II. An old stretcher, however, cannot be regarded as being in the nature of a certificate of authenticity, but, paradoxically, a new stretcher can often be regarded as a sign that a painting is as old as it purports to be.

Until the end of the eighteenth century canvases were woven by hand, and it is not difficult to distinguish between a hand and a machine weave, once both kinds have been studied. The forger usually solves the problem of stretcher and canvas in one of two ways. Either he buys a poor painting of the right period, or very near to it, and cleans off the paint-layer as far as possible, executing the new work over the remnants of the old (Plate 30 illustrates an X-ray which clearly shows one painting over another), or he glues his forged canvas on to a new canvas and stretcher, imitating a genuinely old picture on a disintegrating canvas which has been lined. The second method is rarely adopted because it detracts from the general appearance of age which the forger desires to simulate. Lining is never undertaken without good reason, and an examination of the condition of the edges of the canvas which purports to be old will enable an estimate to be made of its age and condition. Old works are sometimes put on new stretchers for genuine reasons, but in these cases the canvas ought to show the original nail-holes, since there could be no valid reason for using the same holes. Paint which overflows the border of the canvas on to the sides is also evidence of restretching, and may be evidence of cutting down. This practice is discussed later.

Originally stretchers were only frames, often with reinforcing battens running from one side to the other. In the eighteenth century the present system of loose joints was adopted, at first with a single tightening wedge, and later with two wedges, in each corner. The collector without skill in these matters would do well to leave the tightening of wedges to an expert. Fragile canvases have been torn by careless tightening. It is possible for anyone who has handled a large number of old paintings to date a picture fairly closely from the stretcher alone.

The first paintings intended to be portable were on wooden panels. Vasari, referring to the Bellinis[1] (father and sons, *fl.* 1400-1507), says that painting on canvas was almost invariable at this time in Verona, but elsewhere in Italy, with the exception of Venice, panels of poplar were the rule. The painters of Venice used either canvas or panel, the latter of fir imported from Germany. Oak was preferred in North Germany and the Netherlands. Canvas had the merit of portability, and panels sometimes split or became worm-eaten. Wood is also much more likely to expand and contract under adverse conditions of temperature and humidity, with damaging effects to the paint-layer.

At this time artists often framed the panel before laying the ground, which formed a ridge along the interior borders of the frame, leaving the part covered by the rebate unprimed. The back of the panel was usually planed towards the edges, leaving it thick in the middle, but progressively diminishing the thickness as it approached the borders. The absence of one or more of these bevels is an indication that the panel has been cut down. New bevelling ought to exhibit the usual indications of reworked wood.

Panels of large size were made by gluing several appropriately

[1] Giorgio Vasari: *The Lives of the Painters, Sculptors, and Architects.* Various editions.

shaped pieces together. Theophilus[1] (*fl.* eleventh century) describes how the glue was made from soft cheese and quicklime, resembling the modern casein glues. "When they have dried (he says) they stick together so firmly that neither damp nor heat can separate them." Examples of forgeries of early Masters on such woods as American hickory have been noticed, and examination of a suspected panel by an expert in the identification of woods is advisable.

"Cradling" of split panels is frequently undertaken to preserve them, but in rare instances the exceedingly difficult task of planing away the wood until the priming is reached provides the only practicable solution. This is only done when the condition of the panel makes it imperative, and slight damage sometimes occurs, although this is preferable to complete destruction. Of course the surface appearance of a wooden panel is preserved, and this appears out of place on canvas. The collector is not likely to meet with a painting treated in this way because it has only been undertaken with full laboratory facilities as an emergency technique.

Copper panels can be very deceptive. An analysis of the copper by a skilled metallurgist might be used to find out whether the panel is modern or old, but a clever forgery painted on an old panel might be exceedingly difficult to detect, apart from an evaluation of style. Pictures on porcelain in enamels usually fall to be considered by the criteria of judgement employed for that material, but important work on a ceramic support has been done by a number of noted artists, including George Stubbs, who employed plaques made from Wedgwood's creamware, Gauguin, and Toulouse-Lautrec. Renoir began his career as a porcelain painter.

The case of Van Meegeren will here be cited frequently, not only because he was a forger of more than usual acumen and knowledge, but, since he was playing for high stakes, he took great pains to see that his work was deceptive at all points. His forgeries have been minutely studied by Dr Paul Coremans[2] and we know much

[1] Theophilus: *De Diversis Artibus*. English translation as *The Various Arts* by C. R. Dodwell. London, 1961. This welcome translation is of a book which, like Pliny's *Natural History*, is exceedingly important to the student of art-history, but not always trustworthy in its descriptions of technical processes.

[2] *Van Meegeren's Faked Vermeers and de Hooghs—a scientific examination.* London, 1949.

more about his methods than those of any other forger of paintings.

Van Meegeren purchased old and relatively worthless paintings for his work. These already had the numerous cracks (*craquelure*) which arise from shrinkages and movement of the ground, the paint-layer, and the varnish relatively to each other, and these old cracks assisted the later formation of the *craquelure* which was artificially induced by Van Meegeren. *Craquelure* is an important aspect of the detection of forged oil-paintings and one which will later be considered in greater detail.

Van Meegeren removed much of the old paint-layer with a solution of soda and a hard brush, although he had to leave enough to provide a foundation for the new *craquelure*. Perhaps this made him decide to leave some white lead paint, which would otherwise have been undesirable because this pigment is the most opaque to X-rays. It is possible to estimate the relative densities of lead salts by X-ray from the extent to which the various areas allow the radiation to penetrate. Therefore, even if the ground be of white lead paint, subsequent painting with this pigment will still leave traces on the X-ray photograph.

Pigments suspended in oil *appear* to dry fairly quickly. Actually they may take as long as fifty years to harden completely, and a rough and ready test sometimes applied to a suspected painting is to draw the point of a needle lightly over the paint in an inconspicuous place. New paint will be cut, or drag at the needle-point; it will slide easily over old paint. A cotton-wool swab moistened in alcohol and lightly rubbed over an unvarnished surface will remove colour from new paint, but old paint will be unaffected.

It is quite obvious that a seventeenth-century paint-film is as hard as it is ever likely to get. Various methods of imitating this hardness have been tried, of which heating is one. A London studio of the early years of the nineteenth century, which was devoted to the making of forgeries, became known as the "Westminster Oven". Van Meegeren partially solved the problem by using a vehicle made from a synthetic resin of the phenolformaldehyde class dissolved in spirit such as alcohol or turpentine, to which he added synthetic lilac oil (an essential oil which, unlike the linseed oil of Vermeer, dries rapidly) to give the necessary viscosity to the paint. This paint, when it had been subjected to a relatively mild degree of heat, of the order of 100 degrees Centrigrade, became exceedingly hard and resistant to solvents. Moreover, the old cracks over which it had been painted came to the surface in a convincing manner.

At this point the actual painting of the picture was finished, but it was not deceptive because it had none of the signs of age. These had now to be supplied. Not entirely without reason *craquelure* is regarded as a sign of age. It arises in many different ways. A paint-film will react differently to variations in temperature, for example, from canvas or panel; varnish will contract to a greater or lesser extent than the paint-film. The cracks may be in the varnish, in the varnish and paint-film, or may go down to the support. When cracks are in the varnish-film alone, this tends to curl up at the edges in a manner difficult to imitate, although Professor Laurie, when studying the methods of the forger, succeeded in doing so. The camera is particularly useful in the study of *craquelure*, and if a small area be suitably enlarged it is usually fairly easy to distinguish between genuine and false from this alone.

The Italian painter and forger, I. F. Joni, has given a frank account of his methods of inducing *craquelure*. He used a thick *gesso* priming on his canvas, which he then wrapped round a cylinder, rolling it in several different ways. Another method was to mark the cracks on the back of the canvas after the painting had been finished, thus weakening the priming. By rolling the canvas this was induced to crack at the weak points which had been made.[1] In this case the marks on the back of the canvas made it necessary to glue it to a wood panel, always a suspicious circumstance but by no means a certain indication of forgery.

At the point Van Meegeren had then reached he varnished his canvas before rolling it in the manner described by Joni. This was to protect the paint-film during the next stage—covering the whole surface with ink which seeped into the cracks, making them more obvious and more deceptive. The surplus ink was removed, and the picture revarnished, this last coat being coloured to simulate old varnish. Joni went even further; he developed a method of imitating fly-spots, which he applied with thick paint on the end of a pointed stick. Some old paintings are restored by overpainting and this is later discussed, but in such cases *craquelure* is usually *painted* over the final varnish-film—easily detected under a magnifying glass.

[1] I. F. Joni: *The Affairs of a Painter*. London, 1936.

The dirt in old cracks is accumulated in the form of solid particles. The ink used by Van Meegeren not only filled the cracks but tended to spread out slightly on either side under the varnish-film, similar to an ink line on blotting-paper. This is especially obvious in Dr Coreman's enlarged photographs, and made the method of application obvious.

It is impossible in the space available to do more than add a few brief notes on this important subject. *Craquelure* is not an invariable feature of old painting, although it is exceedingly common. In a few cases paintings by a particular artist have developed an idiosyncratic *craquelure* which is fairly distinctive, and can be used to assist attribution. Usually it arises from faulty technique.

Generally, very wide cracks which exhibit a "lizard skin" effect indicate nineteenth-century work, perhaps the result of using bitumen or megilp. Max Friedländer records noticing a similar effect in the work of the portrait painter, Anton Graff (1736–1813), who painted at great speed, and, in the course of his working life, executed about 1,250 portraits and nearly 500 replicas. His scale of fees has survived to us—fifty thalers (about £12 10s)[1] for a half-length without hands or with one hand, and one hundred thalers (£25) for a half-length with two hands, and proportionately higher for more elaborate work. He was also obliged to train an assistant without charge, and to supply a free portrait each year to the Regent of Saxony, Prince Xaver. Small wonder that he wrote: "I had to paint very many portraits."

Arc-like cracks looking like a spider's web, hardly to be made on rollers, are nearly always seen only on eighteenth-century canvasses. Genuine *craquelure* not only penetrates to the priming, and even beyond it, but it is entirely fortuitous and irregular. *Craquelure* is an important indication, but the mistake of putting on it a greater weight than it can bear should not be made. To quote Dr Friedländer once more: "There exist many genuine paintings which show no cracks; they are never absent in forgeries."

The importance of accessories and interior decoration to anyone examining appropriate paintings can hardly be overestimated. This aspect can be used both to date a genuine painting and to expose a forgery.

In a genuine work everything will belong to a period which is not

[1] About £150 in modern currency.

later than the year of execution. It is often possible to date costume, furniture, pottery, rugs and wall-hangings with accuracy to within a few years. Even domestic utensils of one kind or another can often be placed fairly closely in their period. While it is safest to consult a specialist on such points, much can be done with reliable repertories of illustrations of the kind to be found in a first-class reference library, and some of the books noted in the Bibliography have been included for this purpose.

Chinese porcelain, which is to be found in paintings from the seventeenth century onwards, is worth particular attention if it has been rendered with anything like fidelity. Forgers rarely know anything about it; the specialist can sometimes give a very close estimation of the age from shape alone. A Ch'ien Lung vase in a seventeenth-century painting is an obvious anachronism.

Costume is also worth close study by comparison with illustrated works, with other paintings of undoubted authenticity, and with old prints. Contemporary books of costume exist in some cases. Wenceslaus Hollar engraved a series of plates of this kind in the 1640s which were published in London.[1] Fashion was, perhaps, a little slower in changing in former times but change it did.

Forgers have also made the mistake of copying detail from early costume as it appeared in much later works in a revived style. The medieval costume in some nineteenth-century paintings of the kind is, for instance, usually inaccurate.

Maurice Rheims[2] has drawn attention to the impossibility of reproducing the clothes of the late nineteenth or early twentieth centuries in such a way that a photograph of them would be convincing, and of fabricating a scene in which costumes appear in a manner close enough to deceive anyone who has memories of the period. Even those who are acquainted only with early photographs would be difficult to mislead, and few costume-films succeed in recapturing sufficient of the flavour to lull the critical sense of those with an eye for anachronisms.

[1] *The Several Habits of Englishwomen* (*to which is added 48 plates of Continental Costume*). Plates by Wenceslaus Hollar. Published by H. Overton, London, 1643. Curiously enough the title page of my edition appears to be a forgery. The plates are genuine, but are probably later reprints.

[2] Maurice Rheims: *La vie étrange des objets*. Paris, 1959.

(*Top*) The art-dealer, Otto Wacker
entre, behind chair) during the course
his trial in April 1932. He was subse-
ently sentenced to a year's imprison-
ent. X-ray photographs played a
table part in his detection.
[*Ullstein*

. (*Centre*) The experts confer. Some
the Wacker "Van Goghs" displayed
the trial. [*Ullstein*

. (*Right*) Vincent Wilhelm Van
ogh, nephew of the painter, gives
idence at the trial of Otto Wacker.
[*Ullstein*

35. The trial of the Bank directors. *Geheimrat* Dr Max Friedländer, one of the experts who gave evidence, is seen in the foreground in profile. [*Ullstein*

This remark by Rheims is especially apt. Differences in the mechanics of photography, and the appearance of old photographs, account for some of it, but facial expression, and the carriage of the body, are responsible for much more. It would be impossible to dress a girl of today, accustomed to the freedom of light clothing and a different social *milieu*, in the enveloping dresses of the period without the unconscious adaptation of carriage to their unfamiliarity becoming obvious.

The forger, however, is likely to make his worst blunders in other things, apart from costume, because he is less alert to the danger. Interiors often depict many objects, each one the province of a specialist, which are naturally correct in a genuine painting, but which are, to a forger, fraught with the possibility of an anachronistic mistake capable of instantly revealing the fraud to the sufficiently skilled observer.

Perhaps the most dangerous is the Oriental rug. These were imported into Europe from early times, and were much treasured. They are, for this reason, often depicted. A specialist in rugs can usually say whether or not the pattern agrees with the period. Furniture is comparatively easy to date accurately, often within a few years. Carved ornament is a useful indication, and such things as picture-frames or mirror-frames appearing in a painting should be carefully scrutinized. *Rococo* carving in a seventeenth-century painting at once stamps it as spurious.

Readers of the Sherlock Holmes stories will remember the significance of the dog which did not bark in the night. Equally significant in some cases is the omission of detail from paintings purporting to be by artists who normally rendered this aspect carefully and with enjoyment. Blurred detail, also, suggests that the painter was not sure of his ground. It is not proof of forgery, but a sign that additional care is needed.

This is an aspect of looking at questioned works of art which deserves a great deal more attention than it gets, and an acquaintance with the broader aspects of the history of interior decoration is undoubtedly an asset of considerable importance to anyone who collects paintings. In cases of doubt it is often worth asking a specialist to give an opinion on certain details, especially rugs, pottery and porcelain, and furniture. For instance, out of forty plates in a standard work on Vermeer it is possible to see that thirty contain enough of this kind of detail to express an opinion on their authenticity from this standpoint, and three of them (it would be invidious to name them on this evidence alone) emerge very badly from the test for one reason or another.

It is a valuable exercise to examine the details of the various Van Meegeren forgeries. The plate numbers in parenthesis are of those in Dr Coremans' book already mentioned, since this is the most accessible and comprehensive work on the subject.

The "Christ at Emmäus" (Plate 1) has a representation of a mounted *faïence* jug which purports to be either Dutch or German. The base is concealed, as it is in a genuine Vermeer painting,[1] but sufficient of its form can be seen to be certain that it could not have been painted by Vermeer, or by any competent seventeenth-century painter, all of whom used such jugs daily as a matter of course. The discrepancy in Van Meegeren's version is not only in the shape itself, which is subtly but definitely wrong, but in the handle. This, at first glance, appears to be missing altogether, but closer investigation shows it to be in the hand of the standing figure and projecting at an impossible angle. The handle on Vermeer's jug can be well seen in the painting referred to in the footnote, and in the "Sleeping Woman" of the Metropolitan Museum, New York. Van Meegeren's "Blessing of Jacob" (Plate 11)[2] also shows this jug again in a slightly different position. The form of the handle is accurate, but the profile varies from that of a seventeenth-century jug sufficiently to cause an expert in *faïence* of the period to pause for reflection. When we come to Van Meegeren's forged de Hoogh, "Interior with Drinkers" (Plate 17),[3] we find a jug which is completely unlike any appearing in genuine paintings by Vermeer. Its body is globular, and it has a waisted, spreading foot apparently based on metalwork. Dr Coremans illustrates the jug found in Van Meegeren's studio, on which it must have been based, in Plate 45 of his work. This appears to be of eighteenth-century manufacture, and I was able to match it for form with a similar blue-painted jug in the Reitlinger Collection bearing a mark of Hanau which, according to

[1] "Das Mädchen mit dem Weinglas." Brunswick (Herzog Anton Ulrich Museum).

[2] See frontispiece.

[3] Plate 24 in this book.

Behse,[1] was in use from the latter part of the eighteenth century onwards. This is precisely the date and provenance which I would have awarded to it from its appearance in Dr Coremans' plate.

An equally interesting series of comparisons can be made with a Chinese deep dish, like a soup-plate in shape, which appears in several of the Vermeer paintings. From the "Sleeping Woman" of the Metropolitan Museum it is possible to see that it belonged to the late Ming period, the reign of Wan-li, and was decorated with the so-called "aster" pattern. It appears again, also filled with apples, in "Die Briefleserin" in the Dresden Staatliche Gemäldegalerie (1939), and it is possible to see what one would naturally expect—slight decoration on the exterior which was almost invariable on dishes of the kind. This dish appears in a Van Meegeren, "Woman playing Music" (Plate 23), done in 1936 but not sold. Not only is the form inaccurate, but no trace of decoration appears on the exterior.

The glasses used in various forgeries by Van Meegeren appear to be correctly of the period, although someone more expert in the field of Continental glass might be able to detect inaccuracies. The "Interior with Drinkers" (detail, Plate 18) illustrates a woman holding a glass in an extremely peculiar manner which it would be difficult to associate with de Hoogh. The peculiarity is due to the fact that the glass does not have a stem, and could not, therefore, be held in such a way. The drawing of the hand and the position of the glass, however, are very similar to those to be seen in the figure of the girl in the Brunswick Vermeer already mentioned. In the Vermeer, however, the glass has a stem, and the pose of the hand is quite natural. It is certain that this detail was adapted from a reproduction known to Van Meegeren. (See Plates 23 and 24 in this work.)

Generally, in most of the Van Meegeren forgeries details of interior decoration which might be used as a test of authenticity are avoided. But Vermeer did not avoid detail of this sort. On the contrary, in one painting after another, he rendered it so carefully that he obviously enjoyed doing it.

When detail of this kind appears in a genuine painting it will not only have been painted from a model, but it will have a different significance for a painter of former times than for the modern forger. These things were rarer, and treasured with greater care. They were

[1] Arthur Behse: *Deutsche Fayencemarken Brevier*. Braunschweig, 1955.

often works of art in themselves which appealed to an artist in a different medium.

Vermeer obviously delighted in the pattern of Oriental rugs. He had a Ushak from Anatolia which must have been one of his prized possessions, because it appears in several paintings and there is little difficulty in identifying it. Van Meegeren avoided rugs, and only in the unsold "Woman Playing on Music" does one appear. The pattern is too indeterminate to permit identification, but it was certainly not Vermeer's Ushak. No doubt Van Meegeren realized the danger of depicting rugs which might not have been in existence in the seventeenth century.

The examination of a large number of photographs of paintings attributed to Vermeer when these lines were being written brought to light the fact that one work attributed to him, apparently of the late seventeenth century, included a piece of mounted Japanese blue-and-white porcelain of a kind which records suggest was not imported until after his death in 1675. The attribution of this painting, therefore, deserves second thoughts.

A comparison of Vermeer's "Das Mädchen in Blau" in the Rijksmuseum at Amsterdam with Van Meegeren's "Woman Reading Music", done in 1935 or the year following, is instructive. From a photograph the Van Meegeren is much more deceptive than the "Disciples at Emmäus", but there is sufficient material for anyone acquainted with Vermeer's painting to pause for reflection. The general composition is very similar, but the young woman in Van Meegeren's version is seated instead of standing. It is an old trick of the forger to make minor alterations to a genuine composition, and fraudulent paintings of this kind are usually much more difficult to detect.

I have elsewhere commented on the danger-signal provided by the appearance of a number of similar works on the art-market within a short time of each other. It is, therefore, instructive to look briefly at this aspect of Van Meegeren's forgeries. From the day of Jan Vermeer van Delft's death in 1675 until 1938 only one religious painting had been attributed to him. This was the "Christ with Mary and Martha" in the Edinburgh National Gallery. This not only has nothing in common with Van Meegeren's forgeries, but the attribution to Vermeer is not universally accepted. I have heard Terbruggen suggested.

Vermeer's work was not in demand among collectors. Pilkington's

*Dictionary of Artists* (the edition of 1810 with additions by Fuseli) did not think him worth including among hundreds of minor artists, most of whom are now almost forgotten, and until 1872 no painting by Vermeer had made more than £250. Very few appeared on the market after this date, and some light is thrown on the former position of Vermeer's paintings in the estimation of the collector by the existence of one with the faked signature of Pieter de Hoogh.

Then, quite suddenly we get the following:

| | |
|---|---|
| 1937 (December) | "Disciples at Emmäus" |
| 1941 | "Christ" (head and shoulders)—Plate 22 |
| 1941 | "The Last Supper" |
| 1942 | "The Blessing of Jacob"[1] |
| 1942 | "The Woman taken in Adultery" (sold to Hermann Göring) |
| 1943 | "The Washing of the Feet" |

Finally, in 1945, "Jesus among the Doctors"[2] was painted by Van Meegeren for the Dutch Field Security as proof of his authorship of those listed above. The last bears no resemblance whatever to a Vermeer, but was, perhaps, the best that could be done in the circumstances.

The bust portrait of Christ is almost a replica of the central figure of Christ in the "Disciples at Emmäus", and was probably intended to be taken for a study for the larger picture. It does not resemble any extant Vermeer in its handling of the subject.

It must have been obvious, whatever the conditions prevailing, that these fantastic discoveries of "lost" Vermeers were all of religious subjects, of which only one example had previously been attributed. It was quite impossible for this to have been coincidence, particularly as they all lacked a history which was in the slightest degree convincing. A searching inquiry should have been held long before half a dozen had been completed and sold. For instance, the chance that a discovery of a painting like the "Disciples at Emmäus", presumably lost to history for three centuries, could be followed in three years by what was, apparently, a study for the central figure of Christ, was so slender that this alone was cause for grave suspicion. The circumstances of the time cannot be blamed for the situation. The discovery of hitherto unknown

[1] See frontispiece. [2] See plate 21.

Vermeers must have been fairly well-known among Continental art-experts, and it was equally obvious that each new discovery was of the same kind. Yet no one stopped to calculate the odds against such repeated discoveries, which are astronomical.

Dr Coremans is kinder to the experts responsible for the acceptance of these works than they deserve, pointing out that several of them were expecting the discovery of Vermeers with religious subjects which they were convinced must once have adorned the premises of a secret religious society in the seventeenth century. This seems to be an example of the kind of conjecture based on slight foundation which has so often provided an opportunity for the astute forger. It illustrates the fallacy of distorting facts to fit a theory instead of trying to evolve a theory to fit the facts. Art-critics have rarely been noted for the ability to think logically and to follow a train of facts to its conclusion. The whole sordid Van Meegeren episode emphasizes how essential it is that the expert should possess a mind trained to check and evaluate evidence.

How closely did Van Meegeren imitate the style of Vermeer? The verdict, so far as the religious paintings are concerned, must surely be, *Not at all*. If the faces of all the figures in the six paintings listed are examined they will be found to resemble each other to a remarkable degree. The structure is the same, and in most cases the eyes are hooded by unusually drooping lids, an exaggeration of a peculiarity to be observed occasionally in the work of Vermeer. The faces have the neurotic appearance of twentieth-century work which Vermeer would not have understood, much less rendered in terms of paint. The shape of the mouth, always a revealing point, is weak and tremulous, and varies but little in the shaven figures. In the "Last Supper" (Plate 7) the face of one of the disciples can hardly be distinguished from that of Christ, whilst a disciple with distinctly feminine features rests a hand reassuringly on the hand of Jesus, a gesture which, in the seventeenth century, would not have been contemplated because of the divine nature attributed to the principal figure.

Van Meegeren's figures are obviously posed with care, and even with difficulty. The composition is an intellectual construction which is never particularly successful. It certainly does not resemble Vermeer's almost instinctive placing of the figures in his own compositions. From this aspect Van Meegeren's worst painting is the "Last Supper", where the grouping of thirteen figures (all, apparently, close relations to judge from the facial resemblance) has obviously given a great deal of trouble. Looked at dispassionately the composition is ludicrous. His best work is the "Disciples at Emmäus", but here he closely followed a known painting of the same subject by Caravaggio, and his departures from it are hardly an improvement.

It does not detract from the value of Dr Coremans' inquiry, which was surely a pattern for all future investigations of the same kind, to say that it was possible to recognize the spurious nature of Van Meegeren's work from inspection alone, and that the result of the scientific tests served to emphasize what ought to have been apparent without them.

It is essential to avoid relying on the advice of an "authority" who makes attributions by a kind of inspiration welling up from the depths of the subconscious mind, unaided by scientific tests or systematic methods of examination. There is a marked tendency in some quarters to foster the development of a mystique, both in the vital matter of attribution and in art-criticism. The resistance to the introduction of more exact methods has been strong, those supporting their use being stigmatized as cultural barbarians or Philistines, and this has been accompanied by the insidious suggestion that it really does not matter whether an attribution is correct or not provided the object fulfils the particular critic's definition of a work of art. This, of course, is a fairly obvious method of evading the consequences of a mistake, and it marches hand in hand with the modern tendency to avoid the necessity for craftsmanship in the making of works of art. It has also played a notable part in creating the neurotic bypath which art has been following for the past few decades. Like the theologian, this kind of critic considers faith to be more important than works, but the hard fact remains that a painting attributed entirely by intuition is far more likely to be a doubtful object than one which has been properly examined. It is this attitude that, in one case after another, has been responsible for spectacular errors of judgement which have provided material for sensational writers on art-forgery. No matter how certain one may *feel*, it is much safer to reinforce opinion with such facts as may be gleaned from a systematic and objective examination.

It is, however, essential to remember that although exact methods can be used to confirm the date of the object under examination, the final attribution to a particular artist is much more difficult, and here science is a less reliable guide.

Every genuine painting will fall into one or other of five well-marked categories, conveniently listed as follows:

(*a*) The untouched work of a master.
(*b*) Partly by his hand, the remainder the work of pupils or assistants.
(*c*) Studio-piece, painted in the style of a master by an assistant.
(*d*) School-piece. Painting by an independent artist of lesser stature influenced by the master.
(*e*) Contemporary replica executed either as a studio-piece, or by another artist as, for instance, the copy of Raphael's "Leo X" by Andrea del Sarto.

The expert needs to be able to separate (*a*) from all the other categories convincingly, a task which is always difficult and in many cases completely impossible. He is in a quandary which has largely been created by the collector and the public, who both want to see a definite label at the bottom of a picture. This not uncommonly leads to the making of attributions which are unwise, and which the expert himself would prefer to avoid.

A painting falls in its owner's esteem if it is labelled a studio-piece or a school-piece, although it is still the same picture and no worse for the change of label. Nevertheless, all kinds of previously hidden defects suddenly become apparent. In the words of Dr Friedländer: "The eye sleeps until the spirit awakes it with a question." After the question, what previously satisfied is no longer enough.

The only way in which the final selection between all the categories can be made is the style in which the work has been executed, and to this problem we can apply objective methods, such as those of Morelli; intuitive processes, which mean making an attribution from the general impression given to the mind by the painting; or a combination of both. Either of these by itself is dangerous, and my own predilection is in favour of combining them, allowing intuition to suggest and objective examination to confirm.

Perhaps the greatest safeguard is an understanding of the nature of quality,[1] a term not easily understood nor a faculty acquired without

[1] See plate 37.

the expenditure of time and effort. All appraisals of quality are ultimately a process of comparison between work of all kinds, between good and bad, between genuine and spurious. Much might be written on this word which would be applicable not only to painting but to the other things already discussed in this book, but as a general statement good quality is a combination of excellence in design, craftsmanship, and materials in this order. The surest way to make an error of judgement is to invert the order in which these have been taken. To put materials first would be to rate an object of gold more highly than one of bronze, irrespective of design and workmanship. It remains certain, however, that good craftsmanship was rarely lavished on bad design or poor materials, and a skilled craftsman was seldom capable of bad design.

Objective methods in the appraisal of style are principally concerned with the study of detail. The ear, for example, is difficult to draw well, and because the student lavished a great deal of time and attention on learning to do so, he developed an idiosyncratic method of depicting it. Therefore, if photographs of ears from as many genuine paintings as possible are compared with the same feature in the painting under examination, and the handling is recognizably similar, then the chances are greatly in favour of both being by the same hand. Depiction of hands is also characteristic. Some artists found them singularly difficult. I have not yet seen a portrait by Lely in which hands were well drawn. Apart from portraits, the treatment of drapery is often revealing, although there is less room for individual expression in the handling of the details of costume.

The face and its expression is an important guide to the nature of a work. I have not had an opportunity of comparing the Hahn version of "La Belle Ferronnière" with that of the Louvre, except from photographs,[1] and for this reason it would be invidious to express an opinion one way or the other on the attribution of either, but there is a decided difference in the facial expression of the two which makes it extremely unlikely that they are both the work of the same hand. Max Friedländer recalls an amusing instance of the occasion when he acted as adviser to the German Government on the design of its bank-notes. A member of the Committee urged that the portraits on the notes, which were regarded as lacking in taste, should be replaced by an

[1] Harry Hahn: *The Rape of La Belle.* Kansas City, 1946.

ornamental device. Whilst agreeing with the criticism a bank official strongly resisted the suggestion because the portraits were precisely the point which the currency-note forger found it impossible to reproduce deceptively. They were, for this reason, used by cashiers as a test for the genuineness of a note. As Dr Friedländer remarks, a very slight alteration is sufficient to change the whole expression, and it is much easier to make a judgement from this than from a detailed examination of ornament.

This is no less noticeable in Chinese copies of European figure-subjects. A glance at the face immediately reveals whether the painting is by a Chinese hand, and forgeries of export porcelain with European figures are rare in consequence. Those with flowers and armorial bearings are fairly common, and more difficult to detect.

Features, and the hair, are all revealing in their own way, and it is often possible to date some paintings fairly closely from the expression of the mouth. If details of this part of the face taken from paintings of the eighteenth, nineteenth, and twentieth centuries are examined, it will not often be difficult to separate them into their respective periods. Earlier than this it is usually possible to assign the latest date, but the earliest is a little more difficult until one reaches medieval times. This is not peculiar to painting. I have noticed the same thing on many occasions in the course of examining porcelain figures.

A good many modern forgeries are influenced by Hollywood, which, until the advent of television, created the modern female face. The celluloid version bore little resemblance to its prototype, and it is a salutary experience to examine genuine unretouched portraits of film-stars side by side with those made for publicity purposes. The expert cosmeticians of the studios produced an enamelled mask which demanded a rigid economy of expression to preserve it from cracking. I was once able to meet a lady of some reputation in this field who, to quote the words of the American friend who introduced me, was "pushing back fifty with both hands", but, in her public appearances, the years fell away, and, painted and corseted, she became the familiar stereotype. The familiarity was strengthened by the achievements of the makers of cosmetics, who put the means of achieving it within the reach of millions, and one was confronted, particularly in the States, with the similitude of this well-known face at every turn. To see something so often means that eventually it makes no impact at all, and it becomes difficult to see this influence even in places where it has no right to be.

The remark of Sepp Schüller referring to a "Vermeer" apparently by one of Van Meegeren's predecessors—"modernen Typ—eine Greta-Garbo-Erscheinung"—is especially appropriate.[1]

This can well be seen on plates 26 and 27, which illustrate two heads by Lothar Malskat, both from wall-paintings done in Schleswig Cathedral. Malskat provides a rare instance of the forgery of wall-paintings, although these have often been faked and overpainted in the past under the pretext of restoration.

In 1948 the restoration of the Marienkirche in Lübeck, damaged during the bombing, was undertaken. Peeling whitewash had revealed traces of unsuspected medieval frescoes about sixty feet above ground level, and the work of cleaning and restoring these was given to a well-known restorer, Dietrich Fey. The authorities were to some extent to blame for what occurred subsequently, because they wanted the figures to be religious symbols as well as works of art, and for this reason they gave tacit assent to a greater degree of restoration than would normally have been regarded as either desirable or legitimate.[2]

Fey employed Malskat to carry out the actual work, and in the process the walls were cleaned bare and the old painting completely replaced by forgeries. These were regarded as remarkably well-preserved and important Gothic frescoes of the thirteenth and fourteenth centuries, but Schüller comments,[3] very appropriately, that since photographs existed of the paintings before and after the restoration it is surprising that the fraud was not discovered before Malskat's confession in 1952. The "Madonna and Child" reproduced here (Plate 28) obviously has nothing to do with any century but the twentieth. So far as the Schleswig restorations are concerned, Malskat admitted that he took Plate 26 from a photograph of the film-star, Hansi Knoteck, and that Plate 27 was the result of using his sister, Frieda, as a model. The hat worn by Frieda Malskat is as up-to-date a piece of millinery as one could hope to find, and the hair-style bears little relation to the medieval book-illustration on which the

[1] *Falsche oder Echt? Der Fall Van Meegeren.* Bonn, 1953.

[2] Sepp Schüller: *Falscher, Handler und Experten.* Munich, 1959. English translation under the title of *Forgers, Dealers, Experts.* London, 1960.

[3] *Op. cit.*

forgeries were based. Certainly I have been unable to trace anything comparable.

These remarks are no less true of the work of Van Meegeren. At its most obvious the tendency to take the film-star as a model may be seen in the painting of "Jesus among the Doctors", undertaken to convince the police that he was indeed the author of the other forgeries (Plate 21). Because he was using his confession to the lesser charge of forgery as a way of escape from the greater one of collaboration with the enemy, the situation was fraught with danger, and Van Meegeren found it difficult to concentrate on the drawing. He was, therefore, unaware of the unconscious tendency for the Hollywood face to creep into the work which meant so much to him. The face of Jesus needs only to be taken from its setting for it to become typically that of a girl of the period, even without alteration to the hair-style. Nevertheless, even the most purblind critic could not escape the implications of this painting. The hand was the same as that of the other "Vermeers", and that hand was completely modern.

Malskat has become so notorious for the Lübeck and Schleswig murals that it is easy to lose sight of the fact that he forged the work of both old and modern masters on a prodigious scale. It was said at the trial that something like six hundred paintings of this kind had been sold to German art-dealers. They were marketed under the names of seventy different artists, which is sufficient proof of the trivial character of most of them, since no one could produce deceptive work on this scale. Some of these paintings were later marked by Court order to prevent subsequent circulation as genuine works, and a number were sent to the County Museum of Schleswig-Holstein for purposes of study. Some may still be circulating, but they are hardly likely to find their way into the hands of reputable dealers accustomed to dealing in genuine works. Plate 29 illustrates an incident in the Malskat trial of October 1954, and shows some of these forgeries which were then being made public for the first time. The one nearest to the camera appears to be a forged Chagall, and it is known that one of Malskat's spurious copies of Chagall's work sent to the artist for authentication was destroyed by him.

The numerous X-ray plates which have been made of genuine paintings during the last few decades in an attempt to gather information about underlying structures and the methods adopted have proved very successful in some cases. Examples of concealed but genuine drawing differing markedly from the finished painting occur; it is evident that some of the greatest works of art of this kind have been attended in the early stages by hesitancy in design, and that the final result has developed and crystallized as the work proceeded. The remarkable differences which can be perceived in the rendering of the same subject by two different hands is very well illustrated by the X-ray photographs of a genuine work compared with a forgery shown here on Plate 31. The subject of the X-ray of the genuine painting is not only recognizable, but the brush-strokes which formed it conform to a coherent pattern. The painting has been built from the priming upwards by someone who, because he was working in his own style, achieved his effect with a minimum of effort. On the other hand, the brush-strokes of the forgery, apart from a spider's web pattern, are incoherent to a remarkable degree because the forger was trying to reproduce a surface appearance as he worked. The two men were, in fact, aiming at fundamentally different objectives which were only incidentally, and to outward appearances, the same. It is exceedingly difficult to recognize this similarity unless the two plates are compared very carefully. That they are both by different hands is plain, but this would not be nearly so obvious in normal lighting conditions.

*Pentimenti* are small errors rectified by the artist at the time of painting, or afterthoughts which have been painted over the original passage. At first the new paint obliterated the old, but time often causes the first intention to appear as a ghostly shadow beneath the subsequently applied paint, and for this reason *pentimenti* can usually be identified. Sometimes they are only revealed by a black-and-white photograph, which is a good reason for photographing important pictures.

These alterations can often be regarded as a sign of original work, although not necessarily of authenticity. A passage is painted, and then, for one reason or another, the artist dislikes it, or it does not fit easily with the remainder of the composition. Therefore, he alters it. *Pentimenti* are less likely to occur in replicas, where everything can be carefully laid in. The composition already exists, and there is smaller reason for error or afterthoughts. In the kind of "original forgery" done by Van Meegeren they are just as likely to be present as in an authentic work, but in such cases the forgeries are not yet old enough for them to appear in the course of normal examination although X-rays may reveal them.

The presence of these alterations when they can be detected is probably more likely to be significant in cases where it is necessary to distinguish between an original painting and a contemporary studio replica.

Copyists are not creative artists; they are making a painting of a painting which already exists. Therefore, their touch is likely to be surer in some ways, although it will also be more laborious. The closest copies are contemporary. The longer the amount of time which elapses between the creation of an original work and the making of a copy the more easily will the difference become apparent. The original artist was working in the tradition of his own time. He knew nothing of what was to come. It is true that he could not entirely avoid, even if he wanted to, the influence of previous styles and that of the work of his contemporaries, but, necessarily, there is no trace of subsequent developments. The later copyist, however, is burdened with knowledge of subsequent styles, and all those tendencies which he has absorbed from his earliest years stand between him and a full realization of the spirit of the work he is copying. This is most easily understood if paraphrases of earlier work by artists of note are examined, such as those of Rubens by Delacroix, or of Velasquez and Hals by Sargent.[1] Intended as exercises rather than copies, they exhibit in exaggerated form the attributes of more carefully fabricated replicas. Look at the mouth of a nineteenth-century copy—it can hardly avoid the sentimentality of the time. The mouth of the twentieth-century copy is often weak, with neurosis hovering at the corners, to be well seen in the work of Van Meegeren, although his paintings were hardly copies.

A vice of the copyist is that he is inclined to lay unwonted stress on passages which appeal to him, and to relax his attention in the painting of what he considers to be unimportant parts, particularly those near the borders of the canvas. He often misunderstands small points of detail altogether, which then become meaningless. There is a loss in vitality which is always perceptible. This, of course, means that a painting must be examined closely and in detail, with a desire to

[1] See K. E. Maison: *Themes and Variations*. London, 1961.

understand each part, and the reason for its existence. Anything which is nebulous must be questioned.

An idiosyncrasy which, in some cases, is even more marked than the handling of detail is to be found in the manner in which paint has been applied. Greatly enlarged photographs of the paint surface, lit at an acute angle from one side, enable brush-strokes to be traced, and the methods adopted by the artist to depict any particular point of detail charted. A beginner to the art of painting experiments with the application of paint from canvas to canvas. The mature artist has long ago given up this kind of experiment in favour of others more concerned with the ideas he wishes to express. The brush-strokes on a nose, for examples, are likely to follow a fairly set pattern for this reason. A forged painting of yachts at sea by Van Gogh sold by Otto Wacker in 1928, which was otherwise fairly deceptive, at once showed great differences in the handling of paint from the genuine work of Van Gogh when both forgery and original were examined by X-ray. As I have said, the imitation of brush-work is completely beyond the capacity of the forger, who can only imitate the total effect by other means, although he may achieve a superficial imitation of such obvious idiosyncrasies as the *impasti* of Rembrandt.

In landscape painting the treatment of foliage is probably the most revealing, both in enlargement and in natural size, and this is the point to which attention should first be directed.

The forger always selects as a victim an artist whose work is in demand, and this naturally varies from one period to another with the state of the art-market at the time. A study of picture prices will suggest which artists are likely to have been forged at any particular period. Not only will the work of popular artists be copied, but the subjects selected will usually be those for which he is most valued, or, as in the case of Van Meegeren, those which are virtually unknown. Landscapes and pretty women are favourite subjects; the former because they have usually been popular as decoration, and the latter because sex-appeal is always a ready seller. Male portraits of undistinguished people are rarely forged. Paintings of nudes need rather more care in examination than clothed subjects. The eye of even the most objective observer is apt to be distracted from the face, which is the weak point of most forgeries.

This is not to be taken to imply that the female nude does not deserve dispassionate study. The fashionable figure has varied almost as much as the costume which clothed it, and it is by no means easy for the forger to reproduce the many subtle distinctions deceptively. The classical nude is an idealized version of the youthful human body. Neither the Greeks nor the Romans ever indulged in the ruthless realism sometimes to be seen in later periods, apart from a few exceptional instances. When the nude reappeared in European art at the end of the fourteenth century it was much more naturally portrayed. The female nude in such works as the "Three Graces" of Raphael in the Musée de Conde closely resembles the classical handling of the subject on the walls of Pompeii, but it bears no relationship to the treatment of the same subject further north. The nudes of Dürer and Cranach often depict a more or less advanced stage of broad-hipped pregnancy, for example, and the plump, mature nude of the High Renaissance gave place to the even more opulent curves of Rubens. That this was the taste of the period may be seen from Rembrandt's "Bathsheba" in the Louvre. During the eighteenth century the nude fined down progressively and became more seductive, expecially in the work of Fragonard and Boucher, although the naked goddesses were still generously proportioned with ample buttocks. The treatment of this subject during the neo-classical period which followed is noticeably related to that of the frescoes of Pompeii. The nudes of the early part of the nineteenth century by Ingres, Courbet, and others, are realistic, with a plenitude of not always subtle curves, emphasis still being on the buttocks. A similar tendency is to be seen in the work of Renoir, and is probably due to the enveloping clothing of the period, which made a relatively sedentary existence essential and led to the deposition of excess fat in the region of the pelvis. Leaving to one side the Tahitian nudes of Gauguin, those of Manet, Degas, and Bonnard all begin to approach the accepted twentieth-century figure. Forgeries of nudes are not especially common. The body presents difficulties which are similar to those to be met in drawing the face convincingly. An acquaintance with the accepted conventions of a period in the delineation of this subject are essential to a balanced judgement. Attention should also be given to various states of mind, such as Puritanism, which at one time or another have influenced the way in which the nude has been depicted. These range from deliberately ungraceful distortion to the addition of drapery and

36. A panel from the Paumgartner altar-piece, the figure by Dürer, the later additions by Fischer. Page 239.

[*Ullstein*

37. Forgery of a portrait by J. E. A. Tischbein. The latter was a skilful portrait painter, and this forgery is betrayed by poor quality. [*Ullstein*

foliage in appropriate places. It is not difficult to trace the antics of the prurient on many paintings of this kind in public galleries.

Hals did not paint many pictures of laughing or smiling subjects, such as the well-known "Laughing Cavalier" (so-called), although they have become associated with him through the efforts of sellers of popular prints. Consequently forgeries tend to be of this kind.

One such spurious painting was accused by modern pigments—artificial ultramarine, first used about 1820, and zinc white which was unknown before 1781. Van Meegeren was well aware of this trap and spent large sums in buying true ultramarine made from lapis lazuli. In the case of the Hals, the forger was obviously much more preoccupied with the possibility that someone would test the paint for freshness with alcohol because he protected the paint-layer with a coat of size (which is insoluble in alcohol) before varnishing. The alcohol test is, in fact, useless unless it is possible to reach the paint-layer, and in cases of doubt the edge of the painting, where it is covered by the rebate of the frame, can be treated first with alcohol to remove the varnish and then with a pad moistened in hot water to remove any size present.

It is essential for the expert to know as much as possible about the life and work of the artists in whom he specializes. As an example, it is possible to trace the gradual evolution of the style of Degas merely by viewing his paintings in chronological order. His favourite subject —the *ballet*—starts in 1868 with the orchestra at the opera, and by 1872 has moved to the *foyer* and the stage. His interest in figures and groups of figures is obvious. But his pictures gradually become larger and less concerned with a number of figures. By the 1880s he is beginning to concentrate on two or three figures, and single figures become more numerous. His style, at first characterized by careful drawing, becomes broader and his drawing less detailed. Oil-paint gives way to pastel, and his handling of colour is increasingly brilliant and impressionistic.

The forger who had studied nothing but his pictures might make the error of giving an early date to a late subject, or his handling of it might combine elements of early and late work, because he did not know the reason for the course taken by the art of Degas. To know, however, that throughout this period his eyesight was failing, and that from the 1890s onward he was virtually blind, makes his work comprehensible. Brilliant colour could be seen by his dimming sight, pastel did not require the detailed technique of application of oil-paint, and one cannot draw if one cannot see.

Some pictures possess a history, some are provided with one, but little is known about the early vicissitudes of many for the reasons mentioned in the Introduction. In the case of apparently valuable works it is worth trying to trace the origin, although this is rarely easy. The more scholarly and detailed catalogues will often provide suggestions for further research. A comparatively recent and useful development is the publication at a modest price of a series of monographs[1] which illustrate in black-and-white all the known paintings of a particular artist with appropriate commentaries. In 1962 only six had been published, but one hundred and fifty are promised, and the series should eventually be a valuable and comprehensive record of the world's paintings. With the aid of such repertories it is possible to review the work of an artist to see where the painting under examination fits in with his complete work, and perhaps to assign to it a tentative date. At any time, no matter how comprehensive the monograph, an author can only claim to illustrate all the *known* paintings. For the reasons previously outlined important discoveries, although unlikely, are always possible.

In the past, many paintings were engraved and the prints sold in fairly large numbers. This is not a late development; Marcantonio Raimondi was engraving plates after Raphael in the sixteenth century. Any painting of importance, therefore, might have been disseminated in this way, and a print may exist in one or other of the museum collections. Old inventories and sale catalogues are worth consulting, although it must be remembered that the title awarded to a painting may differ from that given to it today. If my reader thinks this obstacle likely to be trivial, the "Susanna brought before Daniel" attributed to Giorgione in the Glasgow Art Gallery was at one time called the "Adulteress brought before Christ".

The history of a painting, however well documented, means little by itself, however. Even if it can be traced from owner to owner, there is still no way of ascertaining whether or not a replica has been clandestinely substituted for the original at some point during its existence. But if history, the estimate of its age by the most exact methods possible, and the style all agree in confirming authenticity,

[1] By the Oldbourne Press, London.

then the fortunate owner has a great rarity indeed. Such things do happen. A recent example is the Rembrandt "Aristotle contemplating the Bust of Homer" sold in New York for $2,300,000. Without its impeccable history the price would probably have been less.

The work of David Teniers the Younger (1610-1690) has been useful in identifying pictures on several occasions. He was Court Painter to the Regent of the Netherlands, the Archduke Leopold, who collected paintings on a large scale. Teniers was Keeper of the Archduke's pictures, and produced for his patron "Painted Galleries", of which there are two in Vienna, four in Munich, and one each in Brussels, Madrid, at Woburn Abbey, and Petworth. These depict part of the interior of a gallery, and consist of careful miniature copies of paintings (not always accurate as to size) nearly all of which are Italian. These paintings were the forerunners of the modern *livre de salon* (the "museums without walls" of André Malraux), and were presented by the Archduke to his friends.

These apart, Teniers often made copies of the Archduke's pictures, and produced an album of engravings in 1660 containing about 230 plates entitled the *Theatrum Pictorum*. This was published in several languages, and his brother, Abraham Teniers the art-dealer, also sold the engravings separately.

The painter, Claude (1600-1682), foresaw the possibility that his work might be forged, and he recorded his paintings in a series of 200 drawings called the *Liber Veritatis* which is now in the British Museum.

Particularly dangerous is the *pastiche*. This type of forgery is not a new creation at all, but a combination of elements from several known and genuine works, not necessarily by the same hand. Typical of this type was a profile portrait of two women exhibited at the Burlington Fine Arts Club in 1924, which was copied from two existing single *quattrocento* portraits closely related in date. The tiara of Rouchomowsky, previously discussed, was a *pastiche* because it combined elements closely copied from several known works. The number of works drawn upon in this way may be two or several—the background from one, figures from another, accessories from yet another. These things are much more difficult to detect than the type of forgery represented by the work of Van Meegeren. If the forger is careful in the selection of the work he draws upon for his combination, and is also a careful copyist, he will not be hampered by fear of making mistakes of detail. In former years, when detailed examination of paintings of the kind common today was unknown, forgers were more careless, and sometimes combined *motifs* which did not agree as to period. Most such things are accused by a stiff and stilted composition which may give rise to suspicion, but only detailed examination of the materials can provide a verdict which is entirely trustworthy. Apart from such combinations, the forger commonly juggles with sizes, and reverses figures and detail.

Although it can hardly be regarded as forgery, the buyer needs to be alert for paintings which have been cut from those of larger size. Unwieldy pictures which, because of their size have not found a buyer, are sometimes treated in this way. An attractive female figure is taken from the remainder, put on to a smaller stretcher, and framed. Much the same is done to saleable parts of damaged works.

Many old treatises on painting exist, and it has been possible to gain from these, and from the physical examination of old work, a great deal of information about methods and materials in general use from medieval times onwards. These, however, varied from one country to another, from one period to another, and from one artist to the next. A number of books which discuss these and allied technical matters are listed in the Bibliography. The attribution of old oil-paintings is hardly a matter for the *amateur* unless he is able to bring to the subject the resources enjoyed by the professional. Even then, he will rarely be able to do more than know well a comparatively small area. It is, however, important to understand the general principles, and to know what is possible, even though others must pursue the details.

Certain pigments act as a useful indication of the date of an old painting, provided the specimen tested comes from the original paint-layer and not from subsequent overpainting. The amount needed to verify the nature of a pigment is very small, and its removal does not damage the painting.

Pigments are of many kinds. Their sources may be animal, vegetable, or mineral, as well as synthetic from coal-tar and similar substances. Synthetic pigments were unknown before 1856, and most are considerably later. Many are subject to fading, particularly with exposure to strong light.

Old Master paintings of fine quality reveal that their authors not only took infinite pains in the selection of materials, and the way in which they were applied, but little expense was spared in procuring the best. Two of them—ultramarine and cinnabar—were valued in much the same way as gold and silver were valued among metal-workers. Ultramarine was lapis lazuli finely-ground and treated to remove the grosser impurities which masked the pure blue. For work of lesser quality azurite, a copper ore which also occurs on some excavated bronzes as part of the patination, was in common use.

Natural ultramarine has always been expensive, and towards the end of the eighteenth century it became virtually unprocurable. A synthetic ultramarine was prepared by Guimet in 1824 which is extremely deceptive to all but expert examination. It differs from the natural pigment because this contains crystals which it was originally impossible to remove. These are missing from the synthetic pigment, but, as Thompson points out,[1] if artificial ultramarine be extended by the addition of a proportion of natural ultramarine the result is indetectable by any means at present known. Van Meegeren was well aware of the danger of using artificial ultramarine, because he purchased the entire stock of the only artists' colourman possessing the natural pigment—a few ounces, for which he paid a large sum. He was, however, sufficiently reckless as to adulterate it with cobalt blue (prepared from cobalt oxide, ground flint, and tin carbonate) which, although it had been used for pottery decoration for centuries, was not available to the painter in oils until its development by Thénard in 1802.

Cinnabar was also identified in the Van Meegeren forgeries. This is red sulphide of mercury, frequently used as a valued vermilion pigment in Europe and the Orient from early times. It has one serious defect—very occasionally, and for no ascertainable reason, it turns black, although this is rarely to be seen in oil-paintings.

Not all forgers are as expert nor as painstaking as Van Meegeren, however, and such errors as the inclusion of cadmium yellow (cadmium sulphide) discovered by Strohmeyer in 1817, and the chromium oxide pigments (another nineteenth-century introduction) in the original paint-layer date a painting inevitably. Other dating pigments include Prussian blue (discovered by Diesbach in 1704), and Scheele's green

[1] Daniel V. Thompson: *Materials of Medieval Painting*. London, 1937.

first used in 1778. Other aspects—primings, vehicles, and varnishes—can often be revealing, but it is more difficult to decide upon definite dates for the introduction of such materials and techniques. It is impossible to make general statements of value to the reader; more specialized works must be consulted.

The methods of former years differ remarkably from those of today. The fact that he primed his own canvas, ground his pigments, and mixed them for use, gave the artist a much closer insight into the vagaries of materials. Painting was a traditional craft as well as an art, its secrets handed down from one generation to the next. Paintings were built up according to tested rules of craftsmanship which were slowly modified, and only formulated in the first place after careful observation and experiment.

The artist had a very clear idea of the form and content of his picture when he started because he first made studies and cartoons which were carefully transferred to the canvas or panel. Then, starting with the underpainting, the work was built up layer by layer. Paintings of this kind often needed long periods to complete them. Van Meegeren was astute enough to study these old techniques and to construct his paintings in the same way, although some of his materials differed. Even so, the secret eluded him, and it is evident from his recorded remarks, after he had listened to the expert evidence brought forward at the trial, that he realized the possibility of forgery of this kind, and on this scale, no longer existed. It seems inevitable, therefore, that spurious work in future will be based on contemporary or near-contemporary painting, since the techniques of these artists present the forger with fewer problems. Indeed, some of them present no problems at all.

In a good deal of modern painting the element of craftsmanship is largely absent. It is obvious that if paint is to be squirted at the canvas it matters little whose hand pushes the plunger, neither will it be possible to tell the original from the copy. Much the same applies to paint "dripped" on to a canvas. These, however, are extreme cases. Work of the kind is hardly to be taken seriously; neither, for that matter, are those who buy it.

Craftsmanship, however, is at an extremely low ebb, even in those works painted in a conventional manner. Moreover, canvasses, pigments, and stretchers of precisely the same kind, manufactured from standardized and sometimes synthesized materials, are available equally to the artist and the forger. Since the materials are the same, and craftsmanship is largely absent, there will be little on which to base a worthwhile opinion on grounds of style. An art which can be forged with practically no risk of detection is worthless.

These remarks, however, are not intended to apply to those artists of stature which the age has produced. The style of Picasso, for instance, is strongly idiosyncratic. A forgery of the "Absinthe Drinker" of the Blue Period was recognizable more immediately and certainly than in the case of many Old Master paintings, principally from the weakness and effeminacy of the drawing. Although the subject in each case is a woman, Picasso's drawing has a masculinity and strength which the forger did not understand. Picasso's treatment of the subject shows a peasant woman, crushed by poverty, taking refuge in alcohol. The forgery depicts a woman straight from the psycho-analyst's couch taking alcohol as an alternative to Miltown or Seconal. Much has been said from time to time about deceptive forgeries of Picasso drawings. This may be true of some aspects of his work, but he is undoubtedly a superb draughtsman, and the more ambitious forgeries I have seen have been easy to detect. The conventional work of an artist with so strong an individual style is exceedingly difficult to imitate successfully.

Picasso has been well called the man of many styles. Some of his earliest work, at the beginning of the present century, was strongly influenced by that of Gauguin and Toulouse-Lautrec. Recently I had the experience of flicking the pages of a newly-arrived sale catalogue to see, in passing, something which my mind registered as Lautrec. This was followed almost at once by doubt, and I turned back to discover that second thoughts were best. The artist had been, as I suspected, Picasso. This is not intended as a personal reminiscence, but to emphasize that Picasso's style is so strongly individual that he could not, despite his remarkable versatility, suppress it, even in a study obviously based on the work of Lautrec. Forgers, of course, are even more concerned with suppressing their own style; they are rarely able to do it. We are better acquainted with the characteristics of Picasso's work, and therefore recognize his style, even in disguise, much more easily and certainly.

Another painter whose work resembles that of Picasso in the peculiar difficulties it offers to the forger is Modigliani. His portraits have certainly been forged, but such frauds are fairly obvious if the work is studied for a while. The facial expression is usually the most revealing point.[1] Renoir landscapes are more often forged than portraits or nudes. One portrait of children was accused by a gesture completely foreign to Renoir's style. Particularly common are forgeries of the paintings of Utrillo, although his widow has worked assiduously to keep them from the market, even burning a large number recently. Fraudulent Utrillos are often very deceptive, and exceptional care is needed. Toulouse-Lautrec has been forged, and the increasing demand for his work makes fresh attempts possible. Compositions derived from parts of his larger works are likely to be dangerous but are accused by incompetent drawing. Forgeries of Cézannes's paintings exist, but are not usually unduly deceptive.

Van Gogh's painting has been the target of the forger on more than one occasion, but few forgeries are deceptive if they are subjected to a rigorous examination. Perhaps the most remarkable incident involving the work of Van Gogh, which has led subsequently to ill-judged statements about the number and deceptive nature of existing spurious paintings, was that concerning a dancer named Otto Wacker in Berlin just after the First World War, when every kind of homosexual degeneracy was rife. Wacker opened a gallery on the Viktoriastrasse in 1927 with a large number of Van Goghs reputed to come from our old acquaintance, the anonymous nobleman. Circumstances were favourable at the time to the production of spurious paintings by this artist because his work was just beginning to realize good prices. In 1924, for instance, the Tate Gallery paid £3,300 for "Cypress Trees", although "Vincent's Chair" cost them only £696. Apart from rising prices it was obvious to the forger that Van Gogh had sold practically nothing in his lifetime, that most of his work had been disposed of after his death, and some in extremely unusual circumstances. Therefore, it was not unlikely at the time that a perfectly genuine painting could be discovered without a history.

Superficially, perhaps, Van Gogh appears easy to forge because of his apparently broad handling of his pigments. This is, in fact, untrue. When Van Gogh's paintings are examined by X-ray it is seen that the structure is built up according to a coherent plan. During the course of the trial of Otto Wacker, Dr Ruhemann of the Prussian State

[1] See page 219.

Museums made this very plain when he drew attention to the fact that a Van Gogh under X-ray remains an entirely recognizable Van Gogh, whereas it is often difficult even to distinguish the subject of a spurious painting based on it. There can be little doubt that an X-ray ought to be routine procedure in the course of examining a painting by this artist. Theoretically, of course, a forger could copy such a work with an X-ray photograph in front of him as a guide, but the task of achieving an accurate representation in ordinary light by means which would give a deceptive appearance of genuineness under X-ray is impossible in practice. Van Gogh applied pigment heavily, taking it directly from the tube. To imitate this the Wacker forgeries were built up with layers of *stucco*, painted over. The basic structure, therefore, was completely different. (Plate 31.)

Wacker was fortunate enough to persuade an art-critic, Dr Baart de la Faille, then engaged on a *catalogue raisonnée* of Van Gogh's work, to include thirty of these spurious paintings. This catalogue was published in 1928, but de la Faille later felt impelled to publish a withdrawal. Frank Arnau[1] lists the rejected paintings and comes to substantially the same conclusion as I have done here regarding the "Vermeers" of Van Meegeren. He says: "It is noticeable, even on superficial examination (of the list) that it contains several pictures dealing with the same theme. This fact alone should have put collectors and dealers on their guard. It was astonishing enough that such a collection of Van Goghs had found their way into the hands of one gallery, and a young one at that, but no one should have been credulous enough to accept the fact that it contained four 'Self-portraits', four 'Cypresses', and three 'Olive Trees'."

The courageous withdrawal of de la Faille from a position which he recognized as potentially untenable was made in the face of favourable opinions from others almost as eminent. It was inspired by the suspicions of a noted Berlin art-dealer of high reputation, Paul Cassirer, who organized an exhibition of Van Gogh's work and accepted the loan of four of Wacker's paintings. This provides yet another instance of the forger detected by the art-dealer, and, after careful examination of Wacker's loan by Cassirer and his associates, these paintings were returned as dubious.

It is curious that these paintings should have found so many sup-

[1] *Three Thousand Years of Deception in Art and Antiques*. London, 1961.

porters at the time. Once more we find sceptics in a minority. But the clash of opinion among experts drew the attention of the police to the affair, and they began to accumulate a *dossier*. They soon discovered that none of the suspected paintings could be traced any further back than Otto Wacker. The latter, with an impudence born of fear of the consequences, decided that attack was the best form of defence, and he succeeded in obtaining an injunction preventing the publication of the addition to de la Faille's catalogue which stigmatized thirty of these pictures as spurious. The affair began to assume the proportions of a *cause célèbre*, but desperate manœuvres by Wacker prevented it from being brought to trial until April 1932.

The case was heard in Berlin, one of the witnesses being Vincent's nephew, Vincent Wilhelm van Gogh (Plate 34), who gave evidence on the dispersal of his uncle's pictures, testifying that only during the Brabant period had a significant amount of his work disappeared without trace. Perhaps the most startling statement to emerge during the course of the trial was that of an expert on the work of Van Gogh, Meier-Graefe, art-critic of the *Frankfurter Zeitung*, who had disagreed with de la Faille's conclusion on the spurious nature of the paintings: "Anyone who buys pictures and pays enormous prices for them on the strength of expert opinions alone deserves to meet with disaster." The operative word is "alone". Meier-Graefe is abdicating from the position of the expert who claims to be able to attribute by intuition, and recognizes that more exact methods are essential. One is permitted to question what certificates of authenticity from experts are worth if they have no higher opinion than this of their function and duty.

A Court action arose from the trial of Wacker against the former directors of the Bank für Deutsche Beamte who had been speculating in paintings on behalf of the Bank. Plate 35 illustrates the Court inquiry into the authenticity of some of these paintings.

Overpainting of one kind or another is the commonest method of faking. This ranges from simple restoration with the object of disguising damage and unwise cleaning to major alterations to the character of a work for the purpose of increasing its value. Overpainting can often be detected with ultra-violet radiation, particularly if it is fairly recent. When the varnish film has been removed from the surface of the painting, the fresher pigments yield more quickly to solvents than the old. In this way most overpainting can be removed from the original paint-layer without excessive risk. Damage from incompetent cleaning is often extreme, especially if it was done in the early part of the nineteenth century or before. The extracts which follow from an early treatise on picture-cleaning in my own library are an indication of some of the methods adopted:

> If it be a hard varnish, such as that of copal, which is to be removed, friction with sea or river sand . . . will accomplish the purpose. More violent means are sometimes resorted to. . . . The solvents commonly employed for this purpose are the several alkalies, alcohol, and essential oils, used simply or combined. Of the alkalies . . . carbonate of ammonia is the only one which can safely be used in removing oil and varnish from a picture, which it does powerfully . . . potash and soda ought only to be employed as an extraordinary means of removing spots that will not yield to safer agents. . . . The uniform disadvantage of spirits of wine or alcohol and ether is that they obscure the work, so that the operator cannot see the good he is doing, or the mischief he may have done . . . except by revarnishing and oiling out. . . . Another friend, known to the public as an eminent engraver . . . was equally felicitous in restoring the purity of an excellent Picture by carefully washing it gradually, and in parts, with some of the *aqua fortis* [nitric acid] used in engraving. . . . We have it on the authority of another talented friend that by damping the face [i.e. the surface] of a Picture and exposing it to the action of a frosty night all foulness will be effectually loosened and removed by the subsequent use of a sponge.

The following footnote is reproduced *in extenso*:

> The famous "Descent from the Cross": this Picture of all the works of Rubens is that which has the most reputation. I had consequently conceived the highest idea of its excellence, knowing the print, I had formed in my imagination what such a composition would produce in the hands of such a painter. I confess I was disappointed. However this disappointment did not proceed from any deficiency in the Picture itself; had it been in the original state in which Rubens left it, it must have appeared very different; but it is mortifying to see to what degree it has suffered by *cleaning and*

> *mending*; that brilliant effect, which undoubtedly it once had, is lost in a mist of varnish, which appears to be chilled or mildewed. The Christ is in many places retouched so as to be visible at a distance; the St John's head repainted, and other parts on a close inspection, appear to be chipping off, and ready to fall from the canvas. However, there is enough to be seen to satisfy any connoisseur that in its perfect state it well deserved all its reputation.[1]

The author, in an advertisement at the end of his book, offered his services "to those Noblemen and Gentlemen who may have ancestral portraits or other pictures in their possession, which require restoration". It is hardly to be expected, therefore, that even paintings in good condition will have escaped entirely without restoration, and much depends on when this was done. Modern restoration by skilled and conscientious workmen has much to commend it, although the line of demarcation between restoration and faking is sometimes difficult to draw. Purists prefer all overpainting to be removed; collectors usually demand that damage be repaired as imperceptibly as possible. Perhaps the best kind of restoration is that in which missing parts are broadly indicated but not imitated, but this is more applicable to public collections and those of scholars. Frequently accusations of overcleaning aimed at restorers employed by public galleries are inspired by the removal of old overpainting previously hidden by discoloured varnish. A varnish which is brown in tone is not necessarily original or even very old, because restorers in the past have frequently disguised their handiwork in this way by adding pigments to the varnish.

Fakes which change the character of a work to a major degree can be divided into two kinds. The first is also the most obvious, and is aimed at altering the subject to provide a more saleable painting. In this way soberly-dressed Dutch burghers are given rich robes and become historical portraits, such as that of Henry VIII; plain girls are given beauty-treatment, and elderly matrons have thirty years lopped from their age by deft touches; nudes are sometimes clothed, more often from prudish motives than to enhance the value, which often falls in consequence. A Reynolds portrait of two young girls chaperoned by their mother was completely altered by the removal of the older woman. A Munich painting of St Eustace by Dürer received the

[1] By "An Artist": *On the Preservation of Oil Paintings*. London, 1835.

addition of an extensive landscape and a horse, and a "Last Supper" by Tintoretto was provided with an architectural background and foreground with the aid of canvas added to top and bottom. St. Eustace is part of the Paumgartner altar-piece and is reproduced by Hans Tietze.[1] Another panel is shown on Plate 36. The horse and the landscape background in this case also were apparently added by Johan Georg Fischer who restored the work for the Duke of Bavaria, by whom it was purchased in 1614. Obviously it must have been done with the Duke's consent and approbation. To possess the untouched work of Dürer was a matter of little or no importance to buyers who were accustomed to purchase the studio-pieces of the time.

More deceptive, and demanding a greater degree of skill from the faker, is the conversion of a school-piece to the work of a major master by adding small but characteristic touches. The addition of the *impasti* of Rembrandt to contemporary paintings sufficiently near to his style to make this feasible has often resulted in a temporarily deceptive fake. In the same way the characteristics of both Vermeer and Hals have been supplied to inferior work. From time to time sales of the contents of an artist's studio have been held after his death, and partially finished and discarded canvases have been sold. These are completed by fakers, and since they often bear the stamp of the sale on the reverse, they can sometimes be confusing.

Signatures are commonly forged and added, often inconspicuously, leaving the buyer to find it for himself and rejoice in a discovery which seems to confirm the attribution. It has been said that in nineteenth-century Paris specialists in signatures were employed to do work of this kind. Fashions change, and it is sometimes found that the signature of a once-popular master has been added to the genuine work of an artist who would, today, fetch a higher price. When Hobbema paintings were inexpensive the signature of Ruysdael, whose work was in greater demand, was sometimes substituted. Today, the chances are that Hobbema would realize the higher price of the two.

Nevertheless the replacement of one signature by another is far from easy, because it is difficult to remove the old paint sufficiently for all traces to be invisible to ultra-violet or infra-red light. The original signature is, therefore, sometimes assimilated into the detail of the painting, which should be detectable on close examination, and

[1] *Genuine and False*. London, 1948.

a new signature added elsewhere. Cases in which a signature is in an unusual position, or in which it diverges from that normally preferred by a particular artist, need special consideration.

There remains the problem of the unsigned painting. In whatever position fake signatures are added they are usually *over* the varnish, and this in itself is highly suspicious. Pictures are not varnished for many months after painting has been completed for the good reason that oil-paint must be allowed to harden by contact with the air. If a painting is varnished too soon the surface is sealed from the atmosphere, and this slows down the hardening process and leads to serious deterioration. The artist, therefore, naturally signed a painting when he finished it, and put it on one side to await varnishing.

If a signature has been added recently over varnish it will offer little resistance to a pad soaked in alcohol. It is, of course, possible for a faker to remove part of the varnish, sign the picture, and revarnish, but this will stand out from the remainder under ultra-violet light with startling clarity, and is merely an insult to the buyer's intelligence. The whole of the varnish could be removed; then the most which could be said without a much closer inspection is that the painting has been revarnished. These remarks apply principally to old works; new painting offers a much more difficult problem.

Arnau suggests the possibility of "engraving" a signature by inscribing it into the paint-layer, afterwards varnishing over it. The signature would, in fact, be "inlaid" into the old and hardened paint. It may have been attempted, but it ought to be easily detectable by ultra-violet light. Moreover the operation would be more difficult than removing the old varnish completely in many cases.

Generally, fake signatures are at their most dangerous on previously unsigned work. Monograms are likely, in some cases at least, to prove even more deceptive within certain limits. The letter *P*, for instance, can quite simply be changed into *R* or *B*, and *C* becomes *G* with a few slight touches. Differences in fluorescence between old and new paint or varnish are just as likely as with other forms of tampering.

Drawings are commonly forged. It is not generally difficult to make certain that the paper is old and of a kind likely to have been used for the purpose. The watermark, too, is sometimes a revealing characteristic. Appendix II discusses paper and ink in a little more detail. Studies which purport to be for known paintings and sculptures are a fruitful field for the forger. They do not need to be highly finished, and are frequently no more than rough sketches.

It is often extremely difficult to be certain that a drawing done on the correct kind of paper with the sort of crayon, chalk, or ink in use during the period is a forgery. In such cases only stylistic evidence may be able to distinguish between genuine and false, which is not a particularly satisfactory position.

It is possible to determine the nature of the material in a pencil-drawing. Early pencils were made from a soft alloy of tin and lead; the presence of graphite is reason to assign a drawing to the last half of the sixteenth century at the earliest. Early graphite pencils were not graded, and could not be sharpened to a point.

Fakes are usually limited to the addition of signatures, monograms, and dates. In modern times artists sign and date working-drawings either to make them saleable when their reputation is already established, or from vanity when they are unknown. Artists of former days signed finished drawings as proof of authorship; there was little point in signing working-sketches.

Chalk-drawings are not difficult to forge if the correct type of paper is available, and appraisal must then depend almost entirely on style. Line-drawings give the forger a little more trouble, and detection is often comparatively simple if the line can be compared with that of an example known to be genuine under a high-powered lens or a microscope. It is useful to have some knowledge of the methods used to detect forgeries of handwriting, and the interested reader is recommended to consult Albert S. Osborn's *Questioned Documents* (London, 1929) which has a wealth of fascinating enlarged illustrations of penmanship of value to the collector of drawings.

The following quotation from this source is equally applicable to the forgery of drawings and of signatures:

> Forgeries nearly always show plainly the natural results of the strained conditions under which they are executed; too much attention is given to unimportant details and a slow, hesitating, and unnatural appearance is shown in the writing, even when it is quite an accurate copy of the genuine writing imitated. Usually it is not even a good imitation of form characteristics. . . . The fundamental and usual defect in a forgery is not divergence in

> form, but in quality of the line. . . . Close scrutiny of line quality alone often furnishes the basis for the gravest suspicion. . . .

A later paragraph emphasizes what has already been said elsewhere in this volume in connection with other types of forgery.

> The forger does not, and is usually not able to determine what are the most significant characteristics in the writing which is being imitated, and *even less is he aware of the significant characteristics of his own writing*, and thus may unconsciously include them in the forgery. Simulation in almost every case gives attention to the conspicuous features of form only, and the many other elements entering into the task receive no attention whatever. It is very much more difficult to simulate an unfamiliar form, and to copy unfamiliar forms and at the same time to write freely in an unusual manner is simply impossible. [My italics!]

A study of Osborn's illustrations will suggest to the reader many ways in which his conclusions can be applied to the examination of suspected drawings, and it is significant to find someone working in a different field arriving at similar conclusions to those recorded in the preceding pages. It suggests that the detection of art-forgery need be no more difficult than that of cheque-forgery if the proper methods are adopted.

Water-colour is a difficult medium for the forger because it demands a high degree of skill. Prices, also, are not generally high. Certain artists who have been at one time in great demand have been forged in the past, although detection is not usually difficult. David Cox has been a popular target for spurious works of this kind, and his signature is frequently added to work in his style, most of it originally by enthusiastic amateur water-colourists—keen students of his *Treatise of Landscape Painting in Water Colours*, first published in 1813 and reprinted by *The Studio* in 1922.

deaz ist[illegible] depulsit mario migrino du
alumta . ¶ De sompnis . c.
Sed qin diuinas unde distinx pl
gimib; multoz qes adiibeam sit
augusti sacratissima memoria cum
quaz dies i secut' e quo i capis phil
minerue spes oborta precepit ut illi
usaz ualitudine primo pho ne itter
i acez de sen iussit . vbi du sup uir
cubat castu ei' a bruto capta sunt
effectuz ne destinatuz iaz i mozt gli
uiolentia secuturi Augustuz no nal
uigorez etiaz recens z domestici eve
nuit Audiuerat e iuly pris su ux
egit iqere uidisse mltis eiz afecti
atrocitate uehementez extitaz rogare
nec At illa ne muliebri sopnio mc

38. Ultra-violet radiation. Photograph revealing writing which had previously been erased.

[*Engelhard Hanovia Lamps*

*Chapter VIII*

# *The Collector, the Restorer, and the Forger*

The slow, prudent method must be learnt of not listening to first impulses until they are supported by something better than the innate conceit of the beginner.

RICARDO NOBILI

In a recent work Gerald Reitlinger[1] remarked that not to collect anything was to fall below the level of the squirrels and the marmots. Certainly the instinct to collect is widespread among the human race, and excavations of the remains of civilizations remote in time prove that it is no new thing, but deeply rooted in human nature. The desire to possess objects which have no practical use, and to decorate articles of utility, must necessarily give rise to some kind of machinery for distributing them, whether it be the comparatively simple and straightforward process of endeavouring to impose the will by conquest on those who are weaker, or by the less violent means of purchase. The art-market is now the normal way of providing channels for passing such works from hand to hand. In modern times the incidence of confiscatory taxation has led to the transference of works of art in large numbers to the State in satisfaction of its insatiable demands, but the art-market is even more essential than before because it is the only way of assessing value.

To some, especially to those who appear to seek in art a substitute religion, who were prepared to pay nearly a million pounds for a not

[1] Gerald Reitlinger: *The Economics of Taste* (I). London, 1961.

particularly distinguished cartoon because it bore a fashionable name, and who object to coupling art with what it takes to buy it, the art-market is analogous to the money-changers of the Temple. But despite the cloud of ink, which resembles that of the cuttle-fish inasmuch as it obscures the fundamentals of the problem, the purpose of money is merely to provide a handy means of exchanging unlike objects and services. Art and money are, in fact, inseparable in the present form of society, and the alternative, in which art would become the plaything of the bureaucrat, carries with it far more unpleasant connotations than this. Better the evil of money than the far greater evil of State control.[1]

Nevertheless, like all markets, the art-market has those who manœuvre on the fringe to pick up whatever crumbs they can from a richly-laden table, and who exercise talents for doubtful purposes which would enable them to make a comfortable living if they were honestly inclined.

Those who collect works of art share their pastime with many of the great figures of the past. Few, in fact, have been able to resist the proferred lure. To name those who are well-known to the art-historian since the Renaissance would be to catalogue the outstanding figures of history—Charles I, Cardinal Richelieu, Cardinal Mazarin, Mme de Pompadour, Augustus the Strong, Frederick the Great, K'ang Hsi, Ch'ien Lung, and many more. Louis Quatorze, the greatest European autocrat of the seventeenth century, when he wished to impress the civilized world with his power and prestige turned to works of art, buying immense quantities for Versailles, and creating through the agency of Colbert and Le Brun the means of supplying his requirments. Nations joined this search for prestige. The French armies looted works of art under Napoleon, and Hitler's Germany followed the same path. Hermann Göring assembled a large collection, for some of which he paid. With the rise of the *bourgeoisie* and the *entrepreneur* we find vast fortunes made by such men as Pierpoint Morgan, Mellon, William Randolph Hearst, and others largely being expended in this way, as were the fortunes of the Medicis, the Fuggers, and the Rothschilds before them.

It is only to be expected that, in such conditions, various forms of fraud will flourish, just as they flourished at one time in the stock-

[1] A sentiment which demands much wider application than to art alone.

market, and still do in sections of the property-market, as a comparison of the advertisements of some estate agents with the property itself will speedily prove. The activities of various professional associations, however, are having a salutary effect on the problem created by those who seek to make a dishonest living, and, so far as works of art are concerned, it is incontrovertible that forgery is now more difficult than at any other time in the history of the art-market. It is being increasingly limited to small and relatively inexpensive objects which can be manufactured comparatively cheaply, and which are not valuable enough to warrant expert examination.

Whatever is accomplished, however, the problem of the gullible buyer will remain. It will seem incredible to the reader that in the nineteenth century a forger[1] actually succeeded in selling letters *in French* signed by Plato and Mary Magdalene. It is true, nevertheless, just as Brooklyn Bridge, the Eiffel Tower, and Trajan's Column in Rome have been "sold" at one time or another to unsuspecting dupes. In the latter instance the buyer arrived with a hired gang of workmen, and actually erected a scaffolding before he was restrained by the police.

It is arguable how far such people ought to be protected. In France the law was (and probably still is) that fraudulent transactions are not *criminal* unless they would deceive a man of ordinary prudence—presumably the person referred to in English legal circles as "the man on the Clapham omnibus". The current fashion for grandmotherly legislation, however, has produced elaborate machinery, erected at no small cost to the taxpayer, to preserve the gullible from the "mock auction". I hold no brief for this kind of swindler, and taken at its face value legislation is, perhaps, desirable, but a little thought given to the subject leads to doubt. People swindled in this way may lose five pounds or so, but is not the lesson they learn worth very much more to them? The effect of being deceived, like buying a forged work of art, ought to lead to redoubled vigilance and an ultimate saving of much more than five pounds. I know that the ten pounds or so which I spent on my first forgery has since saved me many times this sum. Had I not done so, I might later have been persuaded to part with a great deal more for something equally worthless.

A useful parallel is provided by modern medicine. It has become

[1] Vrain Lucas of Paris.

customary to fill the unfortunate individual for quite trivial reasons with antibiotics, vaccines, and prophylactics against almost every conceivable disease. The body's natural resistance to invasion is lowered, and ultimately the disease or infection against which no precautions have been taken comes along and its course is rapidly fatal. Countrymen, and travellers in remote regions, know that it is possible to drink unharmed from a well which would cause serious illness to the townsman. The loss of five pounds may well be regarded as a vaccine which ought to offer a considerable degree of protection subsequently. If it does not, there seems no reason why society should add to its burdens by attempting to protect those who are not prepared to protect themselves. Experience has to be bought, but there is no reason why it should be bought at a high price. To lose money is a salutary way of learning that a desire to make quick profits, or to acquire something cheaply, must be tempered with at least a modicum of caution and wordly wisdom.

It is impossible to safeguard the gullible and the childish if they persist in venturing into worlds inhabited by those who are neither, and no amount of half-baked sociological or political theorizing will ever succeed in depriving the astute and the unscrupulous of their natural prey. This book has not been written for the gullible, but for the serious collector of works of art who wants to know something of the darker side of his chosen pursuit for the purpose of avoiding it. *Forewarned is forearmed* is no less common sense for being hackneyed.

*Caveat emptor*, however, is not a tag which applies only to the art-market. If it did there would be no consumers' associations, no mention of that ugly phrase, "planned obsolescence", fewer mechanical gadgets designed so that trivial damage is irreparable, and much less emetic gushing of lies and half-truths from the advertisers of popular commodities. Whether we like it or not, chicanery and deception are as much a part of life as they have always been, and the work of the art-faker is only one aspect. Ultimately, there is little difference between the manufacturer who produces a shoddy article designed to break or wear out after a specified time, an employee who does slovenly work, and the man who fabricates a spurious work of art with intent to deceive. The latter is, perhaps, the more admirable character, because he pits his wits against those of the collector who need not buy unless he chooses.

The forger, however, is not the only enemy the collector has to fear. Equally dangerous is the unscrupulous restorer, who is usually a faker as well.

The relationship between the collector and restorer has always been an ambivalent one. It is a truism to say that every work of art begins to deteriorate from the moment it leaves the creator's hand, and the process is accelerated by the accidents of time. Legitimately, restoration is aimed at conserving the object without altering its essential character, but how far the process ought to be carried is a matter of controversy. Little objection can be made to such work as the replacement of a missing hand or arm to a porcelain figure where, as so often happens, the original nature of a missing part is well known from other undamaged specimens. I have several times known two specimens of the same figure, damaged in different places, fully restored with accuracy from comparison with each other. It would, however, be very difficult to defend the restoration of a marble statue with the addition of a conjectural head, although lesser repairs may sometimes improve a slightly damaged example of fairly recent workmanship. Much depends on the reason for the restoration. The collector likes to see a near-perfect porcelain figure in his cabinet; he prefers his silver with the dents removed; and he thinks that paintings with bare patches look unsightly. Who is to say that he is wrong? But restoration done for the purpose of deceiving a buyer into thinking that an object is in better condition than it is must always be fraudulent, if only because a much higher price is demanded than for the unrestored specimen.

Equally objectionable is restoration which succeeds only at the expense of altering or modifying the existing work. It may, in some cases, be desirable to fill in or replace missing parts of a painting, or to overpaint those which are damaged and consequently unsightly, but nothing can excuse painting over sound areas to disguise the work. The purist will argue, with truth, that any kind of repair falsifies the artist's intention, but a damaged area also falsifies it, and the choice is really between which kind of falsification one prefers.

Little objection can be raised to much of the restoration in the field of painting. Indeed, one has only to call it by another name, conservation, to put it beyond the realm of argument. Obviously to provide a failing canvas with a fresh support, be it canvas or panel, is essential.

Falling paint may need to be secured to its support; tears can hardly be left because they are a source of additional danger; no one would counsel that a disfiguring scratch remain untouched.

Cleaning is a branch of restoration about which controversy is frequent. There can be no doubt that when the artist painted his picture he did not intend it to be seen through a screen of semi-opaque varnish, and modern methods of cleaning are extremely safe. In the process, however, old and excessive overpainting is sometimes removed, and pigments are found to have altered in shade. The latter defect is unavoidable, and would exist whether the picture were cleaned or not. The objection is not to cleaning, but to the substitution of a picture which confounds the unconsciously accepted idea that Old Master works ought to be dark brown in colour, and should not rival modern work in brilliance. The layer of brown gravy which has hidden old pictures from our view until the more recent developments in the technique of cleaning has proved to be the forger's friend, and forgeries are always covered with varnish of this colour because it has the effect of muting the danger-signals which would otherwise be clearly apparent.

There are, of course, the grave risks inseparable from cleaning done by unskilled hands as may be seen from the footnote on page 237, and from the opportunity occasionally taken by unscrupulous restorers to alter the character of a work into something more saleable in some of the ways already discussed. The restorer has the opportunity to study the technique of the artists whose works are brought to him very closely, and his knowledge of their methods must, if he is a skilled craftsman, be great. If he is dishonest, therefore, his skill may be extremely valuable to a fraudulent dealer, especially in his ability to inflate minor works into major ones. The possibilities are not limited to painting. On page 161 I have mentioned an instance of a porcelain restorer using a rare figure to make deceptive reproductions. The value of the thief turned policeman is counterbalanced by the dangers of the policeman turned thief. In either case they know each other's secret methods.

If an offer is made by a dealer of standing in whom the buyer has confidence, nothing more needs to be done. In the unlikely event of both dealer and buyer being deceived in thinking an object to be genuine which is later found to be spurious, an amicable solution of the problem can undoubtedly be arranged. From any less well-known source it is necessary to proceed with caution because the vendor may be deficient in knowledge or in honesty, and wisdom counsels that both should be assumed until proof to the contrary has been obtained. The beginner who has had little experience of buying works of art would do well to go to a member of a recognized association, not because those who do not belong to it are necessarily ignorant or dishonest, but because membership gives some kind of positive guarantee of fair-dealing. Some dealers outside these associations are extremely reputable and expert, but their reputation will undoubtedly be known to the buyer for other reasons.

If an object is exceptionally important and highly-priced it is often advisable to get a second opinion from an expert in the field. In other cases the buyer can do much to protect himself.

First, consider the nature of the offer. If an attribution has been made by the seller, then it is necessary to do whatever is possible to be certain of its accuracy. The collector should beware of making his own attribution unless he has had a great deal of experience. The experts of the Louvre made their own attribution when they bought Bastianini's bust of Benivieni. This effectually prevented any recourse to the seller, who had made no claims for it.

If an attribution is made, the price should be considered carefully. Is it a fair one, or is it below market-price? If £500 is asked for an object which would normally change hands for about £1,000, then extreme care is needed. If, on the other hand, £100 or less is asked, the chances are that the vendor does not know what he is selling, or he is offering stolen property. If the object is spurious then, at such a price, it will be a fairly obvious fraud which would not deceive anyone but a beginner.

Before an object can be examined, some kind of attribution is essential because only if date and provenance are known or assumed does it become possible to compare it with other things of a like nature. A photograph is useful because it enables comparison to be made easily with repertories of illustrations, such as those to be found in standard works in a good reference library. The comparison should aim at establishing whether the suggested provenance and date is likely, or, if this proves difficult, if the object can be related to those made elsewhere at the same time. The prevailing style of the period is a useful key to the dating of objects, and this is briefly mentioned in Appendix 12.

The material of which the object is made should be studied in relation to that of genuine specimens. For example, it is necessary to see that a porcelain figure is hard where it should be hard, and soft if it ought to be soft; that the colour of the porcelain agrees with that of a genuine figure; and that the usual manufacturing idiosyncrasies are present. An object which does not agree with the characteristics of one known to be of the provenance and date attributed is not necessarily spurious, however. The attribution may be wrong. It may come from another factory, another country, or may belong to a different period.

Next, design and construction should receive attention. If a piece of furniture is under examination, not only should the nature of the wood be considered but care should be taken to see that the methods of construction used are those of the period, and that unpolished wood is present in the right places. The vendor ought not to object to unscrewing a lock-plate, for instance, to show the colour of the wood beneath it. Signs of age need special attention, and care should be exercised in cases of specimens in unusually good condition. Repairs should also be noted, and if any are exceptionally obvious, others more cleverly executed should be looked for.

The style of decoration should be considered with care. Bear in mind the date attributed and look for anachronisms—features which were introduced at a later date than that suggested. Remember, too, the possibility of added decoration for the purpose of increasing value.

Lastly, consider the general impression. Is it convincing, or does it raise lingering doubts? The collector of experience would be well-advised to listen to the promptings of intuition. A close copy will often have many small points of discrepancy, too slight to be noticed easily at first sight, all of which contribute to a feeling of uneasiness which is nearly always justified. Feelings of this kind suggest that the object ought to be examined afresh with even greater care.

If the buyer already has a collection of similar objects, and can persuade the dealer to let him make a comparison, this is often advisable. If the vendor is willing, it is a good sign. It proves that he, at least, has confidence in what he is offering. An object which looks fairly convincing in a shop where it is cheek by jowl with other unlike specimens will nearly always reveal its nature one way or the other if it is examined in company with genuine pieces of the same kind. On the other hand, the shop of the specialist dealer, where many objects of the same kind are sold, is a much easier place from which to buy, because spurious examples can hardly bear such comparison. The buyer must, of course, realize that he can hardly regard the dealer with suspicion without also being in the same position himself, and that the dealer is entitled to inquire as to his *bona fides* before parting with a specimen on approval, and even to ask for a cheque to be deposited against its value.

The safest way for the collector to avoid buying forgeries is to learn as much as possible about the methods and materials of craftsmen, both old and contemporary. Time spent in visiting pottery and porcelain factories, especially those which still work to some extent in the old ways, is never wasted. To be able to watch an experienced restorer of old furniture, and to discuss his work with him, will do more to make a collector proof against forgery than any number of handbooks. Art-schools teach the craft of the silversmith, and even a few months of spare-time activity spent in learning its rudiments will be of the greatest value later.

The collector of paintings is in a more difficult position, because materials are now produced commercially and not in the studio. But experimenting with the basic materials will undoubtedly teach a great deal which it is impossible to learn in any other way. Professor Laurie, whose invaluable work on the methods and materials of the Old Masters is well-known, reproduced experimentally some of the effects of time on old paintings to find out what the forger might be able to do.

There is, in fact, no substitute for some kind of practical experience, and it is not usually difficult to devise a way of getting it. A note of caution, however, is necessary. The trained craftsman of long experience can produce results which to the novice seem almost incredible. Skill is even more important than materials in producing the desired result. Generally, however, an attempt to carve wood with a good and a bad chisel will make plain the importance of the right tools.

This book is primarily addressed to the collector. The buyer of interior decoration does not mind very much whether his commode be genuine Louis Quinze or a good reproduction, provided he has been charged a fair price for it. But even the buyer of decoration wants to be certain that he is not paying more than he need, or more than the market value of the object regarded solely for what it is.

It is essential to take into consideration the probable first cost of the object based on a "time and materials" basis, with a fair allowance for profit. Obviously it will be expensive to make an accurate replica of the work of an eighteenth-century Paris *ébéniste* or a fine piece of Chippendale. These will not be bought for a few pounds, however they are described. Nineteenth-century or modern tapestry coverings of good quality will be priced highly because they are expensive to make. A recent quotation from one of the French tapestry manufacturers for modern work is £200 a square metre. On the other hand a Van Meegeren forgery, whatever it cost to make in the first place, is no more than a curiosity. It has little decorative value, and serves no useful purpose. This is principally due to the fact that Van Meegeren had small reputation as an artist in his own right. A replica by an artist of greater stature would be worth more, as witness the prices given for studies after Velasquez and Hals by Sargent which are sold as his work.

The making of forgeries has always been influenced by the potential profit, and for this reason those works which were most in demand at any particular time are precisely those most likely to have suffered. The pottery of Palissy, for instance, was much copied in the nineteenth century when his work realized high prices; it has not been forged since. Vermeer, on the other hand, was not forged until the twentieth century because his work was not sought until relatively modern times.

Prices for good reproductions will fluctuate more widely than those for genuine works. Even when the latter are unfashionable they will find buyers who admire the period and know that they, or their heirs, will reap the benefit of temporarily low prices. Reproductions of an unfashionable period, however, interest no one. They are not wanted by the collector, and certainly not by the fashionable decorator. Reproduction tables will not even be wanted in the mass-market, because this is interested only in cheap, flashy, and commercial versions of the modern idiom.

It is, of course, obvious that in a world where craftsmanship of all kinds is disappearing, to be replaced by sketchily assembled machine-made parts, any work of craftsmanship will have a price which will become increasingly a scarcity value, and the price of even unfashionable reproductions will tend to rise accordingly, but it will remain far below that asked for those things which are in demand.

Paintings are more difficult to assess than most other things. Prices are now highest for those which can reasonably be regarded as solely the work of a particular artist, irrespective of the school to which he belongs. The value also varies with size and condition. Obviously works which will fit easily into a particular scheme of decoration will be most in demand, and therefore most expensive. Paintings of an awkward size must be extremely important if they are to realize a high price. Subject, also, must be considered. For example, religious subjects are at present unfashionable, and a painting of this kind by anyone but a major master will cost less than one with secular appeal. Even in the case of Leonardo, a "Leda and the Swan" would be more readily saleable than a subject from Christian hagiography. These considerations would undoubtedly influence choice of subject and so forth in any modern attempts at forgery.

Lower prices are usually paid for school- and studio-pieces. Not only are they not by the hand of the Master, but they are much easier to reproduce successfully because some of the signs by which authenticity can be established are missing. The amount of overpainting, and the extent of repairs present, must bear on value to a greater or lesser extent, but, as in the case of restoration to other kinds of work, due consideration must be given to the scarcity or otherwise of works in perfect condition.

Experience will teach how likely it is that any particular object will exist in an unrestored state. In the case of Persian pottery a perfect specimen is a great rarity. Therefore, the desirability of any specimen offered must be deduced from the *amount* of restoration present. A clock-movement with the original escapement can hardly be found, and the experienced collector will not reject an otherwise interesting specimen on this account. Rather will he focus his examination on the remainder. On the other hand, restoration to an Impressionist or Post-impressionist painting ought to give rise to a long pause for reflection, and many of the less fragile and more recent works need to be in reasonably good condition if they are to be worth buying at anything like full market value.

When all has been said, something must be left for the individual judgement and preferences of the buyer, who best knows his intention in seeking to acquire a particular work. It may be that he finds it sufficiently attractive in itself to want to own it, regardless of authorship or authenticity. There is much to be said for buying in this way, provided one is not deceived as to the nature of the purchase, and the price is fair.

In the course of this book it has been difficult to avoid the implication that the art-market is a potentially dangerous place for the buyer without expert knowledge. This is far from true, nor has it been my intention to suggest such a thing. Every market in which purchases have the nature of an investment is speculative. The buyer of pre-1939 Government stock (aptly termed "guilt-edged") knows by how much the "safe" investment can decline in value. An equivalent amount invested in old silver or porcelain would, by now, be showing a very handsome profit. The share certificates of many companies, once regarded as sound, could now be used as an expensive form of wallpaper. Investors in works of art not only have much greater control over their investment, but their chances of capital appreciation in an inflationary world are far greater than those of the investor in most other things. Governments can avoid paying their debts by depreciating currency, or they can dip predatory hands into the till of the public or private company. The work of art is much less susceptible to bureaucratic control and interference.

The art-market, however, has its disadvantages. Even though the profits are tax-free they can rarely be taken quickly, although the rapid advance in the value of old silver during the past few years tends to belie this statement. The dealer, who buys and sells to live, takes a profit on turnover; the collector ought to look for long-term but steady appreciation which will be the greater for wise buying. The art-market, in fact, is only dangerous to those who look for bargains without being properly equipped by knowledge, experience, and the practical handling of objects to recognize the spurious when it is offered. Those who prefer to pay a reputable dealer for his knowledge and skill have little to fear.

The forger flourishes because people who have sufficient business acumen to avoid the "bucket-shop" and go to a member of the Stock Exchange to buy shares, are nevertheless often sufficiently ill-advised as to buy antiques from dubious sources. It is flattering for a collector to be approached by an unknown person with a specious story of a work of art for sale by an anonymous but aristocratic and impoverished family, but in all such cases the buyer must rely on his own unaided judgement which, unless he has had long experience, is likely to be much more fallible than that of a dealer or an auctioneer. If he makes a mistake he is rarely in a position to take legal action. The person who proffers the bait often has no money, and no reputation assiduously built up over years of satisfactory trading to lose. He will also be careful to see that no statements which could later be produced as evidence of fraud exist in permanent form.

There is no reason why even an aristocratic impoverished family, anxious to preserve anonymity, should not offer a genuine work of art in the sale-room. Privacy can be preserved, the work will be catalogued appropriately, and they will receive its full market value in free competition. If they are reluctant to do so, it is almost certainly because they fear the expert examination to which it will be subjected.[1] They may not *know* that it is not what it purports to be, but they are obviously unwilling to take the chance of finding out, because, if it should be rejected, either they or their agents can only offer it subsequently under its former description by becoming parties to what may well be fraud.

There is, therefore, little that the buyer of works of art need fear from the activities of the forger if he buys wisely from accredited sources, because few forgeries are capable of deceiving the expert who knows his limitations, and whose own money is at stake. Beware of the expert who claims a flair. A clever forgery can only be detected by long inspection and consideration of all the factors involved, and anything can be a clever forgery until it has been duly examined and pronounced genuine.

It would be unfair to the dealer of repute if I failed to sound a note of caution against irresponsible suggestions of forgery from the kind of acquaintance we all make sooner or later—the man who delights in casting doubt on the acquisitions of his friends. Occasionally this is the genuine scepticism of the scholar, and it is then worth careful consideration. Just as often it is an attempt to display a rudimentary knowledge, or, to borrow from Stephen Potter, to indulge in a form

[1] This is often the reason for the words, "no dealers", appearing in newspaper advertisements.

of one-upmanship. The simplest way to find out what the criticism is worth is to ask the reasons for it. If they appear to be sound they can be discussed with the dealer who sold the object.

The expert of great experience, however, is worthy of attention if he confesses to an intuitive feeling that an object is spurious, even if he cannot advance a definite reason. Often many small discrepancies which are difficult to explain clearly and in detail may arouse vague feelings of disquiet which are frequently justified. It would be unwise to stigmatize an object as spurious on such evidence alone, but it suggests the need for much closer investigation. The greatest danger of intuition is that it may be accepted as fact, especially when it works in reverse and regards as genuine an object which may be false.

A word of caution will not be out of place regarding the practice of some provincial auctioneers, who allow antiques and other *objets d'art* which are not the property of the original vendor to be put into house-sales. This fact ought to be stated in the catalogue, but it is rarely done. Most such auctioneers are not specialists, and they are likely to be strongly influenced by a vendor's description. It is, therefore, possible for these circumstances to be used as an easy and profitable way of disposing of spurious objects to the public.

It is not usually difficult to detect when objects have been interpolated. The sale ought to be regarded as a whole for the purpose of estimating whether everything in it appears to be related to the taste of the owner. I always look closely at the library. If a man has been a collector, he will certainly have had some books on the subjects which have interested him. As a rule, the more complete the library, the more likely it is that the contents of the house have belonged to one owner. On the other hand, to find a collection of Chinese porcelain, for example, without a single book, or with a few pamphlets and popular expositions, strongly suggests that it has been added. The question then arises: Why was this done, when there are more profitable ways of disposing of it? A man cannot be a collector without knowing the principal dealers and the larger specialist sale-rooms. Of course, the circumstances may have an honest and genuine explanation, but the prospective buyer would do well to examine everything with special care, and to mark on his catalogue the maximum prices he is prepared to pay and see to it that he does not exceed them in the heat of the moment. The principal difficulty of buying from provincial sales is the impossibility of examining objects properly. Often the light is bad, and the room is crowded with dealers and members of the public. Many of the latter regard a sale as a free show, and some of the more reputable sale-rooms try to arrange a private view for dealers and those members of the public who are genuine buyers. This is a practice which ought to be greatly extended.

All catalogue descriptions, whatever the sale-room, should be examined carefully. The auctioneer has a duty to his client to put the most attractive gloss on the object offered; he also has a duty to the buyer to make his description accurate. The larger sale-rooms walk this tight-rope with great skill, and it is nearly always possible to deduce from a description the sale-room's own opinion of an object. For instance, if a picture is described as by "Turner" one gathers that it is in the style of Turner, but only doubtfully by his hand; a painting by "J. M. W. Turner" is almost certainly by his hand but there is slight room for doubt, or the quality does not equal his best work; "Joseph Mallord William Turner" means "This picture is well-known, of fine quality, and we expect it to fetch a lot of money." The same custom does not hold good in the provinces however, and heavy type and lush descriptive prose usually mean little more than that the object has caught the auctioneer's eye or that it is one of the vendor's family heirlooms.

Lastly, it is impossible to bring together within the compass of one volume a discussion of all the ways in which a forgery may be recognized. I have examined many kinds with the intention of providing the reader with information sufficient for him to continue where this book ends. Like the criminal in other fields, the forger is always renewing his attack from different and unsuspected angles, and it is essential to be constantly on the alert for new methods and new approaches.

*Appendix 1*

# *Early Chinese Stoneware Glazes*

The Boston Museum of Fine Arts printed in the *Far Eastern Ceramic Bulletin* for September 1953 (Vol. V, No. 3) an interesting and informative account of an investigation into the sub-surface structure of Kuan and Kuan-type glazes by Robert T. Paine Jr. and William J. Young. Starting from the investigations of Hetherington (op. cit.) into the bubble structure of the Sung glazes, and using shards from the Suburban Altar site at Hangchou which, situated in the grounds of the Imperial Household, may be accepted as undoubtedly of the Sung period, they proceeded to take upwards of 1,500 photomicrographs of surfaces and sections. It emerged that the bubble structure of very deceptive eighteenth-century copies, the date of which had been disputed in some instances, differed to a remarkable degree from that of genuine Sung glazes. The presence of large numbers of bubbles in a glaze, together with that of minute particles, tends to cause opacity and a scattering of the light falling upon it. Equally well-marked differences were observable in the glaze-structure of Northern Celadons and the apparently somewhat similar Yüeh ware, the bubbles in the former being larger, with small adherent bubbles, and those of the latter tending to sink to the bottom of the glaze and to remain in close contact with the body. The text is worthy of study by those technically equipped to do so; the accompanying photographs tell their own story and do not need expert interpretation.

*Appendix 2*

# *Corrosion of Metals*

Strictly defined, corrosion is the gradual conversion of a metal into a compound substance, usually an oxide, as a result of contact with various reagents in the presence of water. Normally, in a reasonably pure atmosphere, corrosion is the result of contact with oxygen, carbon dioxide, and water, but town-atmospheres since medieval times have often contained such substances as sulphuric acid from coal-smoke.

Corrosion is most rapid when the metal is buried in the soil because it comes into contact with a variety of substances capable of starting the necessary reactions, as well as with water. The process proceeds much more slowly in dry conditions, and may even be arrested altogether for long periods. This, however, is unusual.

The metal most liable to attack is iron; copper, lead, and silver are less seriously affected, but bronze, for reasons later discussed, is prone to a serious degree of corrosion. Silver usually tarnishes, with the formation of silver sulphide, whilst gold and platinum are unaffected.

Few objects of iron have survived from early times. In many cases all that remains of an iron implement or a weapon is rust in the soil, and Roman leather sandals have been excavated with pits of rust in the leather to represent the nails. The purer the iron, the greater its resistance to corrosion, which is the reason why wrought iron is often better preserved than cast-iron. Iron rusts exceptionally quickly if it is in contact with another metal which offers a greater resistance to corrosion. Slight pits in the original surface induce an excessive amount of rusting at these points, which rapidly leads to the formation of much larger and deeper pits. Much the same happens with scratches. It is this kind of effect which the forger finds difficult to reproduce convincingly.[1]

The oxides formed from metals by the process of corrosion differ considerably in appearance from the original state. Rust, for instance, is iron hydroxide; cuprite is copper oxide; and so on. Many oxides have the appearance of earthy powders. Salts are also formed, either from the interaction of acids and metals or acids and oxides.

For corrosion to take place there must be present, in addition to the metal, impure water capable of conducting electricity (pure water does not), air, and another metal or carbon. The two metals copper and tin are present in bronze,

[1] Fakers induce rusting with iodine.

but sufficient traces of one metal or another are usually present in soils, and there is no lack of carbon. When two dissimilar metals (or metal and carbon), immersed in a conducting liquid such as impure water, come into contact, an electric current is induced. If salts or acids are present in solution, the current flows more strongly. For this reason metals buried in soils which have a high salt content are sometimes corroded to a point where the metallic nature is completely lost. What happens, in fact, is that conditions create a weak electric battery, and most of my readers will know what occurs when sulphating starts at the terminals of an accumulator.

Corrosion, therefore, is the conversion of the metal to another form, and bronze which has been buried for long periods has sometimes disintegrated completely into copper and stannic oxide. In other cases, when bronze has been buried in well-drained alkaline soil, there may be little more than a light surface corrosion, and even parts which are almost completely unaffected, although this is very rare. Nearly always the factors governing the extent of the corrosion are not constant on all surfaces and in all positions. The effect, therefore, is likely to be uneven, to vary in depth and extent; some will be cuprite, with perhaps part malachite and part azurite. Bronze vessels with gold and silver inlay will show certain differences, because both gold and silver induce a more rapid rate of corrosion in the bronze, and such inlays are often concealed beneath an excess of corroded metal.

The subject, of course, could be pursued in much greater detail. It has been briefly reviewed here because an understanding of the broad principles makes it easier to detect attempts to reproduce patination by artificial means.

*Appendix 3*

# *Ultra-violet Radiation*

Examination of questioned works of art by scientific means is the Achilles' heel of the professional forger. Most such methods are technically beyond the resources and skill of the average collector, and he must therefore go to the specialist. Ultra-violet radiation, however, is proving not only increasingly useful as a general-purpose tool for the collector, but it can be employed to good effect without a great deal of specialized knowledge.

Apparatus of any kind can always be used more intelligently if the principles by which it functions are known, and these are briefly described. Ultra-violet light (often called "black" light) cannot be seen by the human eye. Light is propagated in the form of electro-magnetic waves which vary in their length (measured from crest to crest). This wave-length is always quoted in Ångstrom units, signified by the suffix, A.U.[1] The longest visible radiation is that of red light; the shortest, violet. Beyond this, radiation becomes invisible, and is termed ultra-violet.

The usual source of ultra-violet light is a quartz tube containing mercury-vapour. When an electric current is passed through the tube it provides an intense visible illumination which is also rich in invisible ultra-violet. The visible light has to be screened off, which is done by interposing a filter of suitably dyed glass between the source of light and the object examined. In theory this should filter out all visible light. In practice a certain amount of visible red and violet light passes through the filter and is reflected from the surface of the object.

Examination needs to be carried out in a darkened room. Complete darkness is desirable but not absolutely essential. The observed effects can be divided into two kinds—genuine fluorescence, and a reflection of the visible light passing the filter. Genuine fluorescence is a glow, similar to phosphorescence. Reflection of visible light may partially modify or mask true fluorescence.

Some years ago I was able, through the kindness of Mr J. King of the Department of the Government Chemist, to witness an experiment on porcelain fluorescence using an apparatus he had devised to eliminate visible light completely. Throughout the experiment there was a total absence of visible illumination except that exhibited by the object as a result of true fluorescence. In these circumstances some specimens which exhibited marked differences

[1] 1 A.U. is equivalent to 0·003937 millionths of an inch.

under standard filters did not react at all, whilst others, such as certain kinds of early Chelsea porcelain, gave a reaction not unlike that to be seen when examined by normal commercial apparatus, except that it appeared a little weaker. It is obvious, therefore, that both genuine fluorescence and the reflection of visible light play a part in the observed effects. This, however, does not in the least detract from the value of the results.

The phenomenon of fluorescence is exhibited when ultra-violet light, which is invisible, falls on to certain materials that are able to transform the short waves into those of greater length, which then become visible. Fluorescence is by no means universal, and the substances which give rise to it often exist only as traces, probably in the form of impurities. If two objects which have the same physical appearance by ordinary light also exhibit the same fluorescence under ultra-violet radiation, the chances are overwhelmingly in favour of their being made from the same materials.

If an object is added to in the course of restoration, it is virtually certain that the original surface and that which has been added will fluoresce differently, or one will fluoresce while the other will show merely a reflection of visible violet light passing the filter. The difference between the two colours or shades is often startling. The glaze of a porcelain figure, for instance, will show a soft violet illumination in most cases; some restorations glow with a vivid yellowish white, like a phosphorescent watch-dial. This is due to the varnish with which the glaze is simulated, and the same effect is to be seen from other newly-varnished surfaces. Caution, however, is necessary. Fats, such as those present in soap, fluoresce even more brilliantly, usually with bluish-white, and if the porcelain has been recently washed residual soap can be mistaken for restoration. This, however, may be removed with a handkerchief; varnish is irremoval, except by scraping or with a solvent. The exact extent of surface tampering can easily be traced, but this is sometimes greater than the restored area because the varnish is carried beyond the repair. It is certainly never less.

Ultra-violet light can be used for the swift detection of restoration of all kinds to pottery and porcelain. Usually the missing parts are made from plaster, or some similar material, painted to simulate the original. Varnish is used to imitate the original glaze. Although it seems unlikely to the inexperienced, a skilful restorer using these simple materials can sometimes produce work which almost defies detection in ordinary light, especially when newly done. Of course, it is much simpler to test the difference between glaze and varnish by drawing a needle-point across the surface, but the circumstances in which this can be done without someone objecting strongly are very few. Restoration is quite legitimate. Few specimens of antique pottery and porcelain are now perfect, although many collectors (most unreasonably) demand what is termed "mint" condition, or at least its appearance. Restoration, however, should be limited in extent to the actual part needing it. A specimen becomes progressively less valuable as the area of restoration increases. One or two restorers have attempted to defeat examination by ultra-violet light by spraying the whole of the object with varnish. This, however, is clearly to be seen, since the resultant fluorescence is quite unlike that of a glaze, and from its appearance one may legitimately deduce that the restored area is so great that the vendor would prefer it not to be known. Such things are better rejected out of hand. Painted enamels are restored in the same way as porcelain, and ultra-violet light is equally useful in revealing the extent of the repair.

This, of course, is useful enough, but about fourteen years ago it was noticed that the colour exhibited by certain varieties of porcelain not only differed from that of others, but was, as far as could be seen, constant. Usefully enough, several specimens by Samson of Paris yielded a mustard-yellow when examined in this way—a colour which does not appear, in my experience, on any other porcelain. Examination of a large number of specimens of Chelsea porcelain suggested the possibility of allocating them to specific periods of the factory's life by fluorescence alone. This is particularly likely when a factory, as in the case of Chelsea, changed its formula, and possibly its sources of raw-material supply as well. The earliest Chelsea specimens fluoresce with a well-marked peach-colour, whilst later specimens give a characteristic dark violet. Porcelain from some other factories was also found to exhibit fairly characteristic colours, although not in so marked a degree.[1] In Chelsea porcelain fluorescence was certainly not a glaze effect. Examination of the unglazed interior of a damaged figure gave precisely the same result. This investigation is still in its early stages, but it has progressed far enough to make the acquisition of an ultra-violet lamp worth-while for every serious collector. Examination of suspected forgeries should be carried out side by side with genuine specimens, and the fluorescence carefully compared. It is essential, if the test is to be reliable, for the genuine object to come from the same factory and period as the suspected specimens. If both are not from the same source some differences, which may be extremely marked, are inevitable.

The ultra-violet lamp is not like a computor in the sense that information can be fed in at one end, the answer emerging at the other. To the collector it could best be described as a new kind of vision, with a language of its own which has to be learned. Differences in fluorescence are never meaningless; their real meaning, however, has to be interpreted, and experience can only be acquired by using the lamp on all kinds of materials and studying the effects. The lamp is also a personal tool, because the information it gives cannot be measured objectively. Colour-photographs have been made, but in most cases they are not particularly successful in reproducing the exact effect.

Ultra-violet radiation has been used extensively by porcelain collectors, but those in other fields are not always aware of its advantages, although it is now employed by museums, dealers, and the large auction-rooms. The remarks which follow record the observed effects on a variety of materials.

Some old glass, particularly lead-glass, merely reflects visible violet radiation. Not infrequent, however, is an orange fluorescence which appears in leadless glass, perhaps the result of traces of uranium oxide, and also in some modern laboratory glass. The older the glass, the more likely it is that some fluorescence will be present as the result of degenerative changes, either in the material itself or on the surface. Perhaps the most significant results have been obtained from

[1] George Savage: *18th Century English Porcelain.* London, 1952.

coloured glass, particularly stained glass.[1] The examination of a forgery of Syrian glass side by side with that of genuine specimens showed marked differences, the genuine specimens fluorescing with the orange-yellow referred to. Glass has not yet been the subject of a systematic investigation, and more work needs to be done in classifying the observed effects before anything significant can be said to have emerged. The instances cited above, however, suggest ways in which ultra-violet radiation can be used.

Newly-cut wood fluoresces only slightly. Some fluorescence is exhibited by old furniture which arises from the treatment of the surface. Whilst old varnish does not fluoresce, new varnish does so more or less brilliantly. Fluorescence by itself cannot be used to tell the difference between old and relatively new work, but it will reveal alterations and additions with much greater facility than daylight. It is certainly worth subjecting furniture to an examination of this kind, but lack of a positive result should not be regarded as a certificate of authenticity.

Restorations to objects of bronze are often easily detected, although the metal does not fluoresce. This is especially true if bronze is well-patinated. As an example, I arranged the repair of a fragile Chinese bronze of the Han period for a friend. A number of pieces had been broken from the rim. An expert restorer so skilfully cemented them back into position and filled the visible cracks with a simulation of the patina that the repair defied detection, even with a moderately-powerful hand-lens. In fact, it became a pastime to hand the vessel to those who did not know it and invite them to point out the repaired area, which no one succeeded in doing. Under ultra-violet radiation a number of dark violet lines leapt into prominence, standing out from the lighter ground. They exactly marked the position of the fractures.

In this case, and in certain others, a genuine fluorescence did not appear to be present, but it is noticeable that, even when it seems to be absent, repairs can often be traced simply from the shade and quality of the reflected violet light.

The bronze referred to was an example of repair without solder, but ultra-violet radiation has been used to trace soldered repairs to early bronzes, even when great care has been taken to disguise the work with fake patination. It is worth remembering, too, that solder is a much softer metal than bronze, and the point of a needle can be used to detect its presence in places where it cannot be clearly seen.

Of course, if the entire surface of a piece has been covered with a patina faked chemically (see page 67), then ultra-violet light cannot do very much to detect the fraud. It can only show the difference between materials which are alike in their surface appearance. I have not yet had an opportunity of examining by ultra-violet light the kind of spurious patina made from mixing the products of bronze corrosion with lacquer. Superficially this can be very deceptive unless it is possible to scrape it off with a pen-knife. It seems almost certain that it would fluoresce differently from genuine corrosion if the spurious

[1] James J. Rorimer: *Ultra-violet radiation and its use in the examination of works of art.* New York, 1931.

object were placed side by side with one of undoubted provenance. This, incidentally, is a particularly important aspect of much examination carried out in this way. Until experience has been gained it is essential to have a genuine object of the same kind with which to compare the one suspected, so that any divergence in the results obtained can be seen and evaluated.

The examination of stonework is often illuminating in more senses than one. The best results have been obtained from the softer stones, such as marble, alabaster, and limestone, and it is necessary, first, to be reasonably well acquainted with the effects to be observed on genuine specimens.

Marble is a crystalline form of limestone, and old marbles develop degenerative changes with age and weathering. These start on the surface and penetrate inwards. Professor Laurie investigated limestone from Lincoln Cathedral, and found that aerial-borne sulphur had converted lime carbonate into lime sulphate to a variable extent, ranging from 4½ percent. at one-quarter of an inch below the surface to 2½ percent. at one inch. This result is the more useful because it was possible to examine limestone from the original quarries, which was found to be virtually free from lime sulphate. In addition to this, carbonic acid gas was found *in excess* of the amount needed to form lime carbonate in the outer layers, and it was evident that the stone had been absorbing it from the atmosphere. Professor Laurie suggested drilling statuary and architectural marbles of known age, in order to assess depth of penetration, which would provide valuable information whereby age could be approximately estimated in doubtful cases. Such tests, of course, could be carried out on buildings where the date of erection is known exactly and the amount of weathering estimated from the position of the work.

This is departing slightly from the subject in hand, but it must be remembered that forgeries of old stone-carving are freshly-cut, and would not, therefore, reveal these effects. It is to be expected, therefore, that new work will show some differences from old in the fluorescence to be observed under ultra-violet radiation. Faking, which means the recarving and restoration of old specimens to make a more saleable object, also necessitates cutting through the weathered layer into the hitherto untouched stone beneath, and whatever precautions may have been taken to match the surface effect, this is usually revealed by ultra-violet light, new work exhibiting a different colour from old. Restorations, being in a different material or in marble from another source, will also fluoresce differently, and the joints should be apparent. One method of repairing holes in marble, often used by sculptors, is to melt borax and use it as a filler. This is fairly difficult to detect when freshly-done, but it becomes increasingly obvious with age.

Rorimer reports that with the Corex A filter, made by Corning, marble gives a uniform purple under ultra-violet light when freshly cut, and a mottled white (with occasional patches of yellow and blue) when the surface has been undisturbed for a long but undetermined period. A twelfth-century capital from France was compared with freshly-cut marble from the same region, and the result confirmed this observation.

Different filters, however, are inclined to give different results, and I have observed that American filters will sometimes vary markedly from those made of Woods glass used in England in the effects to be observed. The essential fact is that they agree in revealing differences, whatever the shade or colour. The most usual filter fitted to commercial apparatus passes maximum radiation at 3,660 A.U., but those passing short-wave radiation (for which a different type of glass is essential) at 2,537 A.U. have some applications to the present purpose, although their use does not seem to have been investigated on a systematic basis. Certain substances which will not react to one wave-length will do so to the other.

Dr Plenderleith has commented amusingly on a walk through the sculpture galleries of the British Museum at night carrying a portable ultra-violet lamp, which revealed the repairs with startling clarity.

There is nothing intrinsically wrong with the practice of restoration; it is only desirable that its extent be known, since this must affect value. The use of the ultra-violet lamp to detect restorations to old marble and limestone carving, therefore, is undoubtedly valuable, and similar results have been noted from alabaster. Neither sandstone nor granite have yielded comparable results so far as forgeries are concerned, although it has been possible in some cases to detect recarving. Restoration by addition, of course, can be detected fairly easily.

Rorimer notes that recently-cut jade has been found to give a different effect from old jade, but he does not differentiate between jadeite and nephrite, between which I have noticed a dissimilarity. Nephrite was used for the earlier Chinese jade carvings, and this fact needs to be borne in mind.

Ivory and bone are substances which have yielded useful results. Both undergo an ageing process which leads to alterations in the surface colour to be seen under ordinary light, ranging from pale yellow to dark brown. Newly-carved ivories, as I have already recorded, are stained in various ways to imitate these colours. Interference with an old matured surface by scraping and recutting, or pieces inserted as restoration, can be detected by differences in fluorescence, recent work exhibiting a purple reflection whilst old work will normally give a mottled yellow, although restorations are often treated with some additional substance, perhaps that used to colour the surface, which may tend to mask the result. In such cases it is probable that a solvent, such as alcohol, could be used with good effect. The result, of course, is unlikely to be very deceptive unless the colouring matter has been carried over the whole surface, and even in cases such as these, the fluorescence of the old ivory may be sufficiently strong to detect the difference between old and new work. A Chinese ivory which had been uniformly covered with a brownish stain exhibited a brown colour under the lamp, which, of course, is a danger-signal.

It has been said, with what truth I do not know but it is likely, that forgeries of old ivory are sometimes given to young girls of more than average plumpness to wear between their breasts for a few months, the object being to give the surface a mellow patination from absorption of oily substances secreted by the skin. Oily substances of this kind fluoresce brilliantly with much the same effect as that to be seen in the case of other fats and soaps, and they can be removed by a preliminary wash of alcohol. Incidentally, it will be noticed that natural teeth, which are a kind of ivory, will fluoresce brilliantly, whilst artificial teeth will not fluoresce at all.

The fluorescence of old paper is much more obvious than that of new, and comparison of a suspected document with another known to be old can often be revealing. The condition of prints and drawings is comparatively easily ascertained by examination in this way. Holes in water-colour drawings are often repaired ingeniously and almost invisibly with paper patches. The likelihood of the original paper and that used for the patch exhibiting the same effect is fairly remote. Since the sizing of the paper has to be replaced, often with a cellulose acetate varnish, the difference will become even more obvious. Additionally, the paste used helps to reinforce the difference. Such defects as fox-marks removed by bleaching are often apparent, and erased signatures and altered dates have often been detected under the fresh ink, a fact of which criminal investigation departments make use in examining documents of all kinds for signs of forgery. The practice among medieval scribes of erasing old writing in order to use the surface afresh can always be detected, and the original writing appearing underneath the superimposition has often been read. Documents damaged by fire have been deciphered under ultra-violet light. Plate 38.

Repairs to textiles—rugs, tapestries, and so forth—will usually be found to exhibit a somewhat different colour from that of original work.

Oil-paintings are difficult subjects for investigation in this way, and in many cases X-rays have proved to be more useful. Some paints have a characteristic fluorescence, and varnishes mostly fluoresce strongly, usually with a whitish-yellow colour. Painting over varnish will immediately be apparent, but such crude repairs are not usual. It is possible to detect repairs and repaintings *under* varnish, but much will depend on the type and condition of the varnish and the thickness of the varnish-film. Oil-varnishes can be distinguished from spirit-varnishes, a fact which has been used to examine violins attributed to Stradivarius, who used oil-varnish exclusively.

Some progress has been made towards the dating of pigments by fluorescence, and Grant[1] mentions the case of a painting bearing a signature asserted to be that of Pissarro which, on examination by ultra-violet light, proved to have been painted over that of another artist. In this case the slight traces of paint remaining after the erasure were fluorescent. Results of ultra-violet ray examination in this field need to be interpreted with the eye of experience, and it is difficult for anyone otherwise unskilled in the techniques of oil-painting, and the restoration of old canvasses, to obtain significant results. For the skilled worker, however, the subject is worth pursuing in detail.

Ultra-violet examination is an art, not an exact science. It is impossible to say beforehand what can be expected from an examination of any particular material. Results in each case, therefore, must be considered on their merits. The investigator must first establish a standard by examining accredited

[1] J. A. Radley and Julius Grant: *Fluorescence analysis in ultra-violet light.* London, 1939.

examples, and then strive to account for the departures from it. The use of ultra-violet radiation should go hand in hand with a study of the nature and properties of the materials used and the original methods of manufacture. Properly employed it is an invaluable piece of equipment.

Suitable apparatus for the collector, dealer, and museum, which has the merit of being inexpensive, is made by Engelhard Hanovia Lamps of Slough, Buckinghamshire. Various models are produced for different purposes, but the most useful for the examination of works of art is No. 16, which can be used to illuminate almost anything from a porcelain figure to a large oil-painting. The filter is designed to pass maximum radiation at 3,660 A.U., and this is sufficient for all normal purposes. For experimental investigations, a model with a special filter passing the short-wave radiation of 2,537 A.U. is also made. The company concerned will supply information to *bona-fide* inquirers.

*Appendix 4*

# *X-rays*

The use of X-rays is largely confined, in the arts, to the examination of paintings. Such radiation is of much shorter wave-length than ultra-violet, and is completely invisible to the eye, although its effects can be recorded on a photographic plate. It is so short that it penetrates light materials very deeply, and is only stopped by those which are dense. A familiar illustration is the use of this radiation to photograph fractured bones. The rays pass easily through flesh, but are stopped by the much denser bone, providing a shadowgraph which reveals plainly the site of the fracture. All X-rays are, in fact, shadowgraphs in depth, recording the amount of radiation which various materials have allowed to pass.

In the examination of paintings much depends on such factors as the voltage of the current used, and variations in these will affect the result. If a high voltage is employed only such substances as white lead, or a mercury pigment such as cinnabar, will absorb the rays; the other pigments will pass them to a greater or lesser degree. At lower voltages other pigments will absorb the rays to a greater extent, increasing the amount of detail exhibited by the shadowgraph. It is usually possible to adjust voltage so that it penetrates to the desired amount, and to take several photographs showing different degrees of penetration. In this way old pictures which have been overpainted are sometimes discovered. A recent instance of this sort of discovery was provided by a Holbein cartoon which became perceptible under layers of eighteenth-century overpainting. Dr Coremans, in his investigation of the Van Meegeren forgeries, was able, by using X-ray photography, to confirm the latter's statement regarding areas of white lead paint remaining on the canvas by Hondius used for the "Last Supper". A hound and some game emerge clearly from beneath the new paint.

Although this method has sometimes revealed the spurious nature of a painting in a dramatic way, it still needs to be regarded with caution. An Old Master painting may be over a discarded canvas, either because the artist was short of a canvas or because he was economical enough to use rejected materials. Shadowgraphs of a spurious Van Gogh marketed by Otto Wacker made the nature of the work immediately obvious because Van Gogh's highly indivudual technique proved to be remarkably susceptible to examination of this kind.

There are, however, many variable factors. To name only a few—voltage, energy of the current, exposure time of the plate, focal-length, and the development of the plate. An X-ray used for serious study ought to be accompanied by information on these points.

Undoubtedly this form of examination will be more widely employed in the future, and its value will increase as experience accumulates. Meantime, it is often useful in a limited sphere.

*Appendix 5*

## *The Use of Photography and Infra-red Radiation*

Photography can be used for more purposes than the mere making of a record. In the course of the hearing of Hahn v. Duveen one of the witnesses for the defence was severely handled by counsel for the plaintiff because he admitted giving an opinion on the authenticity of the disputed painting from photographs. His claim that this was common among dealers and art-experts elicited a certain amount of incredulous comment which was quite unjustified. A good photograph is a potent weapon in the hands of someone able to put the correct interpretation on what it has to show.

Photography presents the subject, be it painting, sculpture, or anything else, in terms of black, white and shades of grey. The eye is not distracted by colour, and the mind is free to concentrate on other aspects.

A photograph is not a faithful representation of any object; it falsifies colour-values especially, and in this respect it is unreliable. The mere fact that the colours are falsified, however, gives an entirely fresh view of the object, and this sometimes makes plain small discrepancies which would otherwise have been overlooked. I have several times observed that forgeries which were difficult to detect in normal light became extremely obvious in a photograph. Filters, of course, can be used to vary the colour-values of any particular type of negative.

There are many ways of using a camera, and of arranging the lighting. Powerful lights directed straight at the object give the clearest, simplest view in most cases, and the best results are obtained by using a small aperture and a long exposure. The small aperture centres the light passing to the negative in the middle of the lens where there is the least amount of distortion. A wide aperture and a short exposure tends to blurr detail, and enlargements are apt to be distorted.

It is essential to remember that the physical appearance of any work of art is a product of the intensity and type of light falling on it. Daylight, rich in visible violet and blue light, will give one result; an electric-bulb, with far less violet and much more red, another. Not only colour-values alter, but even the form of three-dimensional objects can vary according to the quality and angle of the illumination, which suggests the importance of examining a suspected object with light from every angle. Most people tend to work in light of much too feeble an intensity; a thousand watts is not too much for important observations. I remember an instance in which the reviewer of a book irresponsibly queried the colours of an object illustrated in one of the plates, only to draw a retort from the owner that it was exceedingly accurate. Obviously the plate was accurate in one light but not in another, and the reviewer foolishly did not stop to consider this elementary fact. Of course, a poor colour-plate is wrong in every light. Proper lighting, therefore, is essential not only to photography but to the examination of works of art generally, and especially to that of suspected forgeries.

The camera should be carefully focussed by adjusting the lens with reference to a page of type resting against the object, or something of the same kind. The image in the viewing-screen can be examined with a magnifying-glass to get the sharpest possible image. If the camera lens is of good quality, properly focussed, and the film of fine grain, the negative ought to allow a great deal of magnification, and enlarged prints can be made which will enable the finest details to be examined in a version which is superior to the use of a powerful hand-lens.

Background is important, and variously coloured papers can be employed for this purpose. The best are black, white, grey, or some neutral shade. High-lights on such surfaces as silver and porcelain can be reduced by interposing a screen of tracing-paper or grease-proof paper between the object and the light-source, with a proportionately longer exposure. Dark shadows can be eliminated by placing cardboard covered with tin-foil in a position to reflect the light on to the appropriate place. Reference photographs should include a rule placed to one side to give the scale.

Photography is especially valuable in the examination of drawings and documentary material because it often reveals aspects which are not visible to the unaided eye. In drawings, for instance, a signature subsequently added in ink which is of different composition from the remainder will often appear to be different in intensity in a photograph, although it may seem exactly similar to the eye. The position of the light-source is important. A flood-light placed to the side of the object, so that it is illuminated at an acute angle, gives an entirely fresh view which is often helpful. Police laboratories use it to read such things as impressions left on a blank sheet of paper from a pencilled sheet above it. The same technique can sometimes be usefully applied to the examination of paintings, when the irregular surface of the modelled paint appears in light relief. Divergences from the general appearance can then be queried. The technique can also be used for the photography of inscriptions, and indistinct inscriptions can sometimes be read in this way. Surface defects also become much more apparent under this kind of lighting.

Photographs enable an object easily to be compared with others. Obviously it is impossible to take an object into a library to compare it with illustrations in works of reference, neither would such a comparison be easy, since it would be between a coloured, three-dimensional specimen and a black-and-white two-dimensional half-tone block. It is important in the detection of forgeries to be able to make accurate comparisons with other things of the same kind, since it is vitally necessary to discover possible sources of inspiration.

Infra-red radiation may conveniently be considered here, because—unlike ultra-violet—it is almost useless without photography, although if an object is viewed by the eye through a filter passing light of a wave-length of about 7,200 A.U. and above, its appearance is approximately the same as it will be on a photographic plate. Powerful illumination of the object is necessary.

Photography with plates sensitive to infra-red radiation is not very different from that in ordinary light. Focussing should not be troublesome at short distances with small apertures, since the same setting as for photography in ordinary light can be used. The ordinary lens of good quality is sufficient for most purposes, although special lenses can be obtained. It is necessary to use a filter to exclude the short-wave end of the spectrum, but large suppliers of photographic apparatus can advise on suitable equipment. Exposure times are apt to be much longer than for work in ordinary light.

Photographs made by infra-red radiation show remarkable differences from those made with ordinary plates and films. Just as—detergent manufacturers notwithstanding—there is no such colour as pure white, so completely black pigments are very rare. They tend to be blue-black, brown-black, or red-black. An assortment of black materials seen through the agency of an infra-red photograph will exhibit a wide range of shades of grey, but only rarely a deep black. The whole colour-scale is altered, and this presents a fresh view of certain objects, particularly paintings, which can be revealing. Paintings badly obscured by old varnish will often yield photographs in this way which are much clearer and more detailed than any other method of examination could procure.

Success has been particularly experienced in the examination of documents. For instance, a book from which several lines of type had been heavily obliterated in ink could not only be read clearly, but the ink virtually disappeared on the plate taken in this way. The application to illegible signatures on paintings is obvious, and infra-red photography has succeeded where ultra-violet light has failed.

Colour-photography is rarely of much value for our present purpose. It is, of course, a record of the appearance of the object in light of one particular kind, and the colours, even in the best examples, are only approximately correct. If it is being used, however, the transparency is better than the print, and can be projected to give a greatly enlarged picture. Black-and-white negatives can be turned into positives and projected in the form of slides to enlarge them.

Photography is also used for recording the results of examination by ultra-violet radiation and by X-rays, as well as in spectroscopy. A good camera, and the ability to use it, is an invaluable aid to the art-expert.

*Appendix 6*

# *Chemical Analysis*

This is probably the most useful and informative kind of examination for many purposes, but it has the drawback that a small part of the object must be sacrificed. It also usually demands a high degree of skill and technical knowledge, although there are simple tests which can be carried out by the novice to ascertain the nature of materials.

The object of this kind of analysis is to obtain an accurate estimate of the substances which go to make up the material under examination. It has been especially useful in determining the nature of certain varieties of porcelain, and this aspect will be briefly examined here not only for its usefulness to the collector of old porcelain, but as an illustration of the way in which such methods can be applied to other things.

As I have recorded earlier, true porcelain is made from china clay (kaolin) and feldspathic rock (petuntse), whilst artificial porcelain is basically clay and ground-glass. If representative specimens of these two kinds are examined the result will be approximately as follows:

| *Chinese true porcelain* | |
|---|---|
| Silica | 69·43 |
| Alumina | 26·20 |
| Lime | nil |
| Magnesia | 0·14 |
| Soda | 1·72 |
| Potash | 2·51 |
| | 100·00 |

| *Artificial porcelain* | |
|---|---|
| Silica | 64·76 |
| Alumina | 6·00 |
| Lime | 25·00 |
| Magnesia | trace |
| Phosphoric acid | 0·23 |
| Lead oxide | 0·55 |
| Potash | 2·58 |
| Soda | 1·82 |
| | 100.94 |

Even the novice is able to see that, however closely the two may resemble each other superficially, they are in fact very different objects. Those more skilled in reading porcelain analyses will recognize them at once for what they are.

Chinese clay is a decomposed form of feldspathic rock. Both clay and rock are similar in composition. Silica and alumina are the main constituents, in approximately the proportions in which they appear above. The magnesia is an impurity; the alkalis, soda and potash, were deliberately added as a flux to promote the fusion of the rock.

In the second analysis the three-to-one relationship of silica and alumina is not preserved. The amount of clay can be estimated at about 25 percent., deduced from the 6 percent. of alumina. The remainder of the silica, therefore, must come from another source. Glass is made from silica (sand), lime in the form of chalk (calcium carbonate), and alkalis. The excess of silica and the presence of lime, therefore, both indicate the use of glass in place of rock.

The English factories developed a major variation in the clay-ground-glass formula by including massive quantities of bone-ash (about 45 percent.), which reveals itself on analysis in the quantity of phosphoric acid (usually about 17 percent.) and of lime (about 24 percent.) present. Both these substances are the major constituents of bone.

At Worcester a clay-soaprock porcelain replaced the clay-feldspathic rock formula. This is revealed by about 13 percent. of magnesia, and soaprock porcelain can be identified with certainty in this way. Lead oxide frequently appears in eighteenth-century English porcelain in small amounts which can be estimated by a comparatively simple test, but the "Girl in a Swing" type of the 1750s, associated with the Chelsea factory, is identified by the massive inclusion of 17 percent. of lead oxide—far more than from any other factory—which indicates the use of lead-glass. It will be seen from this, therefore, that English porcelain can be identified quickly and with relative certainty in this way. Other kinds of porcelain have not been subjected to analysis of a systematic kind, but the method is being increasingly used to study certain varieties which are otherwise difficult to attribute.

A good deal of work of this kind has been done on metals, particularly bronze, and it is usually possible to make a reasonably close estimate of age, and even of provenance, by an analysis of the constituents. The method in fact can be extended, in appropriate circumstances, to all inorganic substances and to many of organic origin, although the value of the results obtained will be variable. It is, of course, usually essential to have an analysis of an object known to be genuine for comparison.

At one time it was essential for large and damaging amounts to be removed for analysis if the result was to be accurate. Developments in microanalysis, using extremely small quantities which make little or no difference to the object, have now largely removed this objection.

*Appendix 7*

# *Spectroscopy*

Although this is exclusively a laboratory method which can only be employed by a trained specialist, it is useful to those who may have to examine the authenticity of works of art to know the principles of the spectroscope, and what information it can be expected to give. This instrument is now commonly used in police laboratories to provide information about suitable materials, and specialized laboratories examining works of art also make increasing use of it.

It is a matter of common observation that if a ray of white light be passed through a prism it is split up into its component light-rays of varying colours, ranging from the short-wave visible violet to the long-wave red. Beyond the violet end of the spectrum there is ultra-violet radiation, discussed in Appendix 3, and infra-red radiation is also invisible, but at the opposite end (see Appendix 5).

The effect of the prism is to sort out light into its component wave-lengths, and if this is thrown on to a screen it will appear as a band of colour, ranging from red through orange, yellow, green, blue, and indigo to violet.

In practice light is admitted to the instrument through a fine slit, and is focussed by a lens on to a prism, which, in turn, reflects the image on to a screen. The type of light emitted by various sources differs in the wave-lengths which are present, and consequently the projected image differs. If existing illumination were always necessary, however, the value of a spectroscope would be very much less than it is. It is possible to detect the presence of an element in a substance by heating its atoms, thus causing them to emit light. This can be done in a variety of ways, usually by means of an electric arc, but there is little point in discussing them in detail here. Suffice to say that each element yields a spectrum which is as unique as a fingerprint. This can be photographed. An unknown element or compound can be identified by comparing its spectrum with that of known substances. Qualitatively this method is extremely accurate; in some cases a quantitative estimation can be made by observing the intensity of concentration of the different colours in the spectrum.

It is possible in this way accurately to identify very small particles of various materials. It has, for instance, been used by police laboratories for the comparison of such diverse substances as fibres of cloth, fragments of paint adhering to vehicles after a traffic accident, poisonous substances, and aniline dyes. If, for instance, a paint fragment on the damaged wing of an automobile gives precisely the same result as that of a bicycle with which it is alleged to have collided, the inference is obvious.

There are, of course, many instances in the examination of works of art where materials need to be identified from a small sample, and for this spectroscopic analysis is probably the most satisfactory. Discussion of a particular problem with an analyst will usually result in a variety of suggestions as to methods to be adopted and what they are likely to prove.

*Appendix 8*

# *"Hall's Box"*

This slightly irreverent term has been applied to an ingenious and impressive apparatus developed by Dr E. T. Hall at the Clarendon Laboratory, Oxford, as a way of obtaining an analysis of objects from which specimens could not be taken for chemical analysis without unacceptable damage. Dr Hall was kind enough to demonstrate this for me, and explain its working, some years ago, and the following brief description is the product of a fallible memory and a certain amount of simplification for the general reader.

Optical spectroscopy, described briefly in Appendix 7, is apt to have the disadvantage in some cases of leaving pit-marks in a specimen. Dr Hall's apparatus avoids this by bombarding the object with X-rays. Each of the various elements which can be detected in this way, from calcium to uranium, reflects the rays at a different but constant angle. The irradiation passes from the object through a collimator tube, and the information is fed to a computor which, in turn, estimates the quantity of the elements present and prints the result, giving a fairly comprehensive and accurate analysis in a relatively short time. The object is completely unharmed.

The apparatus can be used to determine the presence of specific substances in pottery glazes, such as tin or lead, for the analysis of metals and pigments, and for many other purposes. It was used with great success to determine problems relating to the authenticity of the Piltdown skull where, had it been genuine, even the smallest sample could not have been removed, and it greatly assisted in exposing the fraud. It is certain that this apparatus, or some development of it, will play an important part in the examination of suspected works of art in the future.

*Appendix 9*

## *Dating by the Radio-carbon Technique*

Although this is unlikely to be of much assistance in detecting any but forgeries of certain classes of antiquities, it is promising enough to require brief mention here. Carbon ordinarily consists of stable atoms, but carbon dioxide contains an exceedingly small number of atoms of a kind of radio-active carbon formed by cosmic rays penetrating the atmosphere. Consequently these carbon atoms form part of every living organism. The half-life of radio-active carbon is 5,000 years—that is, in 5,000 years half will be converted into stable carbon atoms. In 10,000 years only a quarter of the original amount will persist, in 15,000 an eighth, and so on. The methods of determining the amounts present hardly fall within the scope of this book to describe, but it is possible in this way to date organic remains of from 1,000 to 50,000 years of age with remarkable accuracy. It could, for example, be used to estimate the age of such remains in graves and tombs, and consequently of the objects in them. The forgery involving "old Aboutig" (see page 36) could hardly have survived this kind of examination.

Apparently somewhat similar in broad principle is a method of dating certain kinds of old pottery recently reported from the United States. No definite information is yet available, but according to report it depends on the fact that fired pottery loses its heat much in the same way as radio-carbon loses its radio-activity, and that, even after centuries, measurable residual heat remains which can be detected by extremely delicate tests. Comparison with similar tests on objects of known age, it is suggested, make it possible to date an object within certain useful limits. Another test recently applied to old pottery is to measure its magnetic polarity in relation to that of the earth. It is possible to estimate the date of manufacture from the result, but the margin of possible error is, apparently, wide.

*Appendix 10*

# *Hardness of Materials*

The nature of a stone or a mineral may be ascertained with a fair degree of accuracy by testing the surface hardness. The test depends on the fact that a stone will always be scratched by one which is harder, or will scratch one which is softer. This enables a table to be constructed based on that originally devised by the Austrian chemist, Mohs:

1. Talc, steatite, soaprock.
2. Gypsum, meerschaum.
2·5. Amber.
3. Jet, alabaster (calcite).
3·5. Malachite.
4. Serpentine, fluorspar.
5. Coral, apatite, artifical porcelain.
5·5. Glass, lapis lazuli, obsidian.
6. Haematite, turquoise, opal, feldspars generally, true porcelain.
7. Quartz, agate, amethyst, flint, rock-crystal, jade (nephrite and jadeite), chalcedony, cornelian, tourmaline.
7·5. Beryl, emerald, zircon, garnet.
8. Topaz, spinel, chrysoberyl.
9. Corundum (emery), sapphire, ruby.
10. Diamond.

The materials must scratch each other for the test to be effective. Some leave a streak which can be mistaken for a cut. The average steel file or pocket-knife blade has a hardness of 6 or slightly below on this scale. True porcelain will usually abrade metal from a steel file, to be seen in the metallic dust remaining after the test has been made.

*Appendix 11*

# *Ink and Paper*

The earliest kind of paper to be used for writing was made in Egypt from the papyrus reed, and was obtained by unrolling and flattening thin layers from the stem. Elsewhere parchment made from the skins of sheep and goats were used. Vellum is a finer quality of parchment made from those of calves and kids. Paper may have been made in China from vegetable fibres beaten to pulp as early as the first century A.D., and the Arabs were using cotton and linen rags for the purpose in the eighth century. Rag-paper appeared in England about the middle of the eleventh century, and remained the only variety available until almost the middle of the nineteenth century, although experiments were being made with other materials by the end of the eighteenth. The first paper from wood-pulp appears to have been made about 1840, although its manufacture may have started a little before this date on the Continent. Esparto-grass was first used about 1860. Unsized paper, capable of absorbing ink, probably dates from the fifteenth century, although sand was generally used for this purpose until the end of the eighteenth.

Rags were first cleaned and then beaten to a pulp. The pulp was mixed with water to a creamy consistency and placed on a wire-mesh which allowed the water to drain, leaving behind a sheet of interlocking fibres which was dried under pressure between pieces of woollen material. The surface was then sized with a weak glue made from animal-bones and gristle.

The nature of paper is best determined microscopically, and only a small fragment is needed. Watermarks are sometimes extremely useful in determining the age of paper, and the first known watermark appears in a document of 1310. These can be forged in a variety of ways, perhaps the simplest being the application of a rubber-stamp with a suitable design moistened with a weak solution of acid, followed by careful washing in water. The paper becomes slightly more translucent where it has been in contact with the acid.

This information is useful in the examination of suspected drawings and documents, although forged drawings are often creased and torn deliberately and subsequently mounted in such a way as to make examination more difficult. Staining of forged drawings may be due to the use of coffee, tea, an aqueous solution of tobacco, or to potassium permanganate.

Documents and drawings are often executed in ink. Early inks were made from carbon obtained from the incomplete combustion or charring of organic material. This pigment was usually suspended in a mixture of gum-arabic and water. Carbon-inks can become brown with age, but this is unusual. They can be removed in some cases by washing with water, but are unaffected by such bleaches as chloride of lime and sodium hypochlorite.

Slightly later than carbon-ink is one derived from the secretions of the cuttle-fish, known as *sepia*. In the Middle Ages inks made from decoctions of gall-nuts and an iron salt came into use. These, when applied, were slightly bluish in colour, but later became black by oxidation. With age inks of this kind turn brown, but it is impossible to say how long is needed for this to take place since the time will vary with circumstances. A decoction of logwood and iron tannate was used from the middle of the eighteenth century, and by the middle of the nineteenth the logwood decoction was being employed in conjunction with potassium chlorate. All these inks soak into the paper, and react rapidly to bleaching agents. Aniline inks cannot be awarded a date earlier than about 1860. Coloured inks usually have a coal-tar base, and fade rapidly when exposed to light.

Inks are applied with a pen or a brush. The first steel pen was not made until 1780, and nibs were not produced by machinery until about 1820. The quill-pen was much used, and was made by cutting the quill into the form of a divided nib. In some parts of the world, particularly in the Near East, a reed-pen was employed. The marks left by the various kinds of pen can be distinguished one from the other under a powerful glass.

Pencils are made from graphite—the so-called black lead. This has been known since the middle of the sixteenth century. It is sometimes possible, by means of delicate chemical tests, to distinguish between the marks made on paper by graphite from different sources. Silverpoint is a technique, used mainly during the fifteenth and sixteenth centuries, which superficially resembles pencil. The paper is prepared by washing it with Chinese white, and the silver-grey drawing was made with silver wire in a wooden holder. The mark was indelible. More rarely, gold and lead were used for the same purpose.

So far as alterations and erasures are concerned, these can sometimes be seen microscopically, but ultra-violet radiation, or photography by infra-red rays, are much more revealing.

*Appendix 12*

# *Style in Interior Decoration*

The collector needs to acquire a working knowledge of European styles, and to know the periods of their currency. An acquaintance with the characteristics of *baroque*, *rococo*, and neo-classical *motifs* of decoration is absolutely essential.

Renaissance styles are based on those of Greece and Rome during the classical period, and *baroque* was a seventeenth-century modification of it which grew from the decorative *motifs* of late sixteenth-century Italy. Although classical ornament was commonly used, the style is much more theatrical, and floral and foliate themes which appear, for instance, in such German decoration as the *Laub und Bandelwerke* (leaf and strap-work), and in France in the work of Jean Bérain and the *lambrequins* (drapes and floral motifs in conjunction with themes derived from decorative wrought ironwork), make the style fairly obvious. Both masks and grotesques appear frequently, and are to be found in the decoration of Boulle furniture. Grotesques were originally derived from Roman ornament (in the Golden House of Nero, for example) and consist of figures and half-figures which often terminate in foliage, or parts of animal bodies. *Baroque* decoration is always symmetrical. One side of the decoration will balance the other, and furniture is solidly constructed and architectural in form.

The *rococo* style which followed was predominantly a Court style. It is light-hearted, and much less serious than *baroque*. The introduction of *rococo* followed the death of Louis Quatorze in 1715, and curved and asymmetrical *motifs* became extremely popular. The influence of Chinese art is to be seen, as well as much ornament based on the theme of water—shells, crustacea, sea-weeds, and corals—which can be found alike on porcelain and silver. Pastoral subjects and scenes of gallantry were commonly employed for paintings, tapestries, porcelain painting, and so forth. The light and airy scrollwork associated with the style is almost invariably asymmetrical, and even such formal classical ornament as the acanthus leaf has its tip twisted to one side.

The revival of more strictly classical modes began about 1750 with the discovery of Pompeii, and decoration became much more severe, the *motifs* being taken from Roman frescoes and other work of the same kind. It is, however, a pale shadow of Renaissance classicism, and it gave place at the turn of the century to the Empire style of Napoleon, which was modelled on those current in Imperial Rome.

These styles affected the course of the decorative arts to a greater or lesser degree throughout Europe, and most of them were repeated in a debased version during the nineteenth century. This, however, is easily detected. Forgers make the mistake of introducing *motifs* into their work which were not in use during the period they are copying, and by using them in the wrong way. Once the characteristics of these styles have been learned, however, anachronisms are nearly always obvious. For this reason books dealing with the subject are noted in the Bibliography.

# *Bibliography*

## GENERAL WORKS ON FAKES AND FORGERIES


Arnau, Frank. *Kunst der Fälschen der Kunst*. Düsseldorf, 1959. Translated as *Three Thousand Years of Deception in Art and Antiques*. London, 1961.

Bonaffé, E. *La Commerce de la Curiosité*. Paris, 1901.

British Museum, *Catalogue of an Exhibition of Forgeries, &c. at the*. London, 1961.

Burlington Fine Arts Club, *Catalogue of an Exhibition of Counterfeits, Imitations, and Copies*. London, 1924.

Cescinsky, Herbert. *The Gentle Art of Faking Furniture*. London, 1913.

Cole, Sonia. *Counterfeit*. London, 1955.

Coremans, Dr Paul. *Van Meegeren's Faked Vermeers and de Hooghs*. London and Amsterdam, 1949.

Demeure, F. *Les Impostures de l'Art*. Paris, 1951.

Duveen, J. H. *Collections and Recollections* (1935). *Secrets of an Art Dealer* (1937). London.

Eudel, Paul. *Trucs et Truqueurs*. Paris, 1907.

Furtwängler, Adolf. *Neuere Fälschungen von Antiken*. Berlin, 1899.

Godley, John. *Master Art Forger* (Van Meegeren). New York, 1951.

Gräbke, H. A. *Die Wandmalereien der Marienkirche zu Lübeck*. Hamburg, 1951.

Hahn, Harry. *The Rape of La Belle*. Kansas City, 1946.

Jewitt, Llewellyn on Flint Jack. *Reliquary Quarterly Journal*, October 1867, reprinted as a pamphlet.

Joni, I. C. *The Affairs of a Painter*. London, 1936.

Koppen, Walther von. *Kunst und Kunstfälschungen*. Wiefeld, 1912.

Kurz, Otto. *Fakes*. London, 1948.

Laurie, Professor A. P. *New Light on Old Masters*. London, 1914.

Mailfert, André. *Au Pays des Antiquaires*. Paris, 1935.

Mendax, Fritz. *Art Fakes and Forgeries*. London, 1955.

Mitchell, C. Ainsworth. *The Expert Witness*. Cambridge, 1923.

Munro, R. *Archaeology and False Antiquities*. London, 1905.

Nobili, Ricardo. *The Gentle Art of Faking*. London, 1923.

Oriental Ceramic Society, *Transactions*, 1938-39. Dr H. J. Plenderleith. *Technical Notes on Chinese Bronzes*. 1938-39.

Osborne, Albert H. *Questioned Documents*. London, 1929.

Pars, H. H. *Pictures in Peril*. London.

Plenderleith, Dr H. J. *The Preservation of Antiquities*. London, 1934 and 1956.
Plenderleith, Dr H. J. *Fakes and Forgeries in Museums. Museums Journal* 52. No. 6, 1952.
Schüller, Sepp. *Falsch oder Echt? Der Fall Van Meegeren*. Bonn, 1953.
Schüller, Sepp. *Fälscher, Händler und Experten*. Munich, 1959. Translated as *Forgers, Dealers, Experts*. London. 1961.
Symonds, R. W. *The Present State of Old English Furniture*. London, 1923.
Tietze, Hans. *Genuine and False*. London, 1948.
Treue, Wilhelm. *Kunstraub*. Düsseldorf, 1957. Translated as *Art Plunder*. London, 1960.
Wakeling, T. G. *Forged Egyptian Antiquities*. London, 1912.
Weiner, H. S. *The Piltdown Forgery*. Oxford, 1955.

## USEFUL REFERENCE BOOKS

### THE ART MARKET

Allen, F. L. *The Great Pierpont Morgan*. New York, 1949.
Beard, Miriam. *A History of Business*. New York, 1928.
Chambers, F. P. *A History of Taste*. New York, 1932.
Marillier, H. C. *Christies—1766-1925*. London, 1926.
Reitlinger, Gerald. *The Economics of Taste*. Vol. I. *Paintings*. London, 1961.
Reitlinger, Gerald. *The Economics of Taste*. Vol. II. *Objets d'Art*. London, 1963.
Rheims, Maurice. *La Vie Etrange des Objets*. Paris, 1959. Translated as *Art on the Market*. London, 1961.
Rush, Richard H. *Art as an Investment*. Englewood Cliffs, N.J., 1961.
Saarinen, Aline B. *The Proud Possessors*. New York, 1958.
Sotheby & Co. *Annual Reviews of the Season*. London.
Sutton, Denys. *Christie's since the War, 1945-1958*. London, 1959.
Taylor, F. H. *The Taste of Angels*. London, 1948.
Taylor, F. H. *Pierpont Morgan as Collector and Patron, 1837-1913*. New York, 1957.

### CERAMICS

This Bibliography largely ignores general works. It includes those which are well illustrated or which have something to say about the subject of this volume. The following general works, however, discuss forgeries and include extensive bibliographies:

Hannover, Emil. *Pottery and Porcelain*. London, 1925.
Honey, W. B. *A Dictionary of European Ceramic Art*. London, 1952.
Savage, George. *Porcelain through the Ages. Pottery through the Ages*. Pelican Books, 1959 and 1963.
Leach, Bernard. *A Potter's Book* (invaluable to the student as a discussion of first principles and technical processes). London, 1940.

The following works are reliable repertories of illustrations, for which purpose they have been included:

*The Faber Monographs on Pottery and Porcelain*, edited by W. B. Honey and Arthur Lane. These include monographs on almost every kind of ceramic art by authorities in their own field. Each one contains about four colour plates with about one hundred in black-and-white. The short text is followed by a Bibliography. The illustrations are clear and well selected. For reasons of space this series is omitted from the lists which follow.

EGYPTIAN FAIENCE

Wallis, Henry. *Egyptian Ceramic Art.* (*The MacGregor Collection.*) London, 1898. *Egyptian Ceramic Art* (a further selection). London, 1900. Both works in a very limited edition. Illustrations poor by modern standards; primarily useful because of the shortage of works on this subject. See also Flinders Petrie. *The Arts and Crafts of Ancient Egypt*. London, 1923.

GREEK AND ROMAN POTTERY

*Encyclopédie Photographique de l'Art*. Musée du Louvre, Paris. (See also Faber Monographs above.)

FAR-EASTERN POTTERY AND PORCELAIN

Hetherington, A. L. *Chinese Ceramic Glazes*. South Pasadena, 1947. Hobson, R. L. *Wares of the Ming Dynasty*. London, 1922 (now to be used with care). Hobson, R. L., and Hetherington, A. L. *The Art of the Chinese Potter* (principally illustrations in colour and monochrome). London, 1923. Hobson, R. L. *The Catalogue of the Eumorfopoulos Collection*. London, 1925, and *A Catalogue of Chinese Pottery and Porcelain in the collection of Sir Percival David*. London, 1934. Hobson, Rackham, and King. *Chinese Ceramics in Private Collections*. London, 1931. Honey, W. B. *Ceramic Art of China*. London, 1937. Kim, Chewon and Gompertz, G. St. G. M. *The Ceramic Art of Korea*. London, 1962. Koyama, Fujio. *Céramique ancienne de l'Asie*. Fribourg, 1960. (useful for Japanese wares.) Wu, G. D. *Prehistoric Pottery in China*. London, 1938.

ORIENTAL EXPORT PORCELAIN

Beurdeley, M. *Porcelain of the East India Companies*. London, 1963. Jourdain, Margaret, and Jenyns, Soame. *Chinese Export Art in the 18th Century*. London, 1950. Phillips, J. G. *China Trade Porcelain*. London, 1957.

PERSIA AND THE MIDDLE EAST

Hobson, R. L. *Guide to Islamic Pottery of the Near East*. London, 1932.

HISPANO-MORESQUE POTTERY

Frothingham, A. W. *Catalogue of Hispano-Moresque Ware in the Collection of the Hispanic Society of America*. New York, 1936.

ITALIAN MAIOLICA

Chompret, Dr J. *Repertoire de la Majolique Italienne*. Paris, 1949. Rackham, Bernard. *Catalogue of Italian Maiolica in the Victoria and Albert Museum*. London, 1940.

GERMAN POTTERY

Ducret, S. *German Porcelain and Faience*. London, 1963. Kolschau, K. *Rheinisches Steinzeug*. Munich, 1924. Pazaurek, G. E. *Steingut: Formgebung und Geschichte*. Stuttgart, 1927. Riesbieter, O. *Die deutschen Fayencen des 17. und 18. Jahrhunderts*. Leipzig, 1921.

GERMAN PORCELAIN

Christ, Hans. *Ludwigsburger Porzellanfiguren*. Berlin, 1921. Ducret, S. *German Porcelain and Faience*. London, 1963. Graul, R., and Kurzwelly, A. *Alt-Thüringer Porzellan*. Leipzig, 1909. Handt and Rakebrand. *Meissner Porzellan des Achtzehten Jahrhunderts*. Dresden, 1957. Hayward, J. F. *Vienna Porcelain of the du Paquier Period*. London, 1952. Hofmann, F. H. *Frankenthaler Porzellan*. Munich, 1911. *Geschichte der bayerischen Porzellanmanufaktur Nymphenburg*. Leipzig, 1921-23. *Das Porzellan der europäischen Manufakturen im 18. Jahrhundert*. Berlin, 1932. Honey, W. B. *Dresden China*. London, 1947. Lenz, G. *Berliner Porzellan*. Berlin, 1913. Pazaurek, G. E. *Meissner Porzellanmalerei des 18. Jahrhunderts*. Stuttgart, 1929. *Deutsche Fayence- und Porzellan-Hausmaler*. Leipzig, 1928. Poche, E. *Bohemian Porcelain*. London, n.d. Röder, K., and Oppenheim, M. *Das Höchster Porzellan*. Mainz, 1930. Sauerland, M. *Deutsche Porzellanfiguren des 18. Jahrhunderts*. Cologne, 1923. Savage, G. *18th Century German Porcelain*. London, 1958. Scherer, C. *Das Fürstenberger Porzellan*. Berlin, 1909. Schönberger, A. *Meissner Porzellan mit Höroldt-Malerei*. Darmstadt, n.d. Zimmermann, E. *Die Erfindung und Frühzeit des Meissner Porzellans*. Berlin, 1908. *Meissner Porzellan*. Leipzig, 1926.

FRENCH POTTERY

Gauthier, J. *Faience et Poteries Rustiques*. Paris, 1929. Haug, H. *Les Faiences et Porcelaines de Strasbourg*. Strasbourg, 1922. Lane, Arthur. *French Faience*. London, 1948. Poncettin, F., and Salles, G. *Les Poteries Françaises*. Paris, 1929.

FRENCH PORCELAIN

Alfassa et Guérin. *Porcelaines Françaises*. Paris, 1932. Bourgeoise, E. *Le Biscuit de Sèvres au XVIIIe siècle*. Paris, 1909. Honey, W. B. *French Porcelain of the 18th Century*. London, 1950. Soil de Moriame, E. J., and Desplace de Formanoir, L. *Les Porcelaines de Tournay*. Tournai, 1938. Verlet, Grandjean and Brunet. *Sèvres*. Paris, 1953. Savage, G. *17th and 18th Century French Porcelain*. London, 1960.

HOLLAND

Havard, H. *La Ceramique Hollandaise*. Amsterdam, 1909. de Jonge, C. H. *Oud-Nederlandische Majolika en Delftsch Aardewerk*. Amsterdam, 1947. Neurdenberg, E. *Old Dutch Pottery and Tiles*. London, 1923. Rackham, Bernard. *Netherlands Maiolica*. London, 1926.

RUSSIA

Lukomsky, G. *Russisches Porzellan 1744–1923*. Berlin, 1924.

SWITZERLAND

Ducret, S. *Zürcher Porzellan des 18. Jahrhunderts*. Zürich, 1944. Molin, A. *Histoire Documentaire de la Manufacture de Nyon* 1781–1813. Lausanne, 1924.

UNITED KINGDOM

Barnard, H. *Chats on Wedgwood Ware*. London, 1924. Hodgkin, J. E. and E. *English Pottery Named, Dated, and Inscribed*. London, 1891. Honey, W. B. *English Pottery and Porcelain*. London, 1933. Jewitt, L. *The Ceramic Art of Great Britain*. London, 1878. Nance, E. Morton. *The Pottery and Porcelain of Swansea and Nantgarw*. London, 1942. Rackham, M. *Catalogue of the Schreiber Collection of English Earthenware in the Victoria and Albert Museum*. London, 1930. Rackham, B., and Read, H. *English Pottery*. London, 1924.

ENGLISH PORCELAIN

Bemrose, G. *Nineteenth Century English Pottery and Porcelain*. London, 1952. Eccles, Herbert and Rackham, B. *Analysed Specimens of English Porcelain*. London, 1922. Honey, W. B. *Old English Porcelain*. London, 1948. King, William. *English Porcelain Figures of the 18th Century*. London, 1925. Rackham, B. *Catalogue of the Herbert Allen Collection*. London, 1923. *Catalogue of the Schreiber Collection of English Porcelain, Enamels, and Glass*. London, 1930. Savage, G. *Eighteenth-century English Porcelain*. London, 1952. *English Pottery and Porcelain*. London, 1960.

Most of the books listed above contain bibliographies referring to the large number of specialist monographs on the work of particular factories. Apart from the older works, which are often uneven in value, those of Severne MacKenna on the Chelsea, Worcester, and Bristol factories are worth consulting on points of detail. They are well illustrated. An extensive Bibliography is to be found in the present writer's *Porcelain through the Ages*.

ENAMELS

Cook, Cyril. *The Life and Works of Robert Hancock*. London, 1948. Cunynghame, H. *European Enamels*. London, 1906. Garner, Sir Harry. *Chinese and Japanese Cloisonné Enamels*. London, 1962. Hughes, B. and T. *English Painted Enamels*. London, 1951. Mew, Egan. *Battersea Enamels*. London, 1926. Victoria and Albert Museum. *Catalogue of the Schreiber Collection*, Vol. III. London, 1930. British Museum. *A Guide to the Medieval Antiquities*. London, 1924.

FURNITURE, ETC.

Bell, J. Munro. *Chippendale, Sheraton and Hepplewhite Furniture Designs*. London, 1900 and 1932.

Brackett, Oliver. *An Encyclopedia of English Furniture*. London, 1927.

Brackett, Oliver. *English Furniture Illustrated*. London, 1950.

Cescinsky, H. *Chinese Furniture*. London, 1922.

Cescinsky, H. *English Furniture of the 18th Century*. London, 1909.
Devinoy, Jauneau and Jarry. *Le Siège en France*. Paris, 1949.
Downs, Joseph. *American Furniture*. New York, 1952.
Dilke, Lady. *French Furniture and Decoration of the XVIIIth Century*. London, 1901.
Edwards, Ralph. *Dictionary of English Furniture*. London, 1954.
Edwards, Ralph, and Jourdain, Margaret. *Georgian Cabinet Makers*. London, 1948.
Falke, Otto von. *Deutsche Möbel: Des Mittelalters und der Renaissance*. Stuttgart, 1929.
Feulner, Adolf. *Kunstgeschichte des Möbels seit dem Altertum*. Berlin, 1927.
Jonge, Dr C. H. *Holländische Möbel und Raumkunst, 1650–1780*. S. Gravenhage, 1922.
Jourdain, Margaret. *Regency Furniture*. London, 1934.
Kendrick, A. F. *English Decorative Fabrics of the 16th to the 18th Centuries*. London, 1934.
MacQuoid, Percy. *History of English Furniture*. London, 1938.
Ricci, Seymour de. *Der Stil Louis XVI, Mobilier und Raumkunst*. Stuttgart, 1913.
Ricci, Seymour de. *Louis XIV and Regency Furniture and Decoration*. London, 1929.
Richter, G. M. *Ancient Furniture—Greek, Etruscan and Roman*. Oxford, 1926.
Schotmüller, Frida. *Furniture and Interior Decoration of the Italian Renaissance* (in English). Stuttgart, 1928.
Shapland, H. P. *Practical Decoration of Furniture*. 3 vols. London, 1927.
Singleton, E. *Dutch and Flemish Furniture*. London, 1907.
Strange, T. A. *Historical Guide to French Interiors, &c.* London.
Symons, R. W. *Veneered Walnut Furniture. 1660–1700*. London, 1946.
Symons, R. W. *Masterpieces of Old English Furniture and Clocks*. London, 1940.
Symons, R. W. *Old English Walnut and Lacquer Furniture*. London, 1923.
Truman, Nevil. *Historic Furnishing*. London, 1950.
Wallace Collection. *Catalogue of French Furniture*. London, 1956.
Watson, F. J. B. *Louis XVI Furniture*. London, 1961.

GLASS

Bergstrom, E. H. *Old Glass Paperweights*. London, 1948. (Apparently the only authoritative work on this subject.) Bles, J. *Rare English Glasses of the 17th and 18th Centuries*. London, 1925. Buckley, F. *A History of Old English Glass*. London, 1925. *European Glass*. London, 1926. *Diamond Engraved Glasses of the 16th Century*. London, 1929. *The Art of Glass*. London, 1939. Fremy, E. *Histoire de la Manufacture Royale des Glaces de France aux XVIIe et au XVIIIe siécles*. Paris, 1909. Frothingham, A. *Hispanic Glass*. New York, 1941. Haynes, E. Barrington. *Glass*. London, 1948. Honey, W. B. *Glass*. London, 1946. Hudig, F. W. *Das Glas*. Vienna, 1925. Lamm, C. J. *Mittelalterliche Gläser und Steinschnittarbeiten aus dem nahen Osten*. Berlin,

1929. Lorenzetti, G. *Vetri di Murano*. Rome, 1931. Neuberg, F. *Ancient Glass*. London, 1962. Pazaurek, G. E. *Gläser—der Empire und Biedermeierzeit*. Leipzig, 1923. *Kunstgläser der Gegenwart*. Leipzig, 1925. Schmidt, R. *Das Glas*, Berlin, 1922. Thorpe, W. A. *History of English and Irish Glass*. London, 1929. Thorpe, W. A. *English Glass*. London, 1935.

HERALDRY

Fox-Davies, A. C. *The Art of Heraldry*. London, 1905. *Complete Guide to Heraldry*. London, 1925. (Useful to an understanding of arms appearing on works of art.)

LACQUER

Strange, E. F. *Catalogue of Chinese Lacquer in the Victoria and Albert Museum*. London, 1925. *Chinese Lacquer*. London, 1926. *Catalogue of Japanese Lacquer in the Victoria and Albert Museum*. London, 1924. Willetts, W. *Chinese Art*. London, 1958.

INTERIOR DECORATION

Boehn, M. von. *Modes and Manners*. 4 vols. London, 1935.

*Connoisseur* Period Guides to Houses, Decoration, Furnishing &c., covering the following periods in six volumes: Tudor, Stuart, Early Georgian, Late Georgian, Regency, Early Victorian.

Dilke, Lady, *French Furniture and Decoration of the 18th Century*. London, 1901.

Honour, Hugh. *Chinoiserie*. London, 1961.

Percier, Charles, and Fontaine, P. F. L. *Receuil de Décoration Intérieure, Meubles, Bronzes, &c.* Paris, 1812.

Schönberger, Arno, and Söhner, Halldor. *The Age of Rococo*. London, 1960.

Strange, T. A. *An Historical Guide to French Interiors* (17th, 18th and early 19th centuries). London, 1950.

Tapié, Victor-L. *The Age of Grandeur* (Baroque and Classicism). London, 1960. Originally published as *Baroque et Classicisme*. Paris, 1957. (Has a comprehensive Bibliography.)

COSTUME

Leloir, M. *Histoire du Costume de l'Antiquite à 1914*. Paris, 1935–49. Hartley, D. *Medieval Costume and Life*. London, 1931. Kelly and Schwabe. *A Short History of Costume and Armour, Chiefly in England, 1066–1800. Historical Costumes in Western Europe. 1490–1790*. London.

METALWORK

BRONZES

Bode, Wilhelm von. *Italian Bronze Statuettes of the Renaissance*. London, 1907–8.

Burlington Fine Arts Club. *Catalogue of a Collection of Sculpture and Other Plastic Art of the Renaissance*. 1913.

Fortnum, Drury. *A Descriptive Catalogue of the Bronzes of European Origin in the South Kensington Museum*. London, 1877.

Hill, A. *A Corpus of Italian Medals of the Renaissance before Cellini*. 2 vols. Oxford, 1930.
Karlgren, B. *New Studies in Chinese Bronzes*. Stockholm, 1937.
Koop, A. J. *Early Chinese Bronzes*. London, 1924.
Lamb, Winifred. *Greek and Roman Bronzes*. London, 1928.
Museum of Far Eastern Antiquities, Stockholm. Bulletin No. 8, 1936. Bulletin No. 24, 1952.
Planiscig, L. *Die Bronzplastiken* (Kunsthistorisches Museum in Wien). Vienna, 1924. *Piccoli Bronzi Italiani del Rinascimento*. Milan, 1930. *Venezianische Bildhauer der Renaissance*. Vienna, 1921.
Santangelo, A. *Catalogo delle Sculture* (Museo di Palazzo Venezia). Rome, 1954.
Willetts, W. *Chinese Art*. London, 1958.
Yetts, W. P. *Chinese Bronzes*. London, 1924.

OTHER METALWORK

Ayrton, M., and Silcox, A. *Wrought Iron and its Decorative Use*. London, 1929.
Cotterell, H. H. *Old Pewter—Its makers and Marks*. London, 1929.
Graeme, A. V. S. *Old British Pewter (1500–1800)*. London, 1952.
Hoever, Otto. *An Encyclopedia of Ironwork*. London, 1927.
Laughlin, L. I. *Pewter in America*. Boston, 1940.
Weaver, Sir Lawrence. *English Leadwork*. London, 1909.

The following works on Arms and Armour form an authoritative nucleus for consultation:

Burlington Fine Arts Club. *Illustrated Catalogue of an Exhibition of European Chased and Embossed Steel and Ironwork*. London, 1900.
Cripps-Day. *International Armour Sales 1881–1924*. London.
Hayward, John. *The Art of the Gunmaker*, Vols. I and II. London, 1961.
Laking, Sir Guy. *A Record of Arms and Armour through Seven Centuries*. 5 vols. London, 1922.
Metropolitan Museum. *Handbook of Arms and Armour*. New York, 1915.
Tower of London. *The Inventory and Survey of the Armouries*. C. J. ffoulkes. London, 1916.
Victoria and Albert Museum. *European Firearms*. J. F. Hayward. London, 1955.
Wallace Collection. *European Arms and Armour*. 3 vols. Sir James G. Mann. London, 1924–55.

Most of these have adequate bibliographies.

SILVER AND GOLD

Avery, C. Louise. *Early American Silver*. New York, 1930.
Berry-Hill, H. and S. *Antique Gold Boxes*. New York, 1953.
Bradbury, F. *Collectors' Guide to Marks of Origin on Silver Plate made in Great Britain and Ireland*. Sheffield, 1933. (A handy pocket-size list of marks on silver and Sheffield plate.)
Bradbury, F. *History of Old Sheffield Plate*. London, 1913.

Castro, J. P. de. *Law and Practice of Hall-marking Gold and Silver Wares.* London, 1935.
Currier, E. M. *Marks of Early American Silversmiths.* Portland and London, 1938.
Dennis, F. *Three Centuries of French Domestic Silver.* New York, 1960.
Dent, H. C. *Wine, Spirit, and Sauce Labels of the 18th and 19th Centuries.* Norwich, 1933.
Grimme, E. G. *Aachener Goldschmieder Kunst im Mittelalter.* Cologne, 1957.
How, G. E. P. and J. P. *English and Scottish Spoons.* London, 1952.
Jackson, Sir Charles. *English Goldsmiths and their Marks.* London, 1949.
Norton, R. M. *History of Gold Snuff-boxes.* London, 1938.
Oman, Sir Charles. *English Domestic Silver.* London, 1947.
Penzer, N. M. *Paul Storr.* London, 1954.
Phillips, P. A. D. *Paul de Lamerie.* London, 1935.
Read, Sir Hercules, and Tomachy, A. B. *Catalogue of Silver Plate in the Frank Bequest.* British Museum. London, 1928.
Redslob, Edwin. *Deutsche Goldschmiedplastik.* Munich, 1922.
Reitzner, V. *Edelmetalle und deren Punzen.* Vienna, 1952. (Includes Austrian and South German goldsmiths' marks and a Bibliography.)
Roth, H. Ling. *Oriental Silverwork.* London, 1910.
Taylor, Gerald. *Silver.* London, 1955.
Watzdorf, E. von. *Johann Melchior Dinglinger.* Berlin, 1962.
The series of picture books published by the Victoria and Albert Museum on the subject of English and Continental silver also form a valuable repertory of authoritative illustrations.

CLOCKS AND WATCHES

Baillie, G. H. *Watches: Their History, Decoration and Mechanism.* London, 1929.
Britten, F. H. *Old Clocks and Watches and their Makers.* London. Various editions.
Cescinsky, Herbert and Webster, Malcolm. *English Domestic Clocks.* London, 1913.
Cescinsky, Herbert. *The Old English Master Clock-makers and their Clocks.* London, 1938.
Lengelle, Henri, *La Pendule Française.* Malcolm Gardner, 1963.
Symonds, R. W. *A History of English Clocks.* London, 1947.
Symonds. R. W. *Thomas Tompion.* London, 1951.
Symonds, R. W. *Masterpieces of English Furniture and Clocks.* London, 1940.
Ullyett, K. R. *British Clocks and Clockmakers.* London, 1947.
Ullyett, K. R. *In Quest of Clocks.* London, 1950.

PAINTING

Books on this subject are exceedingly numerous, and very uneven in value. Attributions change, and not all the attributions in some works which are highly regarded would now be universally accepted. Of especial value is the series at present in course of production by the Oldbourne Press which lists and illustrates all the known works of a particular artist. The Phaidon Press has published a number of monographs on the work of individual artists which are extremely useful. *Modern French Painting* by R. H. Wilenski is a general work which may be consulted with profit, and the same author has written excellent introductions to English and Dutch painting. Appropriate volumes in the *Pelican History of Art* are useful works of reference with extensive Bibliographies.

Colour reproductions are not especially useful to the serious student in most cases, because even the best nearly always fall so far short of the originals that they cannot give more than an approximate impression. An exception is the recent work, *Turner Watercolours* by Martin Butlin, where the standard of reproduction is incredibly high, but the texture of oil-paint is much more difficult to imitate exactly. Good black-and-white illustrations are more likely to reveal controversial points. Much information of importance has been published in *Apollo*, the *Burlington Magazine*, the *Connoisseur*, and the *Studio*, of which bound and indexed files exist in large libraries. The most important of these in England are to be found in the British Museum, the Victoria and Albert Museum, the Courtauld Institute, and the London Library (members only). In the case of the latter, volumes may sometimes be borrowed by non-members in special circumstances, but membership is a *sine qua non* for the serious student. The student at the outset of his career could hardly do better than read *On Art and Connoisseurship* by Dr Max J. Friedländer, of which an English translation was made by Tancred Borenius in 1943. In this work a great authority sets out fundamental principles with a clarity and common sense which some of the *avant-garde* critics of the present day would do well to emulate. It is a book which is most valuable on the shelf of the personal library where it can be consulted readily.

The catalogues of the National Gallery are noted for scholarship, and the amount of information they contain. No library devoted to the art of painting would be complete without them.

Antal, F. *Florentine Painting and its Social Background*. London, 1948.

Artist, An. *On the Preservation of Oil-paintings*. London, 1835.

Burnet, John. *A Practical Treatise on Painting*. London, 1827.

Burroughs, A. *Art Criticism from a Laboratory*. Boston, 1938.

Cennino d'Andrea Cennini. *Il Libro dell' Arte* (translation by Daniel V. Thompson). Newhaven, 1933.

Constable, W. G. *The Painter's Workshop*. Oxford, 1954.

Cox, David. *Treatise of Landscape Painting in Watercolour*. London, 1813. (Reprinted by the *Studio* in 1922.)

Doerner, Max. *Materials of the Artist and their Use in Painting*. London, 1949.

Friedländer, Dr Max J. *On Art and Connoisseurship*. London, 1943.

Gettens, R. J., and Stout, G. L. *Painting Materials*. London, 1942.

Hauser, Arnold. *The Social History of Art*. London, 1951.

Laurie, A. P. *The Materials of the Painters' Craft*. London, 1910.

Laurie, A. P. *The Pigments and Mediums of the Old Masters*. London, 1914.

Laurie, A. P. *The Brushwork of Rembrandt and his School.* London, 1932.
Maison, K. E. *Themes and Variations.* London, 1962.
Meder, Joseph. *Die Handzeichnung.* Vienna, 1919.
Moreau-Vauthier, C. *The Technique of Painting.* London, 1912.
Mitchell, C. A. *Inks.* London, 1904.
Reynolds, Sir J. *Discourses.* Various editions.
Schmid, F. *The Practice of Painting.* London, 1945.
Stout, G. L. *The Care of Pictures.* New York, 1948.
Theophilus. *De Diversis Artibus* (trans. by C. R. Dodwell). London, 1961.
Thompson, Daniel V. *The Materials of Medieval Painting.* London, 1936.
Thompson, Daniel V. *The Practice of Tempera Painting.* Newhaven, 1936.
Unesco Publication. *The Care of Paintings.* 1950.
Wilde, A. M. de. *The Scientific Examination of Pictures.* London, 1929.

SCULPTURE

If a substitute for studying the original works exists at all it is to be found in the series of volumes devoted to objects in the Louvre entitled the *Encyclopedie Photographique de l'Art*, published in Paris in the 1930s. These have an English and a French text. They illustrate ancient sculpture, and that of the Middle Ages. An excellent work on Mesopotamian sculpture is *L'Art de la Mesopotamie* by Christian Zervos, published in Paris in French, which is almost entirely a repertory of illustrations in black-and-white. A general work which discusses sculpture is *The Arts and Crafts of Ancient Egypt* by Sir Flinders Petrie (London, 1923), and techniques are discussed by Stanley Casson, *The Technique of Early Greek Sculpture*, Oxford, 1933, and J. C. Rich, *Materials and Methods of Sculpture*, Oxford, 1947. An informative general work by a practising sculptor of note is to be found in the *Lectures* of John Flaxman (various editions). *Ivories* by A. Maskell, and *Carving on Wood* by the same author, are worth consulting. Of more recent works, *Chinese Jade Carving*, S. Howard Hansford (London, 1950), discusses techniques of carving at length, as well as the nature of the material, and is therefore the most useful. *Jade* by Berthold Laufer (reprinted, Pasadena, 1946) is an older standard work which is worth consulting, and still older is the two-volume handbook of *Chinese Art* done for the Victoria and Albert Museum by Stephen Bushell. Much is still to be learned from this excellent work, but care is needed. The more esoteric byways of the subject are explored in the *Transactions* of the Oriental Ceramic Society, which often deal with related arts of China and the Far East, especially bronzes.

Oriental ivory-carvings are discussed in several general works, but no work entirely devoted to them appears to have been published so far. Engraved gems are the subject of a book by C. Newton Robinson in *The Connoisseurs' Library*, published by Methuen in the early years of this century. On the subject of Roman art generally, including sculpture, the *Natural History* of Pliny the Elder (various editions from the first century A.D.) may profitably be consulted, especially Book XXXV onwards. There are various translations, perhaps the best being that of the Loeb Classical Library which is interleaved with the Latin text. Henry Bohn also published a six-volume translation in 1857 which is notable for copious and valuable footnotes, although these are sometimes a little controversial. These sets can sometimes be obtained through the second-hand bookseller. Pliny's remarks on the art-market of his day are not without interest, and he is the source for many of the prices sometimes quoted.

*Style in Sculpture* (edited by Sir Leigh Ashton), London, 1947, is a useful illustrated guide to style in European sculpture from Carolingian times onwards.

RESTORATION, ETC.

Curl and Parsons. *China Mending and Restoration*. London, 1963. Lucas, A. *Antiques: Their Restoration and Preservation*. London, 1932. Plenderleith, Dr H. J. *The Preservation of Antiquities*. London, 1956. Rorimer, J. J. *Ultra-violet rays and their Use in the Examination of Works of Art*. New York, 1931. Scott, Dr A. *The Cleaning and Restoration of Museum Exhibits*. London, 1921, 1923, and 1926. Savage, G. *The Art and Antique Restorers' Handbook*. London, 1954.

TEXTILES

Digby, G. and C. Wingfield (trans.). *Oriental Rugs*. (Haack.) London, 1960. Erdmann, Kurt. *Der Orientalische Knupfteppiche*. Tubingen, 1955. Flemming, H. *An Encyclopedia of Textiles*. Berlin, 1934. Glazier, A. *Historic Textile Fabrics*. London, 1923. Hunton. *English Decorative Textiles*. London, 1930. Kendrick, A. F., and Tattersall, C. E. *Handwoven Carpets, Oriental and European*. London, 1922. Palliser, Mrs Bury. *History of Lace*. London. Marrilier, H. C. *English Tapestries of the 18th Century*. London, 1930. Tattersall, C. *The Carpets of Persia*. London, 1931. Thomson, W. A. *A History of Tapestry*. London, 1930.

See also the numerous small picture books of the Victoria and Albert Museum illustrating Oriental and European textiles.

# *Index*

3 1978 00600 7546